Measurement and Evaluation in the Classroom

John R. Hills

The Florida State University

Charles E. Merrill Publishing Company
A Bell & Howell Company
Columbus, Ohio

To the classroom teacher — may it make her life easier and more satisfying.

Published by
Charles E. Merrill Publishing Company
A Bell & Howell Company
Columbus, Ohio 43216

This book was set in Times Roman.
The Production Editor was Lynn Walcoff.
The cover was designed by Will Chenoweth. Cover photos by Edgar Bernstein.

Library of Congress Catalog Card Number: 75-30445

International Standard Book Number: 0-675-08632-9

5 6 7—81 80 79

Printed in the United States of America

Contents

Preface

To the Instructor

This book is designed to be used as a textbook for a traditional four-quarter-hour or three-semester-hour course on educational measurement for junior or senior education students. Alternatively, it can be used as part of an instructional system for such a course. It is also appropriate for four separate one-credit-hour courses.

The rest of the instructional system which is available includes a workbook for the students entitled *Exercises in Classroom Measurement,* a series of cassette audiotapes which go with the workbook, some reference works such as the *Mental Measurements Yearbook,* which the institution must make available to the students, and an *Instructor's Guide,* which explains various ways in which the course may be organized and which provides evaluation procedures and suggestions. The instructor should read the *Instructor's Guide* for further details.

Certain features of the book were designed to make it especially appropriate for prospective teachers, rather than administrators, counselors, or psychologists, although they, too, should have mastery of its content. For example, the teacher will need to be able to use some statistics, but she cannot be expected to be a budding statistician. Each topic of this kind has been introduced here only after the need for it has been developed. Then it is introduced at the simplest level that will satisfy the needs of teacher. All she needs to solve these statistical problems is the back of an envelope and her ninth grade mathematics. (Reminders of how some arithmetic works are also provided.) However, in deference to those instructors who like to teach all of the statistics at once, the instructional system includes audiotapes with exercises in the workbook which may be selected so as to bring all the statistical concepts together. These tapes could be used by instructors who find this approach congenial, or by students who particularly want to review all these aspects at one time.

Other features of the text were designed to make it especially suitable for use in individually paced instruction. They include the level of reading difficulty (twelfth grade), the level of mathematical difficulty (ninth grade), a certain amount of redundancy between the parts permitting each of them to be taught separately from the others, and the organization of the material. None of these features should inhibit the use of this book as the text in a traditional lecture-discussion format. It has also been found that the system is ideally suited for inservice training, which can be individually paced, using mastery as the criterion for completion.

To the Student

This book has been written for college students who want to become effective teachers. The topics have been selected carefully to be the most relevant topics for teachers. Measurement theory, the history of measurement, and other matters of primary interest to the measurement specialist have been left out unless they are necessary for the teacher's sound use and development of tests and grades for her pupils.[1] The interests of administrators and school counselors have been included only as they interact with the teacher's work. It is assumed that these kinds of specialists will have a thorough knowledge of what is included here and will take further measurement courses to develop the particular additional competencies they need in their specializations,

The topics we take up here are (1) how to make the tests you use in your classes, (2) how to pick and use standardized tests, (3) how to give grades to your students soundly, (4) how to use tests wisely to help with your instruction, and (5) what must be considered and accomplished to deal effectively with evaluations of students' attitudes and opinions. Particular attention is given to the legal aspects of measurement and evaluation by the teacher. Parents are resorting to litigation more frequently than they used to. The treatment of grading is especially thorough. Grading is a difficult area, but it will be a large part of your life as a teacher. You need thorough grounding in it. We will study in detail the use of test results. If they are not used effectively, a lot of time, effort, and money will be wasted. You need to be aware of the weaknesses of tests for some situations in which they are widely used.

We have assumed that teachers using this text are interested in finding out what they should do in their classrooms in order to be effective teachers, rather than being interested in who first noticed a phenomenon or made a useful suggestion. To reduce distraction for the teacher, many of the references that would otherwise be given have been consigned to the *Instructor's Guide* which your instructor will have. A dagger † in the text indicates places for which such references are available. Some particularly important, interesting, or controversial references have been included here, and full documentation is provided for the legal citations, since they are not conveniently available elsewhere.

You will find that the book is divided into five parts, each part on one of the five topics mentioned above. Each part is complete in itself. (There is an exception to some extent for part 4. There we assume that you know something about testing, such as the content of part 1 or part 2, before you become concerned seriously with sound use of tests.) Thus, for example, if you just want to learn about grading, you can read part 3 without having to refer frequently to previous parts. This causes a little redundancy for the reader who goes through the book from start to finish, but the redundancy is always on important topics that you should be able to deal with in a variety of contexts to have a well-rounded elementary competence in evaluation and measurement in the classroom.

We have included for each part and each chapter a set of objectives to guide your study. They closely parallel the text, and you should have little difficulty in developing from the text competence with each of those objectives. Some instructors will provide supplementary instructional help with some objectives, especially through use of audiocassette recordings and associated exercises in the companion workbook entitled *Exercises in Classroom Measurement*. All these materials have been pretested with students, often in several editions on their way to being made available to the public, so we know that they work well for developing competency among students who desire to become skilled teachers.

Acknowledgments

Many people have had a share in the development of this book over the last five years. Some shared their patience, some their knowledge, some their criticism, some their skills

---

[1]Throughout this volume the student who is reading this book has been referred to as being feminine because the writer's experience in teaching this course over the years has indicated that a great majority of the students in it are female. Her pupils are referred to with the general masculine pronoun since they will usually be about evenly divided in sex. It is unfortunate that the English language does not have a general pronoun for a person that avoids reference to sex.

in editing, marketing, and other parts of the task of creating a different sort of an entity within the ancient framework of a book. There are far too many of them to mention each name here. However, some deserve particular note because of their extended effort and their impact on the final product.

Tom Hutchinson, the Merrill administrative editor, nudged things into the form in which they appear, but never nudged beyond my willingness to bend, and encouraged me when I needed it. He obtained careful and thorough critical reviews of the manuscript from two scholars in the field, Charles Dziuban and Darrell Sabers, both of whom I hope to meet.

If this book reaches a new level of effectiveness in helping teachers, it will be partly because I stood on the shoulders of giants like Lee Cronbach, Paul Diederich, Robert Ebel, J. P. Guilford, Frederic Lord, Julian Stanley, and Robert Thorndike, from whom I have learned so much over the years. The students who have taught me how to teach them are owed a debt of gratitude. But perhaps the greatest obligation is to the patience and help of my wife, Myra, who waited, typed, read, edited, and produced an index that should help you as long as you own this book.

Part One

Introduction

Classroom teachers cannot escape the necessity of evaluating the progress of their students. Students should have some "feedback" or knowledge of results of their efforts to learn in order that they may plan the use of their time. The results may indicate that they should spend more time on some things and less on others, and each student should have the best guidance that can be given on optimum use of his time. Knowledge of results also can serve as a reward for successful performance or as a spur to greater effort after unsuccessful performance. Psychological studies of the learning of some psychomotor skills indicate that learning is markedly retarded when students are not informed of the results of their efforts. Imagine, for instance, trying to teach a deaf person to speak. One of the difficulties with learning that skill is that the deaf person cannot easily tell when he is doing the right things to make communicable sounds. In trying to teach aerial gunnery, the importance of tracer bullets lies in the knowledge of results they present to the gunner. The same phenomenon is present in all kinds of learning; so the evaluation of student progress cannot be avoided if we wish to provide optimum conditions for learning.

For additional reasons, the teacher cannot escape evaluation of student progress. Many parents want to know about their children's performances. Administrators must keep records of the progress of individual students so that the whole school enterprise can be evaluated and so that prompt responses can be made to queries about individual students.

Obviously, teachers can evaluate student progress through means other than achievement tests. They can observe performances, rate their students, have students rate each other, have students produce products that can be evaluated or displayed, and so on. However, achievement tests have certain clear advantages such that it would be a rare teacher indeed who would perform optimally without using tests she built especially for her own students to take.

The two major advantages of the tests a teacher makes for her own class are (1)

Making Traditional and Criterion-Referenced Tests

the test permits greater consistency in evaluation than most other kinds of evaluation procedures, and (2) the test designed for a specific class can be tailored carefully to the teacher's own objectives and to the material that has been emphasized in her class.

Tests made by a teacher can be designed so that they can be scored by a scoring machine or so that two independent scorers can produce similar evaluations of individual students. Most other kinds of observation and evaluation techniques, such as ratings, anecdotal records, peer evaluations, and so on, suffer from serious degrees of inconsistency from one measurement to another or from one scorer to another. Tests made by commercial publishers (called standardized tests) suffer in that they seldom reflect the particular set of objectives of an individual teacher and the emphasis that she gives to various topics. The teacher can make tests for a small unit of content, or a specific behavior, for which no published test is available.

The sacrifices that are made to obtain the increased consistency and the precise fit to objectives are (1) the use of a test seems to be less natural than some other kinds of observation; (2) the answering of multiple-choice or other kinds of objectively scored items only approximates the teacher's objectives in most cases; (3) no easy comparison is possible between the scores students make on a teacher's tests and the scores made in the same content by similar students in the classes taught by other teachers.

The advantages noted have been recognized for years and are still recognized as being so important that no teacher should be permitted to practice without a thorough grounding in the fundamentals of building and scoring tests for use in her classes. Those fundamentals will be taught in this part of this book and its accompanying exercises. During all of this learning we will be guided by a set of behavioral objectives. You should be able at the end of this unit to do everything that is listed. The following list of objectives can be used effectively as a study guide or as a guide to reviewing the material before an examination or before commencing to construct a test for a group of students.

Behavioral Objectives for
Making Traditional and Criterion-Referenced Tests

The purpose of this part is to teach the prospective teacher to develop sound class-room achievement tests and to evaluate and improve classroom achievement tests efficiently.

A. Planning the Test — You should be able to:
1. Prepare a satisfactory table of specifications for a test;
2. State the main benefit to be derived from use of a table of specifications;
3. Explain how a list of behavioral objectives for a unit functions similarly to a table of specifications;
4. Explain the meaning of test validity, especially content validity.
B. Preparing the Test Items — You should be able to:
1. List or recognize various kinds of items and describe their faults and virtues;
2. State the common flaws in each type of item;
3. Write sound items of each kind: multiple-choice, true-false, matching, completion, and brief-essay;
4. State a rule or basis for deciding how many alternatives to use for multiple-choice items in teacher-made tests;
5. Describe appropriate procedures for and advantage of item review;
6. Describe the procedure for correcting for guessing and its role in classroom tests;
7. Discuss the role of the number of items in a test;
8. Estimate the reliability of classroom tests and interpret the results;
9. State the optimum difficulty levels for multiple-choice items with various numbers of options.
C. Preparing the Test Form — You should be able to:
1. Explain the effective use of item cards;
2. Describe sound practice in arranging items in a test;
3. Arrange alternate responses to multiple-choice items soundly;
4. Write satisfactory test instructions;
5. Describe effective procedures for reproducing a test;
6. Prepare a satisfactory key for a multiple-choice test.
D. Administering and Scoring the Test — You should be able to:
1. Describe sound administration procedures;
2. Describe sound procedures for scoring multiple-choice tests with scoring pencils;
3. Describe sound procedures for scoring brief-essay items.
E. Analyzing, Evaluating, and Improving Tests — You should be able to:
1. Describe the role and purposes of item analysis for teacher-made tests;
2. Define difficulty level of a test item;
3. Define discrimination value of a test item;
4. Describe the role that item difficulty and discrimination have on test score standard deviation and why this is important for reliability and validity;
5. Find item difficulty and discrimination indices from tabled responses to an item;
6. Describe how to find item difficulty and discrimination values by three procedures: classroom analysis, teacher analysis, and computer analysis;
7. Draw sound inferences and hypotheses about items from their difficulty and dis-crimination indices;
8. Describe the evaluation of distractors and interpret results of distractor analyses;
9. Contrast the virtues of computer item analyses with classroom item analyses.
F. Criterion-Referenced Testing — You should be able to:
1. Differentiate between norm-referenced and criterion-referenced measurement;
2. State suitable uses of criterion-referenced tests and contrast these with the suitable uses of norm-referenced tests;

3. Describe the differences that might be noticeable between criterion-referenced and norm-referenced test items;
4. Describe the use of criterion exercises;
5. State the virtue and the flaws in use of criterion-referenced measures to evaluate instruction;
6. Describe hierarchical instruction and the use of criterion-referenced tests with it;
7. List four virtues of a criterion-referenced approach to learning and measurement;
8. Describe four problems associated with a criterion-referenced approach to learning and measurement;
9. Discuss three problems associated with the development and evaluation of criterion-referenced measures.

1

Planning the Test

Objectives

This chapter should prepare you to be able to:
1. Prepare a satisfactory table of specifications for a test;
2. State the main benefit to be derived from use of a table of specifications;
3. Explain how a list of behavioral objectives for a unit functions similarly to a table of specifications;
4. Explain the meaning of test validity, especially content validity.

Table of Specifications

Among teachers who are unsophisticated about testing, it is not uncommon for a test to be developed by the teacher's examining the textbook page by page looking for important ideas or apt statements about which items could be written. Some will try to write one item per page or one item for each paragraph or one for each topical heading used by the author. Of course, not all pages or topics are worthy of testing, and some do not lend themselves to testing. Also, the teacher may write several items on topics that are more important or on topics about which items are easy to write. Then at the end, the teacher might attempt to write a few items on topics that were presented but did not appear in the text. These might have been presented in lectures, outside readings, workbooks, or discussion groups. The teacher keeps writing items until she runs out of ideas or until she feels she has enough. She might also check to see if the text author provides test items for the teacher, or if some of her colleagues have items they have written for the same or a similar course. This approach does *not* represent what is recommended as sound test planning.

The recommended procedure for planning a test starts with the creation of a table of specifications for the test. This is usually a two-dimensional chart, as in figure 1-1.

The horizontal dimension, labeled across the top, represents different behaviors that the teacher wants the student to display. For example, she may want the student to display the behaviors of the Bloom taxonomy (1956), i.e., knowing, comprehending, applying, analyzing, synthesizing, and evaluating. If she is testing proficiency in dealing with the literature of a foreign language, Valette (1967) suggests that her headings might be knowing, comprehending, and expressing. In the social sciences, behaviors such as interpreting data and criticizing might be included in the desired behaviors (Berg, 1965). The teacher can list the kinds of behaviors she seeks to teach, using the systems mentioned here as sources of ideas. A useful restriction recommended by some experts is that the behaviors be expressed as action verbs — things the student does that can be observed in a testing situation.

Arithmetic: Use of Decimals
(Number of Items)

Content	BEHAVIORS				
	Knowledge	Comprehension	Application	Analysis	Total
Multiplication		1	1	1	3
Addition and Subtraction			1	1	2
Division		1	1	1	3
Renaming	2	2		1	5
Definitions	2			1	3
Total	**4**	**4**	**3**	**5**	**16**

Figure 1-1
Table of Specifications

The vertical dimension, usually labeled down the left side, represents the content with respect to which the student exhibits behavior. This is the content that the teacher teaches. In a foreign language, it might include such categories as vocabulary, idioms, expressions for the time of day, days of week, money, counting, negatives, exclamations, and questions. In social studies, it might include such things as knowledge of dates, people and their notable achievements, relationships between nations during particular time periods, and important issues during periods of history. Ordinarily a textbook provides a reasonably good outline of the vertical content dimension.

In each cell of the chart there is a number. These numbers are related to the number of items which are relevant to each cell. In the first stages of test planning, a teacher might enter in each cell the number of items she thinks would be appropriate for that cell. She would then sum each row and put those sums in a column on the right-hand side of the page. At a glance she could then see what amount of emphasis in the test would be given to each topic of the content. The columns might also be summed so that a glance would reveal the amount of stress given to each of the various kinds of behavior. As items are written or found for the test, to these cells might be added check marks, one for each item found or written. Often there will be differences between the number of items available and the numbers in the original plan, but that is to be expected. The plan gives the ideal, which sometimes cannot be reached with reasonable effort. Finally, as the test is assembled, these check marks might be replaced with item numbers so that not only the number of items on each topic and behavior would be clear, but also precisely which items were related to each cell would be revealed. This kind of a table of specifications would permit a colleague or supervisor to examine the specifications and the test and to evaluate the fit of the test to the specifications. The first and third stages of specifications appear graphically in figure 1-2.

Subject: French
(Number of Items and Item Numbers)

Content	BEHAVIORS						
	Listening		Reading		Writing		Total
Direct Object Pronouns	1	#4	1	#9	2	#17 #18	4
Indirect Object Pronouns		#2	1		2	#20 #21	3
Expressions of Quantity	1	#1	1	#11	1	#19	3
Time of Day	1	#3	1	#10			2
Dates	1	#5			1	#22	2
Avoir, être, *aller, faire* idioms	3	#6 #7 #8	5	#12 to #16	3	#23 #24 #25	11
Total	7	8	9	8	9	9	25

Figure 1-2
Stages in a Table of Specifications

The purpose of a table of specifications in planning a classroom test is to avoid the hit-or-miss testing that results from the usual practice of leafing through the text and writing items as they pop into mind — but especially, the table of specifications works to reduce the heavy emphasis that otherwise tends to fall on measurement of the lowest level of cognition, knowledge. It is not that tests should not measure how much students know. The problem is that without careful planning, tests often will measure little else. Most teachers would include as part of their objectives that students would also comprehend, be able to apply their knowledge, be able to use it to analyze, to synthesize, and to evaluate.

Items to measure higher levels of cognition are more difficult to write. Unless a plan calls for them, they are likely to be ignored. Usually the content areas will be covered reasonably well by the teacher who leafs through the text catching items as they pop out. But items involving applications of knowledge, analysis, and so on don't pop out — they have to be created.

Sanders (1966) has written a paperback booklet which may help the interested teacher to develop items at higher levels, and Bloom, Hastings, and Madaus (1971), in a larger and more expensive volume, include illustrations of items at various levels in preschool education, language, social studies, art, science, mathematics, literature, writing, foreign language learning, and industrial education. A helpful pamphlet on developing multiple-choice questions that test higher levels of learning is available from Educational Testing Service (1963). These documents, and other descriptions of the same problem and potential solutions, indicate that the writing of good items to measure behaviors other than memory is a taxing art, but carefully developed test plans also indicate that no classroom teacher can be fully effective without developing at least minimum skill in that art and practicing it regularly.

Two examples of tables of specifications have been given in figures 1-1 and 1-2. It should be clear from those examples and from the discussion that no one set of behavior categories or content categories is necessarily better than all others. The teacher should determine for herself what categories fit what she is trying to accomplish. Also, there is no correct number of behavior categories or content categories. There is, perhaps, some advantage in keeping both sets of categories small enough that the table of specifications can fit on one page and be easily examined and comprehended. The best idea might be to start with too many categories and to combine those that seem sufficiently similar. There is no correct number of items for each cell, either. The number of items per cell, per kind of behavior, and per content topic should reflect the weight that the teacher wants to give to that element. A lack of sufficient weight because items are not available suggests that perhaps some other kind of evaluation must be introduced to cover that element, or that items must be written and added to this test to give a segment adequate weight.

List of Behavioral Objectives

Another approach to test planning is available when the teacher has prepared a set of behavioral objectives for her instructional guidance. Well-written behavioral objectives indicate at least what the student is supposed to be able to do in respect to each kind of content as a result of instruction. (Some proponents of behavioral objectives would add that the behavioral objectives also should indicate the conditions under which the behavior should occur and the level of behavior that should be expected. See Mager [1962] and Vargas [1972] for interesting paperback treatments of development of behavioral objectives.)

Since behavioral objectives include both the content and the behavior, each of them corresponds to a cell in a table of specifications. Thus, one might plan a test around a set of behavioral objectives by merely indicating in the margin to the left of each objective how many items are desired for it. The second step in planning would be to indicate how many items are available for it, and the third stage would be listing the numbers of the particular items related to each objective. This procedure would then be parallel to the use of the table of specifications described above. The two procedures are equally feasible and effective. The primary differences are that the table of specifications does not require the phrasing of a list of behavioral objectives, but it does display more clearly what kind of behaviors are receiving how much weight.

While there are no collections of sets of tables of specifications for tests that teachers can simply purchase and then use, there are sets of behavioral objectives and items to go with them that are for sale. The Institute for Educational Research of Downers Grove, Illinois, the Objectives and Items Co-op of the School of Education, University of Massachusetts, and the Instructional Objectives Exchange of the University of California at Los Angeles together have listed as many as 10,000 objectives and nearly 40,000 items for those objectives on language arts, English literature, mathematics, social studies, science, business education, home economics, auto mechanics, electronics, mechanical drawing, woodworking, biology, French, Spanish, music, and physical education and health, as well as some objectives in the affective domain. These objectives are for all levels from primary through high school. It would be costly to purchase all of those objectives and items, but each organization offers the objectives and items on a particular topic and level at reasonable unit prices. Thus, it might be wasteful for each teacher to write her own objectives and items any longer if she chooses to use this approach. Why should everyone reinvent the wheel? On the other hand, until these pools of objectives have been used and evaluated by the profession of teachers, they should not be accepted blindly as adequate definitions of the curriculum or adequate sources of items. It seems highly likely that there will be a large amount of redundancy among even these organizations' offerings. (For example, two of them have nearly 400 objectives each for primary language arts instruction.)

Content Validity

The goal to be sought in planning a test according to specifications or objectives is to insure that the prime requisite of a useful test be met — the test must be *valid*. There is nothing more important to be demanded of a test than validity; if a test is not valid, it is worthless. In order to be valid, it must measure what it is supposed to measure. (It must also have some other qualities to which we will come a little later.) There are several ways of evaluating whether a test measures what it is supposed to measure. Only one of these is very important for most uses that a teacher makes of her classroom tests. This one has been labeled *content validity*. Content validity is evaluated by having experts examine the items of a test and decide whether they indeed appear to be related to the content and behaviors that should be included, whether they adequately cover all the relevant contents and behaviors, and whether the balance among topics and behaviors is sound. That is exactly what is being provided for through use of a table of specifications or a list of behavioral objectives. The teacher's use of her own table or list of objectives does not guarantee that other teachers or experts would choose the same content, behaviors, and balance of items. However, the random leafing through a book and writing items as they suggest themselves is highly unlikely to satisfy an expert who evaluates the test on the basis of any table of specifications or list of objectives.

It might be noted that other kinds of validities are commonly considered with respect to standardized tests of aptitude, achievement, and personality. They include *correlational validity, construct validity, semantic validity, face validity,* and perhaps others. Not all of these are important concepts for the teacher, and only rarely would one of them be relevant for her own classroom tests. Her concern there is with content validity — the extent to which experts in her field would agree that her test measures the subject matter and the behaviors that it is meant to measure. The most important contribution to be made by specifications is to monitor and encourage adequate coverage of higher level kinds of learning that will often be omitted without special effort to include them.

References

Berg, H. *Evaluation in social studies.* Washington: National Education Association, 1965.

Bloom, B. (Ed.) *Taxonomy of educational objectives: Handbook I: Cognitive domain.* New York: McKay, 1956.

Bloom, B., Hastings, J., & Madaus, G. *Handbook of formative and summative evaluation of student learning.* New York: McGraw-Hill, 1971.

Educational Testing Service. *Multiple-choice questions: A close look.* Princeton, N.J.: Educational Testing Service, 1963.

Mager, R. *Preparing instructional objectives.* Palo Alto, Calif.: Fearon, 1962.

Sanders, N. *Classroom questions: What kinds?* New York: Harper & Row, 1966.

Valette, R. *Modern language testing: A handbook.* New York: Harcourt Brace Jovanovich, 1967.

Vargas, J. *Writing worthwhile behavioral objectives.* New York: Harper & Row, 1972.

2

Preparing the
Test Items

Objectives

As a result of study of this chapter you should be able to:
1. List or recognize various kinds of items and describe their faults and virtues;
2. State the common flaws in each type of item;
3. Write sound items of each kind: multiple-choice, true-false, matching, completion, and brief-essay;
4. State a rule or basis for deciding how many alternatives to use for multiple-choice items in teacher-made tests;
5. Describe appropriate procedures for and advantages of item review;
6. Describe the procedure for correcting for guessing and its role in classroom tests;
7. Discuss the role of the number of items in a test;
8. Estimate the reliability of classroom tests and interpret the results;
9. State the optimum difficulty levels for multiple-choice items with various numbers of options.

Kinds of Items

The heart of a teacher's test is the items. Many kinds of items can be used effectively in classroom tests, and there are principles or "tricks of the trade" that can help teachers to develop good test items — items that will be unambiguous to the students who know the material — items in which the correct or best answer stands out clearly as correct or best to informed students but in which uninformed students will have difficulty in guessing correctly the right or best answer. We will examine the most generally useful of these principles after first considering differences among several kinds of items used in classroom tests.

MULTIPLE-CHOICE

The workhorse item of the classroom test is the *multiple-choice* item. It has several virtues. It is, first of all, versatile. It can be used to measure many different kinds of content and kinds and levels of behavior, including the higher levels, such as application, analysis, and evaluation. It is also an easy kind of item to score, usually by a clerk or a machine. It is what is referred to as an *objective* item. What is really meant by that term is that the item, or the test composed of such items, is objectively scorable; that is, no human judgment is required in scoring. It is merely a matter of counting the number of correctly marked answers. With reasonable care, very few scoring errors or disagreements should occur. It is relatively easy to develop a pool of multiple-choice items on a topic, to store and retrieve items as needed to fit a table of specifications, and to modify items as their use and data seem to indicate. Multiple-choice items are relatively insensitive to guessing, as contrasted with true-false items, for instance. However, multiple-choice items are more sensitive to guessing than are items in which the responder must create his answer rather than choose an answer. Multiple-choice items are also more difficult to write than some other kinds of items. Further, if one is teaching students to be able to perform behavioral objectives, it will seldom be the case that the objective is to choose among several possibilities the one correct or best answer. In such cases multiple-choice items are at best only approximations to being direct measures of the desired outcomes of instruction.

TRUE-FALSE

True-false items are a popular form of item and are really just a branch of multiple-choice items — those that have only two alternative responses. These kinds of items are popular because they seem to be easy to write. They seem also to be especially effective at detecting common misconceptions. Unfortunately, to write good true-false items requires knowledge and skill, especially if one is to avoid triviality. Also, these items are sensitive to guessing, i.e., random guessing will yield a score which will, on the average, be 50% of the items correct. The resulting problem can be overcome to a large extent by using larger numbers of items when using the true-false format. This is feasible because in a given amount of time students can respond to about one and one-half times as many true-false items as multiple-choice items. The use of more items also permits wider sampling of content during a given amount of testing time.[†] Scoring is simple and reliable, but some kinds of content cannot be tapped easily by true-false items, and many behavioral objectives will not be stated in such a way that answering whether a statement is true or false will be the limit of the teacher's goal. True-false questions may be only indirect indicators of the attainment of such objectives.

MATCHING

Matching items are essentially an efficient arrangement of a series of multiple-choice items, all of which have the same set of possible alternative responses. Matching items may be used anywhere that multiple-choice items could be used. Many matching items that have been used in classroom tests in the past were poorly

---

[†]See Preface, p. vi.

constructed. By the time that people are in college studying to become teachers, they have such an extensive background of experience with faulty matching items that they have to learn about sound matching items. It is then that they realize that matching items have no special virtues except perhaps relieving monotony or conserving space in a test booklet.

CREATED-RESPONSE ITEMS

Completion items, brief-essay items, and *extended-essay items* all differ from the item forms we have mentioned above in that these three kinds of items require the student to create rather than to choose a correct response. A basic problem in any educational measure is inconsistency of performance from one item to another or one test to another. This inconsistency reduces the usefulness of test scores. Anytime a created response is introduced into a test, inconsistency of scoring is added to the inconsistency of student performance. In contrast to the previously discussed types of items, these are called *subjective* items or tests because scoring requires expert judgments. Technically, inconsistency among scores on the same test for a student is called low *reliability* or lack of reliability. Educational tests should be as reliable as we can conveniently make them.

RELIABILITY

Remember that in discussing validity we alluded to other important properties of tests that would be presented later. Reliability is the most important of those other properties. If a set of scores from a test is not reliable, it cannot be valid — because reliability answers the question "Do I get about the same score every time I measure this person with this instrument?"

It must be obvious that we do not get exactly the same score every time we measure the same person with the same test. We don't get the same score every time we measure a person with a tape measure or with a bathroom scale, either. In fact, a person's weight in the morning will be several pounds less than at night, and a person's height will be noticeably less in the evening, when one is tired, than in the morning when one is rested. However, for the purposes for which we ordinarily measure weight and height of people, such minor differences in scores are unimportant. Unfortunately, in educational testing we never approach the degree of reliability that can easily be attained in most gross physical measurements, so we always have to be concerned that our educational measures might indeed be so unreliable that they are useless. We will learn how to measure the degree of reliability of educational measures, how to improve their reliability, how to avoid introducing unnecessary unreliability, and how to interpret reliability coefficients later in this part. For now, the important concept is that we have so much inconsistency in the best of our educational measures that we cannot tolerate any that is unnecessary. The fact that it is difficult to score created responses reliably is the main problem with completion, brief-essay, and extended-essay tests.

Scoring reliability is not the only problem. Another one is that created-response items require much longer per item for students to answer. Therefore, it is more difficult with these items to obtain a good sampling of all the content and behaviors one might desire to measure. Also, scoring of created-response items cannot be done by machine, or even by a clerk. It must be done by a subject-matter expert, which can be an oppressive or even insurmountable problem in some cases.

VIRTUES OF CREATED-RESPONSE ITEMS

Created-response items have some important virtues, which in some cases override their problems. One virtue is that they are essentially impervious to guessing. They have an infinite number of possible alternatives from which the person with no knowledge might guess, and the odds on a correct guess are so small as to be ignored. (The inexpert examiner may, however, be led astray by clever bluffing.)

These kinds of items seem easier to write than good multiple-choice items. They do not have the problem of trying to find good alternative choices. (In fact, one way to find useful alternative choices for multiple-choice items is to use the items as brief-essay items and see what incorrect answers are common. These make good decoys, although they tend to make the item overly difficult.)

More important than either of the above virtues is the fact that a created-response item lends itself to direct testing of the higher-level objectives sought in good instruction. It is much more likely that an objective in a course such as this one would be "Describe the concept of reliability and explain its importance in educational measurement," rather than "Choose which of the following is most closely associated with reliability: (a) validity, (b) consistency, (c) multiple-choice, or (d) variability." While experts in item writing claim with some degree of correctness that they can measure anything with multiple-choice items, they have highly developed specialized skills, facilities for reproduction, and time to give to careful item writing that are not available to the usual classroom teacher. She may find it much more feasible to measure things like application, evaluation, analysis, synthesis, and even organized memory for significant concepts by means of created-response kinds of items.

Some people argue that, aside from the fact that created-response tests may provide more direct measures of the instructional objectives, these kinds of tests cause students to study differently and that one form is superior to the other in terms of ultimate student achievement. The evidence is not entirely clear on this point. Some writers[†] argue that the created-response examinations promote better study habits, but empirical investigations[†] suggest that any differences found may be small, may actually favor multiple-choice examination, if any, and that the kind of examination anticipated seems to have little or no effect on the way students study. One can hardly decide which kind of test to use based on this line of reasoning and evidence.

KINDS OF CREATED-RESPONSE ITEMS

With these things in mind, let us differentiate among the major kinds of created-response items. The *completion* item requires the student to supply one or two words to complete a sentence. It requires some skill to write such items so that there is only one correct response, and they tend to measure only the lowest levels of learning.

The *brief-essay* item usually requires writing — from a sentence to a paragraph. In some fields, the "brief essay" may consist of the working of a problem or display of a proof. This kind of item is the most widely used and most effective of the created-response items.

The *extended-essay* item requires from several paragraphs to many pages of writing. It is seldom as useful as other kinds of items unless one is attempting to measure the student's ability to write well.

Discussions of Item Writing

There are numerous other kinds of items which we will not attempt to present here. A large number of books include instructions on item writing and examples of items for several fields. Large numbers of already written items can be purchased, as noted earlier. For those who wish to pursue the matter further than we do here, the following sources are recommended.

Paperback books on item writing in general include:
Gorow, F. F. *Better Classroom Testing.* San Francisco: Chandler, 1966.
Gronlund, N. E. *Constructing Achievement Tests.* Englewood Cliffs, N. J.: Prentice-Hall, 1968.
Sanders, N. M. *Classroom Questions, What Kinds?* New York: Harper, 1966.
A general detailed treatment of item writing is provided in:
Wesman, A. G. "Writing the Test Item," *Educational Measurement,* 2d Edition. Edited by R. L. Thorndike. Washington: American Council on Education, 1971.
Sources for item writing in specific fields include:
Berg, H. D. *Evaluation in Social Studies.* Washington: National Council for the Social Studies, 1965.
Bloom, B.; Hastings, T.; and Madaus, G. *Handbook on Formative and Summative Evaluation of Student Learning.* New York: McGraw-Hill, 1971.
Preston, R. C. *Teaching Social Studies in Elementary School,* 3d Edition. New York: Holt, Rinehart and Winston, 1968.
Valette, R.M. *Modern Language Testing.* New York: Harcourt Brace Jovanovich, 1967.

Writing Multiple-Choice Test Items

A multiple-choice item has two parts. First, there is the introductory statement that poses the problem, the *stem.* It is followed by a series of possible responses called the *options* or *alternatives* or *choices.* One of these is correct and is called the *answer.* The others are called *distractors, foils,* or *decoys.* The object of the game is to write an item such that any student who knows the material or can perform the intended objective sees clearly that one and only one answer is correct, and can pick that one out. Anyone who does not know the material is reduced to guessing at random among the options.

Of course, we must add some qualifications. First, we seldom reach the ideal of having those who can't perform the objectives reduced to random guessing. They usually have some partial knowledge which permits them to eliminate some of the options as being wrong. They also may have misinformation which leads them to certain distractors. In fact, if one can identify common kinds of misinformation, it is sometimes good practice to include options which will attract those errors. This helps stamp out the misinformation. This is particularly useful if "common knowl-edge" or "common sense" leads to an incorrect response. Then satisfactory eradica-tion requires deliberate and extensive effort.

Second, we don't always require a *correct* answer. It is preferable to instruct students to choose the *best* answer, generally. If we have items in which there is one clearly correct answer, it will also be the best answer. But we may want to include items in which one answer is clearly preferable, even though it may be impos-sible to say that it is more correct than others or that it is the only correct response.

What are some of the important tricks that a teacher should know about writing multiple-choice items?

1. Inexperienced item writers usually have the best success with making the stem a question. Sometimes, however, a stem is written as an incomplete statement, such as:

> The Declaration of Independence was adopted in
> a. 1620
> b. 1776
> c. 1785
> d. 1812

Ideally the stem should stand by itself, clearly stating the problem for the student. It should be thought of as being usable as a completion item. In fact, one might use it that way in order to locate effective distractors. If one used the stem of the above item as written in a completion-item format, he might get responses such as "Philadelphia," "Pennsylvania," and "Congress," all of which would be correct. When phrased as a question, it is more natural to write:

> In what year was the Declaration of Independence adopted?

which stands alone and clearly presents the task to the student.

2. There is no "correct" or even optimum number of options for a multiple-choice item. If standard answer sheets are to be used in conjunction with a scoring machine, that may set an upper limit on the number of options that can be used. However, the usual problem is to find more than about three reasonable decoys. There is no virtue in including distractors that are not plausible — that even the ignorant students do not choose. That is simply wasted effort. In fact, one useful idea is to give a test to students before they are taught a unit to see which decoys they fail to choose even in guessing. These should be pruned from the item.

Unless you are attempting to measure reading ability, it is good practice to reduce the amount that the student must read to a minimum in order to measure more purely that which is desired. So, write a good concise stem, write a correct or best answer, and then write several distractors that are as plausible as possible, including common errors, errors that you think might be likely, incorrect solutions to a problem that could easily be made through carelessness or incomplete understanding, and erroneous "common sense" solutions. Stop adding distractors when you have run out of good ideas. Don't beat your head trying to get four or five choices for each item.[†]

CORRECTION FOR GUESSING

Note that commercial tests often contain only items with the same number of options. That practice grew up when it seemed very important to correct for guessing on the part of students. If there is a possibility that some students might guess entirely at random on a large proportion of the items of a test, a correction for this behavior is in order. That would be the case when a test is too long to be completed in the allowed time. In such a situation, a slow student would be well advised to spend the last minute of the testing time answering at random any item he has not yet answered. He can do that without even reading the items, simply by marking one answer space for each item. Another situation in which random guessing might occur is when a test is entirely too difficult for examinees. If there is no correction for guessing on such tests, these unprepared examinees can gain a substantial number of points through random guessing on multiple-choice items. However, no classroom teacher should ever put herself in the position of giving a test that is too long for the testing time or that is so difficult that her students are reduced to random guessing. So for teacher-made tests, there is really no point in correcting for guessing. The correction for guessing makes the test effectively longer, sometimes to a marked degree.†

With standardized tests, the prescribed procedure for a particular test may include a correction for guessing. In that case there is no choice but to use it. The correction is made by estimating from the number of wrong responses how many "guesses" turned out to be correct and got counted as right responses. One acts as though all wrong responses were due to guessing (rather than to misinformation), and reasons that random guesses would be randomly distributed across all the response alternatives. By dividing the number that are counted as wrong by the number of wrong alternatives for each item, one estimates the number of guesses that would also have fallen on correct responses and been counted as right. This number is then subtracted from the number right to adjust or correct for guessing. The usual formula is:

$$\text{Corrected score equals Rights minus } \frac{\text{Wrongs}}{\text{Alternatives minus one}}$$

or

$$S_c = R - \frac{W}{A\text{-}1}$$

where

S_c is the score corrected for guessing,
R is the number correct,
W is the number wrong (not counting omits), and
A is the number of alternatives for each item.

It can be seen that the application of this formula is simplified if A, the number of alternative responses, is the same for all items. This is one reason why commercial tests tend to use items with a uniform number of alternatives. A little thought will also reveal that application of the formula requires that one count all wrong answers for each student and get a score for wrongs as well as a score for rights. Further, it is true that if no student omits any question the corrected score will agree perfectly with the uncorrected score except for being a little smaller. The students will be in exactly the same rank order with or without correction as long as every student marks a response for every item. In classroom tests, every student should make a response for each item, so there is no point in making a correction for guessing. (For the usual kinds of tests, a test-wise student should mark an answer for every item whether there is a correction for guessing or not. The correction for guessing will only adjust for completely random guessing, and on the average it will not overadjust. But usually, a student who reads an item will have at least some idea about it. If he can eliminate even a single alternative as being known to be incorrect so that he guesses among the remaining alternatives, he will tend to pick up points that the correction for random guessing will not remove.)[1]

Now to return to our set of tricks in writing multiple-choice items, we have just elaborated on writing the options, indicating that there is no correct number of options and that there is no point in using a correction for guessing on classroom tests. Therefore, there is no point in trying to have the same number of options for each item. There are arguments that having larger numbers of equally plausible distractors increases reliability, but in practice it is nearly impossible to find large numbers of equally plausible distractors. There is some empirical[†] and theoretical[†] evidence that three options is the optimum number, but the evidence is not compelling that three is enough better than other numbers to make the matter of much concern to the classroom teacher.

3. Since you should reduce the "reading load" of the items as much as possible, material that would appear in every alternative response should be included, instead, in the stem. For example:

In what condition was the territory of Arkansas admitted to the Union?
  a. as a balance state, part free and part slave
  b. as a free state
  c. as a slave state

Rewritten, the item could appear as:

In what condition was the territory of Arkansas admitted to the Union? As a
  a. balance state, part free and part slave.
  b. free state.
  c. slave state.

Untrained item writers often increase the reading burden of their items by putting instructional material in the item in a belated attempt to prepare the students for the question.[†] The instruction should have been done before the examination. The following item is improved by removing the instructional material which appears in italics.

Andrew Jackson defeated John Quincy Adams for the Presidency of the United States in 1828 by virtue of the vote of the common man. Jackson is recognized as the President who:
  a. authorized the Louisiana Purchase.
  b. created the second Bank of the United States.
  (c.) introduced the spoils system into national politics.
  d. was fondly called the "log cabin candidate."

---

[1]An audiotutorial (Number 1 in *Exercises in Classroom Measurement*) entitled "Correction for Guessing" is provided for students who want additional practice with this topic.

4. The item should be grammatically consistent. Each alternative response should fit the stem so that there is no clue to the examinee that some distractors are incorrect. Grammatical clues have been shown to make items about 10% easier.[†] Students as early as the sixth grade have been found to use them.[†] They also tend to reduce test validity.[†]

The alternative responses should be parallel in structure and content. For example:

>Which of the following is a prepositional phrase?
>a. inside
>b. on the house
>c. Prepositions are parts of speech which modify.
>d. when they were done

The person who does not know what a prepositional phrase is should still be able to eliminate *a* because it is not a phrase, and he should be able to eliminate *c* because it is a complete sentence and thus not parallel to the others.

5. Certain words when used in items give clues to the examinees. They have been named *specific determiners* because they are so common in the items of untrained item writers. They are the such words as *all, none, always,* and *never,* which make strong statements that are rarely unambiguously true. The test-wise examinee who does not know the content will usually recognize statements with those words in them as false and unlikely to be correct responses. Words like *often, sometimes, seldom, usually, typically, generally,* and *ordinarily* are also specific determiners and are most often found in statements that are true, and the ignorant but test-wise examinee increases his score by choosing statements with those words. Specific determiners also are noticed by pupils as early as the sixth grade in some cases.[†] However, the good item writer avoids using specific determiners, and when he does use them he often deliberately arranges so that they function to mislead the ignorant but test-wise examinee. For instance,

>For optimum reliability of measurement, when should a test include some hard items?
>a. All tests should end with a few hard items.
>b. No test should include hard items.
>c. Some hard items should be used when some students are much more competent than most of the others.
>d. Some hard items should be used when the material is familiar to most of the students.

is likely to be answered incorrectly by the person who does not know the answer because usually statements as strong as alternative *b* are incorrect.

Some students might object to such use of specific determiners as trickery, but this is not the case. The objective of a good item is to have the persons who know the material choose the correct answer easily and to have all others choose incorrect answers. Use of specific determiners in the manner described above does exactly that and is good testing practice.

6. While items can be written as negatives, and sometimes it seems hard to test a concept readily without using a negative form, such items tend to be more difficult and confusing and therefore should be avoided. If a negative must be used, it should be emphasized by putting it into capital letters and as near the end of the item as possible. Often an item stem can be written in the form of "All the following are . . . EXCEPT:" which emphasizes the negative nature of the item. No negatives should be used in alternative responses for items stated negatively, since that involves the examinee in sorting out double negatives. For example,

> To increase the reliability of a test, which of the following is NOT recommended?
>   *a.* Do not put the items in order of difficulty.
>   b. Increase the discrimination indices for the items.
>   c. Increase the number of items.
>   d. Use items of equal difficulty.

For most readers, the first alternative so boggles the mind that it is hard to decipher the rest of the item to be sure that the first alternative is the best response.

7. You should avoid other giveaways in items, such as (a) routinely having the correct response longer than the others (or shorter),[†] (b) failing to use certain alternative positions for the answer (such as the first one),[†] and (c) letting use of indefinite articles and singular vs. plural verb forms tip off the clever examinee.[†] For example,

> Which of the following are basic assumptions for correcting for univariate selection in the three-variable case?
>   a. The error made in estimating either of the incidental selection variables from the explicit selection variable is not altered by selection.
>   b. The partial correlation between the two incidental selection variables is not altered by selection.
>   c. The slopes of the regressions of the incidental on the explicit selection variable are not altered by selection.
>   d. All of the above are necessary assumptions.

Even though the subject matter is highly technical, only response *d* fits the grammar of the verb form in the stem, and the correct response is easily chosen by someone who understands nothing of the content.

8. The two major problems in writing multiple-choice items seem to be locating enough good distractors and writing items that are not ambiguous. The first can be reduced as a problem by the simple practice mentioned above of writing only as many distractors as one can readily find. Each should be a potentially good distractor for some reason. There is no need to search for other distractors in order to have the same number for each item in a classroom test.

The second problem is best reduced by two practices. First, discuss the items with your students after they have taken the test and received their scores and information as to their errors. Often good students will see things in items that the item writer never intended, and sometimes students can make cogent suggestions to improve the items. The second useful practice is to review each item, looking for obvious flaws such as stems that do not pose a problem, material in responses that should be in the stem, use of articles *a* and *an* that give away answers, use of singular and plural verbs that give away answers, lack of parallelism in alternatives, and so on. You should also check to be sure that upon looking at the item again after several days, you can clearly choose the correct answer and that no alternative is so close to being correct as to pose a problem. Then, ideally the careful item writer will have a colleague who is also expert in the subject matter examine her items (preferably with the key hidden) and advise whether the stem is clear and unambiguous, whether the keyed response is clearly the best answer, and whether the item seems to tap the behavior and content for which it was designed. Such review is not always easy to obtain from busy colleagues, but when it can be obtained it is usually possible to improve many items before they are ever tried out on students.

The most frequent thing that item reviewers detect is ambiguities that the writer fails to recognize. It is not easy to write items that someone will not misconstrue somehow, and it is hard for a writer to anticipate what various viewers will read into her items. Often the changing of a few words straightens out the problem once the writer recognizes it.

9. Sometimes it seems that a good way to write an item is to have none of the alternative responses the correct one, but to use as the last alternative *None of these*. The informed examinee recognizes that the correct response is not present and chooses the nonparallel response. Of course, this form cannot be used unless there is an absolutely correct answer to the question, and if it is to be used at all, it must also be used as an alternative sometimes when it is not the correct alternative. Research on the use of this alternative indicates that it is neither clearly more nor clearly less effective than the use of parallel alternatives for all the responses.[†]

Some item writers try to use the response *All of the above* as the last alternative. While it may be effective now and then, it has the problem that if any two of the options can be recognized to be correct, then *All of the above* has to be the correct answer. This lets the examinee ignore the other alternatives and is, in this sense, a giveaway. Also, if the examinee can find one alternative that is not correct, he can immediately eliminate *All of the above*. Therefore, this device should certainly not be recommended for frequent use.

With this much attention being paid to the details of item writing, it is essential to reiterate that the basic consideration for any item is that the question is worth asking and that it measures the student's grasp of an important objective of the instruction. Items of the best form that test trivia are of no value. The item writer should ask of any item "Is it worth knowing?" If the answer is negative, the item should be discarded.

Writing True-False Test Items

To make good true-false items, a teacher must avoid triviality. Since few broad generalizations are without exception, the examiner cannot readily use the true-false format to test those important concepts directly. This is a major weakness of true-false items.

Some kinds of triviality are obvious, but some are more subtle. An item is obviously trivial if experts judge it as not worth knowing. It is also trivial if the concept is worth knowing but students can get it right by remembering that the statement was a statement in their textbook. Good true-false items cannot be generated by simply taking sentences from a text, and sometimes adding the word *not* on occasion to make false statements. This kind of item writing is what has brought true-false items into disrepute, but it is not necessary.

Some procedures which can be used to write effective true-false items follow.

1. Convert the information presented to the student into a different form, such as an alternate wording, an application, or an implication which may or may not follow from the information.

2. True-false items should be easy items. As will be seen later, the fewer alternatives an item has, the higher a proportion of persons should get the item correct for the item to be at optimum difficulty level. Many people find it difficult to believe that optimum true-false items should be answered correctly by 85% of the examinees, but this has been demonstrated empirically.

3. Use true-false items to force examinees to respond correctly to sound statements that contradict common sense or popular opinion. This is often a dramatic way to stamp out "old wives' tales." It is especially effective if, when test results are reported to students, these items are discussed and if those who answer incorrectly are invited to defend their choices. For example, the following statement is false, but most naïve readers will believe it is true, and it is often difficult to dislodge that belief:

Good tests should have most items of modest difficulty, with a few easy items at the beginning and few hard items at the end.

In reality, good tests have items all of equal difficulty, and hard and easy items added to such a test are essentially wasted for measurement purposes. To get students to understand this and to answer correctly a true-false item on this topic on a test correctly is no modest achievement. Another example:

Sophisticated test constructors try to obtain normal distributions of test scores.

This statement is also false, but naïve people with a little bit of dangerous knowledge about measurement will usually mark it as correct. Again,

Kuder Preference Record (Vocational) scores are easy to interpret soundly,

is often used as justification for teaching school counselors about an interest measure called the *Kuder Preference Record*. Due to the nature of scores on this test, they are nearly impossible to interpret soundly (Bauernfeind, 1963). It is an accomplishment when one's students understand why that item is false and are willing to mark it thus in spite of common misinformation.

4. Make true-false items as simple in form and as brief and concise as possible, but remember that such items must be unequivocally true or false. If there are any exceptions, the good student does not know whether the teacher had the exceptions in mind when she made up the key and the student does not know how to answer.

5. Ebel (1971) makes some useful suggestions about writing true-false items. He suggests that such items be written in pairs, one true and one false, to help clarify what the item is testing and whether it is worthwhile. For instance,

Sophisticated test constructors seek score distributions that are normal in shape.   (F)

Sophisticated test constructors seek score distributions that are flat or rectangular in shape.   (T)

is a pair of items that clarifies what is being tested. Both items can be used, though most beneficially in different tests or forms.

6. Ebel also suggests that a useful kind of true-false item requires comparison between two specified alternatives. His example is,

> "The beneficial effect of a guessing correction, if any, is more psychological than statistical."   (T)

7. It is generally regarded as sound to make a majority of true-false items with false as the correct answer since students seem to prefer to say a statement is true if it sounds sensible and if they do not know the answer. Making such items have false answers tends to throw the students who do not know the answer onto the incorrect response, which is what is desired of a good item. Research indicates that the effect of this practice is small[†], and the practice makes the items more difficult, but a test composed of them more reliable.[†] The best practice may be to balance the numbers of true-keyed and false-keyed items within each test.

8. Specific determiners can often be used in true-false items to separate students who know from those who do not. For example, in the first item below the specific determiner "always" is used in a true item. The test-wise but ignorant person would be led to mark the item false. In the second, the determiner "no" would lead one to mark the item as false, but the knowledgeable person would mark it true.

> In a norm-referenced test, a large standard deviation is always preferred over a small one.
> There is no occasion in classroom testing in which measurement is improved by use of items with difficulty indices (p) less than 0.50.

There has been a considerable amount of discussion in the literature concerning whether true-false items were as useful as multiple-choice items. Recent studies[†] suggest that about three true-false items can be answered in the time it takes to answer two multiple-choice items. However, this is not enough advantage in speed of answering to make up for the loss in reliability from using true-false. It would take about four times as many true-false items as multiple-choice to yield the same reliability. (Only about 2.5 times as many are needed if the keyed answer is *false*.) So, there seems to be no doubt that there is a place for true-false items, but for equal reliability a true-false test will have to have many more items and take longer than a multiple-choice test. In doing so the true-false test may cover the content better, but it may not be able to ask about certain kinds of content, i.e., issues on which there is no clear true or false answer.

Writing Matching Items

Matching items should perhaps be called matching exercises because several items are combined for economy of presentation. A matching item usually presents the examinee with two columns of statements. For each statement in the left column, he is to identify the most appropriate statement in the right column.

One of the problems with matching items is that there is a tendency for one part of the exercise to give away the answer to another part. For instance, if there are exactly five statements on the left (*premises,* they are sometimes called) and five statements on the right, and if each of the responses is to be used once and only once, then when a student has correctly answered four of the premises, the fifth response has to be the correct answer for the remaining premise. This is called *perfect* matching and is not a recommended procedure. It is better to arrange the item appropriately and to tell the students that any response may be used more than once or not at all — *imperfect* matching — and thus to avoid one kind of clue for the test-wise student.

Another way that matching items give away clues comes about through the use of heterogeneous material in the premises and responses. When that is done, even with little knowledge of the content many of the responses are immediately recognizable as inappropriate for some of the premises. An example of a matching item with heterogeneous content is the following:

Premises	Alternative Responses
egregious	Billy Budd
Herman Melville	flagrant
HNO$_3$	measures blood pressure
sphygmomanometer	nitric acid
	Whisperjet

Many people should be able to match the alternative responses with only a vague idea of the various content backgrounds, such as medicine, literature, vocabulary, and chemistry. A matching item with homogeneous content is likely to be much more demanding. Consider, for example, the following:

Premises	Alternative Responses
barometer	air pressure
hydrometer	blood pressure
hygrometer	humidity
sphygmomanometer	pulse strength
	specific gravity

It is likely to be much more difficult for the average person to match the last premise correctly in this item than in the previous item. To write a sound matching item, one should think of matching items as a set of multiple-choice items, each of which has the same set of alternative responses. Then each response is appropriate for each premise, and what is gained is economy of presentation, and perhaps the test is made a little more interesting.

Matching exercises can be of any length, but the longer they are, the more difficult it is to avoid giving inadvertent clues. If a machine-scorable answer sheet is to be used, the number of responses is limited to the number of choices per item available on the answer sheet.

One problem with matching items is that since each set should contain homogeneous content, one matching item can easily use up all of the item material that is desired for a particular content category of the table of specifications. In fact, it may overweight an area without giving very adequate coverage to that area. For this reason, matching items are more appropriate for longer tests or for tests that concentrate heavily on limited amounts of subject matter. The behavior that seems to fit best the matching format is that of associating or remembering, naming, and identifying. The best kinds of content for it are probably events and dates, events and persons, terms and definitions, vocabulary in a foreign language, and similar pairs of elements.

Premises and responses in matching items should be put into some systematic order so that they are easy for the examinee to find, and, as with all test items, all of each matching exercise should be placed on a single page.

A common flaw in matching items written by beginning teachers is to allow or require several responses for a premise. Such items require very complicated or arbitrary scoring procedures and should be avoided. For example, in the following item:

Premises	*Alternative Responses*
Columbus	explorer
Mississippi	geographic area
Mojave	river
St. Louis	state
	town or city

how does one score Columbus if the examinee only indicates that Columbus is a town or city, but not an explorer? Or how does one score if St. Louis is identified as both a town or city and an explorer. The complications of scoring make this approach to matching items too burdensome to be useful.

Writing Completion Items

The usual practice in writing completion items is for the item writer to leave blanks in place of one or two key words in a sentence. The examinee is to indicate what should be placed in the blanks. The problems in writing such items are (1) making certain that the examinee who can perform the objective being measured will give the correct answer, (2) making certain that the incompetent examinee will not be given clues, and (3) making the test as easy as possible to score. It is a common mistake to write a completion item so that many answers can be given that are correct but are not the desired response. For example, we noted earlier the ambiguity in the question,

The Declaration of Independence was adopted in _____.

A teacher must be definite enough in her incomplete statement that there is only one correct answer.

Another common mistake is to have too many blanks in the same completion sentence — to overmutilate the sentence. For example,

A _____ has _____ of _____.

could be answered with *hurricane, winds,* and *100 mph,* or with *butterfly, wings, gold.* Lesser degrees of overmutilation present sufficient scoring problems that they, too, must be studiously avoided.

It is also common for the item writer simply to lift a sentence from the textbook to construct a completion item. This, of course, measures rote memory, or perhaps verbal fluency, and encourages the undesirable practice of memorizing the text. Some careless item writers make the mistake of leaving a blank for a trivial word in such lifted sentences, perhaps the worst possible kind of item writing.

Clues such as using the indefinite article *an* where *a(n)* could be used and clues based on associating the length of the blank with the length of the intended response are considered undesirable.

To make scoring easy, some arrangement which requires the student to write his answers along the right-hand margin is helpful. One practice is to number each blank in the completion item and to have similarly numbered blanks along the right margin, as in:

The reliability of a test is the ratio of ____1____ variance to ____2____ variance.

1 _____

2 _____

Writing Brief-Essay Items

The brief-essay item is comprised of a question or problem statement which requires from a sentence to a paragraph (rarely more than a page) to answer. This might include a word problem in mathematics, the writing of a definition, the listing of important characteristics of a phenomenon, the listing of the steps in a procedure, the listing of assumptions, implications, or results, and so on. Unlike the completion item in which a well-written item specifies almost entirely what particular words will be acceptable as responses, the brief-essay item permits a wide variety of kinds of expression, and a subject-matter expert is required to decide whether any answer is a sound answer. The unfortunate thing about this is that subject-matter experts are prone to disagree on the quality of answers to essay questions. Early in this century, research[†] indicated that for several different school subjects a given response to an essay question might receive marks from different raters all the way from failing to highest honor. Thus, one of the important considerations in writing essay questions must be to phrase them so that the competent student will know precisely what he is to write and so that the scorer will know precisely what is expected in a sound answer.

To start with, the instructor must know what it is that she intends to measure, and this means that she must have clearly formulated objectives. It also suggests that if an instructor has a list of objectives, essay questions might be soundly based on those objectives. Some writers would even suggest that an appropriate brief essay question would be to require the student to perform the objective. For example,

State the main benefit to be derived from the use of a table of specifications.

The second element in preparing sound brief essay questions is the stating of an explicit task that will be interpreted in the same way by all examinees. A favorite trick of the poorly prepared examinee is to claim that he misunderstood the question and to write an answer to some other question for which he was better prepared. Thus one might ask

List three claimed advantages of brief essay tests over multiple-choice tests,

instead of,

Discuss essay tests.

The third step is to write out a model answer to the question. The model answer should permit the examiner to indicate specifically which parts of the answer must be present in a student's response. If partial credit is to be given, the credit to be allowed for each scored aspect should be determined at this point. (Research[†] suggests that use of this kind of a key results in higher average scores.) At this point, the test constructor can form an idea of how long the question will take to answer. Usually it will take her, as an expert, much less time than it will take the examinee, perhaps only one fourth as long. The time should be noted so that when a set of items is assembled, the total test length will not be too long for the available time. Most users of essay tests find it difficult to prepare an examination that can be answered well within the time limits because the coverage of the instructional objectives seems so skimpy with the few specifically focused items that can be answered well within an hour's testing time.

Finally, if at all possible, a colleague should answer each item so that her answer can be compared with the model answer. Even better, if it is possible, the item should be pretested on at least a few persons for whom it might be appropriate as an exam. Often such experience with an item can reveal serious ambiguities or can indicate acceptable alternative forms for the answer that should be given credit.

It is not good practice to let the examinees choose among several essay questions. Some examiners attempt to do this because they recognize that with so few items, a student who is otherwise well prepared might receive a low score just due to the bad luck of having to write on a particular part of the content in which he was weak. However, allowing students to choose their questions effectively results in each student taking a different examination. This makes comparisons between students less meaningful. The exception to this rule might be when the student's ability to write is being evaluated, and the kind of content on which he displays his competence is irrelevant.

Writing Extended-Essay Items

There is little to recommend the extended-essay format of item writing for measurement purposes except in cases where one wishes to measure ability to write. Other than having him write, there seems to be little one can comfortably do if he wishes to evaluate a student's competence in organizing his ideas, presenting them carefully, making proper transitions, using sound sentence structure, and so on. However, it is very difficult to prepare a model answer for an extended essay in order to judge its quality as an item or in order to provide a scoring guide. In fact, it is hard for judges to agree on quality, and it is rather easy for the clever student to bluff on this type of item if it is used to measure competency in a subject matter other than writing. It is not even easy for examiners to agree on quality of writing. In light of these problems, perhaps the best advice for item writing in the extended-essay format is not to do it if you want to use the results as measures. Coffman (1971) suggests that the extended composition is better used as a learning exercise, which seems to be in agreement with most other experts on the topic.

Number of Items in a Test

So far we have considered how to prepare a test by planning what its items should cover, by deciding what kinds of items to use, and by learning how to write effective items of different kinds. We must also consider how many items to include. In general, the more items there are in a test, the higher the reliability of its scores will be. This assumes that as new items are added to a test, they measure about the same things that the old items were measuring, so we are essentially taking more observations as we add new items. While the generalization applies to all types of items, i.e., the more brief-essay items the greater the reliability of the brief-essay test's scores, it does not necessarily imply that scores from a true-false test of a given length will be as reliable as those from a multiple-choice test of that same length, or that scores from a longer true-false test will be more reliable than those from a shorter multiple-choice test. However, if we add to a true-false test more items like those already in it, the scores can be expected to be more reliable. If we consider more grades in a grade-point average, the average will be more reliable. If we give a two-hour brief-essay test with eight items instead of four, the scores from the test will be more reliable. So, a basic principle of good measurement is to use as many items as one can. Of course, this must be tempered by considerations of how much time should be devoted to measurement and by the fact that eventually fatigue and boredom will begin to distort results.

Estimating the Reliability of Classroom Tests

As noted earlier, reliability refers to consistency — does the examinee get the same score from repeated measurements of his achievement in the subject matter under study? If a test can't be expected to result in reasonably similar scores for a person when he is measured repeatedly with the same test, or with equivalent tests, or with random halves of a test, then the scores cannot be very useful — just as measures of the weight of an amount of sugar are not very helpful if different scales give different numbers of pounds and ounces. Thus a teacher should try to arrange so that her measurements are reliable, and she should evaluate the reliability of her measurements routinely. For objective classroom tests except those composed of brief-essay or extended-essay items this is usually not hard to do, but we will have to learn a few preliminary concepts before confronting reliability estimates, themselves.

RANGE OF SCORES

First, it should be no surprise to a teacher when her different students obtain different scores on a test. This is what she wants — ideally for traditional classroom measurement she would want each student to have a score different from every other student. There would be no tied scores, and the test would discriminate well among the various levels of achievement attained by her students. If the teacher listed each possible score on her test and entered beside each score the number of students who obtained that score, she could easily see to what extent she had spread out the scores for the group with her test. This spread of scores is readily, if roughly, quantified by subtracting the lowest score from the highest score on the test. The resulting number is called the *range,* symbolized as R. If the lowest score on a test was 12 and the highest was 45, the range would be $45 - 12 = 33$. To estimate reliability we need to convert the range to a different scale — technically, we need to use it to estimate a statistic called the standard deviation, a widely used and important measure of the spread of scores in a frequency distribution.

STANDARD DEVIATION

The standard deviation is estimated from the range by dividing the range by a number, call it K, which depends on how many people took the test or are represented in the frequency distribution. The appropriate divisors are given in table 2-1, in which N is the number of scores in the distribution (Pearson & Hartley, 1966). The most important divisor for the classroom teacher to remember is 4, since most classrooms are about 30 pupils in size and this is close to 27 in the table. Thus, if a teacher has a set of test scores on her class of 30 pupils with a range of 12 to 45, or 33 points, she would divide 33 by 4 and obtain 8.25 as the estimate of the standard deviation. For our purposes, there is little to be gained by using fractional divisors for groups which lie between the sizes in the table. Actually if one wanted a more precise value for the standard deviation, there are much more complicated and laborious but routine methods for computing it. These are usually

Table 2-1

Divisors for Estimating Standard Deviation from Range

N = Number of Examinees	K = Divisor
4	2
9	3
27	4
98	5
444	6

taught in a first course in statistics. The estimate we are learning here is adequate for evaluating the reliability of classroom tests.[2]

VARIANCE ERROR OF MEASUREMENT

We also need to estimate another statistic in evaluating reliability; this is the *variance error of measurement*. (The square root of the variance error of measurement is the *standard error of measurement*. This concept is discussed in Part 2 on standardized tests.) For classroom tests which are not too hard or too easy, the variance error of measurement is easily estimated as one-fifth of the number of items in the test, i.e., n/5, or 1/5 n, or 0.2n, where n is the number of items (Lord, 1959).

RELIABILITY COMPUTATION

Once those two elements have been estimated, reliability is simply

$$r_{xx} = 1 - \frac{VEM}{SD^2}, \text{ or}$$

$$r_{xx} = 1 - \frac{0.2n}{(R/K)^2},$$

where,

r_{xx} stands for reliability,
VEM stands for variance error of measurement,
SD stands for standard deviation,
n stands for number of items,
R stands for range, and
K stands for the appropriate divisor for R depending on the number of scores available.

Here are some examples of using this formula. Ms. Jones gave a 30-item test of naming capital cities of states to her geography class of 27 students. The lowest score was Billy's; he got only 6 correct. Jane got every one of the items correct, for a score of 30. The range, then, was 24. Since there were 27 students in the class who took the test, the range should be divided by 4 to estimate the standard deviation. Dividing 24 by 4 gives 6. In our formula, this must be squared. Six squared is 6 times 6 or 36. There were 30 items, so our estimate of the variance error of measurement is 0.2 times 30, or 6. The reliability of this set of scores is then

---

[2]Audiotutorials are provided to clarify and allow practice with this concept. The student may want to use numbers 2 and 3 in *Exercises in Classroom Measurement* at this point. These cover several concepts but culminate in the standard deviation. Number 2 is entitled "Frequency Distributions and Frequency Curves," and number 3 is entitled "Normal Curve, Mean, and Standard Deviation."

$$r_{xx} = 1 - \frac{6}{36}$$

$$= 1 - 1/6 = 1 - 0.17 = 0.83 \text{ or } 0.8,$$

since we are only using a somewhat rough estimate.

To understand what a number like 0.8 implies for reliability we need to know what kinds of numbers are to be expected in reliability estimates. Unless there has been an error in computation or a very unusual set of circumstances, reliability estimates will be numbers between zero and $+1.00$. If the number is greater than $+1.00$ or is negative, the first thing to suspect is that an error has been made. (Using the formula above, only errors could produce reliability estimates greater than 1.00, but some other ways of estimating reliability can yield numbers greater than 1.00 with correct computations. Those values require an expert for interpretation, however.) Using our formula, if the VEM was greater than the SD^2, we could get a negative value. This would be most likely to happen if a test was very easy so that nearly everyone got the same score — a perfect score. There would be little variability in their scores, but the VEM, estimated by $0.2n$, would still be of some size. For very hard or very easy tests, the procedure outlined above should not be used. Again, the teacher trying to estimate the reliability of an atypical class-room test needs the help of an expert advisor who knows more than we will attempt to cover in this treatment of reliability.

Now what does a reliability of 0.8 tell Ms. Jones? First, it indicates that this test worked unusually well for a classroom test. Most teacher-made tests don't reach such high levels of reliability, so she should be satisfied with the quality of measurement she has obtained this time. A reliability of 0.8 also indicates that she should expect to have relatively few tied scores, and the highest scores clearly reflect different degrees of learning than the lowest scores. If these scores are to become part of the students' grades, Ms. Jones should feel confident that grades based on scores such as these reflect true differences in achievement and are not just random fluctuations due to poor measurement of achievement.

Let's try another example. Mr. Brown did not have much time to prepare a pop quiz for his general science class. He used 10 true-false items, and in his class of 25, students got scores from 4 to 10 correct. Mr. Brown was pleased with the performance of the class as a whole, the average being 7, but when he analyzed the test in terms of whether he should rely on these scores as telling him much about the different achievement of different students he found that the reliability was

$$r_{xx} = 1 - 2/2.25 = 1 - 0.89 = 0.11.$$

This reflected the fact that there were many ties among the students, and there were not many items. The measures from this test are not very helpful at discerning which students are doing better than others. However, Mr. Brown should not discard these results. When these test scores are added to scores from other tests in determining the final grade, they will add to the reliability of the total. For example, if Mr. Brown gave 10 of these short tests during the term so that the total number of items was 100, and if the sum of the scores for the student with the lowest total was 61 and the sum for the best student was 93, then the range would be 93-61 = 32. The standard deviation would be 32/4 = 8. The standard deviation squared would be 64. The variance error of measurement would be 0.2 times 100, or 20, and reliability would be estimated at

$$r_{xx} = 1 - 20/64 = 1 - 10/32$$

This is about 1 minus 1/3 or about 0.67. While not high yet, this may be about as good as Mr. Brown can do using true-false tests. Remember, it takes more true-false items to get a given quality of measurement because by answering at random one can get at least half of the items correct. That is why in the example we suggested that the lowest total score on these tests might be as high as 61. If Mr. Brown had used multiple-choice items, the lowest score might easily have been as low as 38. This would yield a larger range — in this case 93-38 = 55. This divided by 4 to estimate the standard deviation gives about 14. Squared this becomes 196. Now reliability would be

$$r_{xx} = 1 - 20/196$$

which is about 1 — 20/200 or 1 — 1/10 or about 0.90. This roughly illustrates the manner in which using items with more alternatives generates higher reliabilities from a given number of items, all other things being equal. The moral is if you use the true-false format, use large numbers of items.

Another general principle to remember is that to increase reliability, use more items, and conversely, if you reduce the number of items, reliability will also be reduced. This is not evident in the formula we have been using to estimate reliability because when items are added to or removed from a test it has an effect on both the variance error of measurement and the standard deviation. In fact, test theorists have shown that as the number of items in a test is multiplied by a given factor, say f, the additional items being parallel in difficulty and content to those already in the test, the variance error of measurement is multiplied by the factor f. However, the standard deviation squared is multiplied by the *square* of f. Since the variance error of measurement is divided by the square of the standard deviation, as more items are added, this ratio becomes smaller. Thus less is being subtracted from 1.0 in estimating reliability, and reliability becomes larger as more items are used.

Before going on, you should be aware of the most common errors in estimating reliabilities this way. The most frequent error is to forget to square the standard deviation. Probably the next most frequent is dividing the number of items by K instead of dividing the range by K to estimate the standard deviation. Third most common is to forget to subtract the ratio from one. If you avoid these three errors, you should have little problem.[3]

Optimum Difficulty Level of Items

A topic about which there is much unnecessary confusion in test construction is the difficulty level at which items should be set. For traditional tests, which are meant to

---

[3]A set of problems on this topic is provided in *Exercises in Classroom Measurement*. It is number 4, entitled "Estimating Reliability of Traditional Classroom Tests."

discriminate among the achievements of different students and to have high reliabilities, there is a clear answer. All items should be of the same difficulty, ideally. There should not be "hard" items and "easy" items, and there is no question of whether the items should be arranged from easier to hardest (it has little effect[†]) or in some other way. Hard and easy items are simply wasteful, as far as measurement goes. In some situations, a teacher might want to have a few easy items at the beginning of a test to help students relax, or a few hard items at the end to keep good students from becoming restless while waiting for the others, but students in today's schools should have enough test experience so that they do not need to be relaxed for their teacher's tests. There is little need for very easy items. For classroom tests, everyone should be allowed to finish. If hard items are put at the end to take up time for good students, the poor students may never get done. So, hard items at the end do not work out well for classroom tests either. Thus, theory, empirical evidence, and careful logical analysis all agree that for good measurement, all items should be of equal difficulty in a test.

How difficult the items should be depends on the number of alternatives each item has. It has been shown empirically[†] through careful analysis that good items should always be relatively easy, and that the ideal difficulty levels for items with various numbers of alternatives are those presented in table 2-2. Since the most difficult items that should be used in the usual multiple-choice tests should be gotten correct by 69% of those taking the test, it is clear that the best tests are easy tests, and

Table 2-2
Optimum Difficulty Levels for Test Items

Number of Alternatives	Proportion Getting Item Correct
2	0.85
3	0.77
4	0.74
5	0.69
Infinite	0.50

there is no value for classroom measurement purposes in a "tough" test! Only for tests in which there is little chance for a correct answer by guessing (e.g., completion tests) does one aim for a difficulty level such that half of the students get each item correct; it is never desirable for items more difficult than that to be used.

The principles to be learned here are (1) never aim to have test items of varied difficulty in a test and (2) never try to write hard items.

References

Bauernfeind, R. *Building a school testing program.* Boston: Houghton-Mifflin, 1963.

Berg, H. *Evaluation in social studies.* Washington: National Education Association, 1965.

Bloom, B., Hastings, T., & Madaus, G. *Handbook of formative and summative evaluation of student learning.* New York: McGraw-Hill, 1971.

Coffman, W. E. Essay examinations. In Thorndike, R. L. (Ed.), *Educational measurement,* (2nd ed.) Washington: American Council on Education, 1971, p. 289.

Ebel, R. How to write true-false items. *Educ. psychol. Measmt,* 1971, **31**, 417–26.

Gorow, F. *Better classroom testing.* San Francisco: Chandler, 1966.

Gronlund, N. *Constructing achievement tests.* Englewood Cliffs, N.J.: Prentice-Hall, 1968.

Lord, F. M. Tests of the same length do have the same standard error of measurement. *Educ. psychol. Measmt,* 1959, **19,** 233–39.

Pearson, E. S. & Hartley, N. O. *Biometrika tables for statisticians,* Vol. I, (3rd ed.) London: Cambridge University Press, 1966. Table 27, p. 189.

Preston, R. *Teaching social studies in the elementary school,* (3rd ed.) New York: Holt, 1968.

Sanders, N. *Classroom questions: What kinds?* New York: Harper & Row, 1966.

Valette, R. *Modern language testing: A handbook.* New York: Harcourt Brace Jovanovich, 1967.

Wesman, A. Writing the test item. In Thorndike, R. L. (Ed.), *Educational measurement,* (2nd ed.) Washington: American Council on Education, 1971.

3

Preparing the Test Form

Objectives

Study of this chapter should enable you to:
1. Explain the effective use of item cards;
2. Describe sound practice in arranging items in a test;
3. Arrange alternate responses to multiple-choice items soundly;
4. Write satisfactory test instructions;
5. Describe effective procedures for reproducing a test;
6. Prepare a satisfactory key for a multiple-choice test.

Item Cards

Preparing the test booklet or, for a very short test, the sheet on which the items and instructions are given, is a simple matter compared to preparing objective items to include in the test. However, there are some common errors to be avoided and some recommended procedures for simplifying this step in testing.

First, objective-test items are usually written on scratch paper of some kind because there is a lot of erasing and rewriting before the first draft of an item comes into existence. However, after an acceptable idea has been developed, the tentative item should be transferred to an *item card* — a 5″ by 8″ card of about the weight of a manila folder. A card is used because it is much easier to file than is paper, and the 5 x 8 size gives enough room but not too much. It is, of course, anticipated that items will be used several times and will be improved based on data gathered from their use, as will be explained when we take up item analysis.

The item card should have space on the front for the following:

   a. Identification, such as a code to indicate where the card should be filed after it has been used in a test. The code might be the number of the behavioral objective to which it corresponds, for instance, and the card file would be organized by behavioral objectives.

b. The item, itself, should be given space on the front of the card; usually about half of the 5 x 8 area should be reserved for the item and the alternative responses.

c. The key. Usually it is sufficient for the number or letter of the correct response to be underlined. Some people put the key on the back. Then if the teacher or someone who reviews her items can't pick the correct answer, one is alerted to the item as having a problem.

d. The specific behavior and content for which the item is designed should be stated concisely in a space on the front of the card.

e. The source of the item should be identified so that the examiner can easily find the reference which demonstrates the correctness of the keyed response. If the item comes from a set of items provided by the publisher of a textbook, this can be indicated.

f. A space for comments, such as the item number and test in which the item has been used previously, should be provided.

An example of an item card with these elements appears in figure 3-1. In this illustration the back of the card is left blank so that the results of analyses of the item's effectiveness in use can be entered there.

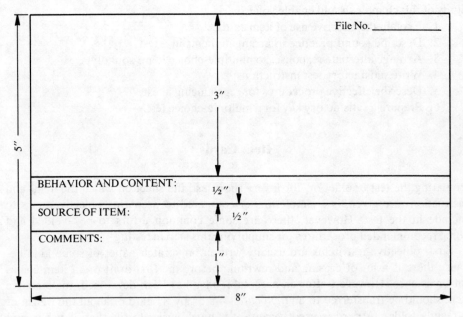

Figure 3-1
Example of an Item Card

Arrangement of Items

Once the items for a test have been placed on item cards, the cards can be arranged in any desired order prior to typing the test booklet's stencil for duplication. In the past it was recommended that the items be placed in order of difficulty, from easiest to hardest, but since in a good test we want all items of nearly the same difficulty, this is no longer a useful recommendation. (Several studies[†] indicate that item order has little effect, anyway.) It seems best now to group together sets of items of the same form, such as multiple-choice items, true-false items, matching items, etc., and within sets to group items according to the sequence in which the material was presented, that is, the content outline. This makes the examinee more comfortable as he proceeds through the test.

Whoever types the material from the item cards onto the stencil for duplicating the test booklets should be firmly instructed to number every item of a test and never to split an item at the bottom of a page so that part of it appears on one page and the rest on the next page. It is better practice to have large blank areas than to have split items.

Arrangement of Responses

It is important that you take into consideration, as you assemble the items for a test, the fact that each possible answer position should be used about equally often. (Research suggests[†] that teachers tend not to use the first and last alternative as the keyed one.) If a set of items does not have this pattern, then a good way to achieve it is to rearrange the alternative answers for a few items as needed. However, when one is transferring items to item cards, it is easy to rearrange the alternative responses according to the alphabetical order of the first word in each response. If this is done routinely, there should be little problem with disproportionate numbers of incorrect responses falling in the first and last positions. Of course, where there is a logical order to responses, such as an increasing order of numbers in numerical items, or a sequential progression of years in a field where dates are of interest, the natural order should be followed regardless of the effect this has on equalization of correct responses across answer positions. If every alternative response that is offered for this kind of item is based on a rationale as to why the student might choose it, even though it is incorrect, there will be enough fluctuation of position of the correct response so that the astute student will not be able to guess correctly more often by figuring out a pattern among the positions of correct answers.

Test Instructions

Every test should have written instructions (except perhaps for very young children who must have the instructions read to them), even though one might suppose that students are familiar enough with tests to know what to expect. The instructions may be brief, but they should cover at least the following points:

1. How to identify the test and the examinee on the answer sheet or on the test booklet if answers are to be entered on it directly,
2. Where answers are to be entered, and how — by circling, crossing out the correct answers, filling in blanks on a machine-scorable answer sheet, and so on,

3. Whether there is a correction for guessing, and if so, what the correction is,
4. How much time is allowed for the test,
5. What the student should do when the test is completed,
6. Any peculiarities about the test, such as use of scratch paper for solving problems, showing work on mathematics problems, weighting values of various items if different weights are used in brief essay items, and
7. The number of items and pages for a test of any length. (It is disastrous when a person turns in a test only to find out later that his booklet had the last page and its items missing. If he had known how many items to answer, this would have been detected during the test, and a complete test booklet could have been provided.)

The following set of instructions can be used as a model for many tests, with appropriate alterations.

Mid-Term Examination

Introductory Algebra
Form M1A-B

First, please put your name at the top of the test booklet's first page where it says NAME _____. This is a twenty-five item test of your knowledge of algebra as we have covered it this far. You should show your work for each problem, and enter your answer in the space marked ANSWER _____ in the right-hand margin for each item. Each item is worth two points, one for a correct method and one for the correct answer, so show all of your work. If you can only guess at the answer and guess correctly, you will get a point. There will be no adjustment for guessing. You will have 50 minutes. If you finish early, check your work carefully. Then raise your hand and I will pick up your paper. Then you may read or study quietly at your desk until the end of the period. The test is two pages long.

Reproducing the Test

Most classroom tests that are prepared by teachers are reproduced by means of a spirit duplicator, such as Ditto, or mimeograph. The spirit process is less expensive for up to 50 copies, and some typists prefer to work with it. It has the problem of direct sunlight's fading the copies, but this is seldom important for classroom tests. It seems a little easier to make a drawing or illustration on a spirit-process master than on a mimeograph master, because the latter are quite subject to tearing by a stylus. Experience yields good corrections of errors in either process, but neither will reproduce details effectively. Drawings must be rough; the correct answer cannot depend on elements such as shading and fine artwork. At the college level a rather common trick of devious students is to examine office trash for used stencils for tests. Needless to say, stencils, unused sheets of questions, and similar materials should be kept as securely as the item cards and the actual copies of the test that will be given.

Usually tests are reproduced on standard 8½" x 11" paper. The question arises whether to use one column of items or to divide the sheet into two columns. Experts disagree on the point. Some argue that the shorter lines of two half-page-width columns are easier to read. On the other hand, two columns are harder to prepare and often result in narrow margins and crowded appearance, as well as less wasted space. The principle to be followed is to make the mechanics of taking the test as simple as possible for the student. Sometimes a combination of single and double column layout is effective, such as when one set of material, such as a table or paragraph, is to be used in connection with several items. The table or paragraph may be spread across two columns, but individual items may be restricted to single half-page-width columns beneath the common element. For younger children it may be advisable to use half-page-width columns to avoid the difficulties of long lines of type.

One kind of item style that is to be avoided is the presentation of the alternative responses one after another in the same line or lines occupied by the stem, as in figure 3-2. Instead, the stem should be presented and the alternative responses listed separately beneath it, as in figure 3-3. Double space is used between stem and responses, but single spacing is used between responses and within the stem. This

Figure 3-2

Incorrect Pattern for Presenting Alternative Responses

> A common device for helping students to remember the difference between latitude and longitude is to get them to remember that both latitude and _____ are associated with cold climates. (1) altitude, (2) conifers, (3) lakes, (4) northern hemisphere.

Figure 3-3

Correct Pattern for Presenting Alternative Responses

> A common device for helping students to remember the difference between latitude and longitude is to get them to remember that both latitude and _____ are associated with cold climates.
>
> 1. altitude
> 2. conifers
> 3. lakes
> 4. northern hemisphere

helps differentiate the parts of the item. Double space should be used between items, also. Of course, no item should be started at the bottom of one page and continued at the top of the next, and every item should be numbered. Every alternative should also be numbered or lettered. Letters are usually better unless the machine-scored answer sheet to be used has numbered alternatives. In that case, the alternatives on the test booklet should be labeled to agree with the answer spaces on the answer sheet.

Scoring is more convenient if the students place their answers along the right-hand margin. Then a strip of paper with the correct answers at the correct point on the strip can be matched with the test booklet, and scoring is a matter of crossing out with red pencil the answers that don't agree. On the other hand, while scoring is not quite so simple, more feedback is communicated to the student if he does something like circle or cross out the letter or number for the alternative he thinks is correct and if the scorer circles or crosses out the correct answer with a red pencil. This immediate feedback keeps the instructor from having to read the key to the class in order for them to find out what they should have answered on items that they got wrong, and it makes certain that some of the less aggressive students do not fail to find out what response they should have chosen to get the questions correct. If the examiner decides in favor of simplified scoring with strip stencils, an item layout such as in figure 3–4 results in all the answers being lined up on the right-hand margin.

Figure 3-4
Pattern for Presenting Items for Use with Scoring Strip

1. A common device for helping students to remember the difference between latitude and longitude is to get them to remember that both latitude and_____are associated with cold climates.

    a. altitude
    b. conifers
    c. lakes
    d. northern hemisphere   1._____

With tests for little children some of these rules may well be bent. Often items are not numbered because some children do not deal with numbers very well. An item may be identified instead by having a drawing of some common object beside it, such as a shoe, a flower, a star, or a box. The child can be directed then to the line with a star at the left. The item may be read to the students, and the alternative responses alone may appear on that line in the test booklet. The alternatives are usually short— one word, letter, figure, color, or something like that. The child may mark through the response he thinks is correct, may point at it, or may make a mark in a circle or box beneath the response he chooses. The classroom teacher is the best judge of whether her pupils can do such things as deal with numbered items, read stems for themselves, and use separate answer sheets.

4

Administering and Scoring the Test

Objectives

The goals for this chapter are that you should be able to:
1. Describe sound administration procedures;
2. Describe sound procedures for scoring multiple-choice tests with scoring stencils;
3. Describe sound procedures for scoring brief-essay items.

Administering the Test

The administration of classroom tests is simpler than the administration of standardized tests because it usually is not intended that the results from one set of examinees be compared with the results from another set. Thus it is less important that precise timing of tests, and parts of tests, be enforced. Conditions of temperature, noise, lighting, and distractions usually influence equally all persons taking a teacher-made test. However, no examination should be given under conditions that are less than the best available. This implies that the room should be quiet, comfortable, well lighted and ventilated, with seats well arranged so that writing or marking answer sheets is convenient. Research has indicated that scores are higher on the average for students using desks than for students using chairs with desk arms,† and it is generally accepted that lap boards are an improper testing arrangement.

SEATING ARRANGEMENTS

Several kinds of seating arrangements are undesirable since they make copying from other students' work easy, and all reasonable effort should be made to reduce such temptation. Having several students sit at a table while taking a test is unsatisfactory on this score. Using a room in which the seats are placed at different heights or tiers is similarly tempting to students who need help with particular items. The general recommendation in such situations is to proceed with testing only if at least five feet of empty space can be maintained between students. In classrooms with rows and columns of desks, the recommended procedure is to seat students in rows, from front to back of the room, with an empty row of seats beside each row of filled seats, as in figure 4-1. This is better than the old practice of seating students alternately,

_'s are Seats; X's are Occupied

```
X  _  X  _  X
X  _  X  _  X
X  _  X  _  X
X  _  X  _  X
X  _  X  _  X
```

FRONT

Figure 4-1
Recommended Seating Arrangement

as in figure 4-2, since copying from directly behind a person is more obvious than copying from someone seated diagonally. Left-handed students should be seated on the left edge of the room so that they do not face other students' desks.

Sometimes in crowded classrooms it is not possible to provide this much empty space between examinees. A useful practice in such cases is to prepare two forms of a test, using the same items but in different orders. Each form is put on paper of a different color. Then each row of students, from front to back of the room, is given booklets of one form and color, and the adjacent row is given books of the other form and color. The use of different colors prevents examinees from exchanging books from row to row, and the rearrangement of items frustrates all but the most diligent efforts at profiting from one's neighbor's attempts. The drawback to this

_'s are Seats; X's are Occupied

```
X  _  X  _  X
_  X  _  X  _
X  _  X  _  X
_  X  _  X  _
X  _  X  _  X
```

FRONT

Figure 4-2
Formerly Recommended Seating Arrangement

method is that the test must be typed twice, and if machine procedures are used to analyze the test, it is inconvenient to combine the work of the entire class for a single analysis.

It is standard practice to permit nothing on the desk top except the test booklet, the answer sheet, and the pencil in order to make it more difficult for anyone to bring to the test notes that might help him with the items. When students must work problems, colored paper can be provided for scratch work, and the scratch work can be handed in so that students cannot write down questions and pass them on to others who might face the same test. Since students can still remember items and reconstruct tests afterwards, especially if the students are at all organized, it may be useful to simply file copies of used tests in the library so that all students have equal access to prior tests. As a teacher is developing a pool of items that are to be reused, the filing of used tests may not be optimum, but when the pool has become large, say 1,000 or more, a student who learns the correct answers to all those items will learn a lot of the course material anyway. He will just have chosen a very awkward and disorganized means of doing so.

ERRORS IN FINAL COPIES OF TESTS

Only the very lucky teacher can always have her tests typed and proofread so well that there are never any errors in them. The teacher should read carefully a copy of the test booklet before the administration, noting all the significant errors so that they can be called to the attention of all the students at the same time before the test starts. After the test starts, there should be few questions, and little help should be given to any individual student. The questions that do arise about ambiguities in wording that have not been caught in item writing, editing, and review should be carefully noted so that the items can be improved for further use.

Testing is itself highly motivating for most students. More than a moderate amount of anxiety can reduce complex performances, so the teacher's manner during testing should be relaxed and genial, rather than foreboding. She should indicate by her attitude that the test is important, but an opportunity rather than a trial.

CHANGING ANSWERS

At the end of nearly any test administration there will be a few students who take far longer than the others unless they are told to stop. Often they are going back over their papers looking for answers they may want to change. Sometimes they ask whether their answer-changing efforts are known to be helpful or harmful. Not much research has been done on this question, but one study[†] indicates that changing answers tends to improve one's score. The improvement occurs from changes made in easy and moderately difficult items, not hard items. It is as though one guess was as good as another on hard items, but on easier items a review sometimes alerted the examinee to a careless error. Interestingly, the improvement from changing answers does not seem to be related to general mental ability, as had previously been suspected. So, the sound advice to students with this problem is go ahead and change answers if you think you ought to, but do not labor interminably over items that baffle you.

Training with Answer Sheets

Young children must be tested with a procedure that prevents proficiency with the testing situation from distorting the measurement of whatever the test is designed to measure. This implies, of course, that if the children cannot read, the items should be read to them, and if they do not know numbers, the items should be identified in some other way. It also means that the very young cannot be expected to use separate answer sheets. When children's manipulative skills reach a level that they can handle test booklet, answer sheet, and pencil, and can learn to keep track of items by their numbers, the convenience of the separate answer sheet can be introduced. However, it is a sound idea to give children practice in using separate answer sheets on "fun" tests that don't count until few if any children in a group lose any points due to difficulty with the way they are being tested. The teacher can best judge when the changeover should be attempted and, after practice, introduced.

Scoring the Test

The scoring of objective tests, such as multiple-choice and true-false tests is straightforward. Since every student should have the opportunity to attempt every item, there is no point in using corrections for guessing, which were discussed earlier. The best procedure is the simplest—count the number correct. Alternatively, count the number incorrect and subtract that from the number of questions. A list of the correct answers can be used in scoring test booklets which have been marked by classes of the usual size, say 25 to 30. For longer tests or more examinees a strip key can be used with the item layout described earlier for use with strip keys. If a scoring machine is available, machine-scorable answer sheets may be purchased for use with it. A wide variety of answer sheet types is available for some of the scoring machines, but most scoring machines will score properly only answer sheets designed for the specific machine. A machine-scorable answer sheet is a very delicate and precise device. It must be very carefully cut to exact dimensions, and the answer blanks on it must be positioned exactly. Some of them have black "timing marks" down one edge which control the machine. These have to be made precisely and with the proper ink. It is usually disastrous for anyone to try to economize by producing his own answer sheets for use in a test scoring machine. The outcome is likely to be that the answer sheets can be scored only by hand; thus a penny is saved for a dollar wasted.

Sometimes machine-scorable answer sheets may be used even if a scoring machine is not available. This will permit reuse of test booklets, providing that each booklet is visually scanned for stray marks between uses and stray marks are erased or marked booklets are destroyed. The machine-scorable answer sheets may be scored easily if the special punch for creating scoring stencils from answer sheets is purchased from International Business Machines (IBM). The special punch is needed to punch holes for items in the middle of the sheet without crumpling the paper. In this procedure, the keyed responses are punched out, and the key is placed over each answer sheet in turn. Any hole that does not have a blackened space is crossed with a green (or other contrasting color) mark. The green marks are then counted and subtracted from the number of items to obtain the score for number correct.

Without the punch a similar procedure can be used with a light source such as a mimeoscope. The answer sheet to be scored is placed over a key on which answers have been blackened correctly. Then both answer sheet and key are placed over the light source. Any item for which a blackened space shows through the answer sheet which has not been blackened on the answer sheet has a green mark placed in the space which has not been blackened on the top (answer) sheet. These green marks are counted and their sum subtracted from the total number of items to yield a number-correct score. An advantage of marking wrongs and subtracting them to get the score is that the green marks indicate to the examinee what the correct answers were for each item he missed.

Another procedure for developing a key that may be convenient is the use of a sheet of clear plastic in the shape of the test booklet (or the answer sheet). The correct answers are marked with a china-marking pencil on the plastic overlay. To score, the overlay is placed over the test booklet (or answer sheet), and the number of answers that agree with the marks of the pencil on the plastic are counted to obtain a number-correct score. The china-marking pencil key can be rubbed off the clear plastic after all the copies of the test have been scored, and the plastic can then be reused for the next test.

Of course, the teacher or school can make up a stencil from which separate answer sheets that are not to be machine scored can be prepared. The usual identification spaces are provided at the top, e.g., name, class, subject, date, school, teacher's name, and name of the test. Then, in columns, answer spaces are numbered, each followed by letters A, B, C, D, and E. The student is told to cross out the letter corresponding to his choice of the answer for each item. The same procedures can be used for hand scoring these answer sheets as for hand scoring machine-scorable answer sheets. For true-false items, students can mark space A for true and space B for false, so the answer sheet is very versatile. If items are commonly used with more than five responses, letters beyond E can be provided on the answer sheet. In most cases, use of more than four distractors is wasteful. However, particularly for matching items, there may be occasions in which larger numbers of alternative responses are readily available. For example, in history more than five dates may be reasonable alternatives for a series of events, and in geography more than five names of places may be relevant for a series of premises.

Sometimes teachers are tempted to develop elaborate scoring schemes for objective test items. One possibility is to give different negative values for different kinds of errors. Another obvious possibility is to give more credit for correct answers to some items than to other items. There is abundant evidence that if there is a reasonable number of items on a test, and if the test is of appropriate difficulty level for the examinees, it is largely wasted effort to give more weight for some items than for others. Use of a table of specifications should insure that the numbers of items for various behaviors and contents are in about the desired proportions, so rough weighting by content and behavior has already taken place as the test was assembled. Further weighting is ineffective unless a test is very short. In such cases, usually it is better to lengthen the test than to weight the items, because lengthening the test permits better sampling of the content. In a sound test then, the number-right score is the most appropriate score for the classroom teacher to use.

A problem that often arises when separate answer sheets are used that require the examinee to blacken a space to indicate his choice among the alternatives is that of multiple marks for a single item. Sometimes it seems that the student has not erased carefully. Sometimes it seems he has just carelessly let his pencil rub the paper. Sometimes it looks as though he has put his pencil down marking a dot as he considered each alternative. And sometimes it looks as though he may have deliberately marked two choices hoping that one would be the correct one and the other would not be noticed through an opaque key with holes punched for the right responses. The recommended procedure for handling multiple marks is to scan all the answer sheets looking for them before scoring any of the papers. Where multiple answers are found, if one is darker it is considered to be the examinee's choice, and the other is erased if the paper is to be machine scored, or marked through with a colored pencil for hand scoring. If two or more marks are equally dark, both are erased for machine scoring, or both are marked through and neither is counted in hand scoring. The most modern scoring machines will choose the darker of unequally dark marks and eject for hand scoring answer sheets which cannot be decided that way.

Scoring Brief-Essay Items

We noted earlier that a fundamental problem of test items that require a student to write more than a few words is that the responses have to be judged by experts, and even the experts fail to agree on the quality of the responses. Judges disagree on the level of performance they require for a given mark or number of points. Judges are not even consistent with themselves if they grade the same papers twice. Judges' standards become higher (and grades lower) as they continue the judging task. Different judges look for different things as they score the same items (that is, one might judge in terms of the quality of the ideas presented, while another might judge in terms of the quality of the presentation of the ideas, for example). Some aspects of the responses that are irrelevant for the content which is being examined may influence the score given by the judge. The most common and noteworthy irrelevant aspect is the quality of the examinee's handwriting. A neatly written and legible paper usually gets a higher score, especially from a teacher with neat writing†, even if the content is no better handled than that presented in an untidy illegible handwriting.†

Another noteworthy irrelevant aspect has only recently been reported—that is the fact that a student's first name may markedly influence the grade a teacher gives his essay. In one study, 80 female elementary school teachers and 80 female first-year and second-year college students were asked to grade eight brief essays written by ten-year-olds. The papers were identified by first names and last initials. It was found that boys' papers with the names David and Michael got scores from elementary school teachers 2 to 5 points higher (on a 100-point scale) than the identical papers when headed by the names Elmer and Hubert. For girls, the name Adelle resulted in 6 to 8 points higher grade than the names Karen and Bertha, when the graders were elementary school teachers. The names did not influence grading when the graders were college students. It may be that teachers develop a bias toward certain given names as a result of their teaching experience.

An illustration of the problems involved in grading of essays is available in studies of the grading of essay examinations in law schools. Klein and Hart (1968) and Linn, Klein, and Hart (1972) studied the scores assigned to a common one-hour essay question on contract law that was included as part of a course final examination at 16 different law schools. Professors from all 16 law schools graded 80 representative essays from the law schools. Lay people also graded the papers according to the quality of the English composition and also according to their impression of correctness of responses according to legal principles. The papers were also scored for many characteristics such as quality of handwriting, length (total number of words written), use of legal jargon, citation of legal authorities, whether the examinee reached a conclusion about the case he was presented, the strength of the argument for the conclusion, and whether he presented both sides of the argument. Several "readability" scores such as number of words per sentence and number of uses of transitional phrases were used. Several composition scores such as number of grammatical errors and number of spelling errors were included. (Spelling and grammar errors were found[†] to lower essay grades in high-school history.) Number of construction errors and inconsistencies in English usage (such as changing person or tense) were two more scores.

The salient findings of these detailed studies were that even though in this case the professors agreed with themselves and with each other in rating their students' papers, only one school of thought about what should be evaluated seemed to be present, and standards seemed to remain constant through the grading of all 80 papers, there were still some doubtful elements in the grading. Some professors were more lenient than others; that is, they gave higher grades on the average than did others. The average grade for the 80 papers was modestly related to the quality of the handwriting. Further, the average grade on the essays was quite well predicted by the length of the essay and the lay person's impression of how correct it was. It was found that length of essay was not highly related to intelligence; the relation with length was not just a function of the more intelligent person using more words. It turned out that using intelligence and length also was a good way to predict essay grades; that is, good essays were written by intelligent, verbose students. More detailed analysis indicated that it was not just the number of words that was important, but the number of words that were written on issues in the case that law professors viewed as especially significant. Further, the use of legal jargon was given positive weight by the professors, and grammatical errors and construction errors were given negative weight. So to get a good grade on an essay question in contract law in these 16 law schools, a student would be well advised to write neatly, use legal jargon in his answer, avoid errors in English composition and grammar, and also demonstrate at length his competence in matters directly legal in nature.

Notice that this conclusion comes from studies of essay grades that are basically of good quality—that avoid many of the more common pitfalls in essay grading. Obviously the grading of essays in a manner that will be reliable, will avoid common errors associated with fluctuating standards, and will reflect the content to be examined rather than extraneous elements such as handwriting, English usage, verbosity, and so on, is no simple matter. We turn next to some procedures that may be useful in producing the best essay grades that we can obtain when essays are chosen as the measurement procedure.

One of the basic problems in scoring essay material is to keep one's standards reasonably constant. We know that teachers tend to let their general opinion of a student (called *halo*) influence their grades unless they are very careful. We also know[†] that standards tend to vary depending on how long the teacher has been working on a set of essays she has to grade (the standards become higher). It is also highly likely that after reading a poor paper a grader will be more generous on the next paper, and vice versa (called *adaptation level*). It has been found† that if a pupil writes several essays in poor handwriting, teachers give lower grades to the essays after the first as though they tolerated a little bad handwriting but retaliated after they became sufficiently exasperated by it.

A routine for reducing these problems consists of:

1. Removing from the papers the names of the students so that the grader will not be influenced by the name or by knowing whose paper is being graded,
2. Grading all of the answers to one question before going on to the next question, instead of grading all of one student's answers before going on to the next student,
3. Shuffling the papers between the grading of different questions so that no student ends up having his answers always graded first, last, in the middle, or after some other particularly able or inept student, and
4. Using an *analytic* method of scoring instead of a wholistic method.

By *analytic* method we mean using a model answer that is broken into the main elements to which points are to be given instead of merely reading the whole answer and making a general judgment of quality and total number of points to be given. The latter would be the *wholistic* method. Large scale commercial testing programs which use essay tests have found that by having several graders for each question and averaging their results, and by having each student answer several questions for which only brief responses are required, a wholistic method of scoring can give good results. However, teachers seldom can arrange to have a number of different graders for their students' papers, so that approach is not available very often. Thus, for classroom purposes, it is more effective to use analytical scoring based on a model answer with predetermined numbers of points for critical elements. The analytical method will ordinarily yield higher scores and more reliable scores.

It is good practice and improves quality and reliability of scoring if more than one person scores each brief essay response and the scores of the several readers are averaged together for each student. This helps to reduce the effect of idiosyncracies of individual scorers. Thus, when a teacher can, she should get one of her colleagues to score her students' papers independently. If the first scorer anticipates that the papers may be scored again, she should make no marks on the papers which might influence the second scorer. Instead, her comments or marks should be written in a separate notebook, or on a separate sheet that can be attached to the student's paper after the second scoring but before the paper is returned to the student.

Finally, if she wants to consider such things as good English, or accurate computation, or quality of handwriting, or neatness in evaluating brief essay papers, these elements should be given separate grades, and every attempt should be made to keep them from influencing the level of grade the student is given on his achievement of the subject matter of the examination. Only in this way can the score for achievement of the subject matter retain any useful meaning for the student or for grading purposes. Even if they are not to be used, a teacher who finds it difficult to ignore such characteristics of essays which are important but not directly relevant to the subject matter may find it easier to restrict her subject-matter grade to the student's achievement in the subject if she gives a separate grade for each characteristic, such as neatness, that bothers her.

For an interesting exercise in essay grading, try grading the following English paper, a brief essay on "My Pet." Work with several of your fellow students to see how you agree on scoring and what you must do to achieve close agreement.

MY PET

When i was a little boy I wanted a pup and my dady gave me a brown and wite one with one black ear and a tail that waged like my sisters pony tale behind. I called him Rip cause he ripped around the house but mostly thro my moms legs when she tried to catch him and made her mad but not mad like my sister wen he ripped her formal behind but he does not rip when he sleps with me he only scratches flees in my bed

Legal Aspects of Classroom Testing

A few aspects of classroom testing sometimes come up for scrutiny outside the school. For example, in New Jersey, a young woman reportedly was given a blank piece of paper instead of a diploma at her school's graduation ceremonies because she failed written badminton and tennis tests given in her high school's gym classes. Her legal representative was reported in the news media in 1974 to be taking up her case with the local education authorities because these tests were given only to girls in that high school. Three of the young woman's five brothers had already graduated from that high school without having to pass the tests that prevented her graduation. It is highly likely that sexual discrimination, such as this appears to be, will not be acceptable any longer in our society.

Cheating, or the suspicion of it, poses another legal problem in classroom testing. The teacher should make reasonable efforts to avoid the problem, of course, and when she detects its occurrence, she should make sure that she has clear and convincing evidence before making a charge. In the case of Kathleen Ryan, in 1926 (*Ryan* v. *Board of Education*) her history teacher thought Kathleen might have been using notes to assist her with her final examination. The teacher stopped Kathleen during the exam, and Kathleen was denied credit in history and therefore was also denied graduation. When the case was taken to court, the court directed that she be given a passing grade and the diploma. It was not clear that Kathleen had ever looked at the notes which were on top of her desk under her ink well.

In another case, Royal Anne Carter was accused of cheating on a college makeup examination in Latin I at the University of North Carolina in 1961 (*In re Carter*). The Honor Council found her guilty and suspended her, but after various appeals the issue found its way into the courtroom. There the judge determined that all the evidence offered failed to rebut the presumption of innocence, and that to deny her readmission was arbitrary and capricious. After legal appeals, the university was ordered to rehear the case to determine whether cheating did occur. If so, all parties agreed that cheating on an exam was adequate cause for expulsion or suspension from the university.

In still another case, Patricia Bluett, a medical student at the University of Illinois in 1953, was accused of having another person write her examination for her (*People ex rel. Bluett* v. *Board of Trustees*). She was suspended and eventually expelled without even having a formal hearing. The court ruled that there were appropriate precedents for expulsion without formal hearings.

These are not many cases upon which to base generalizations about what courts in different jurisdictions will decide in specific cases, but carelessness in developing evidence of cheating seems to be unwise, and certainly the problem is better forestalled than struggled with after it has occurred.

References

In re Carter, 262 NC 360, 137 SE 2d 150, 1964.

Klein, S. & Hart, F. Chance and systematic factors affecting essay grades. *J. educ. Measmt,* 1968, **5**, 197-206.

Linn, R., Klein, S., & Hart, F. The nature and correlates of law school essay grades. *Educ. psychol. Measmt,* 1972, **32**, 267-79.

People ex rel. Bluett v. *Board of Trustees*, 10 Ill. App. 2d 207, 134 N.E. 2d 635, 1956.

Ryan v. *Board of Education*, 124 Kan. 89, 257 Pac. 945, 1927.

5

Analyzing, Evaluating, and Improving Tests

Objectives

For this chapter the objectives are that you be able to:
1. Describe the role and purposes of item analysis for teacher-made tests;
2. Define difficulty level of a test item;
3. Define discrimination value of a test item;
4. Describe the role that item difficulty and discrimination have on test score standard deviation and why this is important for reliability and validity;
5. Find item difficulty and discrimination indices from tabled responses to an item;
6. Describe how to find item difficulty and discrimination values by three procedures: classroom analysis, teacher analysis, and computer analysis;
7. Draw sound inferences and hypotheses about items from their difficulty and discrimination indices;
8. Describe the evaluation of distractors and interpret results of distractor analyses;
9. Contrast the virtues of computer item analyses with classroom item analyses.

Obtaining Reliable Scores

Probably most teachers construct the tests they give their students with little thought that a study of the results of using the tests might result in their improvement. It should be obvious after our consideration of the techniques in writing items that one has goals, such as writing items of the optimum difficulty level, items that will discriminate between those students who have learned more than others and those who have learned less, and, in general, items that will yield reliable measurements. After all, without reliability there is no hope for validity, and we must have valid measurements or we will be deceiving ourselves and our students.

The logic goes this way. We make sure that we have material that is relevant, and thus potentially valid, by relying on our table of specifications or our list of behavioral objectives as we write items. We make sure that our test is reliable, and thus potentially valid, by estimating the reliability of its scores. If we have relevant items and reliable scores, we are safe in assuming that we have valid measures—that we will not be deceived by having measured irrelevancies or by having scores that are random numbers, based on chance rather than student knowledge.

However, to get reliable scores we have to do two things, basically. We have to use a sufficient number of items, and we have to have a reasonably large spread of scores, i.e., standard deviation. For classroom achievement tests, the standard deviation will usually be values between 10% and 20% of the number of items. The nearer we get to the 20% figure, the higher the reliability will tend to be, and relatively large standard deviations are what we are after as we write items. The relative size of the standard deviation is closely related to the level of discrimination of the items — and that is why we will learn to compute a discrimination index for each item, why we seek items with large discrimination indices, and why we learn to improve the discrimination of the items we have used. The alternative is simply to write other items, but study has indicated that more is to be gained by time spent in improving items than by simply writing other items which themselves may need improvement.[†]

The effect of size of standard deviation can be seen by reconsidering our expression for estimating reliability

$$r_{xx} = 1 - \frac{VEM}{SD^2}.$$

Remember, VEM is determined by the number of items, i.e., 2/10 of the number of items. SD^2 is estimated from the range of scores. To the extent that we can make SD^2 large for a given number of items, the ratio of VEM to SD^2 becomes smaller, and less is being subtracted from 1. The result is higher reliability from a given number of items.

One more aspect needs mentioning. There is greater potential for high discrimination from items that are at the optimum difficulty level; so as we analyze items and evaluate them, we should consider their difficulty levels as one possible avenue of improvement and resultant increase in reliability.

Thus, the effective teacher seeks to analyze the results of her tests, item by item, in order to revise the items and to reuse the best ones on future classes. Eventually she will develop a sizable pool of tested and evaluated items from which she can build future tests efficiently and with confidence that her measurements will be sound guides instead of wastes of time or, at worst, deceptive indicators of student development.

We are going to examine in detail three methods of test and item analysis. Many different methods and techniques are possible, but these three should satisfy the needs of most teachers. One is a method for use in the classroom. The students are involved in the process, saving the teacher time and effort while at the same time reviewing and perhaps learning. The strategy is to capitalize on student interest in test results in order to explain and elaborate on concepts that analysis suggests need additional work.

The second method is useful in situations in which the teacher cannot or does not want to involve the students. It may be used for analysis of a test given to an earlier or different class, or for doing an analysis when students are not available. To make this kind of analysis feasible with groups of typical class size, certain short-cuts are taken, and this results in a different approach to some matters.

The third method to be considered is available to teachers in many large systems in which there are computer facilities. Computers can analyze tests and items very efficiently, at little cost, and with more extensive and refined results than are reasonably obtainable any other way.

Item Analysis in the Classroom[1]

There are three levels or degrees of analysis of items. The first level reveals how difficult each question was. This serves two purposes. First, it indicates which items were very difficult (less than half of the class got them correct). These items need revision or else the instruction needs improvement for the future. Second, it indicates which concepts need further discussion and elaboration with a given class before proceeding with new material.

The second level of analysis indicates not only the degree of difficulty of each item, but also the degree to which the people who get the item correct also get other items on the test correct, and the people who get the item wrong also get other items on the test wrong. This is the discrimination value of the item. The underlying idea is that most tests are fairly homogeneous in content, and one might reasonably expect that each item would help evaluate the degree to which a student has learned the homogeneous body of content. Each item can be thought of as a sample of the possible items that might be asked on the content, and by accumulation of items one gets a more thorough sampling of the content. The best students are the ones who can answer correctly items on any aspect of the content. If an item does not agree with the rest of the items in this sense, one wonders whether something is wrong with the item. This lack of agreement would be reflected by a low or negative discrimination index.

The third level of analysis indicates not only the difficulty level and the discrimination value for each item but what happened to each of the decoy responses. The best items have a pattern of responses in which every alternative is chosen by at least one examinee, the correct alternative is chosen by more of the students who get good scores on the total test than by students who get poor scores, and the reverse is true for the decoys, i.e., they are more popular for the poor scorers than the good scorers. Any alternatives that do not fit that pattern are candidates for revision before subsequent use of the item in another test.

The teacher ordinarily chooses the level to which she wishes to go in her analysis before she starts, but she may decide to use the third level only for items that look suspicious after evaluation at the second level. Ordinarily she would not use both the first and second levels of analysis because the second level includes the first, and to use both is wasteful of time and effort.

---

[1]The author is indebted to the presentation of these procedures by Paul Diederich in *Shortcut Statistics for Teacher Made Tests* (Princeton, N.J.: Educational Testing Service, 1960).

DIFFICULTY ANALYSIS

The difficulty level of an item is expressed in terms of the proportion of examinees who get the item correct. NOTE: There is a problem here in that tradition somehow got backwards, and the index which really tells how *easy* the item is (proportion who get it *correct*) is called the *difficulty* index. You must simply learn to keep this straight because it is too late to change the tradition. Hard items have low difficulty indices — near zero. Easy items have high difficulty indices — near 1.00. It is too bad that this problem exists, but it does, and there is no solution except to keep your thinking straight about what the difficulty index is — the proportion who get the item *correct*.

To do an analysis of the difficulty levels of the items of a test in the classroom with the help of the students is easy. The first step in any analysis of items, of course, is to get the papers scored. A common way of doing this is to have the students exchange papers and score each other's papers. The students should mark each item that is wrong.

At the next step the teacher has a choice to make. To get the proportion correct for each item, she is going to ask to raise their hands all students with papers on which a particular item is correct. She will count the hands that are raised and put this number in the margin beside that item on her master copy of the test. When these numbers are divided by the number who took the test, the result is the proportion correct for each item. These are the difficulty indices for the items. The choice the teacher has to make is whether to have the papers returned to the persons whose answers are on them, or to leave them with some other student while the hands are being raised. If she returns them to the original examinees, there is the potential objection that astute but snoopy students will look around and find out how their fellow students performed. This seems like an invasion of privacy. If the teacher does not have the papers returned to the original examinees during the item analysis, it is less easy for students to look around and find out how each other did, but every student then knows from the paper in his hand exactly how at least one other student performed. Although no research on the topic is widely cited, it seems more palatable to students to use the procedure in which the papers are not returned before the show of hands for item analysis.

The teacher can make the procedure more interesting to the students if she posts on the chalkboard the difficulty level of each item, as well as entering it on her master copy of the test. Then the students can clearly see which items were hardest, and the teacher can readily move into discussion of those items. In her discussion she will be trying to accomplish two things. First, she will be finding out from the students why they got a particular item wrong. This may indicate how the item can be improved — or that the item should not be used any more. Second, she may discover that the item is good, but the students have not learned something they should know. She will never find a more opportune time to reteach that material than just after a test when the students are usually as highly motivated to learn as they ever will be.

As the teacher goes over the difficulty indices for the items of her test to see what might be done to improve the test, she needs some guidelines. Items are too hard if the difficulty value (usually called the p value as shorthand for *proportion correct*) is below 0.50. For two-choice items, in which the optimum difficulty level is 0.85, as you remember, items are too hard if the *p* value is below about 0.60. Items are too easy if the *p* values are above 0.90. They are too easy in the sense that they don't have much potential for effective discrimination and thus increasing the standard deviation. However, a teacher may want to keep easy items in a test if their purpose is to check to be certain that important basic concepts are mastered by nearly everyone. She must realize that those items do not contribute to sound measurement in the sense of discriminating among students. They serve a different purpose, which may indeed be worthwhile.

Sometimes it is found that some items which are too difficult or too easy by these standards still help in discriminating among students. This is determined by means of the second level of analysis. Such items may be retained in spite of their extreme ease or difficulty, but it is likely that they may be made even more discriminating if the difficulty level is adjusted by careful revision.

We have said that items may be easy if they test important concepts that everyone should know. They may also be easy if there are giveaways, such as specific determiners, grammatical cues, and so on, that have not been removed in the item writing and editing phases of test construction. Items may be hard for several reasons. A very low difficulty index should always suggest that the key be checked to be sure it is not in error. A second possibility is that there are two correct answers, or that a distinction is being required among several alternatives that has not been taught clearly in class. Ambiguous stems also make items harder, and items on minor or trivial points may show up as difficult. They may also be worthless from the point of validity.

DISCRIMINATION ANALYSIS

As with analysis for difficulty, for discrimination analysis the tests must first be scored. But this time we must also put the papers into rank order according to the score, because now we want to select the papers with the highest scores and the papers with the lowest scores and see whether the people in the former group got a particular item correct while those in the latter got the item wrong. For classroom item analysis we use all of the papers so that all of the students will be interested and involved. Usually the teacher has to find the paper or group of papers that have the middle (median) score in the class. She can either collect the papers and do this quickly, or she can create a frequency distribution of scores at the chalkboard. She merely calls off each score, starting with the highest possible score and asks everyone with a paper receiving that score to raise his hand. She counts the hands and puts that number by the score and then does this for every score until everyone in the class is accounted for.

Then she counts down from the top or up from the bottom until she reaches the score which divides the class into two equal parts. Suppose that score were 17, there were three students obtaining that score, and only one of them was needed to account for the low half of the class. The teacher would pick up those answer sheets and have a student draw one at random from the three. That answer sheet would then go into the lower group, and the remainder would go into the upper group. If there is an odd number of students in the class, then one of the papers in the middle should be selected at random and set aside so the upper and lower groups are equal in size. The student whose paper is set aside can become the teacher's assistant at the chalkboard, recording the results of the analysis. If there is an even number of examinees, the teacher can do the recording at the chalkboard.

Now the teacher needs to arrange so that it will be easy to count the papers in the upper and lower groups which have the correct answer. The easiest way to do this is to find the line through the people in the classroom that divides the number of students into halves. Then all of the answer sheets in the upper group should be passed to one side of the line, and all those in the lower group passed to the other. This is much easier than trying to have people move from one side to the other. Any papers that were assigned at random due to ties at the dividing score should be returned to the correct sides of the room. At this time one person toward the back of each of the upper and lower groups should be chosen as the counter — someone who can count hands for you.

After the room is set, the next thing is the chalkboard, where there should be a vertical list of numbers, one number for each item of the test. Next to each item number there should be entries for the number of papers in the upper group with the correct answer, the number of papers in the lower group with the correct answer, the difference between those two numbers, and the sum of those numbers. Headings for those columns should be set up, like this:

Item	U	L	U−L	U+L
1				
2				

The procedure for making the analysis is that the teacher (or student assistant when there is an odd number of students) stands at the chalkboard and calls out the number. (She may also have to call out the key if answer sheets do not have individual items marked right or wrong.) Then she says, "All students whose papers have the item correct raise their hands." After a moment she says, "Upper group." The counter for the upper group counts the raised hands in his group and calls out the tally. At the same time the counter for the lower group is counting his hands. After the teacher has marked the tally for the upper group she says, "Lower Group." The counter for that group then gives his count. The teacher writes these counts on the board and quickly makes the subtraction and the addition. Then she calls out the next item number and the process continues until all the items have been tallied. This sounds complicated, but after a class gets used to the procedure it proceeds quite rapidly with a rhythm that makes the exercise more fun than work.

The result on the chalkboard is numbers that indicate the difficulty and discrimination values for each item. The teacher should transfer them to her master copy of the test, writing the $U+L$ and $U-L$ values beside each item. If there is an odd number of papers, she can be doing this while the student assistant is putting the numbers on the chalkboard.

Of course, $U+L$ is the number of students in the class who got the item correct. When each $U+L$ sum is divided by the total number of students in the class, we have our difficulty index or "p value" for the item.

The $U-L$ value for each item indicates the difference between the number in the upper group and the number in the lower group who got the item correct, and this indicates the ability of the item to discriminate between students who do well on the whole test and those who do not perform well on the whole test. The guide recommended for interpreting $U-L$ values is that for good items they should be at least

10% of the class. For example, in a class of 36 students, for good items $U - L$ values would be about 4 or larger. At least four more students in the upper group than in the lower group would get the item correct. For items that are very hard or easy, with p values of less than 0.05 or more than 0.95 let's say, we might accept lower discrimination values, say only 5%. Remember that items that are very hard or easy are handicapped for being good discriminators.

The values of 10% and 5% are useful guides, but they cannot be followed rigidly. First, we usually have very small numbers of people for classroom item analyses. The big testing companies would not trust item analysis data on fewer than three or four hundred people because with small numbers there is too much fluctuation from one group of examinees to another. In other words, with classroom-sized groups you might get a discrimination value of less than 10% one time and more than 10% another time even from two random samples from the same class. So with classroom-sized groups, the item analysis results can be thought of only as guides or cues.

Certainly a negative discrimination value would cause us to look carefully at the item to see why the better students should have more trouble with it than the weaker students. Sometimes it will be obvious once we are led to the problem by the item analysis. If not, one can ask the students why they answered the way they did, and see if better wording of the item would solve the problem. They may tell you that you confused them in teaching the concept. Then you reteach right on the spot so the concept is clarified for this group. You also alter your approach for subsequent groups so that the problem won't arise again. The item may be perfectly alright.

Of course, an item which is keyed wrong or has more than one correct answer is unlikely to discriminate well. If it is so hard that most students are just guessing at it, it won't discriminate well either. (Obviously, you would *not* want to use discrimination indices of the sort we have calculated here to improve items from a pretest before instruction because you expect most students only to be guessing at that point in their study!)

If an item covers an important point, and if you can detect no obvious problem with it even though it gets a low discrimination index, the best thing to do is to try it one or two more times on different classes. Maybe it will turn out to be satisfactory. Sometimes the only thing to do is to discard the item, however, and replace it with another or with a different kind of evaluation technique. Research on the use of discrimination indices to evaluate the quality of items indicates a substantial relationship between size of discrimination index and lack of flaws in the item.[†]

One other possible cause for a low discrimination value is that an item may be a good item but unrelated to the other items in the test. This should not happen very often in teacher-made tests, but if you do have only one item on a concept that is different from the other material in the test, there is no reason to expect that those who perform well on the rest of the test will also perform well on this single unrelated item. Thus, it may get a low discrimination index that does not really describe the quality of the item. The item would have to be given among other similar items in order to evaluate its discrimination value.

The usefulness of this kind of analysis of the discrimination values of items is indicated in a study[†] in which it was found that it only took one-fifth as much time to improve an item as it did to write a new replacement for it. However, the discrimination values of improved items were noticeably higher, on the average, than the values for replacement items. In other words, it is wasteful to throw away the work that has already been done on an item that does not discriminate well. It is better to polish it up than to go back to the drawing board and start all over.

DISTRACTOR ANALYSIS

For some items, further analysis will assist in evaluating the items or in improving them. This consists of an analysis of the effectiveness of each alternative response to the item — especially of the effectiveness of the distractors. As we have said, ideally the alternatives of an item show the following pattern:

1. Every alternative should be marked by at least one examinee.
2. More examinees in the upper group than in the lower group should answer the correct alternative.
3. More examinees in the lower group than in the upper group should answer each distractor.
4. More than half of the examinees should answer the correct alternative, and the nearer the proportion is to the optimal proportions that were presented earlier, the better.

It is not really necessary to analyze the functioning of the distractors of every item in a test. Items that seem to have appropriate p values and reasonably large discrimination values can be accepted as sound until other evidence indicates they should be questioned. However, the items that have low p values or the items that have low or negative discrimination values may be improved through distractor analysis, and even the very easy items may be improved through the removal of distractors that are unused. These items are the ones that should be examined in the manner we will look at next.

For distractor analysis, the same upper and lower groups are used that were used in discrimination analysis. Therefore it is a good idea for the teacher to proceed to distractor analysis immediately after discrimination analysis if she intends to use distractor analysis at all. By doing so, she avoids having to reassemble the upper and lower groups. So she should quickly examine the p values and discrimination values from the discrimination analysis and decide on which items it would be particularly helpful to get distractor analyses.

She proceeds by having the person at the blackboard set up a new table for the first item to be further analyzed. This table has a column for each distractor, and rows for the upper and lower groups, as in table 5-1.

Table 5-1

	Alternatives				
	1	2	3	4	5
Upper					
Lower					

The teacher asks for all the students on whose papers alternative number 1 is marked to raise their hands. She then asks, "Upper Group?" and the monitor tells her how many in the upper group raised their hands. Then, "Lower Group," and the lower group monitor gives her that number. These numbers are entered in the appropriate rows under alternative 1. The same procedure is followed for each of the remaining alternatives. When the table is complete, the teacher copies it beside the item on her master copy, and the next item to be analyzed in this manner is taken up in the same way.

The pattern of results for a good item for thirty students might be as in table 5-2, where alternative three is the correct answer.

Table 5-2

	Alternatives				
	1	2	**3**	4	5
Upper	1	0	14	0	0
Lower	3	2	7	1	2

This item follows our characteristics of the ideal item. There are 70% choosing the correct answer, approximately optimal for a five-choice, multiple-choice item. The $U - L$ index would be 7, well over the 10% required for a good item. Every distractor was chosen at least once, and more in the lower than in the upper group chose every decoy.

An item that is too difficult may have a distractor that receives more choices by both the upper and lower groups than does the correct answer. If the item has not been keyed incorrectly, and if there are not two correct answers, then this result is a clear clue that either this distractor needs to be revised or eliminated, or else the instruction must be modified so that the concept represented by this distractor is learned to be an incorrect choice in the situation represented by the stem of the item. If such a popular distractor is chosen more often by the upper group than the lower, we have perhaps the worst possible result. It suggests that there is more than one correct answer, or at least instruction is failing to eliminate a popular misconception.

Sometimes a distractor will not be more popular than the correct answer but will be more often chosen by the upper than the lower group, a reverse kind of discrimination. Such distractors may be ambiguous, and clarifying their wording may reduce their popularity with the upper group. If that does not seem feasible, the best alternative may be to eliminate that distractor or replace it with a different one. With this situation and with the situation in which a distractor is not chosen by anyone, reuse of the distractor with additional groups of examinees may reveal that the results including more people are not the same. That is, given enough examinees, someone does choose the distractor or the lower group finds the distractor more attractive than does the upper group. If further use produces the same results, the distractor should be dropped or replaced. Distractors which are never used simply waste time and effort, adding nothing to measurement. Further tentative use of the distractor is a good idea whenever examination of the item does not reveal why it is faulty.

Some item writers insist that every distractor for an item should have a rationale — the item writer should be able to state just why someone would choose that alternative instead of the correct answer. If that practice is followed in writing items, the most likely remaining failure in item writing is ambiguity. With experience in item writing and item analysis, one is continually surprised by the observation that what seemed perfectly clear and unambiguous to him as he wrote the item turns out to be confusing to the examinee. Having items reviewed by a colleague is, of course, one way to reduce the problem, but colleagues are not students, after all, and they, too, see things differently from the vantage point of their experience.

Distractor analysis in class is a good way to get clues as to the location of the flaw that makes the item less effective than is desired, but the item analysis results do not tell us what is wrong or what change should be made. Here is where one of the great virtues of item analysis in class comes in. The teacher can simply ask the students why they chose the wrong answer or did not choose the correct answer. Often they can tell why they made the error, and when the teacher asks how the item should be written to measure the same concept effectively, the students can present useful ideas for item revision. At the same time that this process is taking place, the teacher has an unusually good opportunity to clarify the concept, essentially to reteach the material, if that is necessary, to a group of students whose interest is high. The combination of getting students to reduce the labor of item analysis, getting their help in improving items, and getting their attention for reteaching of important concepts makes item analysis in class a very attractive procedure, well worth the time it takes.

As a result of item analysis in class, or other item analyses, the teacher may find items that are so defective for a group that fairness suggests that they should not have been in the test at all. If there are very many items like that, the teacher may decide to rescore the test leaving those items out. This shortens the test, but it usually does not reduce reliability since the items being left out were ineffective items, anyway. If the teacher uses a large number of items during a course of instruction, the deletion of bad items and rescoring of tests probably has little effect on final evaluations such as grades. In that sense it probably is not worthwhile. Sometimes students feel very strongly that a test should be rescored without the faulty items, however. Often they do not realize that when a test is rescored this way, the only thing that happens is that some students lose some points. No one gains any points. When this is explained, for some reason many times the students when allowed to vote as to whether the test should be rescored will vote against rescoring. Thus, it is hard to give a recommendation about scoring that is satisfactory. It's hardly worth the effort. Students do not agree among themselves that they want it. Probably the reason they don't agree is that they don't understand the whole process, which often includes evaluating a score in terms of its level relative to the scores of other students.

Item Analysis by the Teacher[2]

A second approach to analysis of test items is necessary for those situations in which the teacher does not want to involve the students or perhaps cannot involve them. For example, she may have a test given to a previous class whose items she wants to analyze. Or for some reason she may feel that it is more beneficial for her to use her

---

[2]The author is indebted for some of these ideas to the filmstrip *Making Your Own Test,* developed by the Cooperative Test Division of Educational Testing Service, Princeton, New Jersey. Used by permission.

own time to analyze items and use the class time for other activities. For classes with 20 students or less, the teacher can proceed in a manner parallel to the procedure described above. It is parallel, rather than the same, in that the teacher must do her own counting of responses. For example, for difficulty level analysis, she merely counts the number of student papers on which the correct answer is marked. Dividing these counts by the total number of examinees gives her the *p* value of each item. These values are then compared with the optimal *p* values for items of the same kind to see whether the item is too hard or too easy and whether further analysis of the item is indicated.

For discrimination analysis, the teacher must divide the papers into two groups, those who scored above the median on the test and those who scored below the median. (The median is the same as the fiftieth percentile, i.e., the score that divides a group into two equal sized groups, half above it and half below.) Then she should prepare a summary sheet, like the answer sheet but with the columns, U, L, U−L, and U + L, so that these data can be recorded for each item, as shown in table 5-3.

Table 5-3

Item Number	U	L	U−L	U+L
1				
2				
3				

Now the teacher should stack the answer sheets for the upper group on top of the key and put the summary sheet on top of the answer sheets, doing this in such a way that the keyed response for each item is visible on the key and the response spaces on each answer sheet are visible. Since there are 20 or fewer students to be considered, she never has more than 10 answer sheets in such a stack.

She then counts the number of answers that agree with the key for the first item and records that number under the column labeled "U" for that item. She does this with each of the other items in succession. She then removes the answer sheets for the upper group and puts in their place the answer sheets for the lower group. She counts the number of answers that agree with the key for each item again, but this time she records them under the column labeled "L." Then she adds U+L, and subtracts L from U, for each item on the summary sheet, and she has completed her discrimination analysis. For this kind of analysis, with 20 or fewer students, she should apply the standards suggested for classroom item analysis, i.e., discrimination values of 10% of the class encourage her to think that an item is working well, and 5% is encouraging if an item is unusually easy or difficult. The *p* values (U+L divided by the number of examinees) are compared with the optimal values for items of that number of alternatives.

To analyze distractors by this method for 20 or fewer examinees, the only change is in the form of the summary sheet. Instead of having columns U, L, U−L, and U+L, a blank sheet of paper with the item numbers on it should be used. When the papers for the upper group are being recorded, the number who choose each alternative for an item are entered in small numbers in the upper half of the line for an item; when the papers for the lower group are being recorded, the number choosing each alternative is entered in the lower half of the line for the item. The result is a pattern like the following:

	7	0	1	2	0
Item 1					
	4	0	2	3	1

If the first alternative in the example is the correct answer, we would have a p value of 0.55 for the item, which is a little hard but not bad, and a $U - L$ index of 3 which is more than 10% of the group, and indicates the item is functioning rather well. The only concern indicated by the analysis is that alternative 2 did not attract anyone. However, with only 20 cases, this may be misleading; the item should be tried several times more on groups of this size to see whether that alternative ever is attractive to anyone. If it never seems to draw any takers, it might as well be eliminated and the item shortened to one with four alternatives. Or, possibly another useful distractor could be tried in the place of alternative number 2.

For tests with more than 20 examinees, we take some shortcuts to save labor for the teacher. The main one is that we choose our upper and lower groups to be those *ten* students with the highest scores and those *ten* with the lowest scores, leaving out of our analysis the rest of the students who are in the middle. (This procedure will probably be adequate for classes up to 65 or 70 in size. Above that size one should seek the help of a computer or the advice of someone with advanced training in educational measurement.) In choosing the upper ten and the lower ten, if there are ties at the critical scores, we choose the number we need to constitute our ten by a random method.

Once having set up our upper and lower ten, we proceed just as we did with 20 or fewer students, with the following differences in standards. First, we compute the p values just as with 20 or fewer students and we accept them as adequate indicators of difficulty level, even though we left out the students in the middle. (Our divisor for p values is 20, not the number of students in the class.) Experience indicates that the approximation which results from this shortcut is satisfactory for evaluating whether items are so extreme in difficulty or so far from the optimal values that they deserve further attention. Second, for the discrimination analysis we set different standards for $U - L$ in determining whether discrimination level is high enough that we need not be concerned that the item is wasted. Now we ask that $U - L$ equal 3 or more for items of near optimal difficulty and 2 or more for items with very high or very low p values. The differences between this standard and the standard of 10% and 5% that we used before occurs because we are leaving out the cases in the middle in this approach.

There is no essential difference in distractor analysis for the case of more than 20 students. You are still looking for alternatives that no one chooses, that are more popular than the correct choice, or that function backwards, i.e., are wrong but are more often chosen by the upper than the lower group.

One thing that you can do that is an advantage over the case with 20 or fewer students is to look among the left out middle students for cases in which an apparently unattractive distractor does draw a response. For example, if the upper 10 vs. lower 10 analysis indicates that no one chose alternative 2 to item number 1, you could look through the remaining papers to see whether any of these people chose response 2. If someone did, then the item passes muster on this account. If no one did, and if there are a large number of papers, say 30 or 40, in the middle, then it becomes doubtful that alternative 2 is a worthwhile distractor, and it might well be eliminated.

Item Analysis by Computer

Most universities, many colleges, and many large city school systems have available to their teachers computerized procedures for analysis of tests and test items. Often the better organized facilities can provide the results of test and item analyses within four to eight hours of the time the answer sheets and keys are turned in for analysis. (The actual analysis by the computer may take only a matter of seconds, but assembling the materials, conveying them to the computer, waiting in line for processing, returning them, etc., take up minutes and hours.) The computer procedures are usually exceedingly accurate, and they can be used on any number of cases with no adjustment for sample size.

The only thing the teacher has to do is arrange to have the examinees mark their answers on standard answer sheets with pencils that make satisfactory marks, and to assemble the answer sheets with another sheet, the key, on which the correct answers have also been marked with an appropriate pencil. These are turned in to the agency that provides the item analysis service, and a few hours later a computer printout with the results is returned to the teacher along with the answer sheets and key she turned in.

To get the best results, the teacher may want to scan the answer sheets to be sure that each student has made dark enough marks and has not made stray marks on the answer sheet. Most modern facilities have machines to read the answer sheets that automatically score whichever mark for an item is the darkest if a student has made more than one mark, so even scanning is not too important except perhaps with third or fourth graders or students who have never used machine-scorable answer sheets previously. (For children below the third grade, it may be unwise to try to use separate answer sheets in giving tests. There is evidence that these children may not be very successful in avoiding making errors in the answer-marking process.[†] If the teacher wants to use machine scoring and analysis, she might do well to transfer the students' marks from the test booklet to machine answer sheets, usually not too great a task for short tests.)

The virtues of computer analyses are, of course, the accuracy, the elaborate results, and the absence of concern about using special procedures to allow for sample size, but perhaps more important are the saving of teacher and class time, and the fact that approximate methods are no longer used to save effort. While class time is saved, there is the drawback that the students are not so intimately involved in study of the items as they would be during item analysis by show of hands in class. This drawback can be overcome if the teacher discusses the test in class, using the computerized item analysis to direct attention to the most difficult items and the items with the lowest (or negative) discrimination indices. If she takes up each item that fewer than half of the class got correct (p less than 0.50), she will have covered nearly all the problems that the students will want to bring up and that deserve further elaboration or reteaching.

It should be realized that our earlier use of p values based on upper and lower 10 cases instead of on all the examinees, and our use of $U - L$ as a discrimination index, were shortcuts to save labor. The computerized item analysis will usually compute a p value for each item based on all of the examinees no matter how few or many. Naturally, if the p value is based on only a few examinees, one will have to remember that the obtained p value is "wobbly," i.e., further analysis on more examinees may change the p value markedly. Computer analysis does not make up for small groups of examinees.

CORRELATION

The computer will ordinarily use as a discrimination index some form of a *correlation coefficient* between success on the specific item and success on all the items in the test, i.e., total test score. Correlation coefficients are statistics that describe with numbers the degree of relationship between sets of pairs of numbers. For instance, we might find the correlation coefficient (symbolized by the letter r) between the height and weight of all the students in a class. The height and weight of an individual form a pair of numbers. Similarly we might assign the number 1 to each person who answered a particular item correctly, and the number zero to each person who answered that item incorrectly. Pairs could be formed of each student's score on that item (zero or one) and his total score on the test which includes the item. A correlation coefficient could be calculated between those paired sets of numbers. If ones go with high scores, and zeros with low scores, the correlation coefficient will be high and positive. That is what we would want.

The correlation between two sets of numbers is on a scale which ranges from -1.00 to $+1.00$. A coefficient of zero indicates that there is no relationship between the pairs of numbers, that when one number is high the other is not more often high or low — it may be anything. A high positive correlation, near $+1.00$, indicates that if one number is high, the other is most likely to be high. A high negative correlation, near -1.00, indicates that if one number is high the other is most likely to be low. The correlation between height and weight of children of the same age is probably modestly positive, maybe about $+.25$.

There are a number of different procedures for computing correlation coefficients, and they have different names. They may be identified as biserial r, point-biserial r, tetrachoric r, etc., but that need not disturb the teacher who uses the computer results. The same index will be used for all of the items on a test, and invariably values near zero or less than zero are causes for concern while the largest positive values indicate the best items on the test in terms of discrimination. Discrimination values of $+1.00$ are the largest possible, and many experts look with disfavor in items with correlation discrimination values less than $+.30$. Teachers often will not be as good at writing items as experts are, however, and acceptable items may have discrimination values in teacher-made tests as low as $+.15$. If all the items in a test have discrimination values that low, it would require a great many items to reach a satisfactory level of reliability for a single test. However, most teachers are going to make major evaluations not on the basis of one test, but on the basis of the results of many tests during a term. So low reliability of a single teacher-made test is not as serious a matter as low reliability for an intelligence test or other commercial standardized test.

Furthermore, the numbers of examinees with which teachers deal will often be small, and for one class an item may have a discrimination value of only .15, but for the next class it might rise to .45. Even negative discrimination values may reverse themselves on new small groups of examinees. But the negative values often are very useful clues to flaws in the items that, once signaled by item analysis, are easily recognized and corrected. That is the beauty of item analysis for classroom teachers — a good way to get useful clues on test-item revision, rather than a means of evaluating the quality of items or tests.

It is not possible to catalog or describe all the varieties of results that might come from the various computer programs and machine configurations that exist. We will try to describe below the general nature of output that might be found, but the teacher may find that for understanding the computer facility available to her she needs to discuss the item analysis program with an expert in the computer center.

RESULTS PROVIDED BY COMPUTER ITEM ANALYSIS

The better computer item analysis programs provide the following kinds of information from an item analysis. First, they will identify the test, the teacher, the date, and provide other information desired by the teacher to identify her material. Then the computer output will provide the average test score for the examinees whose papers have been submitted for analysis, and the printout will give the standard deviation of those scores. Somewhere the printout will give an estimate of the reliability of the scores.

Then the analysis will turn to each item and report the number of people in the upper and lower groups who chose each alternative response. It will indicate the keyed response also. The form might be as shown in table 5-4.

Table 5-4

Item Number 1						
Response	1	2*	3	4	5	Omit
Upper 50%	5	21	2	0	0	2
Lower 50%	8	18	0	0	4	0

This result would be interpreted by the teacher as follows. The keyed response was alternative 2. Since each row totals 30 cases and since the analysis is based on upper and lower 50%, there were 60 papers. The Omit column indicates that 2 students in the upper group did not answer the item. The numbers under the keyed response indicate that 39 of the 60 got the correct answer, so the item was near optimal difficulty level. Alternatives 3 and 4 are worrisome, since 3 was more popular among the upper group than the lower, and no one chose 4. Discrimination was not particularly good since nearly as many in the lower group as the upper group chose the correct answer. Maybe alternatives 3 and 4 can be revised to be more attractive to the lower group, luring them away from number 2, without also luring the upper students away from the correct response. That would make the item more discriminating. To do that one might replace alternatives 3 and 4 by alternatives that were more common errors among students who do not really grasp the concept examined with this item. Or perhaps alternative 2 should also be modified — maybe it is somehow a giveaway. And maybe alternative 4 should just be dropped altogether. If no one in 60 students chose it, why bother with it? Then the next time the item is used it would be a 4-choice item with no loss in measurement but a reduction in reading time and reading load for the examinees.

A good item analysis program might also provide the same information in terms of percents of the upper and lower group so that the teacher would be looking at similar table values regardless of the number of examinees. It might also have a row called total which gave the total number (or percent) of examinees choosing each alternative.

Furthermore, in a good program beside each item would be printed the p value and a discrimination index. For the item above, the latter value would probably be small but positive, perhaps $+0.10$.

The better computer item analysis programs would go further and provide a summary analysis of all the items in an abbreviated form, so that as many as 40 items would be reported on a single page. The output might appear as follows:

1	5-8	21-18*	2-0	0-0	0-4	0-2	.65	.10

which shows that for item 1, 5 in the upper group and 8 in the lower group answered alternative 1, etc.; the p value is 0.65; the discrimination index is 0.10. The objective of such a summary analysis is to provide condensed information on one page that can be conveniently filed with the test booklet for later reference.

The best computer outputs also print up a gummed label for each item designed to fit on the back of the teacher's item card, and these labels have on them the same abbreviated results we just described. Thus every time an item is used the teacher can attach the appropriate label to the item after analysis, and have all her item analysis information permanently available with no need for her to copy results from computer printout to item cards or to a master copy of the test.

Good programs provide other services. One is to list the items in order by their p values, so the hardest items are listed first, down to those that nearly everyone gets correct. The teacher knows quickly from such a list which items require discussion and reteaching. Another listing is of the items in order of their discrimination indices. With this list the teacher can discover at a glance how many of her items had negative or near zero discrimination values and which ones they were; so she is led quickly to the items most in need of revision.

Another listing service that good computer facilities provide is alphabetizing the students by name and listing for each name the total test score. This makes it very simple for the teacher to enter the scores into her grade book or other permanent record. The computer may also list the scores by student number, leaving off the student name. This permits the teacher to post a list of the test scores so students can find out their results without having their results revealed to anyone else who happens to look. Finally, the computer may list the scores in rank order with the students' names so that the teacher can quickly determine which students are doing the best and may be used to help other students, and which students are doing the worst and may need help from other students or the teacher.

As you can see, the thorough and careful teacher who wants to make the most effective use of her classroom tests can get so much help from a good computer item-analysis service that it may be a better choice than the analysis of tests in the classroom with the students. The expert teacher will know all the possibilities and make the decision that is best in a particular set of circumstances.[3]

---

[3]An audiotutorial that provides for practice in item analysis is included in *Exercises in Classroom Measurement*. It is number 5, entitled "Exercise on Item Analysis of Traditional (Norm-Referenced) Classroom Tests."

References

Cooperative Test Division. *Making your own tests*. Princeton, N.J.: Educational Testing Service.

Diederich, P. *Shortcut statistics for teacher made tests*. Princeton, N.J.: Educational Testing Service, 1960.

6

Criterion-Referenced Testing

Objectives

You should be able to do the following as a result of study of this chapter:
1. Differentiate between norm-referenced and criterion-referenced measurement;
2. State suitable uses of criterion-referenced tests and contrast these with the suitable uses of norm-referenced tests;
3. Describe the differences that might be noticeable between criterion-referenced and norm-referenced test items;
4. Describe the use of criterion exercises;
5. State the virtue and the flaws in the use of criterion-referenced measures to evaluate instruction;
6. Describe hierarchical instruction and the use of criterion-referenced tests with it;
7. List four virtues of a criterion-referenced approach to learning and measurement;
8. Describe four problems associated with a criterion-referenced approach to learning and measurement;
9. Discuss three problems associated with the development and evaluation of criterion-referenced measures.

Kinds of Measurement

Up to this point in our discussion of measurement, we have defined good measurement as that which *discriminates well* among examinees, i.e., reliably and validly. We have deliberately sought to have few tied scores on a measure, a large standard deviation, a flatter than normal distribution (which is a natural consequence of good discrimination and, thus, of a large standard deviation) with few perfect scores and few very low scores. We wanted these characteristics in our score distribution because having few ties means we can distinguish each examinee from anyone else, at least roughly. We wanted no perfect or very low scores because at the upper end we would not know how much better a person might have scored if there had been more items. At the lower end, we do not feel we have measured well if guessing behavior might account for differences among examinees, or, at the extreme, if we do not know how much worse they might have done had there been even easier items.

This kind of measurement, which has been most common in schools during this century, is called *norm-referenced* measurement. It is called norm-referenced because we tend to decide whether any score is good or bad on a norm-referenced measure by seeing where the score stands in the distribution of scores on the measure. A score of 20 is good if it is higher than 90% of the scores, but bad if it is higher than only 2%. That kind of interpretation of a score is what is meant by norm-referenced. The word *norm* here probably comes from the common use of distributions of scores in norms groups and the use of norms tables in interpreting the usual standardized test scores. This kind of measurement is often called *traditional,* although other kinds of measurement may be equally as deserving of that name.

There is another way to define measurement that is just as important as identifying "good" in terms of position with regard to a group of scores. We could define measurement as a procedure which identifies reliably and validly which individuals have reached an established level of performance, regardless of how well any other individual performs. This is called *criterion-referenced* measurement. An intriguing illustration is that of the parachute packer. The measurement is whether he can pack a parachute so that it opens when desired. It does not matter at all how much better than that standard he performs, or how much worse, and it does not matter whether he is the best parachute packer in the class if his parachutes do not open. It has been said that the criterion for graduation from parachute-packing school might be having the packer take one of his own parachutes up in a plane and jump out. If he makes it to the graduation exercise, he passes.

Other illustrations are perhaps useful. Norm referencing is inappropriate for the surgeon, when the criterion is whether he can perform an operation successfully, such as an appendectomy. The best in the class would not be good enough if no one in the class could perform the operation successfully. Criterion referencing is common in physical education — in fact, whenever *skills* are involved. In typewriting, the criterion of importance is being able to type a number of words correctly per minute, rather than being the best typist in the class.

For this kind of measurement, there are some differences in our objectives. We still demand reliability and validity, as is the case in any measurement —in education, in the grocery store, in surveying, or anywhere else. But with criterion-referenced measurement we do not deliberately seek few tied scores, large standard deviations, flat distributions, and few perfect or low scores. We also must consider a cycle of measurement, that is, measurement before instruction and measurement again afterwards. The ideal in criterion-referenced measurement is that with ideal instruction scores on a test given before instruction would be uniformly low, and scores on the same measure after instruction would be uniformly high. Uniformity in scores implies small or zero standard deviations. Low and high scores of uniform size suggest that distributions will not be normal or flatter than normal. Scores will pile up on one end or the other depending on whether the test is given before or after instruction. All this makes a lot of difference in the way we construct, analyze, and evaluate tests — matters which we will consider soon.

Uses of Criterion-Referenced Measurement

Although there has been a recent increase of interest in criterion-referenced measurement, the idea is not a new one. It was a common notion early in the twentieth century. In fact, the swing to norm-referenced measurement probably was closely associated with the movement to compulsory education through high school. As a larger number of students, especially larger numbers who formerly had not seemed suitable for "book learning," began to appear in schools, rigid standards based on criteria set for the academically elite could not reasonably be maintained. Norm-referenced measurement, curve grading, broadening of the curriculum, and other changes came about in response to the changed clientele. However, although these various ideas emerged in school settings at about the same time and in response to the same cultural changes, they are not necessarily tied together. That is, curve grading does not depend on norm-referenced measurement, nor does norm-referenced measurement imply curve grading. Norm-referenced measurement does not imply that some specified percentage of students will get high grades and a corresponding percentage low grades. The belief that they are inherently inseparable is a mistake that is often made, even by authorities on measurement and education when they are not thinking clearly. The distinctions that must be made for effective use of the two kinds of measurement are more subtle and important than that.

The cultural development that has brought renewed attention to criterion-referenced measurement is the interest in evaluating effectiveness of education. If we want to contrast a new instructional procedure with an older one, it seems to make more sense to ask a question like "What proportion of the students taught by each method are able to perform accurately such-and-such an activity after a given amount of time?" than to ask "What proportion of the students taught by each method are in the top 15% in scores on text X measuring such-and-such an activity after a given amount of time?"

Obviously, 15% will be in the top 15% regardless of the teaching method, but that is not the whole problem. A test that functions so that 90% of the students will get perfect scores will be regarded as a poor norm-referenced measure, while it may yield just the results that the instructor wants if 90% of his students are shown by it to be able to perform accurately such-and-such an activity after the given amount of time! So, when a criterion level can be preset and when measures of degree of proficiency below or above the criterion level are relatively unimportant, criterion-referenced measurement seems the sounder procedure. Tests for this kind of measurement should be constructed differently and must be evaluated in a manner other than the procedures we have learned for norm-referenced measurement.

On the other hand, when a criterion level cannot easily be preset and when measures of degree of proficiency are important all along the scale, rather than just at a selected point, then norm-referenced measurement may be more desirable. Obvious examples would be situations in which people were to be selected for openings and not all could be chosen. You would want the "best" to be selected, even if all were above a cutoff score that was indicative of failure. In school subjects, when it is important how much a person knows, say of history or English literature, and the more he knows the better, one is interested in who knows the most. It is not easy to set a cutoff score which indicates that the person knows enough. These cases suggest the use of norm-referenced measurement. Sometimes, you really want to know both kinds of information — so both kinds of measurement are significant, as for example, in English. You might want to be sure that each student had mastered the minimum essentials of grammar, punctuation, usage, and so on, but also be interested in which students knew the most about more sophisticated points.

Thus, we will probably be primarily interested in norm-referenced measurement when we want to compare students with other students for purposes such as:

1. Selecting students for honors, remediation, advanced education, special education, etc.;
2. Comparing students in one educational program with those in another, such as "national norms";
3. Guiding students into the areas in which they can expect the greatest satisfaction through successful or superior performance;
4. Motivating students to enjoy the satisfaction of outstanding achievement — of excellence.

We will probably be primarily interested in criterion-referenced measurement when we want to compare students' performances with a preset standard of performance judged for some reason as the performance that is adequate. (Notice, nearly all such preset standards are also based on norms, i.e., on the performance of others. The four-minute mile is important only because not many people can run a mile in that little time. It has no intrinsic value. Ability to cure cancer 100% of the time is not a preset standard in schools of medicine because no one can do it. Ability to perform a successful appendectomy in a very high percentage of routine cases is a reasonable standard because it can be done by many.) Situations in which criterion-referenced measurement will be of primary interest include:

1. Evaluating the extent to which standards have been met by students;
2. Evaluating the effectiveness or quality of instruction and comparing the effectiveness of different instructional procedures;
3. Placing students at the appropriate level in hierarchies of instruction.

Each of these three situations appropriate for criterion-referenced measurement will be discussed in more detail.

THE MEETING OF STANDARDS

Even during the period in education when little attention was given to measures like those we now call criterion-referenced, there was an interest in knowing whether students were performing as well as they should be expected to perform. Often norm-referenced measures were used as though they were what we now think of as criterion-referenced; that is, some arbitrary standard was set on a norm-referenced measure, and students were judged according to whether they met that standard. The standard might have been set in terms of a percentile score for a norms group or in terms of a grade-equivalent score or even in terms of a raw score. This is criterion-referencing of a measure — the problem is that the norm-referenced measures were not particularly well designed for the kind of measurement for which they were being used. The difference that occurs when one sets out to create a criterion-referenced measure for a certain purpose is that he uses a different rationale for selecting items to retain in the final form of his test.

The items of a norm-referenced test and a criterion-referenced test of the same objective do not look different. The tests could not be sorted into the two types by examining the items in the test booklet. Both kinds of tests, if well made, include representative samples of items covering all important aspects of the performance of interest. As you recall, this is achieved through use of a table of specifications or a list of behavioral objectives.

The significant difference between the two approaches is that for norm-referenced measurement items are selected for a final form by choosing items of optimum difficulty level and maximum discrimination index, using total test score on an administration after instruction as the criterion. This is subject always to the constraint that if all the items for a given important aspect of the performance are faulty, then new items will be created for that aspect or a different measurement procedure will be used for it. For a criterion-referenced instrument, items are selected for a final form by choosing items based on two testings, one before instruction and one after instruction. Two difficulty levels are involved; the difficulty index should be low (a low proportion of correct responses) before instruction, and the index should be high after instruction. Items with this pattern should be retained. Of course, the same constraint applies here — that no important aspect of the performance should be deleted during item selection without being replaced by other items or by a different measurement procedure.

Note that the effect of the item-selection procedure should produce slightly different tests in terms of the meaning of the scores. The norm-referenced test will tend to be homogeneous in the sense that people who score well on one item will tend to score well on others, and vice versa, and items may tend to be more detailed and subtle and demand more meticulous and thorough learning. That is what makes it possible for the test to discriminate well among the students and gives a large standard deviation and a high internal-consistency reliability coefficient. The criterion-referenced test, on the other hand, will delete any items that many people know before instruction (since they need not be taught what they already know), and it will tend to include items that are very subject to instruction — that everyone can learn from the given instructional procedure. The items will probably not concern subtle points, fine distinctions, and details that the best students master but that many students do not. These would probably be unreasonable elements to require as part of a criterion of mastery that would make sense for large-scale educational enterprises.

It would seem, then, that for instruction organized into units in each of which it was desired that every student reach an arbitrary level of performance called mastery, and organized to be efficient, i.e., to avoid reteaching what was already known, either norm-referenced measures (with an arbitrary preset criterion) or criterion-referenced measures could be used. But the criterion-referenced measure would be preferred since it was developed for this specific purpose.

Another aspect of this kind of instruction that is well suited to a kind of criterion-referenced measurement is the provision of student exercises by which the student may judge whether or not he is proceeding well. These might be called *criterion exercises* instead of tests. (Some people would call them *formative evaluations*.) They might consist of relatively few items, from two to five depending on the subject matter, and the exercises might be provided at frequent intervals — a sort of monitoring of progress. For some highly organized and sequential kinds of instruction, such as arithmetic, only two or three items of a particular kind are needed to ascertain reasonably well whether mastery has been reached — particularly if the items are of the completion or brief-essay type instead of the true-false or multiple-choice type. For other kinds of subject matter, such as reading, social studies, and science, five to ten items may be needed to be certain that a particular part has been mastered.

Extensive use of criterion exercises in the form of brief criterion-referenced tests will tend to produce a distinctive style of teaching. Testing activities will be prominent and consume a large part of the instruction time.[†] Since some students will reach mastery sooner than others, this style of instruction will invite individual pacing, and this, in turn, will create problems of trying to keep track of where each student is and what he should learn next. Some day all this may be simplified for the teacher through use of computers, but until then the typical teacher cannot let herself be carried away into chaos without her eyes open. This is not to say that criterion-referenced, testlike exercises should not be used frequently to check mastery of particular units or objectives, but rather it is to say that the complete reorganization of teaching along these exciting lines introduces a whole new set of problems that must be carefully planned for if disaster is to be avoided.

You should take note of the fact that preliminary evidence indicates that students have more favorable attitudes toward the *content* (but not the method) of instruction after criterion-referenced tests than after norm-referenced tests.[†] It is not yet clear whether this is simply a result of criterion-referenced items being easier.

THE EVALUATION AND COMPARISON OF INSTRUCTIONAL PROCEDURES

There are a variety of ways to teach anything to anyone. We speak of the Socratic method, the discovery method, the lecture method, programmed instruction, drill and practice, and so on. Educators used to try to determine which method was best, but sufficient failure in that attempt has caused us to recognize that different methods may be best for different people and for different subject matter. Now the search is for such combinations, called *aptitude-treatment interactions,* or even *content-trait-treatment interactions.* It hardly seems possible that any method is as good as any other for anything. Thus for economy, efficiency, a good showing in studies of accountability, and so on, it makes sense to try to use the "best" method for any given situation, or at least to avoid an inferior method. This kind of thinking is what brought criterion-referenced measurement back to the surface after many years of submersion.

The key to measuring in order to make comparisons between educational treatments (kinds of instruction) seems to be the establishment of clear objectives and clear standards for each of those objectives. If the teacher does not know clearly what she is trying to accomplish, it is unlikely that she will accomplish it well, and it is unlikely that anyone will be able to tell whether she accomplished more by one procedure than by another. Carried to the extreme, everything a teacher tries to do can be spelled out as an objective, and teachers could negotiate with administrators as to what objectives would be attempted in a given learning situation. Teachers and methods could be evaluated in terms of success in reaching the agreed-upon objectives. A catalog of all the reasonable objectives in elementary and secondary education would have thousands of entries, and there would need to be thousands of criterion-referenced measures to evaluate them. In fact, there would need to be multiple thousands of measures if each student is to be given repeated chances to try to reach the criterion. The number of items required for all these multiple measures is staggering to imagine, but work is proceeding to develop just such catalogs of objectives and pools of items, as was mentioned in chapter 2.

A simpler approach is to consider a number of objectives together as a unit, to set a standard for the unit as a whole, and to build criterion-referenced measures and set criteria for the units instead of for each objective. Not all educational authorities approve of this simplification, since reaching the mastery criterion on a unit test could be accomplished without necessarily mastering each objective in the unit. The missed objectives could be important for some future learning and require reteaching or else result in failure. This might be especially important in sequential subjects such as mathematics. On the other hand, the bookkeeping problems of checking mastery for every one of thousands of objectives is likely to be overwhelming with the resources available in most schools.

Much of what was said about using tests to evaluate the meeting of standards by students is also true of comparing instructional procedures. Norm-referenced measures could be used, and, indeed, have often been used. An arbitrary score is set as the standard. It is no more arbitrary to do this with a test designed to be norm-referenced than with a test designed to be criterion-referenced. Norm-referenced tests can also be designed to reflect units of instruction. The fact that norm-referenced tests discriminate more finely among the examinees than is needed does not preclude them from use as criterion-referenced instruments. Notice, incidentally, that criterion-referenced instruments are probably useless for purposes that are best served by norm-referenced instruments.

However, measures that have been designed to be criterion-referenced will probably function more effectively for instructional evaluation since the items included will be those that reflect the objectives or the table of specifications and have been shown to be amenable to instruction. Norm-referenced measures may include items that would be answered fully as well without instruction as with instruction since those items are not eliminated by the item-selection techniques used in conjunction with creating norm-referenced measures. On the other hand, it is disturbing to note that when different kinds of instruction are differentially effective with various topics, then a criterion-referenced measure which has been developed from pretesting and posttesting in conjunction with one instructional technique may include items that are effectively taught by that technique, and it may not contain items that would be effectively taught by a different technique. The measure is then biased in favor of one of the instructional techniques. This precludes a sound conclusion about the relative effectiveness of the two instructional procedures. The comparison of instructional techniques is no simple-minded problem, solved merely by use of criterion-referenced measurement.

We should not need to repeat at this point that either criterion-referenced or norm-referenced measures should include all the important objectives, but some writers criticize norm-referenced measures on the ground that blindly selecting items with item difficulties and discrimination values that are optimal for norm-referenced measurement but without attention to the coverage of objectives may result in measures that are incomplete. These writers are, of course, criticizing poor test construction, whether norm-referenced or criterion-referenced. It is attacking a straw man to criticize just one kind of measurement rather than both on this issue. On the other hand, there are very few published criterion-referenced measures available for anyone to use for the purpose of evaluating or comparing teaching strategies or instructional procedures. Thus, the norm-referenced measure with an arbitrary criterion set for mastery may be all that is available for those who do not have the resources to conduct a test development program before conducting the evaluation of instructional procedure.

PLACING STUDENTS IN HIERARCHIES OF INSTRUCTION

Some kinds of subject matter lend themselves more readily to sequential instruction — to a pattern of instruction in which one can state the elements necessary to reach any objective, and the order in which they should be learned is relatively obvious. For instance, it seems logical that before a student should be taught multiplication, he should be taught addition, and before that he should be taught to count, and so on. Actually, people who try to find such clear-cut hierarchical orders even in mathematics often have difficulty; the task in mathematics seems infinitely easier than in social studies.

When such a hierarchy of objectives can be delineated, a prespecified system of instruction can be created with criteria set for each objective. Then one problem is to place each student at the point in the hierarchical system at which he has mastered all previous objectives but no subsequent objectives. That seems a sound place for the student to commence his next learning task. For this purpose, good criterion-referenced measures seem to be ideal. In fact, a system of measures could be invented such that some measures tested over whole units. A student would be judged to be beyond any unit for which he reached the criterion score on the test. He would be given additional criterion-referenced measures within the lowest unit for which he failed to reach criterion. These additional measures would locate the highest specific objective which the student had mastered, and he would be invited to commence his learning anew with the next objective.

Obviously such a system of hierarchical objectives is no simple thing to create. Even more obviously, organizing instruction about such a system requires a tremendous amount of testing and test construction. The work is so great that teachers are no longer expected to do it. They must have aides for this purpose. Computers are brought into play, or some other device or technique is developed to relieve the teacher of the testing and bookkeeping activities involved in this kind of instruction. This is probably the most clearcut case in which criterion-referenced measurement is the way to get the job done, and one could only advocate use of norm-referenced measures for this purpose as a compromise at best. It remains to be seen whether much of education will be amenable to such hierarchical formulation, and whether the resources for attacking educational problems in this manner will become widely available.

Virtues of Criterion-Referenced Approach
to Learning and Measurement

When instruction is organized so that definite, reasonable goals are set for achievement for all learners and a criterion of "mastery" is preset, the teacher and the pupils can function as partners in trying to reach the goals. This is in contrast to the dual role many teachers feel that they are playing in the usual learning situation. One role is that of instructor, and the other is that of evaluator. The teacher tries to help each student learn to a high level of performance, but she also tries to write items that will discriminate, which only 70% to 85% of the students will get correct depending on the number of alternative responses. This poses a conflict for the teacher — no matter how well the students learn, she feels obligated to test them with items which not all can get correct.

The criterion-referenced, or mastery, situation is one in which the teacher hopes, and indeed plans, for every student to be able to get every item on her tests correct. Some students will take longer, of course; and there is the implication that the teacher will *not* simply teach the answers to the items she is going to use in her test. She should be teaching so that whatever items she happens to include in the sample for a test can be answered correctly by the knowledge, understanding, or skill that the student has developed.

This kind of teaching and measurement has been going on continuously over the years in good programs of physical education. The goal for the golf instructor is to have every pupil be able to place a ball on a green from 120 yards out in the fairway with a seven iron at least nine times out of ten. She does everything in her power to help each student achieve that goal and does not feel successful if only the best 15% reach it — or even the best 75%. Of course, some will take longer, and some may just not be interested enough or interestable enough. But even with those pupils, to some extent the instructor has a feeling of failure in that she was not able to create and sustain the needed motivation.

Similarly in swimming, the instructor wants every pupil to be able to keep his head above water enough to breathe comfortably for five minutes in water well over the pupil's head in depth. She does everything she can think of to achieve this, trying different strategies for different pupils, cajoling, threatening, scolding, demonstrating, and trying to drown-proof everyone she can. No one should fail, but the criterion is not raised or lowered because some pupils are slow or because a class of fast learners comes along. The test is not modified so that it remains at a constant difficulty level regardless of the degree of skill developed by the learners.

The reason that these kinds of learnings are so readily developed in a mastery, or criterion-referenced, framework is that their development is not measured by items. Let the physical education instructor start to use test items on such things as the history of golf, the rules of golf, the elements in the golf swing, the current champions of golf, etc., and, if she is not careful, she will start to adjust the difficulty level of her tests to what she anticipates from her students, she will teach to the items on her test, and she will fall into the other traps that plague the uninformed teacher of any subject.

The criterion-referenced approach implies repeated testing with the same test form as one improves items, and with alternative forms as she tests different students at the time when they seem ready to demonstrate mastery. (If the same items were used for each student, the students would soon learn to pass the items on to their followers. Performance on the test would then demonstrate ability to learn the answers to certain items, not the skills or knowledges that underlie correct answers to any of a pool of items that randomly are chosen to represent those skills and knowledges.) Clearly, this kind of measurement is going to require a large number of items — many more items than are necessary for norm-referenced approaches with group testing. If this results in a lot of item-writing practice so that the teacher refines her item-writing skills, it can be a virtue. If it results in careless item writing by disinterested and marginally competent assistants, it is a defect.

A desirable feature of the criterion-referenced orientation to instruction is that it tends to help the student to learn to be responsible for his own learning. Usually the approach combines criterion-referenced measurement with clearly specified objectives, alternative methods of learning, and rates of learning which vary from student to student. The teacher can no longer march the students through the halls of knowledge in lockstep, and, as a result, each student must take greater responsibility for his own success. To the extent that this prepares him for continued successful learning when he is an adult without a teacher, it is very desirable.

From the teacher's point of view, the mastery approach can be a relief when it is time to make out report cards. It is entirely reasonable and justifiable to give high grades to everyone if everyone has mastered the objectives, and most teachers do not like to have to give low grades. Unfortunately, there is a conflict between the mastery approach and the grading system as it usually operates. The usual grading system is defined as being norm-referenced. C is the average grade, and A and F stand for performances far above and below average. If one is to attempt to conform to that definition and use a mastery approach to learning and measurement, if all students reach "mastery," then they should all receive grades of C since no one is performing detectably far above or below the others. This does not seem sensible or practical. The problem is that the grading system and the approach to learning and measurement are inconsistent. The proper solution would seem to be to use something like pass-fail grade reporting in situations in which criterion-referenced measurement was to be used. But, unless pass-fail grades are given on many more objectives than the usual report card includes, simple dichotomous grading does not provide enough information for the needs of many of the users of report cards. If pass-fail grades are given on a large number of fairly specific objectives, the report card and permanent record become unmanageable and an inadequate summarization for many of the users. This dilemma has not yet been solved satisfactorily.

The idea, which seems to be part of a criterion-referenced approach, that students proceed at their own speeds can be a virtue. The fast learners can move on without being bored or they can consolidate their learnings by using them to help the slower ones or they can be rewarded by additional leisure time, etc., and the slow learners can be allowed as much time as they seem to need. It has been estimated that with normal children, the slowest learners will require about five times as long as the fastest on any given objective.

Of course, this becomes a defect if the school system is not organized with the idea that students will proceed at different paces. The most able twelve-year-olds will be ready for college work instead of the usual sixth grade work, and the least able normal eighteen-year-olds will still be trying to learn to read with reasonable fluency and to do simple arithmetic. They may require 20 or 30 years to attain the skills our society acts like it demands. In fact, if

1. The average child takes twelve years to complete high school,
2. A "high-school education" is to be required,
3. The attainment of a high-school education is to be defined by criterion-referenced measures with mastery set at the performance of the average student after twelve years of instruction, and
4. The slowest students take 2½ times as long as the average students to achieve mastery,

then we would anticipate that unless standards are altered, 2½ times 12 would be 30 years of study which would be required for the slowest. Adding 6 years before entry into first grade gives an age of 36 before the slow but normal student finishes high school. Our society does not seem ready yet for this facet of the idea that mastery learning permits the slow students to have enough time so that they, too, can reach criterion performance on the school's educational objectives.

Problems with Criterion-Referenced Approach to Learning and Measurement

As we discussed the virtues of the criterion-referenced approach in the section above, we noted several problems — the requirement of many more test items, the inadequate provision in our society at present to reap the rewards of individualized pacing of instruction, the inadequate communication from criterion-referenced grades, and the requirement that teachers not simply teach the answers to the test items. Earlier we noted the problems connected with creation of hierarchical objectives, with cataloging all reasonable objectives, and with the arbitrary setting of standards of mastery. We also have alluded to the fact that a criterion-referenced organization of instruction requires much more testing and testing time than the usual teaching situation. Some proponents of individualized, mastery-oriented, instruction have reached the conclusion that it cannot be done effectively without the aid of computers to conduct the testing, keep track of the individual students and their accomplishments, and steer each student to the next exercise appropriate for his level of development. The burden is just too much for the teacher, even though the teacher presumably no longer conducts person-to-person or person-to-group instruction. Certainly, if

1. Pretesting, posttesting, and retention testing are to be conducted on each specific objective,

2. The items for all these tests have to be written, used in pretests and posttests, evaluated, rewritten, tried out again, and recycled repeatedly until they perform soundly, and
3. Numerous alternative items on each topic are needed so that the same items are not repeated so often as to be rendered ineffective,

then someone in the school is going to have a heavy load just in conducting the measurement and evaluation implicit in a criterion-referenced mastery approach to education.

Even without those measurement "equipment" problems, the criterion-referenced approach with its individual pacing of students puts the teacher in what is essentially a room full of students to be tutored individually when each needs it. The impossibility of running that kind of education efficiently for large numbers of students is what led in the dim distant past to the idea of taking a few students who were at about the same level and teaching them together, all at one time. And, of course, that led to classes, grades, and the very thing that mastery learning is trying to get away from.

A problem that is easily overlooked with criterion-referenced learning and evaluation is that we do not know how to treat (teach) students who seem to be unable to master a given objective. That is to say, for much of what is considered appropriate to teach in our schools, we do not know effective remedial procedures for the slow learners. Every faculty member who has ever taught a course on measurement for teachers is aware of the college seniors who have not yet mastered long division, multiplying by fractions, or converting fractions to decimals. This is a symptom of our inadequacies in remedying defective instruction — or of providing effective alternate treatments for those who do not learn to a reasonable criterion of mastery from the available treatments. Every college English instructor is aware of the students who have never learned how to spell or the rudiments of grammar. These students are not dumb. Some of them will go on to attain the highest of degrees and make highly significant contributions to their fields, always handicapped by their inability to communicate effectively in writing. This reflects our lack of effective remedial treatments for intelligent people who do not learn these communication skills from the usual kinds of instruction. Until such remedial treatments, or combinations of treatments that are effective for students with known characteristics (trait-treatment interactions), have been discovered and developed, trying to teach to a criterion of mastery will be frustrating to those who set their arbitrary standards for mastery above very low levels. Meanwhile, as was noted in the previous section, we have the problem of not being organized to handle well slow students to give them enough time for mastery — or fast students to move them on at the rate they can go.

Additional Problems with Criterion-Referenced Measures

We have presented a number of problems with a criterion-referenced approach to instruction and some of the problems with criterion-measures, such as the number of items needed and the arbitrary nature of establishing the level of performance that will be considered mastery. (For a cogent argument against mastery learning, see

Ebel, 1973.) There are some other problems with such measures that need our attention. As we mentioned earlier, ideally in criterion-referenced measurement with superb teaching every student should obtain a low score on pretest and all should obtain identical scores representing complete mastery on posttest. This will result in there being no variability among students. On posttest, the standard deviation will be zero. This means that no study of reliability by the usual procedures for norm-referenced measures will be meaningful. The item-analysis procedures for norm-referenced measures will be useless. Since everyone gets the same perfect score on posttest, we can't even talk about the upper group and lower group. So we will have to develop different procedures for test development than we have been used to.

It should also be recognized that the whole idea of criterion-referencing not only fails to fit some kinds of instructional material, as noted earlier, but also is usually inappropriate for measuring aptitude. The teacher cannot simplify her life by just learning about one kind of measurement as though it could be used for all purposes. Aptitude is rarely sensibly measured by criterion-referenced measures, and, on the other hand, placing of students into hierarchical learning sequences is not optimally done by norm-referenced measures.

Finally, it should be recognized that the convenient kinds of items most often used in norm-referenced measures that require the student to choose the correct response from a set of alternative responses may not, and most often will not, be optimum for criterion-referenced measurement. In instruction that is organized into behavioral objectives, there will seldom be objectives stated so that the desired performance is that a student be able to choose the correct alternative from a set of possibilities. Usually he will be expected to present some kind of performance, such as "Compute the area of the rectangle" or "Describe the principle of operation of the reciprocating steam engine" or "Point out on a map the area of California in which gold was found in useful quantities in the middle of the 19th century."

While such skills and knowledges can be measured with items in which the student chooses among alternatives, such items are a compromise. Precise measurement of the objective is sacrificed for the convenience of efficient measurement of something that should logically be related to mastery of the objective. The quality of the compromise should be checked empirically — that is, in developing criterion-referenced measures of objectives that are not stated as choices among alternatives, the test developer should conduct experiments to be sure with a high degree of regularity that those who have mastered the objectives make the correct choices, and those who have not do not. The validity of each item should be verified, and that is a sizable task. This task is not an inherent part of norm-referenced measurement, and it is not required for all criterion-referenced measurement. But because criterion-referenced measurement is so typically tied to instruction based on specific objectives, we call this to your attention as one of the problems of criterion-referenced measurement used by classroom teachers.

The Development of Criterion-Referenced Measures

Finally, let us consider what techniques are available to assist the classroom teacher in developing sound criterion-referenced measures. She will have to develop her own measures because very few can be found for her to purchase or borrow.

ITEM ANALYSIS

The basic step in developing a sound criterion-referenced test from a pool of likely items is to administer the items as a pretest and again as a posttest after instruction. Each item should be written with the following thought in the writer's mind. "What can I ask that will demonstrate that this objective has been met and that will nearly always be answered incorrectly by those who have not had the instruction but will nearly always be answered correctly by those who have had and profited from the the instruction?" What is desired, then, is a comparison of the difficulty level of the item before and after. The desired outcome for a good item is a low p value before instruction and a high p value afterwards.

There is a problem with this technique in that over a short instructional period, students may remember what they gave as answers in the pretest and be influenced by that on the posttest. Or they may remember actual items from the pretest and learn the answers to them without learning much of anything else if they think the posttest will include only those items. To some extent the problem may be solved by giving the items as a posttest to one group who have just finished instruction and promptly giving the same items to the next group who are about to start instruction. The weakness here is that the two groups may not be similar enough to be regarded as random samples of the same population. So one problem is traded for another, and the test developer must decide which weakness is least damaging.

An alternative way to proceed which has the same essential meaning and which will yield almost the same results in terms of which items will be selected (Helmstadter, mimeo. undated) is to consider the pretest results as the "lower group," and the posttest results as the "upper group," and obtain the U − L indices for the correct responses to the items just as in item analysis of norm-referenced measures described earlier.[1]

A little thought will indicate that this method of item analysis involving two administrations of the test is less convenient than the item analysis for norm-referenced measures which involves only one administration. Further, a little thought or experience will indicate that early attempts by a teacher at developing criterion-referenced items that yield chance-level p values on pretest and p values of 1.00 on posttest will not be very successful. In fact, most attempts will yield items that have p values much lower than 1.00 on posttest. That means that even though we are trying to develop criterion-referenced measures, we are far from the degree of perfection in measurement and instruction that results in complete loss of variability in posttest performance. Since we have variability, it is reasonable to use the standard procedures for norm-referenced item analysis. The condition to be observed is that the resulting item statistics be treated with caution.

For example, if an item gets a p value near 1.00 on posttest, and if the item is designed to measure an important objective, the teacher should have no concern at all if the norm-referenced discrimination value is very low or even negative. It is essentially meaningless. Maybe negative discrimination values should result in at least cursory inspection of the item — they may reflect ambiguity that could be

---

[1]An audiotutorial is provided in *Exercises in Classroom Measurement* that makes available practice on these concepts. It is number 6, entitled "Exercises in Item Analysis for Criterion-Referenced Tests."

detected and removed, but they could also reflect the wobble due to small samples of examinees.

On the other hand, if the *p* value is modest, in the 0.50 to 0.70 range, and the item has low or negative discrimination value, there is probably something wrong that could be corrected. The problem may be in the item, or it may be in the instruction. Even if the item has substantial discrimination value, a modest *p* value suggests that instruction may not be adequate, and the combination of modest *p* value and high discrimination value suggests that instruction is not adequate for the weaker students. In a mastery-learning situation, that cries for attention, but the conclusion is not necessarily that the item is faulty and should be modified, discarded, or replaced. However, such a result could be due to having a distractor that was so close to being correct that only the stronger students could avoid it. Unless the distinction is an important part of what is to be mastered, the troublesome distractor should be modified or replaced.

Posttest item analysis of the usual norm-referenced type can, of course, help to locate distractors that are not functioning. A teacher probably should be cautious about deleting unchosen distractors that look promising until she also has pretest data that indicate that the distractors do not draw responses on either pretest or posttest.

It should be clear, then, that even though in theory with perfect instruction and excellent criterion-referenced measurement the usual norm-referenced item analysis procedures would be meaningless for criterion-referenced tests, in actual practice the usual procedures can be very helpful in the beginning stages of item and test development. They must be supported by more refined and complex procedures in the later stages of development, and the results of norm-referenced item analysis of criterion-referenced measures must be interpreted with caution and sophistication.

RELIABILITY

The reliability of criterion-referenced measures is not easy to evaluate. Again, in the ultimate case there is no variability among the responses of the examinees, so the usual procedures cannot be used.

One is not interested in the internal consistency of criterion-referenced measures, unless they are measures of performance on small, discrete, homogeneous units. What one wants to know is whether the same result, mastery or failure, would occur with a different random sample of items, or with the same sample of items administered after a lapse of time. One suggested procedure is to use a third testing — a retention test given one or two weeks after the mastery test just for the purpose of evaluating reliability. The suggestion has some flaws — the students may just try to remember what they answered the first time and repeat it, and they may forget during the lapse of time — but good suggestions are not readily available as solutions to this problem. We just do not have convenient ways of evaluating the reliability of criterion-referenced measures, though we surely need to know how reliable they are before we trust their results. The reliability coefficient we learned to compute earlier for norm-referenced measures is meaningless for many criterion-referenced measures. It may even be misleading. To the extent that one nears perfection of measurement and instruction, reliability coefficients will approach zero instead of 1.00!

Ebel (1973) suggests that reliability for criterion-referenced tests can be evaluated in different ways depending on what the test is used for. If it is used to determine how well a pupil has succeeded in a course, the usual reliability coefficient is appropriate since that coefficient tells us how well the instrument sorts out different levels of achievement. If the criterion-referenced test is to be used (more appropriately) to sort out those who have learned from instruction from those who have not, he suggests that pretest and posttest papers should be combined into a single group, and the reliability coefficient computed in the usual way. That coefficient would indicate how well the test sorted the two groups. Trial of that idea has not yet been reported, but on the face of it a coefficient computed in that way does not seem to be evaluating the same concepts as the reliability coefficients we examined earlier.

It is highly likely that classroom teachers who attempt to develop criterion-referenced tests for their instruction will be far from the ideal instructional situation, and their items will be far from ideal, too. In such cases, the usual estimate of reliability may be helpful as a clue. That is, if students are not getting all of the items correct on posttest and yet the reliability estimate is low, the test deserves careful scrutiny as to whether it is a sound test at all. However, one should not expect reliability coefficients estimated in the usual ways to be in the 0.80's and 0.90's when one has set out to develop criterion-referenced measures.

VALIDITY

Three ideas related to the validity of criterion-referenced measures are available. One is to rely on content validity, the usual standby for teacher-made achievement tests. This is done, of course, by careful attention to having items that reflect the objectives or the table of specifications. The second is to validate each item against its objective by an experiment in which it is determined that to a large extent those who cannot perform the objective get the item wrong, and those who can perform the objective get the item correct. If every item is valid, and if the test meets the specifications well, the test should then be valid. The third idea refers to validly setting the score which represents mastery. In sequential courses in which each course depends on mastery of the previous course (as, for example, to some extent in mathematics), the mastery criterion for an earlier course can be set at the level that usually results in success in the subsequent course. As always, there is a degree of arbitrariness in defining "usually results in success." You can choose any reasonable value between 51% of the people who reach this level on the first course and also reach mastery on the second and 100% of the people who reach this level on the first course and also reach mastery on the second. However, even with this latitude, a criterion for mastery set this way will be more valid than when it is set without any empirical guide based on subsequent performance.

Summary Evaluation of Criterion-Referenced Measurement

Since we have discussed the problems with criterion-referenced measures and their development at the end of this chapter, it is highly likely that some readers will leave with the impression that criterion-referenced measures are inherently inferior to norm-referenced measures, or that one kind of measure is more desirable and useful than the other. That is not a sound evaluation. More correct would be that there are two different definitions of good measurement, each appropriate for different purposes. Both points of view have long histories and ardent advocates. Both make good sense. The trick is to use the right kind of measurement for the purpose at hand, and to know enough about both kinds to recognize the strengths and weaknesses of each. If one has studied this book carefully, she should be well equipped to deal soundly with both kinds of measurement in the classroom and to profit as the future brings improvements in the procedures associated with both of them.

References

Ebel, R. L. Evaluation and educational objectives. *J. Educ. Measmt*, 1973, **10,** 273–79.
Helmstadter, G. C. A comparison of traditional item analysis selection procedures with those recommended for tests designed to measure achievement following performance oriented instruction. (Unpublished paper, n.d.)

Part Two

Introduction

Many classroom teachers need to know the rudiments of working with standardized tests. Often schools will require teachers to administer standardized tests to their pupils. If teachers are knowledgeable about standardized tests, they should be involved in the choice of what particular tests will be used for various purposes with their pupils. If standardized tests are used, and if their results are to have maximum useful effect, the scores must be correctly interpreted to the students, to their parents, and to school and public officials. Often these chores fall on the classroom teacher because she is the one closest to the pupil or his parent or because no one else is available who can be expected to know much about what scores from standardized tests mean.

There are many ways that serious mistakes can be made in dealing with standardized tests. We usually worry about the mistakes that can be made in dealing with pupils, but often the mistakes may be detrimental to the teacher. Scores may be erroneously interpreted to indicate that her teaching is ineffective — or sometimes they can make her look more effective than she is. Teachers should know enough about their educational tools, such as tests, so that they can effectively protest if they are misused. In this unit of instruction we will attempt to help prospective teachers acquire the knowledge and skills that will enable them to deal effectively, if not expertly, with standardized tests.

The approach that is often taken to teaching people about choosing standardized tests is to pick a number of widely used tests, or tests that are widely different, and teach about them in detail. Since thousands of standardized tests are available, instead of doing that we are going to approach the problem by studying the use of two important guides to the standardized tests that are on the market. Teachers who know how to use those guides effectively can choose tests wisely whether they have happened to learn about the specific tests during their formal instruction or not.

Choice, Administration, and Interpretation of Standardized Tests

Other than the use of good sense, there is not much that is very complicated to learn about the administration of standardized tests. The most important thing is to follow the instructions with meticulous care. We will note common errors and try to help the teacher who is involved in the administration of a test for which the instructions are of marginal quality.

Without some training with standardized-test scores, potential users of these tests are not only ineffective, but also dangerous. There are a number of different forms of test scores, devised for different purposes, and with different strengths and weaknesses. A thorough grounding in their proper use will be developed, and practice with tools for their use, such as norms tables and expectancy tables, will be provided here.

During all of the instruction on this topic, we will be guided by a set of behavioral objectives. You should be able to do everything that is listed in these objectives when you have finished the instruction on the topic. The following list of objectives can be used effectively as a study guide or as a guide in reviewing the material before an examination or before dealing with standardized tests as a practicing teacher.

Behavioral Objectives for Instruction on Standardized Testing

The purpose of this unit of instruction is to teach the prospective teacher how to choose, administer, and use effectively the results of standardized tests. A list of detailed objectives follows.

A. Nature and School Uses of Standardized Tests — You will be able to:
    1. Recall how standardized tests differ from other tests in terms of administration, scoring, and test construction;
    2. Recognize situations in which the use of standardized tests is appropriate;

3. Recognize situations in which standardized testing is inappropriate or is being used improperly;
4. Categorize tests from their descriptions as being measures of aptitude, achievement, or personality;
5. Categorize testing situations as being appropriate for use of measures of aptitude, achievement, or personality;
6. Describe the meanings of each of the following terms as they are used in educational measurement:
    a. Assessment
    b. Ceiling and floor effect
    c. Correlation coefficient
    d. Criterion
    e. Diagnostic Testing
    f. Evaluation
    g. Frequency Distribution
    h. Norms: Individual; School-mean
    i. Percentile
    j. Placement testing
    k. Prediction
    l. Reliability
    m. Scatterplot
    n. Validity
7. Differentiate between reliability and validity, giving practical examples to illustrate the differences;
8. Describe the levels of validity and reliability usually regarded as high in educational uses of standardized tests;
9. Differentiate between content, predictive, and concurrent validity;
10. Identify and describe the effects of at least five factors that limit or enhance the size of validity correlations;
11. Describe three different kinds of procedures for estimating reliability;
12. State important ways in which the nature of the group of examinees can influence reliability and validity evaluations;
13. Describe the significant characteristics of a sound diagnostic test and situations appropriate for its use;
14. Describe the usefulness of standardized tests for placement, assessment, and evaluation;
15. Recognize in descriptions of norms development indications that norms are untrustworthy;
16. Compute the percentile associated with a specified score, given the frequency distribution or the number out of a total who obtain that score or a lower score;
17. Use norms tables to make meaningful statements about students' raw or derived scores;
18. Select and defend your choice of norms for a particular interpretation.
B. Administering Standardized Tests — You will be able to:
    1. State at least five important conditions which must exist for a test administration to qualify as standardized;
    2. Recognize in descriptions of testing situations conditions which destroy the standardization of the test.
C. Choosing a Standardized Test — You will be able to:
    1. Identify the most important consideration in choosing a standardized test;
    2. Discuss three considerations of technical quality involved in choosing a test;
    3. Discuss competently the role of the following factors in choosing a test:
        a. Alternate forms
        b. Cost
        c. Recency of revision
        d. Scoring
        e. Storage

D. Locating Information about Standardized Tests — You will be able to:
   1. List four or more sources of information about standardized tests;
   2. Contrast the merits of various sources of information about tests;
   3. Use the *Mental Measurements Yearbook* to locate a test with given specifications;
   4. Use the *CSE Elementary School Test Evaluations* to evaluate a test for a specified purpose.
E. Interpreting the Results of Standardized Testing — You will be able to:
   1. Differentiate among raw scores, formula scores, and derived scores;
   2. Put scores into rank order;
   3. Construct frequency distributions of scores;
   4. Draw the distribution curve of scores;
   5. Locate the mean and standard deviations on the distribution curve;
   6. Indicate the positions of mean and standard deviations on a normal curve;
   7. Indicate the percentage of scores included in each standard deviation unit of a normal curve;
   8. Indicate the percentile equivalents of selected normal deviates;
   9. Indicate the T score and z score equivalents of selected percentile scores, and indicate the percentiles for selected z and T scores;
   10. Recall that stanines are range instead of point scores;
   11. Indicate the stanine scores equivalent to selected percentiles, z scores, and T scores, and indicate the percentiles, z scores, and T scores for selected stanines;
   12. State the principal strengths and weaknesses of:
       a. Raw scores
       b. Percentiles
       c. Stanines
       d. z scores
       e. T scores;
   13. Calculate and interpret a confidence interval for an individual's score, given the standard error of measurement;
   14. Explain the relationship between the confidence interval and the percentile-band score, indicating the strengths of the percentile-band score in interpreting standardized test scores;
   15. Describe the advantages and dangers of using profiles in test interpretation;
   16. Interpret profiles soundly;
   17. Explain how grade-equivalent scores are obtained and give at least three reasons why their use should be avoided due to the strong likelihood of misinterpretation;
   18. State correctly the result to be expected from a specified test score, given an expectancy table for a test;
   19. Locate specified information about a test in the test manual.
F. The Superintendent's Fallacy — You will be able to:
   1. Describe the Superintendent's Fallacy;
   2. State situations in which the fallacy is to be expected;
   3. Indicate sound procedures for preventing occurrence of the fallacy;
   4. Recognize that the Superintendent's Fallacy is called the regression effect in technical discussions of research design.

7

Nature of and School Uses of Standardized Tests

Objectives

The objectives that you should have for this chapter are the development of the ability to do the following things:

1. Recall how standardized tests differ from other tests in terms of administration, scoring, and test construction;
2. Recognize situations in which the use of standardized tests is appropriate;
3. Recognize situations in which standardized testing is inappropriate or is being used improperly;
4. Categorize tests from their descriptions as being measures of aptitude, achievement, or personality;
5. Categorize testing situations as being appropriate for use of measures of aptitude, achievement, or personality;
6. Describe the meanings of each of the following terms as they are used in educational measurement:
   a. Assessment
   b. Ceiling and floor effect
   c. Correlation coefficient
   d. Criterion
   e. Diagnostic Testing
   f. Evaluation
   g. Frequency distribution
   h. Norms: Individual; School-mean
   i. Percentile
   j. Placement testing
   k. Prediction
   l. Reliability
   m. Scatterplot
   n. Validity

7. Differentiate between reliability and validity, giving practical examples to illustrate the differences;
8. Describe the levels of validity and reliability usually regarded as high in educational uses of standardized tests;
9. Differentiate among content, predictive, and concurrent validity;
10. Identify and describe the effects of at least five factors that limit or enhance the size of validity correlations;
11. Describe three different kinds of precedures for estimating reliability;
12. State important ways in which the nature of the groups of examinees can influence reliability and validity evaluations;
13. Describe the significant characteristics of a sound diagnostic test and situations appropriate for its use;
14. Describe the usefulness of standardized tests for placement, assessment, and evaluation;
15. Recognize in descriptions of norms development indications that norms are untrustworthy;
16. Compute the percentile associated with a specified score, given the frequency distribution or the number out of a total who obtain that score or a lower score;
17. Use norms tables to make meaningful statements about students' raw or derived scores;
18. Select and defend choice of norms for a particular interpretation.

What Are Standardized Tests?

All of us have taken tests given by teachers in classrooms. Probably each of us has taken at least one test that might be called a standardized test — a college admissions test, an interest test, an intelligence test. What does the term *standardized* imply that causes us to use it to differentiate some tests from those that teachers make up and give in their classes?

The essence of the implication of *standardized* is that the standardized test is given under the same standard conditions to everyone who takes it.

There are other differences between standardized tests and the usual classroom tests, and many people think of those differences as being the fundamental meaning of the word standardized. For instance, usually a standardized test has been administered to a large group of people, and their performances have been recorded in the form of *norms* with which any new examinee's score can be compared. (We will learn much more about norms a little later.) Usually a standardized test is purchased from a publisher, and is printed, bound, and accompanied by a booklet describing the test, called a test manual. Usually standardized tests are timed. Usually they are given to a number of people at once. Usually they are *objective*; that is, no judgment is required in scoring them. But none of these things is essential to a test's being standardized. What is essential is that the test be given to all examinees under the same conditions.

Some other things are common with standardized tests. Usually a provision is made for them to be sent away to a publisher or a scoring service to be scored. Often reports of various degrees of elaborateness can be obtained from the service along with the test scores. These reports might list all students alphabetically with their scores, might report not only each student's score but also which items he got wrong, might convert the students' raw scores to some "derived" score which is more easily understood or used, and so on. It is usually possible for teachers or teachers' aides to score standardized tests, but that may be found to be more expensive than buying the scoring service from a commercial agency.

Standardized tests are often constructed by an agency which employs people whose profession is writing items for tests. Such agencies may have research units who work on improving the tests, the reporting procedures, the scoring systems, and so on. Often test publishers, instead of having a permanent staff of item writers, contract with experts in measurement to write items for tests. In either system, the items are likely to be of higher average quality than those made by teachers who rarely have much instruction or guided experience in item writing. Expert item writers can often devise items that measure more subtly or measure more complex objectives than teacher-made items. Not only are the experts more skilled, but they have more time and are willing to spend more time on each item, and they are willing to throw away many abortive attempts in order to get one effective item. Teachers can seldom afford to put that much effort into preparing their classroom tests.

Finally, standardized test items have almost always been pretested to check on their effectiveness and to permit editing to improve their effectiveness before they are used in a commercial test. Most teachers have not learned how to use experience in this way to evaluate and improve their items.

Why Use Standardized Tests?

Even though we have just seen that it is often the case that the items in standardized tests may be of higher average quality than those of informal tests, and we have seen that scoring and reporting services that may be very helpful can be obtained for standardized tests, these are not the primary reasons for deciding to use a standard-ized test in a particular situation. There are three main reasons why one would decide to use a standardized test.

First, a standardized test may be chosen for use in a school because it measures something other than achievement that a teacher or the school wants to know about — or it may measure achievement in a particular way for a particular purpose. Standardized tests exist that measure, or purport to measure, a variety of human characteristics. Among these characteristics are educational achievement, aptitude or potential for learning, interests in various school subjects or in vocations or occu-pations, and personality characteristics.

Some achievement tests are specially designed to attempt to measure details of what has *not* been learned so that problem areas for individual students can be dis-covered and remedied. These would be called *diagnostic* tests. Some achievement tests attempt to measure details, not to permit remedy of defective learning but to optimize future learning by placing a student at the right level in a subject or in the best kind of instructional setting for him. These would be called *placement* tests.

Few teachers are sufficiently skilled in measurement or have the resources to develop their own instruments to measure aptitude, interest, or personality, or to develop sound diagnostic instruments to analyze students' learning problems and direct an instructor to the correct remedies. Thus, a teacher would ordinarily turn to standardized tests for these purposes.

Second, it may be that a teacher can find a standardized test that fits her instructional objectives as well as any test she could devise. To use a standardized test then saves her the effort of test construction and probably gives her the added benefits of expert item construction, edited items, comparative scores from other schools, statistical evaluations of the test's performance for a variety of purposes, and perhaps other virtues. By the very nature of things, however, such a good fit of a standardized test to the instructional objectives of a particular teacher is not very common.

Third, and perhaps most important for classroom teachers, is the fact that the teacher may want to be able to compare the performance of her students with the performance of some other group. It is nearly impossible for her to arrange for her test to be given to the students of some other teacher. If all teachers asked their colleagues to give extra tests for comparison purposes, there would soon be little time for instruction. So on occasion, perhaps at the end of the term or year, a teacher may want to find out whether her students are as competent in her subject matter as students in other schools and other communities. To find this out, she might give a standardized test on the subject. That is about the only way such a comparison can be made.

In the rest of this chapter we will consider each of these reasons for using standardized tests in greater detail.

MEASURES OTHER THAN USUAL MEASURES OF ACHIEVEMENT

While teachers may occasionally consider the wisdom of use of personality or interest measures for their students, the most common kind of test, other than an achievement test, used in schools is the aptitude test. There is a great deal of confusion about what an aptitude test is and how it differs from an achievement test. The naïve person is likely to believe that an aptitude test measures "native ability" or "brains" or something that a person is born with, rather than something that has been developed. However, we do not know how to do that. In fact, all aptitude measurement is basically measurement of achievement, and students who have achieved more by a certain period in their life span are usually judged as having more aptitude. We act as though their experience has been uniform, which obviously is not true. For decades students of human development and of measurement have struggled with the question of the relative roles of heredity and environment in development of achievement, and the struggle has, if anything, intensified in recent years, but there is no unanimity among professionals as to the best answer.

One leading scholar in the field (Carroll, 1974) has argued that if he set up an experiment in which he was concerned with the learning of Mandarin Chinese by U.S. schoolchildren, he could give a battery of tests of ability to learn pairs of words, to learn and apply rules, etc., and he could give an initial test of Mandarin Chinese fluency to the students. On pretest the children would vary in their scores on the ability tests, and all would get zero on the Mandarin Chinese test. After extensive concentrated training in Mandarin Chinese, retesting would reveal that the average score on Mandarin Chinese was much increased, while the scores on the ability tests were, on the average, at about the same level. Further, those who scored highest on the ability tests in the beginning would tend to be the persons who got the highest scores on Mandarin Chinese at the end.

If you agree that he could perform an experiment with these results, then you should find acceptable his claim that the ability tests are measures of aptitude, and the Mandarin Chinese tests are measures of achievement. In fact he would define aptitude tests as measures that change only a little with instruction but are related to degree of success in other kinds of instruction. He would define achievement tests as tests that change markedly with instruction, but in situations like the one described (pretest on Mandarin Chinese of people with no experience with Mandarin Chinese), they would not predict degree of success in learning. That seems like a convincing illustration of the difference between aptitude and achievement measures — until another expert points out that the tests of ability to learn pairs of words, to learn and apply rules, etc., were measures of achievements. That is, people learn how to learn pairs, and they learn how to learn and apply rules. They are not born with these abilities. So, he claims, there are no real measures of aptitudes — only measures of achievements. And so the battle continues.

While it is good to realize that the confusion that a teacher feels on this point is shared by the experts, there are some rules of thumb that can be helpful in everyday work. The rules we will recommend here are that we will think of aptitude measures as being used primarily for prediction of future achievement, and we will think of aptitude items as being only loosely tied to instruction. We will think of achievement measures as being used primarily for evaluating what has been learned (though they can be and often are used for prediction, also), and we will think of achievement items as being closely tied to subjects recently learned in school. We must always remember that the distinction can be tenuous, and care must be exerted if anything depends on that distinction (Cleary et al., 1975).

JINGLE AND JANGLE FALLACIES

While teachers may not need to get very excited about the heredity vs. environment controversy as they think about measurement of their students, there are other kinds of mistakes that can be very serious that are related to the difficulty of distinguishing between aptitude and achievement. Two that have received attention since the early days of modern testing are called the *jingle fallacy* and the *jangle fallacy*.

The jingle fallacy is assuming that two tests with the same name measure the same thing. An extreme example of how fallacious this can be is the tests given beginning in the early 1970s to reexamine people for driver's licenses in the states of Florida and California. Both have been called driver reexamination tests, and have been given to people who already have licenses to see whether they should be allowed to keep their licenses. The California test contains a number of items requiring the examinee to know how to make signals for turns, which lane to turn from and into, how far behind another car he must remain to be safe at various speeds, etc. The Florida examination requires only that a person be able to do such things as read a red sign that says STOP on it and indicate that it means one should stop. Obviously the two tests can be expected to measure different things, to give different results, and to yield scores that have but slight relationship to each other.

The same kind of thing can happen in tests of history if one test emphasizes dates, names, and places, while another emphasizes major historical trends, cultural developments that influenced the historical developments, and so on. It can happen in spelling if one test emphasizes especially difficult words or uncommon words, while the other emphasizes routine spelling tasks. It can happen in foreign languages if one test is based entirely on reading the language and another includes speaking the language. An especially troublesome instance of the jingle fallacy in educational measurement occurs in connection with measurement of IQs. There the naïve lay person and the untrained teacher expect not only the thing measured but the actual score to have the same meaning from one test to another. Later on we will consider IQ scores in detail and find that for the same person, different tests given at about the same time can give results that differ by as much as 20 points, due only to the difference between the tests, not to fluctuations in the intelligence of the person who takes the test.

So, the jingle fallacy warns us that tests with the same name do not necessarily measure the same thing.

The jangle fallacy warns us that measures with different names do not necessarily measure different things! A "reading comprehension" test and a test of achievement in social studies may measure essentially the same thing in spite of their different titles if the social studies achievement test uses items which require the student to read a paragraph of social studies material and then answer questions about what he has read, not an uncommon practice in the field.

In several kinds of aptitude testing, it turns out that very similar test items are used for "aptitude" tests and for "achievement" tests. For instance, it might be hard even for an expert to sort the items from a pool of items on arithmetic into those which should go into an aptitude test and those which should go into an achievement test. As we have noted, we often judge "aptitude" by how much one has achieved compared to others who have had approximately the same opportunity, that is, are the same age or in the same grade. In one important testing program in a country other than the United States, *mathematical aptitude* has been arbitrarily defined as involving concepts taught at the eighth grade or below, and *mathematical achievement* has been defined as involving concepts taught above the eighth grade.

The important problem arises when someone asks how well students achieve in relation to their aptitude. Some people would suggest that students should be graded in school according to whether their achievement was high compared with their aptitude, for example. If the items on the aptitude test and the achievement test are essentially the same kinds of items, there is little chance that differences in scores on the two kinds of test will represent other than the errors one might make in measuring the same thing twice. We call these *errors of measurement*. The result of failure to recognize the jangle fallacy (in this case the error in assuming that achievement tests measure different things than aptitude tests just because their names are different) is that students are graded on the basis of errors of measurement instead of on some useful reflection of their achievement of the objectives of the instruction.

Mathematics tests are not the only area in which the jangle fallacy is a problem. For example, vocabulary items are used both in measures of verbal aptitude and in measures of achievement.

It is not necessary for aptitude and achievement always to be measured with similar items. In foreign language instruction, aptitude might be measured by using items concerning a pseudo-language that is created just for the test. Achievement would be measured by one's ability to use a specific language such as Spanish. There would be no jangle fallacy here.

APTITUDE MEASUREMENT FOR PREDICTION OF FUTURE ACHIEVEMENT

We have said that for our purposes we will think of aptitude tests as being measures that are only loosely tied to instruction and are used primarily as predictors of future achievement. By loosely tied to instruction, all we mean is that the contents of the aptitude tests are not usually the same as the instructional material in school. The items may require the student to recognize words that are synonyms, but we do not teach courses in synonyms in the same way that we teach courses in biology. People who have had more and better instruction in general can be expected, on the average, to perform better on synonyms items, but the effect is rather incidental.

When we consider what is meant by the idea that aptitude tests are primarily useful as predictors of future achievement, we need to examine rather closely what is meant by prediction. We will do that now. An example might be the situation in which a student upon entering high school must decide whether he wants to think about going to college or wants to give serious consideration to preparing for a vocation that does not require college. If he makes the decision to prepare for a vocation in high school, he might not take the kinds of courses that would be of greatest benefit if he were to go to college. In fact, he might close the door to the possibility of college by taking a vocational curriculum at the high school level. This might not be sound for a student who could be predicted to perform well in college classes, while it might be very sound for one who could be predicted to have difficulty with college work. An aptitude test which is effective in predicting performance in college courses could be used to help the student evaluate his possibilities for success in college, and it might give him useful information, or corroboration of other information, that will help him make a sound decision or be comfortable with the decision he does make.

Now the concept of a test being an effective predictor of future performance is known in educational measurement as *validity*. A measure that is a good predictor is called a *valid* test. There are some other meanings of the word *validity* and we will discuss them later. This particular kind of validity is called *predictive validity*. It should be noted immediately — and never forgotten — that a test can be called valid only for a specific kind of prediction. In our example, our test was an effective predictor for, i.e., was valid for predicting, college course grades. (Technically, college course grades are called the *criterion*.) It was not necessarily valid for predicting whether our student would be a good football player or would stay in college or would become a discipline problem or any of a host of other possibilities. Thus, any test may have a variety of validities, ranging from high to low, for different criteria.

We need some way to express differences in degree of validity. One possibility is to draw a picture of the relationship between scores on a test and performances on a criterion. If we were to draw a picture of the relationship between a college aptitude test and the average of grades during the first year in college of 20 students at a particular college, it might look like figure 7-1. For each student we have found the point on the horizontal axis that represents his test score and the point on the vertical axis that represents his average first-year college grade, and we have put a dot at the juncture of these two points. This is called a *scatterplot*. The shape of the scatterplot reflects the degree of validity of the test for predicting this criterion.

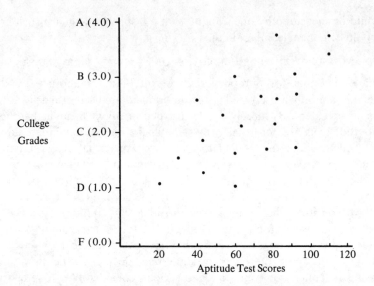

Figure 7–1
Scatterplot of Aptitude Test Scores and College Grades

A high degree of validity goes with a plot in which the swarm of dots tends to rise as scores on both measures get higher, and as this happens it will also happen that the shape of the swarm of dots becomes more like a football or cigar than like a basketball or grapefruit. If there is no relationship between the two measures, the case of no validity of a test for a particular criterion, the swarm of dots will look like a circle with dots more thickly spaced in the middle and tapering evenly in frequency toward the edges.

We could make a prediction for a student by finding his test score on the horizontal axis and then estimating that his most likely college grade will be the grade that corresponds to the middle of the grades received by people with that same test score. This is shown in figure 7-2 for test scores near 60. If there is high validity, the swarm of points is narrower and rises as both scores increase, reflecting the fact that with high validity we predict higher grades for students with higher test scores, and we are also more likely to predict his grades more accurately (the grades received for a given test score are more similar if the validity is higher).

Correlational validity. Scatterplots are not very convenient ways to express validity. We are fortunate that statisticians have developed a way to express by means of numbers the concept we have just developed in terms of scatterplots. The numerical index they have created is called the *correlation coefficient*. The symbol for correlation is the letter *r*. Correlation coefficients range from − 1.00 through zero to + 1.00 and can be calculated through use of complicated formulas that we will not consider. A minus value indicates that as scores on one measure increase, scores on the other measure decrease; a plus value indicates that as scores on one increase, so do scores on the other. A zero value indicates that there is no relationship between increases in value on one measure and increases or decreases in value on the other. In terms of our scatterplots, positive correlation numbers indicate that the scatterplot would be shaped like an oval tipped so that high values on one axis correspond to high values on the other. Correlation of zero indicates that the

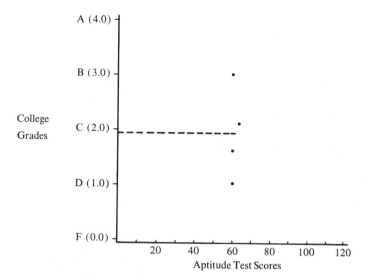

Figure 7–2

Predicting College Grade from Aptitude Test Score
(A Test Score of about 60 Predicts a C Grade)

scatterplot is round. Correlation values that are negative indicate that the plot is oval, again, but this time it is tipped in the other direction so high values on one variable go with low values on the other.

Figure 7-3 indicates correlations of various sizes with the kinds of scatterplots that are associated. The subscripts x and y indicate that the correlation is between variables x and y. Instead of learning how to compute correlation coefficients, which is usually a tedious chore without the aid of computers, you should learn about what shape of a swarm of dots is associated with different levels of correlation coefficient so that when you see a correlation coefficient, you can immediately visualize the shape of the scatterplot, and when you see a scatterplot you can estimate reasonably well the size of correlation coefficient that it would yield.

In some situations there is a relatively simple way to make a better estimate than can usually be made by simply looking at a scatterplot.[*] If the two variables that are plotted are on similar scales and happen to have scores that range over about the same spread of values, we can make some simple measurements and look the results up in a table to estimate the correlation. By covering about the same range of values, we mean that if you subtract the lowest score from the highest score on one measure, you get about the same difference that you get if you do the same subtraction on the scores from the other measure. (Some of you may recognize that we are talking about measurements with about equal *standard deviations*. If that term is new to you, just be patient. You will learn a lot about it soon.)

When we have measures on the same scale with about the same spreads of scores, we can take a ruler and measure on the 45° line from lower left to upper right (for positive correlations) how long the spread of points extends. Call this value, b. We make a corresponding measurement of the width of the spread of dots, that is, on a line perpendicular to the measure of the length of the swarm. Call this value, a. We divide the former by the latter, b/a, and look the value up in table 7-1.

---

[*]This procedure was suggested to the author by W. Angoff.

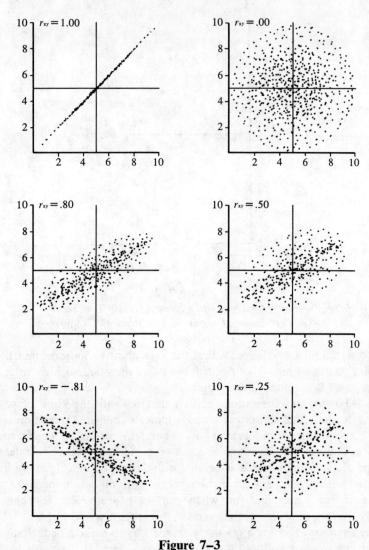

Figure 7–3
Scatterplots of Correlations of Different Sizes and Signs

This is a very simple process compared to calculating a correlation coefficient. To get the simplicity, we give up some accuracy. Except for very high correlations, say above .60, we should probably not consider the second decimal place, and for low correlations and small groups of people, even the first place may be too high or too low by .1 or so, but at least you have a ball-park estimate that is better than the eyeball estimate and does not require a desk calculator or a computer. Remember, though, it only works if the scores on both measures are on the same kind of scale and have about the same amount of spread.[1]

---

[1]An audiotutorial is provided in *Exercises in Classroom Measurement* to help familiarize you with this concept. It is number 7, entitled "Correlation." Those who have not previously studied Part 1 of this text should do audiotutorials 2 and 3 before starting on number 7.

Table 7–1

Estimating Correlation Coefficients

b/a	r (estimated)
1.05	.05
1.11	.10
1.22	.20
1.25	.22
1.36	.30
1.50	.38
1.53	.40
1.75	.51
2.00	.60
2.50	.72
3.00	.80
3.50	.85
4.00	.88
5.00	.92
6.00	.95

In educational measurement we take advantage of the correlation coefficient and the thinking underlying it to speak of *correlational validity* — that is validity that might be represented by the correlation coefficient between two different measures. *Predictive* validity would be one kind of correlational validity, the kind in which one measure is obtained at a point in time prior to the point in time when the other measure is obtained, as, for example, in our illustration of using tests in high school to predict grades in college some years later.

Now, with what we have just been through in mind, you can see why the classroom teacher might want to use a standardized aptitude test that someone else has constructed and whose predictive validity has been experimentally verified by someone else, instead of trying to make up her own tests for the purpose of prediction. Obviously there is a great deal of work involved in creating an aptitude test for prediction purposes. Someone has to wait a period of time, perhaps years, before the criterion data become available in order to determine whether a test is a valid predictor and, if it is valid, how high the correlation between test and criterion is. Teachers are in no position to do this; so they turn to standardized aptitude tests for this purpose.

When teachers turn to standardized aptitude tests for assistance, they need to know a few fundamental things as consumers to be sure that they choose wisely among the available tests and know a little about what they are purchasing. For instance, with regard to validity, how large a correlation coefficient should one expect to find in a "good" aptitude measure? Validity, after all, asks, "Does a test measure (or predict) something well? What does it measure? How well does it measure that thing (or those things in the case of a test that may be a useful predictor of several criteria)?" It is appropriate to consider, then, not just whether it measures what we want it to measure, but how well.

To put this into perspective, let's start by indicating that a good scholastic aptitude test can be expected to have a validity coefficient of about .45 to .50 for predicting first-year grades in college. This knowledge comes from literally tens of thousands of studies of the validity of such tests as the College Entrance Examination Board's *Scholastic Aptitude Test* for use in college admissions decisions. As you can see if you look back at the scatterplots in figure 7-3, that is a rather modest degree of predictive effectiveness. On the other hand, we are really surprised if any single test score is more closely predictive of a criterion of interest than a validity coefficient of, say, .65. Much more common would be predictive validity coefficients of .25. Fundamentally speaking, tests are *not* usually very effective predictors of significant criteria. We use them, however, because to ignore them usually means even less effective prediction!

Several kinds of factors can enter the picture to increase or decrease the general level of validity one might expect from a measure. For instance, in predicting school grades we know from long experience that the grades of girls are more predictable than the grades of boys. So if one were looking at validities of aptitude tests for girls one would expect them to be a little higher, maybe .05 larger on the average.

Research has also indicated that higher validities are to be expected if the criterion measure is of the same form as the predictor variable. Thus, if we were to predict comprehensive achievement-examination scores taken at the end of the senior year of college instead of senior year grade average, we would expect higher validities for an aptitude measure. On the other hand, high school average grade might be expected to have higher correlation coefficients, on the average, with first-year college average grade than the correlations found between aptitude test scores and first-year college grade. In fact, we can estimate that the difference in correlation coefficients for these two predictors will be about .10 in favor of grades predicting grades as a result of thousands of comparisons between the two situations over the years.

We also know that the shorter the time between the measurements on the predictor and the measurements of the criterion, the higher the validity can be expected to be. Thus we would expect larger validity coefficients for predicting first-year college grades than college senior grades from a test given before one enters college.

One could conceive of reducing the time between measures to a very small period, one that would scarcely justify the use of the word prediction. For example, one might want to use a test as a measure of something that is otherwise more difficult to measure. Take the golf instructor. He might want to know whether a student in a golf class could make a sound selection of which club to use for particular situations. He could, of course, follow each student around 18 holes of golf and observe which clubs he chose for what situations and then make a judgment as to his knowledge of proper choice of clubs. But if the teacher could prepare a multiple-choice test, perhaps with pictures of situations, or even movies of scenes on the course, and ask the student to indicate what club he would choose, many students could be examined at once and much valuable time would be saved.

To validate such a test, the test developer would want to conduct an experiment in which he administered the test and then immediately had the golf instructor actually follow a student around the course and grade him on actual club selections. Of course, the test developer would want to do this with many students, and with a variety of instructors, but he would not want appreciable time to elapse between the test and the gathering of criterion data. This type of validation is called *concurrent* validity, instead of predictive validity, because the prediction interval is so short and the interest is not really in prediction as much as substitution of a convenient measure for an inconvenient one. It is a form of correlational validity because the result is evaluated in terms of an average correlation coefficient.

Whether concurrent validity for a measure will be large or small depends on a number of factors, including how good the criterion is, but obviously one would not want to substitute the convenient measure for the inconvenient unless the correlation was rather high, say at least .70, unless, of course, the inconvenient measure was just about impossible to obtain. In the case of the golf instructor it is just about impossible to obtain because it takes so long — at least four hours for each student. And often in school settings we find teachers using substitute measures in this way instead of measuring their real objectives. Usually the teachers have not even been aware of the fact that the concurrent validities of their substitute measures are matters of concern.

Another kind of factor which affects correlational validity is the degree of homogeneity of the group. The same test will have a higher validity coefficient if it is used on a more heterogeneous group of students and a lower validity coefficient if it is used on a more homogeneous group. You would ordinarily get information about the validity of a standardized test from statements the publisher of that test makes, either in advertisements or in the technical manual for the test. You could also obtain such information from research reports on the test, from published critical reviews of the test by testing experts, or from data you collect and analyze for yourself. As you read such information about validity coefficients for a test, you should be considering each time whether the group on whom the coefficient was based is similar to your group in terms of the variety of students included. If you have a special group of gifted students, you should expect a lower validity coefficient than would be obtained from a representative group of all students at a given level. The same would be true if you had a group of disadvantaged students. Unless there are data on validities for such special groups, you might want to go to a testing expert who might determine for you what validity to expect on your group. Often this can be done by certain formulas if the basic data are available.

One factor that can artificially decrease the heterogeneity of scores from a group is known as the "floor" or "ceiling" effect of a test. If a test is altogether too hard for a group, it is said to have too little floor, i.e., there is not room enough for the test to reveal just how poorly some students would perform. If there had been more easy items, some students would have gotten some of them right, while others would have gotten them wrong, and there would be better differentiation among poor students all of whom get the same score (zero) on the too difficult test. The pile up of zero scores reduces the heterogeneity of scores and makes it impossible to get as high a validity correlation coefficient as would be obtained with more appropriate items. This kind of thing happens when an aptitude or achievement test designed for a typical middle socioeconomic class group is given to a disadvantaged group. For example, Hills and Stanley (1970) found that the correlational validities of a test designed for sixth to eighth graders were from .02 to .27 higher for students entering segregated black colleges in the South than the validities of a similar test designed for high school seniors. The latter test did not have enough floor for these college students.

If a test is too easy, on the other hand, it is said to have too little "ceiling," and its validity will also be curtailed, but now because it cannot differentiate adequately among high scorers. Using the usual test to select scholarship winners will often result in low validities for the candidates as a group because they all get similar scores — they are too homogeneous.

Of course, if one wanted to give an exaggerated appearance of high validity, he could give a test to students across a wide variety of grades and ages and lump their scores together in estimating validity. That would be a heterogeneous group of students indeed, but the results would be meaningless since tests seldom are used to deal with such heterogeneous groups.

Reliability. We need to consider one more factor which influences validity. This is the reliability of a set of scores. The *reliability* of a test is most readily thought of as the consistency of the scores. For example, if we measured the height of a table with a yardstick and recorded the measurement, and then measured it again with the same yardstick, we would expect to get very similar measurements. They would be consistent. The yardstick would be considered a reliable measure for tables, in such a situation. Or we could think of two yardsticks, and we could measure a number of different tables with each of them. We should get short measurements for short tables from both yardsticks and long measurements for tall tables from both yardsticks. The two yardsticks are equivalent or parallel in this sense. Again, the yardsticks give consistent results. (We can think of there being equivalent or parallel forms of a test in this same way.)

Obviously, we can measure reliability with correlation coefficients just as we measured validity. It does not make much sense to think of reliabilities less than zero, although once in a while a small negative estimate of the reliability of a set of scores can occur. All we can say in such cases is that the results from using the measure that produced such a value seem so inconsistent with each other as to be meaningless. It is more normal for reliability coefficients to be quite high, .80 or above, and excellent scholastic aptitude tests are expected to have reliability coefficients of .90 or above, indicating that one can expect to get similar results from repeated measurements with such instruments. Short tests, or measures of nebulous characteristics such as attitudes or personality traits, will have lower reliabilities. Ordinarily one gets rather uneasy with measures with reliabilities below .70, which you will remember is higher than we expect most validity coefficients to be.

Teachers' tests in the classroom will often have reliabilities below .70, but teachers should use many tests and combine their results before making a final evaluation. Since the reliability of the composite of many measures is higher than the reliabilities of the individual measures, the lower reliabilities of classroom tests are not a serious problem for a competent teacher. In general, longer tests, or measures with more observations, are more reliable.

Clearly, if test scores for individuals don't agree with each other for the same test, we can't expect them to agree with some outside criterion. Thus correlational validity is limited in size by reliability. Unreliable tests cannot have high validity coefficients. So, one of the things a potential user of a standardized test checks on is its reliability. Unless it is high, the prospect of finding that the test will be useful, except perhaps for research, is dim. A teacher thinking she will use a standardized test because it will measure a characteristic that it would be helpful to know about, but a characteristic which she has neither time nor talent to build a test for, may be disappointed to find that no reliable published measures for that characteristic exist. This will often be the case with such personality traits as motivation, but it may also happen with other kinds of tests, especially if measurement of a lot of different variables is to be crowded into a short time period. The short time permits few items per characteristic, and that results in low reliability which means the individual scores have little potential for useful validity.

Notice, we talk about reliability not as a virtue in itself but only because a test must be reliable in order to be valid. A valid test must be reliable — otherwise it cannot possibly be valid. However, a reliable test need not be valid. It might be valid for some criteria but not for others — or there may be nothing we know of for which it is valid.

We need to mention two more things about reliability. First, it is an abstract concept, and there are a number of ways to estimate the degree of reliability of a set of scores. The usual example is either *alternate forms* like our two yardsticks, or *retest* which would be measuring a set of things twice with the same instrument. We could give the same test twice to a set of students, maybe with a week between testings, and see if the correlation between the scores was high. Another possibility is to think of each item as a miniature test and use the correlations between the items to estimate reliability. Computers have been programmed to do this, and it is a very common approach because it requires only one test administration. Such reliability coefficients are usually called *internal consistency* coefficients, for obvious reasons. No one way of estimating reliability is better than the others, and a good standardized test will usually have reports on all three of these methods, since each tells something slightly different. All should be high in most situations if we expect to have the opportunity for predictive validity.

The last thing that should be pointed out about reliability at this point is that the size of reliability coefficients also depends on group heterogeneity. One can get higher reliability coefficients, say on test-retest, if the group tested ranges over several grades in school and several ages than if all the students are at the beginning of a particular school year and within a month of each other in age. A teacher considering a standardized test should take into consideration whether the group she is going to use it with is similar in homogeneity to the group on which the test was standardized. If not, she can expect higher or lower reliabilities depending on whether her group is more or less heterogeneous.

Now it may seem that we have covered a large amount of ground in order to consider just the first reason that teachers might choose to use standardized tests — because they measured something other than achievement or measured achievement in a particular way. We have chosen this route because it seemed effective to teach some of these immensely important ideas about tests in a situation wherein the learner could see that they had to be understood in order for her to be competent in a common practical situation. Once we have learned these ideas we can use them as we need them later, and we will need them often.

MEASUREMENT FOR DIAGNOSIS

The *diagnostic* test is a kind of test that is not readily constructed by a teacher. By diagnostic test we mean a test that can help us discover why it is that a student is failing to learn as efficiently as others do. By analogy with medicine, from which field we get the term diagnostic, such a test should have a number of different scores, and we would hope that only a few of the scores would be particularly low so we would have a good clue to the source of the student's difficulty. Also by analogy with medicine, a prescription should be available for each low score or pattern of low scores, so that we would know how to treat the student in order for his malady to be remedied. Further, we should know for each treatment any kinds of students for whom it might not be effective, how long it would have to be applied, and what proportion of persons with the malady recover after correct use of the prescribed remedy. Of course, even in medicine there are some maladies for which we have no well understood treatments, but our heavy use of diagnostic procedures in medicine is based on the fact that there are a great many diseases for which diagnosis implies cure.

Notice that a good diagnostic test would have certain characteristics. It would be a long test since it would have many scores, and each score must be highly reliable if we are going to decide on a treatment from its size. Data would have to be collected on a wide variety of both normal people and people with different kinds of problems to be sure that the scores did, indeed, give sound clues to specific maladies. Varied treatments would have to be tried with those people diagnosed by the test as having specific problems so that the relative merit of treatments could be evaluated, the proportion recovering given each treatment could be determined, the length of treatment required could be found, the dosage (hours per day of specific remedial instruction) could be optimized, and so on. Such a test development task is scarcely a suitable project for a classroom teacher!

In fact, though millions of "diagnostic" tests are sold each year, and there are a wide variety of tests with the word diagnostic in their title or description, there are almost no diagnostic tests available that function in the manner described above, analogous to a diagnostic procedure in medicine. Seldom will a diagnostic test be accompanied by a specific prescription, and even less often will the user be told how much remediation to apply for how long and with what expected result. The fact of the matter is, we really don't know how to remedy learning difficulties very effectively. If we did, there would not be students in this course at the college level who were unsure of basic procedures in dealing with percentages, negative numbers, and elementary algebraic manipulations. Those flaws in learning would have been corrected before you got to college. Obviously, they were not, largely because we don't know how to proceed to accomplish the remediation in any reasonable amount of time. And at that, we are more advanced in diagnosis and remediation of problems in arithmetic and reading than in any other field of school learning.

You can see, then, that not only will teachers have to turn to standardized tests if they want to try to use tests to help diagnose students' problems, but also teachers will often be disappointed in the quality of the diagnostic tests available and in the lack of proven remedies to accompany the diagnosis they may get.

A common flaw in the use of diagnostic tests that classroom teachers should know about and avoid is the tendency to give diagnostic tests, like achievement survey tests, to all students in a class, as though they all had problems needing diagnosis. For most students the results of diagnostic testing will be unrevealing. After all, most students are progressing normally, and there is no problem to be diagnosed. Besides that, diagnostic testing implies that each student's problems will be treated individually, or at least that students with similar diagnosis will be grouped together for treatment. If this is not planned for, even the testing for diagnosis of nature of difficulty for students known to be falling behind is simply a futile gesture and a waste of money that could better be spent more productively. In general, diagnostic testing in the present state of the testing art is sufficiently tricky that the classroom teacher without special training in remedial instruction should probably avoid attempting to engage in it without the assistance of a well-trained specialist.

INTEREST AND PERSONALITY MEASUREMENT

Teachers may turn to standardized tests to measure such characteristics of students as their interests or their personality traits. Certainly teachers are in no position to develop tests to measure such variables. There is considerable doubt whether teachers should even attempt to use the instruments that are on the market for measuring them.

Interest tests are much more widely used by counselors than teachers. Usually they ask such questions as "Indicate whether you like, dislike, or are indifferent to the following activities: Making flower arrangements, outdoor sports, preparing a budget." From the student's responses, the scoring key attempts to indicate what kinds of school subjects, or what kind of employment, will be most satisfying. Sound interpretation of such results requires special training, beyond the scope of this course. A well-trained school counselor should have the background necessary for appropriate choice and use of interest tests, but it is too much to expect of the subject-matter specialist.

Personality tests attempt to measure facets of a person such as his ego strength, his aggressiveness, his adjustment, his stability, his motivation, and so on. They may ask questions such as "Do you often feel that you are left out of things?" or "Do you frequently have nightmares?" Though there are more tests of personality than standarized tests of any other kind, they are potentially harmful when used by persons not properly trained in their interpretation. Even many psychologists are quite cautious in the use and interpretation of such instruments. The school teacher is well advised to leave them alone.

MEASURES THAT FIT THE TEACHER'S OBJECTIVES

In our consideration of standardized tests thus far, we have examined the nature of standardized tests and have evaluated the potential for use by a teacher of measures other than the usual achievement measures, i.e., measures designed for prediction and for diagnosis, and measures of interests and personality. Now we want to return to measures of achievement and consider why a teacher might want to use standardized tests of achievement instead of simply building her own achievement tests.

For one thing, a teacher who could find a standardized test of achievement in her subject might save herself a lot of time and effort that she would otherwise have to devote to test construction. She would also have a much finer test than she could build with her limited resources of time, training, energy, and expert collaboration. For another thing, a whole school system might want to use a common standardized achievement test instead of teacher grades in evaluating the effectiveness of some kind of instruction that has been adopted in the system. It might be felt that teachers would not agree in their grading practices, and it is impossible to get one teacher to grade all the students because each teacher teaches in just one school.

In situations such as these there are a number of important considerations involved in choosing to use a standardized test, but the paramount consideration is a kind of validity which we have not yet discussed. This is known as *content validity*. By content validity we mean that experts have looked at the content of the test items, and their judgment is that the items measure what the test purports to measure. Thus, content validity might be established by a teacher's having a detailed outline of a course and examining the items of a standardized test to determine if the test items were nearly all included in the content she taught, and if all the content she taught was included in the test items. If so, the test would have content validity for her course. We would be especially confident of the content validity if several other people compared her course with the test items and agreed that the test measured what she taught. There is no statistical technique to measure content validity, and no coefficient to express it. This kind of validity is the kind that is probably most natural and appropriate to use for achievement tests, though we might be especially happy if a test had both content validity and correlational validity for a criterion that was generally acceptable as being appropriate for the test. Thus, ideally, an achievement test for geometry should have items that experts in geometry agree measure geometry, and it should also correlate highly with the grades students get at the end of a course in geometry.

It may often be the case that there is no published test that fits a specific curriculum well enough to be satisfactory. In such situations it may be wiser to give no further consideration to standardized tests for that specific curriculum and to rely on teacher-made tests or other means of evaluation if they would serve the purposes. You might be tempted to change the curriculum to fit the standardized test, but that is putting the cart before the horse. On the other hand, a good teacher might pick up some good ideas about things to include in her instruction from seeing what the experts include in standardized tests on that subject. Always remember, however, that published tests are there to *serve* those who find them useful. They should not be allowed to *control* what is taught.

PLACEMENT TESTS

By *placement* one ordinarily means determining the point on a continuum of sequential instruction at which the student has achieved mastery so that if new topics are then introduced, eventual achievement of instructional objectives will be maximized or hastened. The clearest examples of placement come in sequential courses like arithmetic. Since some operations are built upon others, as multiplication is built upon addition, one wants to know whether the earlier topic has been learned before introducing the later one. If not, introduction of a new topic prematurely will presumably delay or decrease the attainment of the objective of being able to multiply fluently.

For a placement test to be effective, the scores should reveal clearly the level to which a student has progressed. Most tests result in a total score which could be obtained either by very thorough knowledge of items related to material early in the sequence or by scattered performance on items all along the sequence. Thus even tests called "placement tests" should be examined carefully to see whether it is reasonable to expect them to function as desired. If no data from their successful use for placement in the way placement is to be done are presented by the publisher, you should be very tentative in choosing them for use. Probably a limited number of copies should be purchased and used in an experiment to see whether the test does well what is desired. Or as a potentially sound alternative, you might develop locally a placement test that will perform as desired. There is no intrinsic need for a standardized test for this function. And it should be obvious that no test can do a sound job of placement in a subject matter that is not sequential. It does not make American History any easier to have taken local history or world history first. So placement testing in history or social studies is most likely a waste of testing time and money.

One placement use of tests that has received recent attention occurs in the context of desegregation of schools. On many occasions a school district may be tempted to use tests as a nondiscriminatory procedure that will sort students who are newly housed together into groups which teachers will find it easy to teach as groups. This is often called homogeneous grouping or tracking. Sometimes it has been suggested that whole schools be separated, with the higher scoring students going to one school and the lower scoring going to a different school.

Such a use of tests can be challenged in the courts if the system appears to discriminate by race, ethnicity, or socioeconomic level, as well as test score. All that is required as *prima facie* evidence is that the testing produce a significant difference between the proportion of the minority group in a particular classification (track, school, etc.) and the proportion of that group in the school population. Once that has been established, then those doing the testing have to prove that the testing procedures are rational, sensible, and serve well a useful educational purpose.

There have been many court cases on issues concerned with placement testing which seems to discriminate against minorities. Some issues seem to be well settled by now. For instance, in a series of cases it has been repeatedly decided that tests cannot be used for placement in recently desegregated schools, regardless of arguments in their favor. In one case (*Lemon* v. *Bossier Parish School Board*) the courts even went so far as to indicate that the school district could not assign pupils to schools on the basis of achievement test scores during the first year of desegregation. The court said, "We think as a minimum this means that the district in question must have for several years operated as a unitary system." The case involved schools in Plain Dealing, Louisiana, in which the plan for desegregation provided that students in grades 4-12 be assigned to one of two schools on the basis of scores made on the California Achievement Tests. The outcome of the legal procedures was that the U.S. Fifth Circuit Court of Appeals ruled that the district must discontinue assigning students on the basis of achievement test scores.

In another important case (*Hobson* v. *Hansen*) in which tracking was being done on the basis of aptitude test scores, the court ruled the tracking illegal. The ruling was not that ability grouping is illegal, but when it is done on the basis of aptitude tests which might be biased, and when the result is that black students are relegated to lower tracks and there given an inferior education, the procedure is unconstitutional.

The attempt to use achievement test scores to resegregate in the guise of placement can backfire. In the case of *Serna* v. *Portales* (New Mexico) *Municipal Schools,* the fact that the IQ scores of students in schools having a preponderance of Spanish surnames were low caused the court to decide that this was evidence of unequal educational opportunity, in spite of the presence of equivalent programs in these schools. The court ruled that the schools must reassess their program to provide for the specialized needs of the Spanish surnamed students. By contrast, a year later another court decided (*Lai* v. *Nichols*) that in the case of non–English-speaking Chinese students, equal public education does not imply that the school must provide students with special assistance to overcome disabilities whatever their origin. The school's failure to provide these students with bilingual compensatory education in English did not violate the Civil Rights Act of 1964. So, time and additional cases will indicate what the limits are in using standardized tests for this kind of placement. These cases should alert the teacher to the kinds of legal issues that may be involved and how they might be decided.

ASSESSMENT TESTS

A teacher might be interested in using a standardized test of achievement instead of her own test in order to demonstrate that her instruction has indeed produced a change in the competence of her students during a lengthy period of teaching, such as a school year or term. This is what is meant here by the term *assessment*. The teacher might turn to standardized achievement tests in an attempt to provide evidence that is generally acceptable, without hint of the test just covering topics that are easy to teach or otherwise giving an unfair picture of her success with these students.

Unfortunately, change is much harder to measure than it seems. There are many very complicated technical problems in measuring change, and most school personnel are unaware that they even need to be considered. No widely accepted procedure for measuring change can be recommended. But at the very least, there would have to be some sizable measured change for you to conclude that an educational program was effective. If you examine the average scores on standardized tests from one grade or year to the next, you almost invariably will find that the average performance increase over a year's instruction is only a few items, five to ten, perhaps. For example, on the *Comprehensive Tests of Basic Skills,* the increase in the average number of items correct on Form Q, Level 3, from the beginning of the sixth grade to the beginning of the seventh grade in arithmetic is 12 items; in reading it is 9 items. From grade 7 to 8, the increases are 10 items and 7 items, respectively, and from the beginning of grade 8 to the end of grade 8 the increases are 7 items and 4 items, respectively. It will not be very impressive to a parent or legislator to tell him that after a year's instruction all that has been achieved is that out of a test of 85 to 98 items, the student can get from 4 to 12 more items correct.

The small increase in number of items correct is not a matter of a poorly constructed standardized test. Other tests might show even less average increase in number of items correct over a year's time than the *Comprehensive Tests of Basic Skills.* The reason standardized tests show so little effect over time is that the tests have to be designed to suit a wide audience in order to have sufficient sales volume to justify publishing the test. That means that one test has to cover several years' work, and it has to be suitable for a wide variety of curricula. The result will be that not very many items are suitable for any one curriculum at any one grade. So even when a student has learned all that he was supposed to learn and has met all the instructional objectives, he may not find many more items that he knows at the end of a year than at the beginning. Thus, using standardized tests for *assessment* is likely to be very frustrating.

Using tests designed by teachers specifically for their own curricula and tied closely to their own objectives should show much larger numbers of items gained during a year. It would not be impossible to have tests on which no one got above a modest score at the beginning of the year, and everyone got very high scores at the end. These would be just as legitimate assessment tests and would give a much more impressive *and* realistic picture of instructional effectiveness. If a standardized test is to be used, it should be selected for having most of its items closely related to the objectives of the program being assessed so that a grossly misleading unfavorable impression is not the result.

We should perhaps note that in some cases the results from standardized tests have been used to dismiss teachers on the grounds of incompetence. As you can see already, this is very treacherous ground since growth may be nearly undetectable by standardized tests over as short a period as a single school year. There are other problems with using standardized test scores this way, too. For example, you would want to know not just the scores at the end of the year for the students of the teacher in question, but also the scores at the end of the previous year. That is, what kind of students did she have to work with? You would also want to know accurately just what she did in attempting to work with the children, what resources she had available, and so on.

However, in at least one case, (*Scheelhaase* v. *Woodbury Central Community School District*) that of Mrs. Norma Scheelhaase of Woodbury, Iowa, the school dismissed an experienced teacher because her pupils' scores were too low on standardized tests. Mrs. Scheelhaase was ordered reinstated and paid substantial damages in a ruling by a U.S. District Court. The court said, "A teacher's professional competence cannot be determined solely on the basis of her students' achievement on the ITBS and the ITED (standardized tests), especially where the students maintain normal educational growth rates." On appeal, however, that decision was reversed. The appeals court indicated that since there is no tenure provision for teachers in Iowa where the case arose, and since the dismissal did not seem arbitrary or capricious (even though it might be erroneous), no right had been violated and the court should not overrule the school board's exercise of its discretion. Apparently, then, in a situation like this the evidence from standardized tests can be used legally to determine the competence of a senior grade school teacher.

COMPARISONS WITH OTHER STUDENTS

A teacher might want to compare her students with students in other classes or schools. By *evaluation* as a purpose for using standardized tests in a school we mean the evaluation of a school or a school group by comparison of that group with other, similar groups. This makes a requirement on the test materials that is often unrecognized. The requirement is that there be available norms for *school means*. You can expect that a standardized test published by a major test publisher will provide norms for individual students, but only rarely will provide norms for schools' means. But if a school's mean is evaluated by comparing it with norms based on individual students, erroneous and misleading interpretations will result.

TEST NORMS

Let us consider this in more detail. First, we will have to learn in detail what norms are, and then we will consider the difference between individual norms and school-mean norms.

When a test is given, the result is a set of scores, one for each individual who took the test, as in figure 7-4. To comprehend these scores, it is helpful to put them into some kind of order. Usually we find the highest score and list it at the top of a piece of paper. We find how many people got that score and place that number beside the score. We then find the next highest score, count how many individuals got that score, and place that number beside the score. We continue in this manner until we get to the lowest score, which is placed at the bottom of the column of scores. Using this procedure, the set of scores in figure 7-4 is transformed into the *frequency distribution* in figure 7-5. Now we can more readily see what happened to our students on the test.

Person Number	Score
1	22
2	30
3	24
4	22
5	22
6	24
7	23
8	17
9	21
10	20
11	22
12	19
13	20
14	20
15	30
16	22
17	20
18	19
19	29
20	23
21	23

Figure 7–4
Scores for Persons Taking a Test

To make comparisons even easier, another step is usually taken. The frequencies are converted to *percentiles*. The percentile corresponding to any given score for a specified group of people is the proportion of the group who obtain that score or any lower score. Thus if 31 out of a group of 50 got scores of 17 or below on a test, the percentile for a score of 17 is simply 62, i.e., 31 divided by 50.

In a frequency distribution the percentile corresponding to a given raw score can be found by counting up or adding up the number of persons who scored below that score, then adding in the number who obtained that score, and dividing the sum by the total number who took the test. For instance, in figure 7-5 the percentile for score 22 is found by adding the frequencies for all lower scores, i.e., by adding $1 + 2 + 4 + 1 = 8$, then by adding in the frequency of score 22, i.e., 5, and dividing by the total number of cases which appears beside the word *Total* at the bottom of the list of scores. In figure 7-6, the scores, frequencies, and percentiles for all the scores obtained by these students are listed. You should calculate some of the percentiles we have not discussed to be certain you know how percentiles are obtained.

Score	Frequency
30	2
29	1
28	0
27	0
26	0
25	0
24	2
23	3
22	5
21	1
20	4
19	2
18	0
17	1

Total 21

Figure 7–5
Frequency Distribution of Scores

Score	Frequency	Percentile
30	2	100
29	1	90
28		
27		
26		
25		
24	2	86
23	3	76
22	5	62
21	1	38
20	4	33
19	2	14
18		
17	1	5

Total 21

Figure 7–6

When such a frequency distribution is based on a representative sample of people from some population of people in whom we are interested, we call the distribution a set of *norms*. The population might be all sixth graders in September who are within six months of their twelfth birthday. The sample should have been obtained by means of careful statistical sampling of all such sixth-graders in the country. It would be important in many cases to give the test to all these sixth graders at the same time of the year, say the fall or the spring, because their performance might be quite different at the end of the sixth grade compared to the beginning. Thus one might want separate norms for sixth graders tested in the fall and sixth graders tested in the spring. Norms might be provided for students in urban schools separately from rural schools, public separately from private schools, midwestern separately from eastern schools, and so on. The potential user of a standardized test should be sure that the norms groups provided by the test publisher include the kinds of people with which she wishes to make comparisons. If not, there is usually no way in which the teacher can obtain the norms she needs for evaluation.

The potential user of a standardized test needs to be alert to the quality of the norms provided for a test. The norms are usually found in the *manual* for the test. (We will look at publishers' test manuals in more detail later.) If sound sampling procedures are used, adequately representative norms can be obtained from groups that are not particularly large. Five or ten thousand properly sampled students can represent all sixth graders in the country. However, in the not too distant past, it was common for test publishers to attempt to provide good norms by merely testing large numbers of students with no regard to sampling. To get large numbers, the publishers would ask for their tests to be given in big city schools where a lot of students could be obtained at once with ease. As a result, the norms provided were biased, sometimes rather strongly.

Some tests still do not have norms that can be trusted as being adequately representative of a specific population. The best clue for the teacher who does not know a lot about sampling procedures is to look for a clear statement of the population, some description of how many cases there are in the population, some description of how samples were drawn from the population, and a description of how closely the sample fits the characteristics of the population. If all these things are provided, the user is reasonably safe in assuming that the norms adequately represent the population and were obtained from sound sampling procedures.

If the publisher does not give details of how the sample was drawn, how well it fits the population, and so on, but merely speaks of the size of the sample or gives a vague description perhaps based on equating this test through another test, etc., be careful. If the results seem strange it may be because the norms are not sound.

Percentiles are obtained from publishers' norms tables by looking up the score for an individual student, say Johnny, in a table for some population of interest, say students at Johnny's grade level, and obtaining directly from that norms table the percentile corresponding to Johnny's score. We simply find the corresponding percentile; we don't have to add frequencies or percents. That has all been done for us. That percentile indicates at what level in the norms group Johnny performed. If his score is at the ninety-fifth percentile, 95% of students at his grade level could be expected to make that score or lower. If he scored at the fourteenth percentile, only 14% of students at his grade level could be expected to score at that score or lower. If he scored at the fiftieth percentile, then he scored at about the middle of the scores obtained by people in his grade.

Notice that we never speak of norms or percentiles without indicating the norms group. It is meaningless to say that Johnny is at the ninety-fifth percentile. Ninety-fifth percentile of retarded children, college graduates, Nobel prize winners, or sixth graders? We must always specify the norms group.

We will always talk about percentiles here in terms of our definition — the percent of persons who score at or below a given score. You should be aware that other definitions are in use. A very common one is that the percentile is the percent of persons who score *below* a given score. This leaves out those who score at that score. Another common definition includes half of the persons who score at the given score level. You must look at the test manual to find out what definition is being used for the norms of a specific test. For most classroom purposes, it will not make much difference which definition is being used.

SCHOOL-MEAN NORMS

The percentiles we have just described are for individuals. We could also study the average performance of sixth grades in different schools. The population might be the sixth grades in all the schools in the United States. A sample of these might be drawn, and the average score for each sixth grade in the sample could be obtained for the test in which we were interested. These could be put into rank order and the percentile could be calculated for each mean raw score.

We would find that the percentiles for mean scores would be rather different from the percentiles for individual scores. Mean scores tend to cluster more closely about the grand mean for everyone than do individual scores. No school can have a mean as high as the highest individual's score because the mean is a kind of middle score for a school, and there have to be some people above the mean in every school, as well as some below its mean. The net effect is that the percentiles on *school-mean norms* are higher than the percentiles for individual norms if the school mean is above the grand mean for everyone. If the school mean is below average, its percentile on school-mean norms is lower than its percentile on individual norms would be. The size of this effect can be perceived in the example in figure 7-7 taken from the 1970 information provided for the *School and College Ability Test,* Second

Scores	School Mean Percentile	Individual Percentile
288	95+	82
286	94	79
284	91	75
282	86	71
280	80	65
278	75	60
276	68	55
274	59	51
272	50	47
270	41	43
268	32	39
266	23	35
264	18	31
262	15	27
260	12	24
258	9	20
256	5	17

Figure 7–7

School Mean Percentiles Compared with Individual Percentiles on SCAT-II, Quantitative

Edition (SCAT-II) on which both individual and school-mean norms are available. Notice how far in error it would be to interpret a school's performance in terms of norms for individuals. A school whose *quantitative* mean was high, say 282, would only be at the seventy-first percentile on individual norms but at the eighty-sixth percentile on school-mean norms. To have used the wrong norms would not have treated the school fairly in *evaluation* at all. That is why we stress that if standardized tests are to be used for evaluation of schools, the test must supply school-mean norms. This is important because many tests do not supply such norms, and many schools who try to evaluate their performance by using the wrong norms are not only in error but also may make other incorrect decisions to compound the error. Many test users are unaware that there is even a problem of this sort.

Contents of Publishers' Test Manuals[2]

Earlier we indicated that test norms are found in the publishers' test manuals and that we would take up manuals in more detail soon. Let us turn to them now, since the norms we have just discussed are one of the important elements of manuals, and the instructions for administering standardized tests, which we will turn to in the next chapter, are another important element in manuals.

Often one manual or booklet includes both the instructions for administering a test and the material needed for score interpretation. Sometimes, however, these materials may be published in separate booklets, perhaps called something like "Administrator's Manual" and "Technical Manual." Although the sequence, captions, and style of publication vary from one test to another, for all standardized tests of useful quality the publishers provide information on the following five topics.

1. *Introductory Material.* Usually a description of the test and what it is meant to measure are presented, and positive features of the test are emphasized.
2. *Directions for Administration.* These are usually very comprehensive and detailed, designed so that the teacher who has prepared by reading them and examining the test booklet will have no trouble conducting a standard administration.
3. *Directions for Scoring.* Usually procedures for the teacher to use in scoring the tests locally are provided, as well as procedures for obtaining machine-scoring services. Procedures for dealing with irregularities are sometimes provided here.
4. *Standardization and Norms.* Often the procedure used in developing the test is described, and the methods used in obtaining the sample of students upon whom the norms were developed are presented. In addition, tables to permit conversion of raw scores to derived scores and to relate scores to performances of the standardization group appear here.

---

[2]You should get first-hand experience with several test manuals of different sorts to see what they contain, how they are similar and different, and the different ways norms tables can be presented. An audiotape, used with several manuals illustrating different styles of presentation, is part of the instructional system. However, you need to know more about different kinds of scores of standardized tests before the exercise on test manuals and norms will be most effective. It is, therefore, postponed until near the end of chapter 11.

5. *Statistical Information.* Here will be found estimates of validity and reliability, means and standard deviations for various groups, other statistics, and perhaps the results of research using the test.

A PROBLEM IN USING PUBLISHERS' NORMS TABLES

A common mistake of the naïve is to get the idea that norms tell what ought to be rather than what is. Perhaps they confuse the word *norm* with the word *normal.* (If one uses the dictionary definition of "norm," such a confusion is likely.) However, in the technical use of the word *norm* in testing, there is no implication of a standard being set or a goal being established. In fact, in testing we speak of norms, i.e., distributions — not of a *norm.* It is displaying ignorance to talk about "getting students up to the norm" as though that were somehow good. It is not even possible because, obviously, if all students get "up to the norm" (assuming that "the norm" is the fiftieth percentile), the norm, which is an average, just changes upward so that about half of the group are once again below it. You can't win in a game like that. If you understand what you have just read, for the rest of your life you should wince when you hear someone use the phrase "up to the norm." If you aren't wincing, go back and read this paragraph again and again until you do!

In order to provide some practice in working with test norms to consolidate our learning about them to this point, a fictitious norms table is presented in figure 7-8.

Test X: Form 6 A, Fall Testing, Boys

Score	Grade:	Reading 4	5	6	Mathematics 4	5	6	Social Studies 4	5	6
45				100			100			
44				91			86			
43				76			60			
42			100	52		100	35			
41			95	25		83	14			100
40			86	14		52	1			90
39			64	6	100	22				67
38		100	50	1	88	2			100	43
37		96	31		70				89	11
36		85	16		45			100	65	1
35		65	6		18			96	40	
34		47	1		1			85	9	
33		30						50	1	
32		17						33		
31		7						7		
30		1						1		

Figure 7–8
Norms Table
(Fictitious Data)

If you have understood the discussion, you should have no trouble verifying the following in that figure:

1. The percentile equivalent for a score of 34 on Reading in the fourth grade is 47. The percentile equivalent for that same score in Mathematics for the same grade is 1. In Social Studies, it is 85. This does not, however, imply that fourth graders perform better in Mathematics. That test may have had more items or been composed of items that were generally easier.
2. The increase from year to year on the average in these fictitious tests is only a few items.
3. The Reading scores are more variable than the Mathematics scores.
4. A score of 36 on Reading in the fourth grade is better than a score of 37 on Mathematics in that same grade even though it reflects a smaller number of correct responses

Summary

We have learned a lot about the nature of and use of standardized tests in this chapter. The salient points follow. Standardized tests are tests designed to be administered under as nearly identical conditions as reasonably possible. Usually standardized tests are sold by commercial publishers, have been normed, and are accompanied by manuals which include a description of the test, instructions for administration, technical and statistical information, and norms tables.

Teachers most often use standardized tests in order to be able to compare their students with norms groups, or because the tests measure things for which teachers are not trained to develop tests, such as aptitude for learning. It is easy to be deceived about what a test measures or for what purpose it can be used effectively. Diagnostic tests can be, and often are, misused. Teachers should be careful with them and should probably not even attempt to use personality and interest tests without advanced training in measurement.

Scores from a test for use in schools must be *valid* to be useful; that is, they must measure a characteristic of interest. They must have *content* validity or *correlational* validity for a particular kind of person and situation. In order to be valid, the scores must first of all be *reliable;* that is, the test must yield consistent results. A student must not score high on one testing and low on the next. Reliability is expressed by a correlation coefficient, obtained by comparing scores from a test with scores from a retest, by comparing scores from two forms of a test, or by study of the individual items of a test.

Standardized tests may be used for placing students at the optimum point in a curriculum, but they should only be used for that purpose after study in the local situation indicates their effectiveness. They may be used to assess whether students are improving in their achievement, but they usually are not very effective for this purpose. They may be used to evaluate the performance of a school or class, but only if school-mean norms are provided, and few tests provide these.

Norms for a test should be based on representative samples of students. Some tests still provide norms not clearly based on samples representative of any useful population. Norms are usually reported in terms of percentiles (and perhaps other kinds of scores). The percentile for a score is the percent of people (or schools) in the reference group who receive that score or a lower score. Using a norms table is usually easy, once the principle is thoroughly grasped. However, it is a mistake to speak of getting a pupil or group of pupils "up to the norm." That idea reflects an inadequate understanding of what test norms are.

References

Carroll, J. B. The aptitude-achievement distinction: The case of foreign language aptitude and proficiency. In Green, D. R. (Ed.), *The aptitude-achievement distinction.* Monterey, Calif.: CTB/McGraw-Hill, 1974. Chapter 9.

Cleary, T. A., Humphreys, L. G., Kendrick, S. A., & Wesman, A. Educational uses of tests with disadvantaged students. *Amer. Psychologist,* 1975, **30,** 15-41.

Hobson v. *Hansen,* 269 F. Supp. 401 (DDC 1967).

Hills, J. R. & Stanley, J. C. Easier test improves prediction of black students' college grades. *J. Negro Educ.,* 1970, **39,** 320-24.

Lai v. *Nichols,* 483 F. 2d 791 (CA Cal, 1973).

Lemon v. *Bossier Parish School Board,* 444 F.2d 1400 (5th Cir. 1971).

Scheelhaase v. *Woodbury Central Community School District,* 349 F. Supp. 988, rev. 488 F.2d 237 (1972, 1973).

Serna v. *Portales Municipal Schools,* 351 F.Supp. 1279.

8

Administration of Standardized Tests

Objectives

The objectives that you should have for this chapter are the development of the ability to:
1. State at least five important conditions that must exist for a test administration to qualify as standardized;
2. Recognize in descriptions of testing situations conditions that destroy the standardization of the test.

Instructions

As you have learned, the essence of a test's being what is called *standardized* is that the test is administered under the same conditions to all who take it. This permits comparisons among students who have taken the test at different times and in different places. Therefore, it is important that the teacher who would use standardized tests knows how to administer them to maintain standard conditions.

The most important thing a teacher can do to administer a test soundly is to familiarize herself completely with the instructions for administration, which appear in the manual for the test. She should follow those instructions explicitly. Sometimes a test will have more than one manual, and there will be a separate booklet covering administration of the test. Not all tests are organized so thoroughly, but the best developed have very detailed instructions for administration, and those instructions can be used as models for guidance in administration of less well-developed instruments.

The best sets of instructions involve three levels of information, often presented in different typefaces, in boxes, or in different colors of print. One level of information is that from the publisher to the administrator; it gives such information as the amount of time to be allowed. The second level indicates to the administrator instructions she is to read or to recite verbatim to the examinees. The third level indicates to the administrator the instructions that the examinees read from their test booklets. An example of such a set of instructions appears in figure 8-1. Instructions are given in such careful detail because they are meant to be followed in every respect. That is what produces a standard administration.

Figure 8–1
Sample of Test Instructions with Three Levels

Instructions for Synonyms Test

Time Limit, 10 minutes

The students should have their booklets open to page 2. The number 2 in boldface should appear in the upper right-hand corner. The left-hand page should be blank.

SAY: On page 9 are instructions for the SYNONYMS test. Read them silently while I read them aloud.

This test will show how well you understand words. For each item you are to blacken the space on your answer sheet which corresponds to the word which means the same as the given word. Read the sample item and see how the right answer is marked.

The examiner should *not* read the sample item.

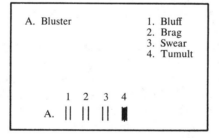

SAY: Since bluster is the same as tumult, blank 4 has been blackened.

Are there any questions?

If not, when I say START, turn to page 3 of your books and start the test. When I say STOP, you are to stop working and hold your pencils in the air.

START

Handling Students' Questions

A test administration in which no examinee wants to ask a question is a rare event. The administrator must be prepared to field questions. Her problem is to do so without seriously modifying the conditions of test administration. The best solution available is to remember the principle that answers to students' questions should not provide any information that has not already been presented in the oral or written instructions to the student. In other words, the teacher may repeat or rephrase what has already been presented but must add nothing new.

One of the most severe problems is that some older tests, which are still in use, did not instruct the students concerning whether they should guess when they did not know the answer to an item. Modern practice is to inform students on this point because it is believed that the less information they have, the more personality differences in guessing behavior will enter and distort the measurement of whatever competency the test measures. But to inform students concerning what they should do about guessing on a test that does not have such information provided uniformly to all examinees through its instructions is to alter the administration in a significant way. The standardization is broken, and the results from the administration may as well be thrown into the wastebasket. They may not legitimately be compared with norms, nor may the reliability and validity data associated with the test be applied to the results of this nonstandard administration. Effectively, it becomes a new and unknown measure.

It is embarrassing, but all an administrator can do when asked "Should we guess when we don't know the answer?" is to reread the instructions that refer to guessing, if there are any. If there are none, the reply must be something innocuous and uninformative such as, "Do the best you can." The teacher should not let herself become defensive or hostile at this point since one of the administrator's duties is to try to maintain order while remaining relaxed and cheerful in order to keep examinee anxiety at a minimum. If the examiner finds such situations distressing, she should try to choose tests which are explicit about what the student should do about guessing!

It should be stating the obvious to say that in no case should the administrator of a standardized test attempt to assist any examinee with any individual item. Even if it seems that the student has a legitimate question, and one that the examiner could help with, no help should be given. If the examiner does provide help, even as much as a nod of the head, the administration is no longer standard, and we are dealing with a new test. Sometimes help with a single item can make an appreciable difference in the percentile rank of a person; so giving even a little bit of help to a student cannot be condoned. It is interesting to note that the percentile rank of a student near the average is likely to be changed most by altered performance on one or two items. This can be verified in any table of norms. On the other hand, with a kind of score called "grade-equivalent" scores, about which we will learn later, the scores at the ends of the distributions of scores (high or low scores) are often changed as much as a whole year by altered performance on a single item.

Timing Tests

Particular attention must be paid to the time limits on standardized tests that are given under time restrictions. A matter of 10 or 15 seconds error in timing can change some students' percentile ranks appreciably if it prevents them from answering an item or permits them to answer one more item than they could answer within the correct limits.

There are several tricks that can be used to handle timing effectively. First, the administrator must remain alert. Second, she should have two timepieces available. One can be the clock on the wall or her wristwatch or some timepiece that is not altered for the test administration. The other should be a clock or watch that can be reset as needed. Some test administration instructions tell the examiner specifically when and how to set this second clock at the beginning of each test. If the instructions do not give those directions, the examiner should pick a convenient hour, such as 12 o'clock and reset the clock to this time at the beginning of each timed unit. This makes it easy to tell when the time period is up. The regular clock's time should also be noted by marking it down. This should be used as a backup device in case something goes wrong with the reset clock. Nothing is more distressing than to notice in the middle of a test that the clock has stopped, and no one knows how long it has been stopped. The backup clock, with starting time written down, saves such situations. It can also ease the mind of a serious administrator who suddenly gets the feeling that too much time has gone by even though her reset clock indicates otherwise.

Some administrators like to use the specially built interval timers that are available for timing tests. They are also used by teachers of such skills as typewriting in which time or speed is a basic element. Usually they can be reset for periods of time up to an hour or two, and they ring a bell at the end of the period. The administrator who plans to use such a device should try it out before the test administration so that she is thoroughly familiar with it. On some of them it is very easy to get confused and set the time period for, say, ten minutes less than the maximum time on the clock instead of setting it for just ten minutes. Since it is easy to get confused with timers, and since sometimes they are not given proper maintenance, it is especially important to record the time of starting a test period from another clock when using these instruments.

Monitoring the Room

In the past the general practice in monitoring or proctoring a standardized test was for examiners to move about the room quietly, supposedly to be readily available to answer questions and to prevent or detect cheating. Currently it seems better practice for the examiner to move about very little. She should not expect to, or be expected to, answer many questions during a standardized test. Unless someone has a faulty test booklet or some other mechanical problem, the examiner should have little reason to move among the examinees. The seating arrangement should be such that collaboration between examinees is ineffective, so moving around the room is only useful at the beginning of a test to be sure that the students understand the instructions. Other movement is considered to do more harm from its distractiveness than it does good.

Seating the Examinees

The recommended practice for seating has changed over the years, also. Of course, one wants to administer a test in a quiet, well-lighted, and well-ventilated room.

It should also be spacious. Ideally, no student should be seated within five feet of any other student. Sometimes that cannot be managed, and then the particular pattern in which students are seated becomes important.

's are Seats; X's are Occupied

```
X _ X _ X _ X _ X
_ X _ X _ X _ X _
X _ X _ X _ X _ X
_ X _ X _ X _ X _
X _ X _ X _ X _ X
```

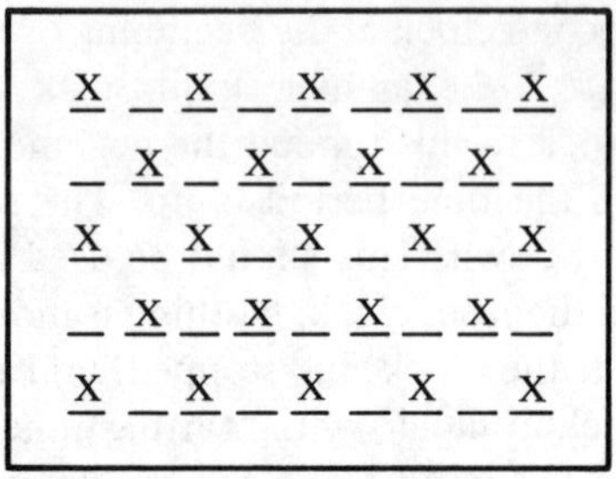

Front

Figure 8–2
Former Practice in Seating for Test Administration

's are Seats; X's are Occupied

```
X _ X _ X _ X
X _ X _ X _ X
X _ X _ X _ X
X _ X _ X _ X
X _ X _ X _ X
```

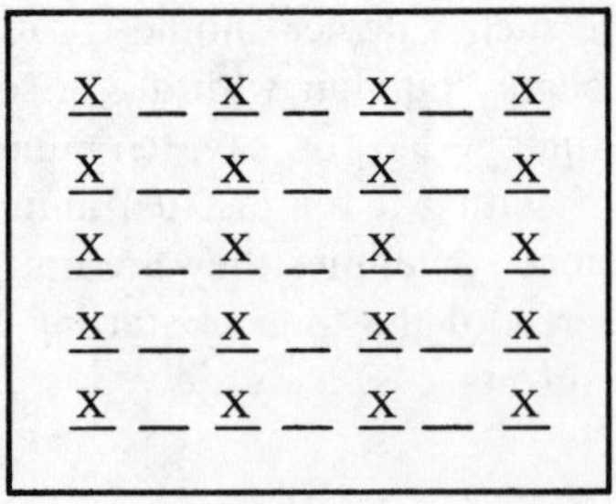

Front

Figure 8–3
Recommended Seating Arrangement

In the past it was the practice to seat students alternately in rows of seats as in figure 8-2. Empty seats were left between each student and the student on every side of him. More recently it has been noted that copying from one's neighbor is more difficult if one must look directly over his shoulder than if one can glance diagonally forward; so currently recommended practice is depicted in figure 8-3. Students are seated directly behind one another in columns. Between each two columns of students is an empty column of seats, giving about the recommended five feet of spacing laterally, while placing students directly behind one another from front to rear.

Most students do not like to be crowded during an important activity such as a test. Rather than feeling offended at being spaced to avoid collaboration, they will appreciate being seated so that they will be as little bothered by neighbors as possible, and they will have a sense of freedom and openness permitting their maximum concentration.

Tiered rooms, in which each row of seats is a few inches higher than the one in front in order to give each student a better view of the front of the room, should be avoided in administering standardized tests. If such a room must be used, the students should be seated directly behind each other, but empty rows of seats should be left between students from front to rear as well as from side to side, and the five-foot rule should be observed carefully.

Examiner's Manner

Since testing is usually an exciting time for students and many of them become quite anxious about it, the examiner should not do anything to increase anxiety even further. Thus, the general demeanor of the examiner should be such as to reduce threat. She should try to be relaxed and cheerful, indicating that she expects each student to do his best and to do well. At such times smiles are more desirable than frowns, and coaxing is more useful than threatening.

Overtesting

A common mistake in testing for certain purposes, such as research projects, the administration of standardized tests for school-wide testing, and for evaluation efforts, is to overtest. There have been cases reported to the author in which as many as 40 tests have been given to students, one right after another, throughout the school day. It is to be expected that students will become less motivated as such testing continues, until they may become completely antagonistic. In one case it was reported that such antagonism continued through an experimental treatment up to the equally lengthy posttest, and the researchers were puzzled as to why the posttest scores were actually lower than the pretest scores. Testing specialists consider that even a three-hour testing period for high school seniors is sufficiently taxing that any longer period is not recommended (though it is not clear that longer periods at that age level produce lower scores). For younger children best results would probably be obtained by giving no more than one hour of standardized tests per day, testing on subsequent days if additional testing time is needed. If a testing program requires more than five or six hours, one should seriously question whether the program is adequately and soundly planned.

Preparation for Testing

Upon finding that their pupils will soon be given their first standardized test, teachers in the early grades wonder how the children should be prepared for it. Should they be given practice in a similar situation? Should the teacher get a copy of the test first and teach the children the answers to the questions? Should they teach them the answers to similar questions?

It makes good sense to give the children practice in a similar situation before they take their first or second standardized test. The teacher can make up items that can be presented in about the same way that the test items will be presented, timing parts of the test if that will be involved, using separate answer sheets if that will be involved, reading the questions aloud if that will be involved, and so on. The test is not trying to measure how well children take tests; it is built on the assumption that all of the children being tested are proficient, and about equally proficient, at the mechanics of being tested. So make sure that yours are not handicapped.

The standardized tests are built on the assumption that by giving each child a random sample of questions appropriate to a subject-matter level, a reasonable measure of his competence in the subject can be obtained. For you to teach him the answers to some of those specific questions would distort the measurement. So you might as well not bother to test at all if you are going to teach answers to the specific questions before the test. However, a test will ordinarily be chosen because it is related to what children are being taught. If you are teaching your children, as part of your instructional objectives and plan, to answer questions that are like those on the test, that implies that the test has been chosen well. So, don't change your instruction to fit the test, but choose a test that fits your instruction, and then make sure your students know how to take the test and feel comfortable doing it.

Summary

Standardizaton of a test implies that the test is always given under essentially the same conditions, so that students tested in various places and times by different examiners can be compared. This requires that administrators of standardized tests follow uniform practices.

Obviously, the first step in a standard administration is thorough familiarization with the established procedure for the test. This is given in the administrator's manual, which should be followed in precise detail. Not all manuals are carefully written; so the administrator must sometimes adopt the sound procedures from well-prepared instructions when in doubt. Students' questions during a test should not be encouraged, and no new information or emphasis should be given in responding to questions. This is especially important, and bothersome, in connection with some older tests that did not advise the student about guessing. Help with even a single item on a test may seriously distort a student's score.

Tests should be timed carefully, if there are time limits. Faulty timing results in worthless scores. Monitors in testing rooms should be as unobtrusive as possible, confining their activities largely to replacing faulty equipment. Examinees should be seated in a manner that provides a sense of freedom from crowding and reduces the possibility of copying from one another to a minimum. The examiner should maintain order in as pleasant and nonthreatening a manner as possible.

Overtesting should be avoided. Results obtained from bored, tired, or otherwise unmotivated examinees are not only worthless, but may be misleading.

9

Choosing a Standardized Test

Objectives

The objectives that you should have for this chapter are the development of the ability to:
1. Identify the most important consideration in choosing a standardized test;
2. Discuss three considerations of technical quality involved in choosing a test;
3. Discuss competently the role of the following factors in choosing a test:
   a. Alternate forms
   b. Cost
   c. Recency of revision
   d. Scoring
   e. Storage.

Intended Use

The first consideration in choosing a standardized test is, of course, for what purpose are we testing? You will remember that we might think of standardized tests for such purposes as measuring aptitude, interests, or personality — traits that require measurement expertise beyond the background of the usual classroom teacher. We might also think of standardized tests for diagnosis because good diagnostic instruments require long periods of development to clarify their relationships with varied treatments and criteria for successful remediation and to clarify the kinds of people with whom the diagnostic and remedial procedures are more or less effective. We might think of standardized tests for evaluation, where we want to compare our students with students elsewhere. We might think of standardized tests for placement or assessment of change, though standardization is not particularly necessary for these purposes. We may sometimes want to use the same standardized test for several purposes. One of the most common is probably the combination of testing for admission to an educational program, such as college, and using the test results to place students into remedial, regular, or advanced sections of such subjects as English and mathematics. In choosing a standardized test, then, the first step is to decide what you want the test scores to do or to help you to do. The most common uses in most school settings are to measure potential for school learning, i.e., aptitude, and to permit comparisons of individual students with students in other schools in terms of measures of achievement of subjects taught in school.

Technical Quality

Since there may be many different standardized tests available for the purpose for which a test is desired, in choosing among tests you should consider the technical quality of the test. We have discussed earlier the fundamental importance of test *validity*. We would like the validity of the test to be as high as possible, other things being equal. This may mean that the correlation coefficient between scores on the test and some criterion such as later school performance is as high as we can find among tests which have been studied on students like our own in spread of talent (heterogeneity) and level of talent (mean). Or it may mean that correlations are as high as we can find between scores on this test and performance on some more difficult to obtain measure when such correlations have been obtained from studies on students like ours. Or it may mean that we have examined the actual items on different tests and have decided that the items from one test reflect what we are teaching — our instructional objectives — better than those of other tests. (You remember that these kinds of validity were called *predictive, concurrent,* and *content* validity in our earlier consideration.)

Most likely we will not find tests with validity coefficients as high as we would like, nor sets of items that reflect our objectives perfectly. We would like to find reported correlations in the .90's, but more likely they will be in the .30's. On the other hand, we never know until we try a test whether it might be more valid in our situation than in someone else's situation. Or it might be less valid, of course.

To give us the potential of having reasonable validity for our purposes, we need a test that is at least *reliable.* So another important technical consideration in choosing a test is that in use with groups of students like ours the scores have been found to be reliable. For aptitude tests, this implies reliability coefficients in the low .90's, or at least high .80's. For achievement tests, they should be about the same level. A teacher must expect appreciably lower reliability cofficients for measures of more subtle things, such as interests or personality traits, if she chooses to use standardized tests in school settings to measure such characteristics. Even if we are only interested in a test because of its content validity, we must still insist that the scores from it be reliable. If they are not reliable, we can't depend on them, and we might as well assign the students numbers at random to represent their scores. That is what unreliability means. Any relationship that might exist between scores on two measures will be obscured to the extent that the scores on either measure are unreliable. Choosing to use an unreliable standardized test is, in a sense, equivalent to choosing a pair of spectacles with the wrong lenses. Whatever you are looking at will be distorted, perhaps beyond useful recognition, by the test or by the glasses.

The third technical issue of great significance is the normative data that the publisher supplies for the test. If you want to use a standardized test because it makes possible comparison of local students with students elsewhere, then the kind of data available on students elsewhere may determine the value of a particular standardized test. Some tests have much more extensive norms than other tests. By extensive, we mean they provide separate norms for a large number of different kinds of students. The students may be divided by their ages, sex, grade, the time of year in which they were tested, their majors, their socioeconomic level, whether they are in urban or rural schools, their geographic region, and combinations of these elements. A test with more extensive norms is more likely to provide a comparison group that is very close to the group with which a school wishes to be compared. On the other hand, if a test has only a few sets of norms, but has the particular set that your school wants to use, it may be a better test in this sense than a test with extensive norms which do not include the set you want.

It is important that the norms data have been collected carefully, with representative sampling of known populations of interest. Further, if you want to compare the performance of a class or school, you cannot proceed unless the test you choose has *school-mean norms*. Comparisons with individual norms, the kind that are provided by most tests, will only lead to erroneous conclusions.

Ease of Administration

Some standardized tests are much easier to administer than others. Of course, the most complicated to administer are the standardized individual tests, such as individual intelligence tests like the Stanford-Binet and the tests developed by Wechsler. They require a specially trained administrator who tests students one at a time, in a private place, taking as much as an hour or more with each student as well as another period of time to score the results and write up an evaluation. The school teacher ordinarily would not be involved in such tests, so we will not consider them further.

Among the standardized tests that teachers might choose, there are still significant differences in ease of administration. Probably one of the most noticeable is the requirement by some tests for many separate timings of small parts. If an administrator has to allow three minutes for one section, five minutes for another, eight minutes for a third, and so on, she has a rather harried time unless she conducts such administrations frequently. In contrast, a test which has blocks of time of half an hour or so provides a much less tense situation for the administrator. Some tests may require materials other than a test booklet and answer sheet for the examinee, and those tests are more difficult to administer.

If the same measurement can be achieved more simply, it may be well worthwhile to choose the administratively simpler instrument. Earlier we mentioned using a test composed of movies of situations on a golf course that would permit a teacher to evaluate soundness of club selection in a standardized manner without taking four hours to play eighteen holes with each pupil. Using the movie may be more administratively convenient if it displays adequate concurrent validity.

Other Considerations

Scoring procedures for a test can make it easier or harder to use. For instance, certain interest inventories are so difficult to score that they are almost always sent away to a scoring service. This involves payment of a substantial scoring charge for each test and a delay of several days or longer for mail service, as well as the risk of loss or damage to the answer sheets in the mail. Some tests are easy to score by the school personnel. Some tests are provided with very extensive *scoring* and *reporting* services by the publisher; these include such things as providing lists of the scores alphabetically for all the students, providing mean scores for various groups, providing frequency distributions, providing not only raw scores but also their associated percentiles, grade-equivalents, and so on. Some services also report item by item for each student whether he got each item right or wrong. Of course, the more elaborate the service, the more it costs, but usually careful thought will indicate that if the results are desired it is less expensive to purchase them from a publisher's service than to use the time of school personnel to obtain them. Further, school personnel will probably make more errors in this boring and unfamiliar task than will the test publisher's computer.

Tests vary in the *costs* of test booklets, answer sheets, and scoring and reporting services. They may also vary in the way the tests may be handled by the user. For instance, the College Board's *College Placement Tests*, offered by the publisher for placing students in the appropriate level of course work in college, must be ordered from the publisher each time they are to be used and must be sent back to the College Board after their use. Thus, each use requires a new fee and the ordering and returning of the test booklets. (Sometimes special arrangements with frequent users can avoid this nuisance.) Many other tests can be obtained by buying the test booklets and using them with separate answer sheets until the booklets wear out. Tests vary widely in their costs, but often there are several possible tests for a given purpose that are priced rather closely to each other. Therefore, in choosing a standardized test, you should be sure that you do enough comparative shopping that you're aware of any unusual price structure and then decide whether the product or service is worth its cost to you.

For some purposes, having *alternate forms* of a test is an important feature. If you want to pretest a group before instruction or at the beginning of the school year and want to posttest them after instruction or at the end of the school year and to compare the results, ideally you would want to use the same test for both. But memory and practice with specific items could easily distort the results since we cannot erase people's memories. So we use an alternate but interchangeable form of the test for the second testing. But some tests don't have alternate forms available, while others may have three or four alternate forms at certain levels. If you expect to give the same test twice to students, you should be sure that interchangeable alternate forms are provided.

Most tests are easy to *store*. They consist of test booklets, answer sheets, and manuals for use. They can be stored on shelves in a storeroom. However, some tests require more apparatus. For the test to remain valid, the apparatus must be in the same condition for every examinee. This requires care in storage and handling and should be taken into consideration in choosing among tests.

Finally, you should consider the fact that many tests are sufficiently profitable to publishers that they are frequently *revised* and modified to keep them up to date and to add new features and improve on old ones. If you are considering purchase of a test that has been on the market in its current edition more than three years, you should attempt to ascertain whether it is contemplated that the test will be revised soon. One way to seek such information is simply to ask the publisher's representative about it. You might also want to inquire of other people who are acquainted with the field. A short delay in ordering might permit you to obtain the newest form or to decide to purchase a similar test from a different publisher that has recently been revised rather than purchase an obsolescent form that is otherwise appealing.

Summary

In choosing a standardized test for use in a school, the first consideration is the intended use of the test. It is imperative that a test be selected that is designed for the purpose we have in mind, or we are likely to be throwing money away. Sometimes no appropriate standardized test is available, in which case we can't use standardized tests and may not be able to achieve our intended purpose at all.

If we find tests that seem to be designed for our purposes, we next examine their technical quality. How valid can we expect them to be? How reliable? Are the norms satisfactory and based on representative samples of the populations with which we wish to make comparisons?

Among the tests which are suitable for the purpose and adequate technically, are some so awkward to use compared with others that they should be eliminated from further consideration?

What will we do about scoring the tests and tabulating the results? Can we do it ourselves? Is that a good use of our time and money? Or do we want to purchase scoring and reporting services? If we choose to purchase these services, what particular kinds of scores and reports do we want? Are those available for the tests we are still considering? How much do those scoring and reporting services cost? How quickly can we get the results?

Among the tests which have passed all these hurdles, we need to compare their costs per use, and finally, we need to note any special considerations that might influence our choice. Are there unusual security requirements? Do we buy the test booklets or just rent or borrow them? Are alternate forms of the test available for pretesting and posttesting, if that is our desire? Is storage or maintenance of testing materials a problem? Is the test likely to be revised soon, or is the edition we are considering very recent and likely to be available for several years?

Now we have a good foundation for choosing a standardized test. In the next chapter we will learn how to obtain the information we need.

10

Locating Information about Standardized Tests

Objectives

The objectives that you should have for this chapter are the development of the ability to:
1. List four or more sources of information about standardized tests;
2. Contrast the merits of various sources of information about tests;
3. Use the *Mental Measurements Yearbook* to locate a test with given specifications;
4. Use the CSE *Elementary School Test Evaluations* to evaluate a test for a specified purpose.

Finding a Standardized Test for a Specific Purpose

Classroom teachers will often find themselves participating in the search for and choice of standardized tests for use in their school's testing program. It is well that they should be involved since, after all, no one is more at the heart of the educational program nor more expert in the objectives of the program and in what is taking place. Teachers who know the things we have learned about standardized tests in the previous chapters should be an important and valuable resource in the development of a testing program, but they must know how to find tests which might fit their needs. This chapter will try to make the search easier and more efficient.

First, let us realize that it may not be possible to find a suitable standardized test for every educational purpose. Just as in the exploration of outer space, we may know that we would like to have materials with certain properties in building a space vehicle, and we may also know that no such materials have yet been invented or discovered, in education we may know that we want a measure with certain properties and may find that it does not yet exist. This may be true even though such a measure might be exceedingly important, as, for example, a sound measure of motivation to learn. When we find that no appropriate test exists, we can do one of several things. We can create one — maybe. We can use the best approximation we can find. Or we can do without. Our problem in this chapter is to learn how to find one if it exists and how to determine its quality once it is found.

134

The skilled measurement specialist follows a fairly standard procedure in trying to locate a test for a particular purpose. The first thing she probably does is obtain a copy of the most recent edition of the reference work entitled *The Mental Measurements Yearbook* and look for a suitable test under the appropriate heading in that guide. She might decide to use the Center for the Study of Evaluation (CSE) *Elementary School Test Evaluations, Preschool Kindergarten Test Evaluations,* or *Secondary School Test Evaluations* handbooks as an alternative to the *Mental Measurements Yearbook,* especially if her intended use is framed in the form of measuring a specific instructional objective.

If a suitable test is not located in these resources, the odds are high that no appropriate test exists — at least no modern test. However, new tests come out periodically, and usually they are reviewed in educational journals shortly after they are published. So the expert would check recent years of a few journals, especially the *Journal of Educational Measurement* and *Educational and Psychological Measurement.*

In the latter, the expert would especially examine the "Validity Studies of Academic Achievement" section that appears in each summer and winter issue. If no suitable test appears after this much digging, it is unlikely that one will be found at all.[1]

If a test is found by the above means, the next step is to obtain more information about it. Both the *Mental Measurements Yearbooks* and the CSE *Test Evaluations* provide the searcher with additional information, sometimes including a rather detailed evaluation. Those references and the journals mentioned above will also indicate which publishing company distributes the test of interest. Usually the next step is to consult the publisher's catalog to see what is said there about the test. This will include prices, possible scoring and other services, ordering information, and so on. Most any publisher will send his catalog, at no charge, to any teacher who writes requesting a copy. Catalogs are ordinarily updated every year since offerings, prices, and services change frequently.

Finally, for the test that is chosen as the best candidate, or perhaps for several of the leading candidates for selection, *specimen sets* are ordered from the publisher. The cost of these is usually minimal, and they include the test manual, a copy of the test, and the answer sheet, and perhaps score reporting forms, keys, etc., so that the potential user can see exactly what she is purchasing. This step enables the teacher to examine the items for content validity for her own objectives, as well as letting her or a testing expert with whom she consults evaluate the correlational validities, the norms, the reliabilities, and so on that we have discussed earlier. After this step, the favored test is ordered from the catalog, using the school's letterhead stationery since publishers are ethically obligated to restrict their sales to qualified and responsible users, and the testing program is underway.

MENTAL MEASUREMENTS YEARBOOK[2]

For the teacher who is not an expert in testing, the two reference works mentioned above deserve extended attention. These are the *Mental Measurements Year-*

---

[1] Buros has recently announced publication of five *MMY Monographs* covering tests in the specific subject areas of English, Foreign Language, Mathematics, Science, and Social Studies (June 1975). These are new resources for the teacher searching for an appropriate standardized test.

[2] An audiotutorial is provided in *Exercises in Classroom Measurement* to develop thorough familiarity with this resource. It is number 8, entitled "Use of the *Mental Measurements Yearbook.*"

book and the CSE *Test Evaluations.* Let us look at the *Mental Measurements Yearbook* first. Without any argument whatsoever, the best single source of information about standardized tests is the series of publications by Dr. Oscar K. Buros who is responsible for seven editions of the *Mental Measurements Yearbook* as well as several other volumes describing and cataloging tests. These volumes are so important and so helpful for a person choosing a published test, that we will discuss them in some detail here. Even this discussion is not enough experience for you to use these publications effectively. You should spend a few hours with a copy of the latest yearbook available in your library or counselor's office so that it becomes a trusted friend.

Buros has cataloged all tests and books on testing published in the English language. Many of the tests are obscure and little used. For those that are more widely used or more important, Buros has asked authorities in measurement to study the test carefully, including all the materials and services provided with it, and to write an evaluation of the test. For some tests he has asked several authorities to write reviews, seeking authorities who might differ in their views in order to give an unbiased total impression. He has been careful to be sure that the authors or publishers of a test are not asked to review their own product, and he has asked reviewers to be critical as well as to refer the reader to competitive tests which should be considered. The seventh edition of the *Mental Measurements Yearbook* contains listings for over one thousand tests. There are nearly 800 reviews. Buros has also gathered reviews of tests from journals and has provided excerpts of 181 such reviews in the seventh *Mental Measurements Yearbook.* There are over 12,000 references provided for the specific tests.

Buros does a very careful job in preparing these volumes. He personally checks every reference for correctness, and he analyzes each review. As a result of this experience over the years since the first volume, which was called the 1938 *Mental Measurements Yearbook,* Buros has developed a very pessimistic view of the quality of standardized tests. He feels that most commercially marketed tests are poorly constructed, inadequately validated, and of unknown value. Even the best tests make some claims that are not supported by research data. Further, even though few tests escape adverse criticism by his reviewers, the rank and file of test users do not appear to be particularly alarmed, and the quality of tests does not markedly improve after so much criticism.

Buros's "Yearbooks" are not really yearbooks in one sense. They do not come out each year. The sixth edition was published in 1965, and the seventh in 1972. Each is larger than the previous one, but each leaves out much that was in the previous ones. The yearbooks are meant to supplement each other, rather than to replace each other. For most efficient use, one should have at hand not just the most recent edition, but the most recent three or four editions, because each frequently refers to its predecessors.

Buros has been attempting to do several things by publishing these volumes about tests. His aims have been to:

1. Provide a bibliography of published tests and books on testing,
2. Make readily available hundreds of frankly critical test and book reviews,
3. Make available bibliographies of published research on tests,

4. Point out dangers that may accompany the uncritical use of standardized tests, and
5. Impress test users with the desirability of being suspicious of all standardized tests.

You will not be able to use the *Yearbook* most efficiently unless you are familiar with some of its important characteristics, most of which are described in the introductory sections of each edition. We will mention some of the high points here to call attention to them and to give you a greater appreciation of the volumes before you study one at first hand.

One of the significant things about the *Mental Measurements Yearbooks* is their size. Until the seventh edition, it was possible to bind an entire *Yearbook* under one cover, though it made a very large and heavy book. The seventh edition had to be put into two volumes, due to its size (1986 pages). It is such an expensive document that most teachers cannot reasonably have copies for their private use; instead they must rely on the school's library for this resource.

By far the largest section of the *Yearbook* is the section consisting of a catalog of tests and reviews of many of those tests. The tests are arranged according to the topics they concern. The plan appears in the Table of Contents in the front of each volume.

It is important to note that each page of the *Yearbook* has two numbers. One number reflects the sequence of pages and increases page by page. This series of numbers is at the inside upper corner. These numbers are referred to in the Table of Contents. The second set of numbers reflects the sequence of items, such as reviews. Since some reviews require several pages, these numbers may not always increase from page to page. Also, since some tests are merely listed and not reviewed, often several items can be covered on one page. When this happens the number sequence on the outside upper corner (right side on right-hand pages, and left side on left-hand pages) will skip a series of numbers.

The numbers attached to items are referred to in several indices at the back of the second volume. There are three particularly important indices — one by test author, one by test title, and one by test content — which parallel the organization in the Table of Contents. Thus, you can find an appropriate test by looking at all tests in its classification. They are found by examining the Table of Contents for that classification or by looking at the Classified Index of Tests. Alternatively, you could locate a test by knowing the author and looking up his name in the Index of Names, or, knowing the name of the test, you could look up the name in the Index of Titles.

You can also look up books and reviews of books on testing by using the Index of Books and Reviews. There is also an index and directory of periodicals on testing. There is a directory and index of test publishers, and finally, an index of book titles.

In the early 1960s, Buros attempted to develop a complete list of all tests that were in print in the English language in 1961 and all tests listed in earlier editions of the *Mental Measurements Yearbook* that were no longer in print at the time. This was published as a book called *Tests in Print*. This volume has been revised and now indexes nearly 2500 tests that were in print as of early 1974. It also provides a guide to test reviews and the literature on specific tests. There is in it a comprehensive, cumulative, author guide to about 70,000 documents on testing. *Tests in*

Print would be helpful to someone who really wants to search for a test, or information on a test, but its cost suggests that if it is needed, it be sought in a library.

Often an edition of the *Mental Measurements Yearbook* refers the user to earlier editions, to *Tests in Print,* or to one of the *Mental Measurements Yearbook* monographs, *Reading Tests and Reviews* or *Personality Tests and Reviews,* for information about tests that are obscure, obsolete, or are appropriate for specialized areas. These tests will probably be of little value to the typical classroom teacher.

CSE Test Evaluations[3]

A different approach to assembling information about tests for use in schools has been taken by the Center for Study of Evaluation at the University of California, Los Angeles. This organization has prepared several more modest paperbound volumes evaluating tests available for kindergarten, primary, elementary, and secondary school students, including tests for higher-order cognitive, affective, and interpersonal skills. The handbooks for different school levels have different prices. The one for tests appropriate for preschool and kindergarten objectives costs about $5.00, as does the one for tests appropriate for elementary school objectives. At the secondary school level, however, there are separate volumes for grades seven and eight, for grades nine and ten, and for grades eleven and twelve. These are sold as a single set for about $22.00. The additional handbook for higher order skills is priced at about $8.50. So the total is approaching the price of the *Mental Measurements Yearbook,* but many teachers would not have to buy the complete set of CSE handbooks to satisfy their needs.

The approach taken by the Center is to consider the objectives of instruction at these levels and to search for the tests on the market that might be thought to be appropriate for measuring achievement of these objectives. They have rated each of the potential tests (and each of its separately normed subscales when those are present) in terms of its validity; its appropriateness for the examinees; its ease of administration, scoring, and interpretation; its reliability; its range of coverage; and the fineness of score gradations.

It takes a little familiarity with these handbooks to be able to use them effectively, and the user must depend on rough numerical ratings as evaluations instead of carefully explained technical reviews by recognized authorities in the measurement field, in contrast with the *Mental Measurements Yearbooks.* No tests not potentially appropriate for measurement of objectives in schools are included, and since separate scales are evaluated separately, one has to be careful to consult a publisher's catalog as well as the CSE handbooks to know what he is doing in trying to purchase a scale that looks appropriate for his school. However, the individual handbooks are much less expensive than the *Mental Measurements Yearbooks,* they provide access to currently available tests by objectives measured, rather than by test title or author, and they concern themselves solely with educational problems. In many ways the

---

[3]An audiotutorial has been provided in *Exercises in Classroom Measurement* to develop proficiency in use of *Elementary School Test Evaluations.* Mastery of this audiotutorial will provide the basis for competent use of the other volumes provided by the Center for Study of Evaluation. The audiotutorial is number 9, entitled "CSE *Elementary School Test Evaluations."*

two approaches complement each other, and the careful user of tests may find both the *Yearbooks* and the CSE handbooks helpful in making a wise choice of standardized tests for specific purposes.

Summary

Finding the most appropriate test to meet a specific school need requires several steps. First, you turn to reference works to determine whether any likely prospects exist, and, if so, what the likely prospects are. The reference works for this purpose are the *Mental Measurements Yearbooks* and the CSE *Test Evaluations*. The former consists of two large volumes, inches thick, very expensive, and usually found in school and college libraries. The latter consists of six paperback handbooks, of more modest size and price, suitable for a personal library.

Use of the above reference works indicates not only the existence of a test for a purpose, but also a good deal of information about the test, including what agency publishes it and the agency's address. These works also provide evaluations of the quality of most of the tests appropriate for use in schools.

Current and recent issues of the few educational journals that include reviews of tests and studies of the effectiveness of tests may enable you to find a new test that meets your need but that has been published too recently to appear in the standard references.

Once suitable tests are located, the catalogs of the publishers of the tests should be obtained and examined to obtain details about ordering, prices, available services, time delays in obtaining scores and reports, the most convenient branch of the publisher from which to order, and so on.

For the main contenders for use in the school's testing program, specimen sets are ordered. These are inexpensive, and they permit the potential user to examine the actual items for their content validity, the alternate forms for their comparability, the keys, the report forms, and the test manuals for their extensiveness and suitability.

From among the tests examined in detail, a test is chosen. Test booklets, answer sheets, and keys or scoring and reporting services, are ordered on school letterhead stationery. Often for a major purchase, a representative of the publishing company will visit the school and help with choosing and ordering, a service provided by the publisher at no cost.

11

Interpretation of Standardized Test Scores

Objectives

The objectives that you should have for this chapter are the development of the ability to do the following things:
1. Differentiate among raw scores, formula scores, and derived scores;
2. Put scores into rank order;
3. Construct frequency distributions of scores;
4. Draw the distribution curve of scores;
5. Locate the mean and standard deviations on the distribution curve;
6. Indicate the positions of mean and standard deviations on a normal curve;
7. Indicate the percentage of scores included in each standard deviation unit of a normal curve;
8. Indicate the percentile equivalents of selected normal deviates;
9. Indicate the T score and z score equivalents of selected percentile scores, and indicate the percentiles for selected z and T scores;
10. Recall that stanines are range instead of point scores;
11. Indicate the stanine scores equivalent to selected percentiles, z scores, and T scores, and indicate the percentiles, z scores, and T scores for selected stanines;
12. State the principal strengths and weaknesses of:
    a. Raw scores
    b. Percentiles
    c. Stanines
    d. z scores
    e. T scores
13. Calculate and interpret a confidence interval for an individual's score, given the standard error of measurement;
14. Explain the relationship between the confidence interval and the percentile-band score, indicating the strengths of the percentile-band score in interpreting standardized test scores;

140

15. Describe the advantages and dangers of using profiles in test interpretation;
16. Interpret profiles soundly;
17. Explain how grade-equivalent scores are obtained and give at least three reasons why their use should be avoided due to the strong likelihood of misinterpretation;
18. State correctly the result to be expected from a specified test score, given an expectancy table for a test;
19. Locate specified information about a test in the test manual.

Raw Scores and Formula Scores

Once a test has been chosen and administered, scoring takes place and the scores become available to those who might use them. Teachers are the most important users. In the course of dealing with pupils' standardized test scores, every teacher will face occasions, probably numerous, in which she will have to explain to a parent, a pupil, or perhaps a fellow teacher or administrator, the meaning of a score on one of these tests. The score might be the sixth stanine or perhaps a *T* score of 56 or a grade-equivalent score of 3.9, or a percentile-band score of 35-67 or an IQ of 112. There are a number of kinds of scores that are commonly obtained from standardized tests, and to be effective a teacher must be able to deal with them fluently. Next we are going to learn about several of the most widely used of such test scores.

In any test, the number of items a student answers correctly is called the *raw score*. Sometimes the number right is modified to adjust for the fact that some items might have been answered correctly by guessing. Such modified scores are usually called *formula scores* because a formula to "correct" for guessing has been applied to the raw score. Modern testing practice seems to be moving away from correcting for guessing, but in the use of standardized tests one has no choice but to use the correction procedure if that is what is prescribed for a standard administration, or not to use it if it is not prescribed.[1] To fail to follow the standard procedures would destroy the usefulness of the scores altogether. Therefore, in a standardized test whether you initially obtain raw or formula scores depends on what the publisher directs you to do, not on your opinion or beliefs about the soundness of correcting for guessing.

Derived Scores

Whichever of those two fundamental scores one starts with, neither has much meaning in the realm of the standardized tests widely available today until it has been converted into some form of *derived score* that compares this score with the scores of some large group of people. To know that Johnny scored 56 correct out of 150 questions on the XYZ test reveals nothing. But once we convert 56 out of 150 to the ninety-fifth percentile for boys of Johnny's age, we know that Johnny is rather out-

---

[1] An audiotutorial has been provided in *Exercises in Classroom Measurement* to familiarize the student in detail with correction for guessing. It is number 1, entitled "Correction for Guessing."

standing in his performance on the XYZ test. We can interpret derived scores readily once we know their characteristics, but we can make little sense at all out of raw or formula scores unless we have had so much experience with them that we can use that experience in place of tabulated data to make the same kind of interpretation. In this sense, derived scores help the inexperienced to make the same kind of judgments that an experienced person would make. Since no one lives long enough to become very experienced with all the thousands of published tests currently in use, you should appreciate the importance of your being competent in using derived scores!

THE NORMAL CURVE

We will take up each of six widely used kinds of derived scores in turn. But to start we need to build some background that is related to all of them. First, remember that earlier (chapter 7) we noted that given a set of scores, one of the first steps in trying to comprehend them is to put them into rank order. A second step was to prepare a frequency distribution of them in which each score was listed in a column on the left side of a sheet of paper, and the frequency with which it occurred was listed on the right. A third step was to convert these data to percentile values corresponding to each score. This was depicted earlier in figure 7-6. (If you do not remember it, please review that figure and the accompanying text now.)

A frequency distribution can be portrayed graphically as a frequency polygon or graph. To do this, a base line is marked off into various score points. The vertical axis is marked off into frequencies. Then for each score value a dot is placed at the frequency level with which it occurs. When these dots are connected with straight lines, we have a graph as in figure 11-1. Such distributions have a variety of shapes.

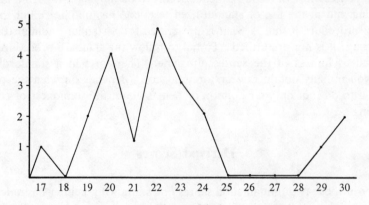

Figure 11–1
Graph of Frequency Distribution in figures 7-4 and 7-5

Often the highest point is near the middle of the score distribution, but sometimes the scores will extend further to one side of the peak than to the other. One "tail" or the other will be much longer. This is especially likely to happen if the number of people whose scores are graphed is small, i.e., less than 100 or so.

There is a curve or graph that seems to occur quite often when measurements of an attribute over a large number of objects of nearly any kind are described this way. It is a bell-shaped graph, with a peak in the middle and tails of equal length and identical shape. An idealized model of this shape is called the *normal curve* and is depicted in figure 11-2. If we were to graph the weights of all tenth graders

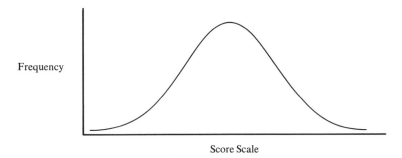

Frequency

Score Scale

Figure 11–2
The Normal Curve

in the state of California, we probably would get a curve shaped like the normal curve. We would get a similar shape if we graphed the maximum temperatures on 4 July at Independence, Missouri, over 100 years. In this sense, the normal curve is often a good approximation to the nature of the real world, as well as being a model that has some convenient mathematical properties, which we will use in interpreting standardized test scores of several different kinds.

You must remember, however, that there is nothing that says measures have to be normally distributed, or that it is better if they are normally distributed. They will very often *not* be normally distributed in small groups of measurements, such as the ordinary class of 30 or fewer students.

What test publishers have done is to give their tests to large numbers — thousands — of students and have found out what their distribution of scores was. On large numbers such as they use, a normal distribution is usually a good enough approximation to the shape of distribution they obtain that it is a useful tool for interpreting test scores.

THE MEAN

We will need to use two major indicators associated with frequency distributions or curves. The first of these is the *mean*. It reflects the central tendency or the middle of the distribution. In a normal distribution, the mean falls at the score corresponding to the highest point of the curve. So one way to estimate the mean is to find the highest point on the curve and determine the score associated with it, as in figure 11-3.

It may comfort you to be told that this mean is the same thing as the arithmetic *average,* which you have been using all your life. Another way to obtain it is to add up all the scores in a frequency distribution and divide by the number of scores. In a distribution that has more than one frequency for any one score, of course, you must multiply the number of times each score occurs by the size of that score before adding all these products together, and then you must be sure to divide by the total number of frequencies, as in figure 11-4. A common mistake to be avoided is to divide by the number of different score levels that students obtain (14 in figure 11-4) instead of dividing by the total number of frequencies (21 in figure 11-4).

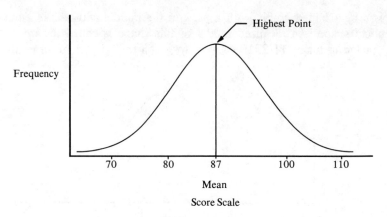

Figure 11–3
Determining the Mean from the Distribution Curve

Score	Frequency	Product
30	2	60
29	1	29
28	0	0
27	0	0
26	0	0
25	0	0
24	2	48
23	3	69
22	5	110
21	1	21
20	4	80
19	2	38
18	0	0
17	1	17
Sum:	21	472

$$21 \overline{)472} = 22.5$$

Figure 11–4
Determining the Mean from a Frequency Distribution

THE STANDARD DEVIATION

The second indicator we need to use in dealing with distributions reflects the degree to which scores spread out about the mean or central tendency. If we think of two archers, one of whom is an expert and one of whom is a beginner, we could expect that the expert would place all arrows near the center of a target, while the beginner might have arrows all around the target's sides, evenly spread from top to bottom and from right to left. Now the mean for either archer might be the center of the target, but what differentiates them from each other is the spread of their performances. That aspect of their performance is measured by a number we call the

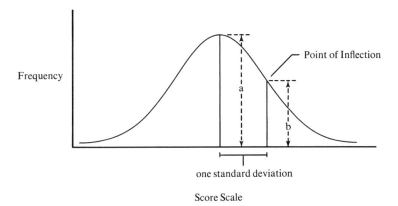

Figure 11–5
Standard Deviation and Point of Inflection

standard deviation. It reflects *deviations* from the mean, and when we think of it in connection with normal curves it has a clear interpretation that perhaps accounts for its being thought of as somehow "standard."

In a normal curve, you can estimate standard deviations by locating the point of inflection of the curve, i.e., that point where the curve changes from curving downward to curving outward. The score associated with that point is one standard deviation from the mean. This is depicted in figure 11-5. Some people have difficulty visualizing where the point of inflection is. The most common mistake is to estimate its location as too close to the mean. A good way to locate the point of inflection of a normal curve more accurately than by simply trying to eyeball it is to measure (with a ruler) the height of the curve at its highest point. The point of inflection is approximately at the point on the curve where its height is 0.6 of its maximum height. The distance between the mean and that point is the standard deviation. In figure 11-5, the height *b* is 0.6 of the height *a*.

Remember that the standard deviation is a distance on the score scale. Once we have found how large one standard deviation is, we can mark off two standard deviations and three standard deviations, and we can do this on either side of the mean, as in figure 11-6. As you will have noted by now, the words *standard deviation* are long and tedious to write repeatedly. Therefore they are commonly abbreviated by the letters *s.d.,* or by the lowercase Greek letter sigma, σ.

There are a number of other ways of determining the size of a standard deviation. There is, of course, a rather complicated formula, but teachers rarely, if ever, use it. However, quite useful approximations to the values that would be obtained by the complicated formula can be obtained rather easily. As you could see from figure 11-6, once you get beyond plus three s.d.'s or minus three s.d.'s from the mean, the curve is so close to the base line that the frequencies are low (on the vertical scale); that is, not many people get scores that far from the mean. So you could estimate the standard deviation by subtracting the lowest score in a distribution from the highest score, and dividing by six. The difference between the highest and lowest score is called the *range,* and this procedure is called using the range to estimate the standard deviation.

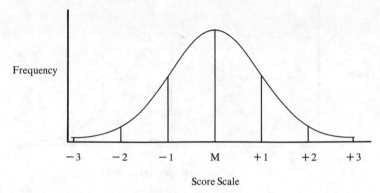

Figure 11–6
Three Standard Deviations on Each Side of the Mean

You must note that dividing by six is fine for distributions which contain large numbers of cases, but distributions with smaller numbers of cases seldom have any values so far away from the mean as plus or minus three s.d.'s. So for distributions based on smaller numbers, we divide by numbers smaller than six. For now, remember that for the large numbers of cases found in norms distributions of standardized tests (over say 250), we would divide by 6, but for the numbers of cases in the usual classroom, say about 30, we would divide the range by 4 to estimate the standard deviation. For example, if we had a normal distribution of 27 scores, and the lowest was 19 and the highest was 35, the range would be $35 - 19 = 16$. The standard deviation would be estimated to be $16/4 = 4$. In doing this you must be careful to use the right divisor for the size of the group that you are dealing with— 4 for ordinary classrooms of about 30 students and 6 for groups of roughly 250 or more scores.[2]

Now the normal curve is particularly useful as an approximation or model or tool because it has some well-known helpful properties. Those that we are going to use in interpreting standardized test scores concern the proportions of the cases in the distribution that fall within various standard deviation distances from the mean. To start with we must learn three numbers—34, 14, and 2. Approximately one-third, i.e., about 34%, of the cases in a normal distribution will fall between the mean and one standard deviation from the mean. About 14% of the cases will fall between the first standard deviation point and the second, or one might say in the second standard deviation, and 2% will fall in the third standard deviation from the mean. The total of $34 + 14 + 2 = 50$, which is as it should be since half of the cases should fall on either side of the mean. This relationship is depicted in figure 11-7. If we think of combining across the mean, we have 68%, or about ⅔ included within plus or minus one standard deviation of the mean, 96% or about 19 out of 20 included within plus or minus two standard deviations, and nearly everyone, or 100%, included within plus or minus three standard deviations, as in figure 11-8.[3]

---

[2]A more complete table of divisors for various group sizes appears in chapters 2 and 18.

[3]An audiotutorial is provided in *Exercises in Classroom Measurement* to develop proficiency in thinking about the normal curve. It is number 10, entitled "Percents under the Normal Curve."

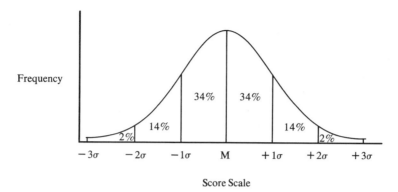

Figure 11–7
Proportions of Cases Included in Standard Deviation Units

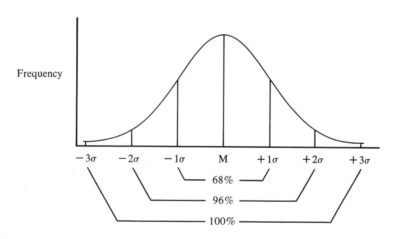

Figure 11–8
Proportions of Cases around the Mean in a Normal Distribution

PERCENTILE SCORES

Now with these tools in our hands, we can turn to the various kinds of derived scores used with standardized tests and develop an understanding of them. First, let us reconsider the percentile score. Of course, you remember that a percentile is not the percent of items correct! A raw score is converted to a percentile, as you recall, by finding the proportion of a reference or norm group who scored at or below that score level. In figure 7-6 we saw how percentile scores were found. For standardized tests it is not necessary to calculate a percentile value for each score. The publisher will have given the test to representative samples of one or more populations of students and calculated from their data the percentile equivalent of each raw score. These will be presented in norms tables in the manual for the test. You can look up the percentile equivalent for any raw score, and you may be able to look up several different percentiles for a given raw score if the publisher has provided norms for different kinds of people for the same test, such as students in different grades or of different ages, or from urban or rural schools, or from different regions of the United States.

Notice that the fiftieth percentile on a normal curve would be the same as the mean, and with our normal curve, the second percentile would be two standard deviations below the mean, the sixteenth percentile would be one standard deviation below the mean, the eighty-fourth percentile would be one standard deviation above the mean $(50+34=84)$, and the ninety-eighth percentile would be two standard deviations above the mean, as in figure 11-9.

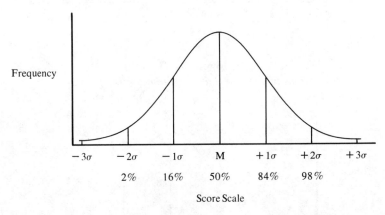

Figure 11–9
Percentiles Corresponding to Standard Deviation Points

Though it is not precisely correct, you can usefully approximate the location on the normal curve of percentile points other than those corresponding to plus and minus one and two standard deviations by linear interpolation. That is, for example, the seventy-fifth percentile is about three-quarters of the way between the fiftieth and the eighty-fourth percentiles, or about at the plus ¾ standard deviation point. $(84-50=34. \; 75-50=25. \; 25/34$ is approximately .75.) Similarly the twenty-fifth percentile corresponds approximately to minus ¾ standard deviation from the mean. Now you should begin to see why it is important to remember those numbers 34, 14, and 2—the proportions of cases falling in the various standard deviations.[4]

ADVANTAGES AND DISADVANTAGES OF PERCENTILE SCORES

There is one important good feature of percentile scores. They seem to be easier than most derived scores to use in communicating with parents. Parents seem to understand what a score means if you say to them that the score indicates that their daughter scored as well as or better than 62% of children tested in the first month of the third grade.

However, there are two troublesome features of percentile scores that have caused other kinds of scores to be invented. First, it is not sound to add percentiles or to average them. If you take two scores and obtain their percentiles and then average

---

[4]An audiotutorial is provided in *Exercises in Classroom Measurement* to develop competence in dealing with percentile scores and standard scores. It is number 11, entitled "Percentile Scores and Standard (z) Scores."

the percentiles, the result will not be the same as that found by averaging the scores first and then obtaining the percentile for that average. For example, in the distribution in figure 7-6, the scores of 29 and 19 were at the ninetieth and the fourteenth percentiles, respectively. Averaging the percentiles gives the fifty-second percentile, but averaging the scores first gives 24, which is about the eighty-sixth percentile, quite a different result! The reason has to do with the shape of the normal curve. For example, the ninety-fifth percentile is a greater distance from the eighty-fifth percentile in test score units than the fifty-fifth percentile is from the forty-fifth percentile. Therefore, you must remember ordinarily not to add, subtract, or average percentile scores. Instead, if you want to find the average percentile for a group who took the same test, you should average the raw scores and find the percentile corresponding to the average. (Of course, it is nonsense to do this for scores from different tests with different numbers of items!) If there is no table giving percentiles for averages, and you don't have the frequency distribution of averages to find the percentile of your average, you simply can't interpret the average as a percentile.

The second troublesome thing about percentiles is that the units are so small that they give a false sense of how accurately a student's performance has been measured. In observing a child one really cannot detect the difference between a performance at the fiftieth percentile and a performance at the fifty-first percentile, and it is misleading to report scores as though there were 100 discriminable differences.

One final note—you should be aware that the fiftieth percentile is often called the *median* score, and that the points dividing the distribution into quarters are called *quartiles*, those dividing it into tenths are called *deciles*, and those dividing it into fifths are called *quintiles*, just as the points dividing it into one hundredths are the *percentiles*.

STANDARD SCORES

To get away from the problem that percentiles cannot meaningfully be added, subtracted, or averaged, another kind of score is sometimes used. It is called a *z* score or standard score. It amounts to no more than determining how many standard-deviation units a raw score is away from the mean, and then giving the score in terms of these standard-deviation units instead of in terms of the associated percentiles or in terms of raw-score points. For scores above the mean, we speak of standard or *z* scores with a positive sign, as plus 1.5 *z*. Below the mean we use a minus sign, as minus 2 *z* scores, or −2*z*. You can convert to percentiles immediately by remembering that in a normal distribution the mean is at the fiftieth percentile, the first standard deviation adds 34%, and one-half of the second standard deviation adds 7%, so +1.5 *z* is approximately the ninety-first percentile. Minus 2 *z* would be at the second percentile. Figure 11-10 shows the close correspondence between standard deviations and *z* scores, and figure 11-11 shows the percentiles associated with each *z* score unit.

DISADVANTAGES OF STANDARD SCORES

While *z* scores have the merit of being averageable sensibly, they also have problems. First, some of them have minus signs, and that is a bit of a nuisance. Second,

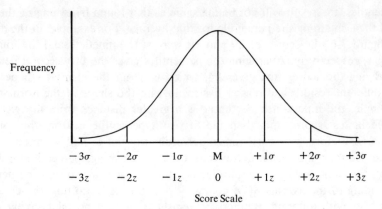

Figure 11–10
Standard Deviations and z Scores

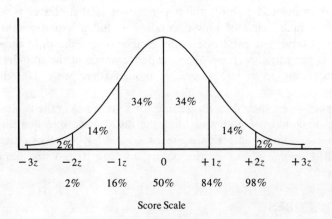

Figure 11–11
z Scores and Percentiles

they have a very large unit—a whole standard deviation. For practical uses this requires that we deal in parts of a unit, or decimals, and that also can cause difficulty. So still another kind of score scale has come into use.

T SCORES

This score is called a T score. What is done is simply to multiply each standard deviation unit by 10, to get rid of the decimals, and then add fifty to each of these scores to get rid of the negatives. Now the mean becomes 50, i.e., $0+50=50$. Plus 1 z becomes 60, i.e., $(10 \times 1) + 50 = 10 + 50 = 60$. Minus 1 z becomes 40, i.e., $(10 \times -1) + 50 = -10 + 50 = 40$, and so on. A z score of 1.5 becomes a T score of 65, and a z score of -0.5 becomes a T score of 45. The relationship between z scores and T scores appears in figure 11-12.

DISADVANTAGES OF T SCORES

Unfortunately, the T score still has one of the faults of the percentile score. It appears to be more precise than the quality of even the best educational measure-

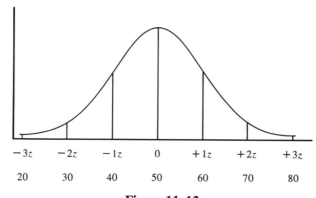

Figure 11–12
Relationship Between z and T Scores

ments justifies. We really can't tell the difference between performances of 59 and 60 on the *T* score scale—or probably even between 55 and 60. We still need a scale with units not as coarse as whole standard deviations but not as fine as tenths of a standard deviation, and we want such a scale in a form in which averaging different scores is sound when the scores are distributed approximately normally.

STANINES

The next score scale that is widely used was created in an attempt to solve these problems in a slightly different way. The scores are called *stanines*, (pronounced "stay-nine") a combination of the word *standard* from standard scores and the word *nine* because there are just nine levels on the stanine scale. The lowest level is number 1 and the highest level is number 9. The middle level, as you might expect, is 5, like the 50 of the *T* score scale. It seems more reasonable to divide educational measurements into 9 levels than into only 6 or into as many as 60 or 100, but historically speaking, the number 9 was chosen because there are 9 standard holes in a column on an IBM card.

The standard score part of stanines comes into play in that each unit on the stanine scale is one-half of a standard deviation wide, except for scores 1 and 9 which extend out as far as needed on either end — technically, extending to plus and minus infinity.

There are two convenient ways to relate stanine scores to the other scores we have studied. Perhaps the easiest is to relate stanines to percentiles. Here you can use the *Rule of 4*, to help you remember how to proceed. The rule goes this way. Starting with either end of the stanine scale, 1 or 9, 4% of the cases in a normal distribution fall into the end stanine. Let's start with stanine 1. Four percent fall into stanine 1. Stanine 2 contains as many cases as stanine 1 plus an additional 4%. That is, stanine 2 contains 8% (4% + 4% = 8%). Stanine 3 is larger by another 4%, for a total in stanine 3 of 12%. Stanine 4 is incremented by another 4%, for a total in that stanine of 16%, and stanine 5 by the same rule contains 20%. Remember stanine five is in the middle. Above that stanine the percentages decrease by the same 4% decrements. So, stanine 6 has 16%, 7 has 12%, 8 has 8%, and 9 has 4%. This is depicted in figure 11-13. If we add these increments together from one stanine to another, we see the relationship between the stanine scale and

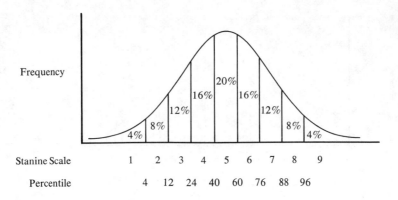

Figure 11–13
Rule of Four with Stanines

the percentile scale. Thus the top of the first stanine is the fourth percentile. The division between the second and third stanines is the twelfth percentile, and so on up the scale as presented also in figure 11-13. (To make use of the rule of 4, we have fudged a little on the stanine scale. Really, the second and eighth stanines have only 7% and the fourth and sixth have 17%. But that is hardly worth quibbling over. Diederich [1960] first called this to our attention.)

Now to find the stanine corresponding to any percentile, you can proceed as follows. Start from the bottom, i.e., stanine 1, and add up the percents included in consecutive stanines until you find the stanine which includes the percentile in which you are interested. For instance, the stanine corresponding to the forty-fifth percentile is found by adding together 4% for the first stanine, plus 8% for the second, plus 12% for the third, plus 16% for the fourth. Now you have 40%. Adding the 20% for the fifth gives 60%, so the forty-fifth percentile must be in the fifth stanine.

To go in the other direction, finding the percentile that corresponds to a given stanine emphasizes an important aspect of stanine scores. They are range scores instead of point scores. Unlike z scores, which could have been scores representing a range but in practice got divided into tenths and hundredths, the stanine score has never been treated as though it could be subdivided. Part of the reason for this, no doubt, is the fact that the holes in a column of an IBM card could not be subdivided. This aspect of stanine scores is considered an asset because stanines more adequately reflect the degree of measurement precision that is attainable with usual educational measures. So the percentile equivalent of a stanine is really two percentiles, the percentiles that are the boundaries of the particular stanine score. For example, the percentiles corresponding to stanine 3 are the twelfth percentile and the twenty-fourth percentile. If Susie's score on a test was stanine 3, and Susie's mother wanted to know what that meant, the teacher might say, "That means that Susie scored between the twelfth and the twenty-fourth percentile, or that from 12 to 24% of the children (in whatever reference group is being used) scored at or below Susie's score."

At first, you may be uncomfortable using such range scores since they don't seem to show where Susie's score is. But that is the truth of the matter — you don't really know where Susie's score is. One knows what one of her scores is, but given another form of the test or tested on another day, she would probably have gotten a slightly different score. Once in a while her scores on two days or two forms might be markedly different, but small differences would occur more often, in a pattern resembling a normal curve. So to act as though we really know Susie's score down to the nearest percentile is misleading and dishonest. The virtue of the stanine scale is that it reduces this kind of misinformation and misconception about Susie's scores.

Another important and often useful way to think about stanines starts with stanine 5 and works out from it in both directions in half standard deviation units. Remember, we said that the stanine scale is composed of 9 units. Stanines 1 and 9 are infinitely wide, but all the rest are one-half standard deviation wide. Stanine 5 is centered on the mean and extends one-quarter standard deviation on either side, as in figure 11-14. Then stanines 4 and 6 extend one-half a standard deviation beyond the limits of stanine 5 on the lower and upper sides, respectively, as in figure 11-15. Similarly, stanines 2 and 3 are one-half standard deviation units lower than stanine 4, and stanines 7 and 8 are half-deviation units above stanine 6, as in figure 11-16. Obviously, the first and ninth stanines extend out as far as there are any cases in the distribution from the lower limit of the second stanine and the upper limit of the eighth stanine, respectively. The whole picture, including lines for the mean and for the standard deviation divisions, appears in figure 11-17. You will notice immediately that the mean splits the fifth stanine into two equal parts, and that the third and seventh stanines are centered on the -1 s.d. and $+1$ s.d. points, respectively. These clues can help in determining stanines quickly from percentiles. Obviously, a score near the mean or median or fiftieth percentile will be in the fifth stanine. We could have recognized this immediately when we tried to find the stanine corresponding to the forty-fifth percentile, earlier. Similarly, scores near the sixteenth percentile must be in the third stanine, and scores near the eighty-fourth percentile must be in the seventh stanine.

It should be recognized that z scores and T scores can be converted to stanines, and stanines can be converted to z and T scores. To go from a stanine of 8 to the associated z and T scores, you must first note that stanines are range scores, and therefore the procedure requires two z scores or two T scores to indicate a given stanine. Then starting from the fifth stanine, we note that it extends ¼ s.d. above

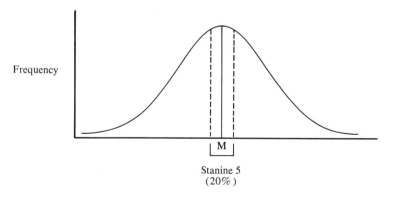

Stanine 5
(20%)

Figure 11–14
Location of Stanine Five

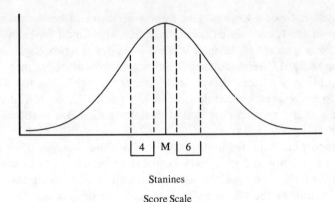

Figure 11–15
Locations of Stanines Four and Six

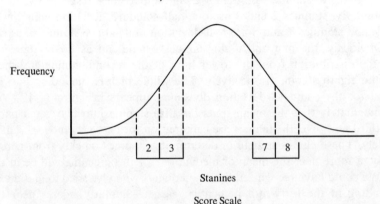

Figure 11–16
Locations of Stanines Two, Three, Seven, and Eight

the mean. The sixth stanine is ½ s.d. wide, and the seventh is also ½ s.d. wide. Adding these together, we find that the lower end of the eighth stanine is 1¼ standard deviations above the mean, and thus corresponds to a z score of $+1.25$. Since T scores are found by multiplying z scores by 10 and adding 50, the associated T score is $12.5 + 50 = 62.5$. The upper limit of the eighth stanine is ½ s.d. more, i.e., 1¾ s.d. above the mean. This corresponds to a T score of 67.5. So the z scores that correspond to the eighth stanine are $+1.25$ to $+1.75$, and the T scores corresponding to that stanine are 62.5 to 67.5.[5]

Different publishers report different ones of these types of derived scores. Nearly all report percentiles; many report stanines also; fewer report T scores; and a few report z scores. Some report other kinds of scores not based on the normal curve. We will turn to those kinds of scores in a moment. It is important that the teacher keep in mind the virtues of these different kinds of scores so she can use the one most suited to a particular purpose. It is also important that she be able to transform one to another fluently, since at any time she may need to make such conversions

---

[5]An audiotutorial has been provided in *Exercises in Classroom Measurement* to develop proficiency in using T scores and stanines. It is number 12, entitled "T Scores and Stanine Scores."

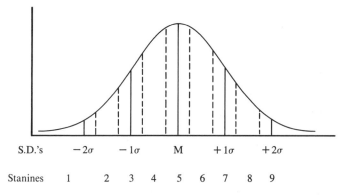

Figure 11–17
Stanines and the Mean and Standard Deviations

without referring to her class notes or her textbook. Thus, you should practice working problems in which you pick a score of one kind at random and convert it to each of the other three kinds until such conversions become easy and you feel confident that you are doing them correctly.

You may notice that proceeding from different starting points in making the conversions results in slightly different numbers. That is because we have used some approximations and taken some shortcuts in this presentation to make the work easier. The accuracy will be satisfactory for classroom purposes, and it is better to have teachers who can make approximations fluently than teachers who simply cannot take the time to learn all the technical details for precise conversions and who cannot keep up the continuous practice with those details that is necessary if they are not to be forgotten.[6]

PERCENTILE-BAND SCORES

Before we can take up the next score scale that is coming into wide use, we need to build up some more background. You will remember that when we choose a standardized test, we are concerned that it be reliable, and that reliability is thought of as reflecting consistency. A reliable test is consistent in that if a person took two parallel forms of the test, he would get similar scores — or at least his rank in the group of examinees would be similar. Or if he took the same test twice with a day or two between testings, he would maintain about the same rank position in his group. Obviously, on a test that was not perfectly reliable, people would not get quite the same score each time they took it. Theoretically, for each person there is a *true score,* but due to errors in measuring him from one testing to another, his *observed scores* differ from the true score that might be obtained if we measured him an infinite number of times and averaged all those measurements.

It is common to assume that frequency distributions of errors are normal in shape. Frequency distributions of random events, or of events in which there are many unrelated causative factors, are often assumed to be normal in shape, and errors

---

[6]An audiotutorial has been provided in *Exercises in Classroom Measurement* to develop competence in transforming from one score scale to another among percentiles, z scores, T scores, and stanines. It is number 13, entitled "Practice in Converting Scores."

of measurement of the kind we are talking about behave like random events. (Errors that are consistently in one direction or another are called *bias,* but we are not talking about bias now.)

STANDARD ERROR OF MEASUREMENT

If these errors of measurement are normally distributed, it makes sense to talk about their mean and their standard deviation, just as we talked about the mean and standard deviation of the observed scores, themselves. If there is no bias in the errors of measurement, their mean will be zero. The standard deviation of the errors of measurement has a special name — the *standard error of measurement,* abbreviated SEM. There are several ways to estimate or calculate the size of the SEM, but in dealing with standardized tests, one seldom has to calculate it. The test manual usually provides the SEM directly. It is related to reliability. All other things being equal, a test with higher reliability has a smaller SEM, and if a test had reliability of 1.00, the SEM would be zero because there would be no errors of measurement. A test with reliability of zero would have SEM as large as the standard deviation of the distribution of scores on the test.

CONFIDENCE INTERVALS

Now if we are again willing to fudge a little bit for convenience, we can use the SEM to estimate within what range a person's true score will fall with a certain probability. (For the technically correct procedure, see Nunnally [1967], p. 220.) We do this by taking a person's observed score as our best estimate of his true score, and then setting up *confidence intervals* around that, based on the standard error of measurement. As with any time we have used the normal curve, an interval of plus and minus one SEM around the observed score is considered to have a probability of containing the true score of about 0.68, i.e., it can be expected to contain the true score about 68% of the time. Plus and minus two SEMs around the observed score would contain the true score about 96% of the time, and plus and minus three SEMs would be expected to contain the true score nearly always.

To give an example for clarification, if Kathleen got an observed raw score on a test of 50, and the SEM of the test (obtained from the test manual) was 5, then we could estimate that there was a probability of 0.68 that Kathleen's true score was between 45 and 55. Ninety-six percent of the time people with scores of 50 would have true scores between 40 and 60, and nearly always people with scores of 50 on this test would have true scores between 35 and 65. A picture of this idea appears in figure 11-18.

We concern ourselves with true scores and with standard errors of measurement because we would not want to interpret Kathleen's observed score on one test to be higher than her score on another test unless we were pretty sure that her true score would also be higher on the first test than her true score on the second. A widely used rule of thumb to reduce the likelihood that we will interpret as different observed scores that are really coming from the same true scores (or even true scores that differ in the opposite direction) is to call two scores the same if their 1 SEM confidence intervals touch or overlap each other. For example, if Kathleen had a score of 50 on a measure of arithmetic and a score of 43 on a test of spelling, and each test had a SEM of 5, we would not conclude that Kathleen was superior in

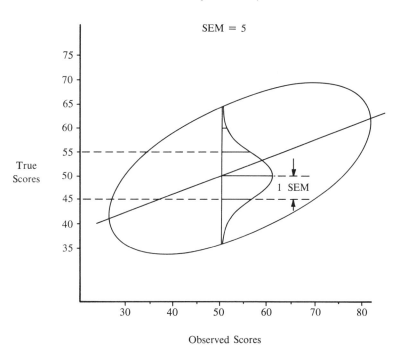

Figure 11–18
Confidence Interval for True Score

arithmetic despite the seven-point difference. The 1 SEM confidence interval for spelling would go up to a score of 48. Since they overlap, the conclusion would be that the true scores might be equal or even differ in the opposite direction from the observed scores; so it is not safe to conclude that there is any real difference between these two measurements. The situation is depicted in figure 11-19.

Even if Kathleen's score in spelling was as low as 40, we would not conclude that she was superior in arithmetic because the two confidence intervals would touch at 45. But if her score on spelling was only 39, we would feel safe in concluding that her arithmetic performance was superior to her spelling performance.[7]

FORMING PERCENTILE-BAND SCORES

With that background, we can turn to the development of the percentile-band score, which uses the concept of the confidence interval based on the standard error of measurement to attain the goals of (a) providing meaning by relating the scores to the performances of other people in a reference group, (b) avoiding negative scores, and (c) avoiding overprecision in scores. The percentile-band score corresponding to a given raw score is found by adding and subtracting one SEM from the raw score and finding the corresponding percentiles for those two raw scores. These percentiles are then reported as a band within which there is a high probability

---

[7]An audiotutorial has been provided in *Exercises in Classroom Measurement* to provide further clarification and practice in using the concepts of the standard error of measurement and confidence intervals. It is number 14, entitled "Standard Error of Measurement and Confidence Intervals."

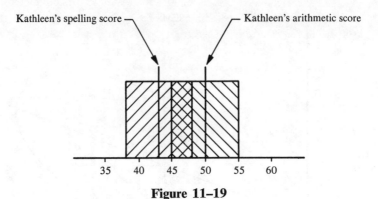

Figure 11–19
Overlapping 1 SEM Confidence Intervals

of the student's true score lying. For example, Kathleen's percentile-band score in spelling would be found by adding 5 (1 SEM) to her score of 43, and subtracting 5 from her score of 43. The percentiles for scores of 48 and 38 would be looked up in the appropiate norms table, and her percentile band score on spelling would be reported as something like thirty-fourth to sixty-second percentile. This is a much more sophisticated way to provide a range score than is the stanine, but to obtain the precision you sacrifice the convenience of a single-digit score.

There are some important things to be noticed about percentile-band scores. The percentile bands for raw scores are much wider in the middle of the score range for a norms group than at the extremes. At the high end, a band might be from, say the ninety-second to the ninety-eighth percentile. In the middle, the band might be 20 or 30 percentiles wide, even on an excellent test. The teacher and the parent are likely to feel frustrated at the width of the band. After all, what good is it to know that Johnny's score is at or above from 34% to 62% of people in his grade? They are likely to ask, "But what is his real percentile?" However, any score system or educational standardized test that seems to give more precision is only misleading the user. With the amount of testing time we ordinarily devote to a given test in educational measurement, we simply don't know any more closely what Johnny's true score is. To pretend that we do is dishonest. One of the greatest virtues of using percentile bands is the fact that it forces us to reognize the limitations of our measures, which are so much less precise than the common measures used around the house. All we have available to us in usual educational measurement are measures that would correspond roughly to gauging room temperature as very hot, hot, about right, cool, and very cold, instead of 72 degrees vs. 71 degrees. To continue to think and act as though educational measurements were more precise than they are is to continue to make needless erroneous evaluations and decisions.[8]

The classroom teacher should be alerted to the fact that her own tests that she makes up and uses to evaluate the performances of her students will probably be even less precise than these standardized tests that are prepared by experts, using all the best procedures for selecting items and usually using a sufficient number of items to insure as reliable a score as is accessible in the time allowed. The precision

---

[8]An audiotutorial is provided in *Exercises in Classroom Measurement* to afford experience in using and interpreting percentile-band scores. It is number 15, entitled "Percentile-Band Scores."

of her arithmetic test score after the unit on dividing with fractions will not really be represented by whether a student got five vs. six items correct. She would have to estimate the SEM and use it to ascertain the limits within which his true score could be expected to lie, and she would then recognize how very imprecise her own tests really are.

BATTERIES AND PROFILES

Before we turn to the last two kinds of standardized-test derived scores that we will discuss here, we will take time to look at an important use of percentile-band scores. Often students are not given just one standardized test. They are given several tests of different abilities or of some abilities and some achievements or of achievement in various areas of the curriculum. It seems useful to compare a student's achievement in the various areas to see whether he has fallen behind in any one or perhaps has shown an unusual capacity for a subject. His various aptitudes might be compared, or perhaps a comparision might be made between aptitude and achievement. When such tests are given together, they are often spoken of as a *battery* of tests.

One way to display the results of a battery of tests is as a *profile,* often in terms of a graph. Each test is given a column on the graph, and the level of the person's score indicates the degree of quality of his performance. Often the vertical scale will be in terms of percentiles. An example of such a form for a profile appears in figure 11-20. The scores for a student have been indicated by a dot for each of the tests in the battery. It can be seen that this student is at the seventieth percentile on verbal aptitude, at the forty-eighth percentile on quantitative aptitude, at the fifty-fifth percentile on reading achievement, and at the seventieth percentile on achievement in arithmetic. We seem to have a clear display of the student's relative strengths and weaknesses — a weakness in quantitative ability, but an anomalous superiority in arithmetic performance.[9]

One might be led to conjecture as to what produced this odd pattern of results. Here the percentile-band comes to our rescue in a most important way. When the profile is plotted with the plus and minus 1 SEM bands around each score, as in figure 11-21, there is no anomaly. All the bands overlap, and the student is recognized as having a rather uniformly good performance across all the tests in the profile. The moral of the story is to regard all profiles that do not present scores in terms of bands as treacherous! The only major exception would be a profile of mean scores for a group of students. In such a case the standard error involved would be the *standard error of a mean.* If the number of cases is large (say over 30) the band may often be so narrow as to be of little help. If you want to contrast the mean scores on the various tests of a battery, you need the help of a person with a basic knowledge of inferential statistics, a topic we will not pursue here.

Two more points should be made with regard to interpreting differences among scores on different tests. First, we used in our example above the comparison between different scores for the same person. We could also use the percentile-band idea to compare the scores of two different people on the same test. For classroom use,

---

[9]An audiotutorial is provided in *Exercises in Classroom Measurement* to give experience in several different kinds of profiles and the restrictions that apply to forming profiles of scores. This is number 16, entitled "Profiles."

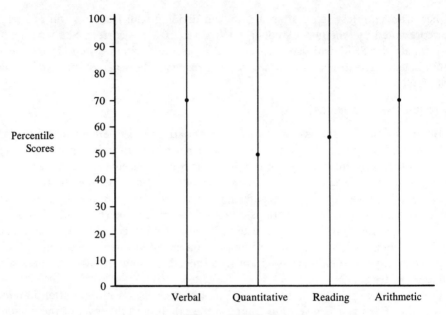

Figure 11–20
Example of a Profile Form

you proceed in the same way, evaluating the observed difference by comparing the bands for overlap. If they overlap, you do not conclude that the true scores are different.

Second, you need to be alerted to the fact that whenever you compare scores on different instruments you are really dealing with a *difference-score*. The difference between the two scores is a new score that must be evaluated as to whether it is really different from zero, and in terms of its reliability. We know one thing very well about difference scores — in educational measurement they are always less reliable than the average of the reliabilities of the two scores. Sometimes they are much less reliable than that average. In fact, the more similar the two scores are (the higher their correlation), the lower will be the reliability of their difference score, all other things being equal. For example, if two tests had reliabilities of 0.90 and 0.80, their average reliability would be 0.85. If the correlation between the two tests was as high as .70, which it might be if one test measured mathematical aptitude and the other test measured mathematical achievement, the reliability of the difference score would be about 0.50. We regard such a low reliability as evidence of an untrustworthy indicator — a measure of low consistency. In general, comparisons between scores on educational measures should be treated with caution. They tend to be very wobbly measures. Repeated testings to get difference scores can be expected to give conflicting results much more often than repeated measurements of the individual variables.[10]

---

[10]An audiotutorial is provided in *Exercises in Classroom Measurement* to give experience in calculating and interpreting reliabilities when decisions are to be made on comparisons between scores. It is number 17, entitled "Reliability of Difference Scores."

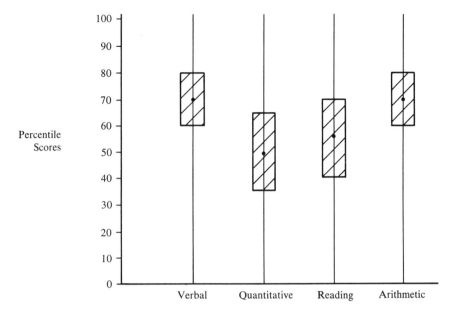

Figure 11–21
Profile with Percentile Bands

GRADE-EQUIVALENT SCORES

Most of the kinds of derived scores we have discussed so far have been introduced in order to obtain some particular advantage. Each has achieved that advantage, but in order to do so has sacrificed something else. One kind of score that is widely used was introduced to obtain an advantage, that of ease of understanding the meaning of each score. But it fails to clarify and instead has caused a great deal of varied kinds of confusion. That score is the grade-equivalent or grade-placement score. The educational world would be a better place if the concept had never been invented. Test publishers, in many cases, supply grade-equivalent scores for their tests only under protest. They urge that these scores not be used. The only reason for publishing them is that uninformed people don't realize how treacherous grade-equivalent scores are. They think grade-equivalent scores possess the easy inter-pretability for which they were invented and insist that tests provide these scores. If a test does not offer grade-equivalent scores, some people will not want to use the test or its scores.

In order to comprehend what is so bad about grade-equivalent scores, you must know how they are created. The test is given to students in various grades, and the mean test score for each grade is found. A graph is made of the trend of mean scores from grade to grade, as in figure 11-22. Notice that the units on the base line are divided into ten parts, from grade 2.0 to 2.9, and then 3.0 to 3.9, and so on. A score of 2.2 indicates the second month of the second grade. Essentially, we have assumed that all increases in test scores are due to the months that a child is in school and that nothing happens in the summer time.

However, students are not tested in each month of their grade. A few points are chosen for testing, and then the remaining grade-equivalent values between those

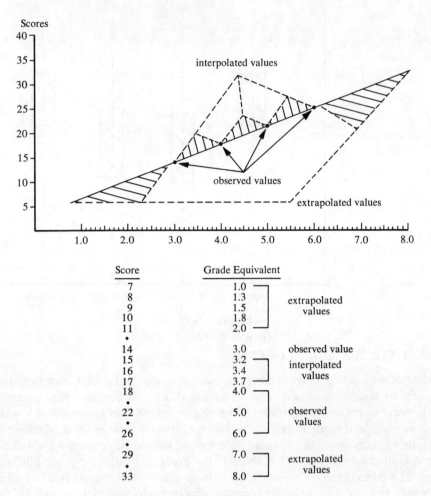

Figure 11–22
Development of Grade-Equivalent Scores

points are found (interpolated) from the graph. Not only that, but once a trend line is found, it is necessary to find grade-equivalent values for very high scores and very low scores. So the line is extended at both ends, and grade-equivalent values are identified (extrapolated) even though no one at those grade levels ever took the test. Indeed, the test might be totally inappropriate at those grade levels. It might be inappropriate because it was too easy or too hard, or because the content is not taught at those levels. After all, a grade-equivalent of nine for reading is nonsensical since reading is not ordinarily taught at the ninth grade. So we have three peculiar things about grade-equivalent scores that should cause us to be wary about innocent interpretations of them as though they really gave us what we think we should get in a "grade-equivalent." There is worse to come.

It might not be so worrisome if tests giving grade-equivalent scores contained items of very similar difficulty. We could think of them as mastery tests, in a sense. However, the usual test which gives grade-equivalency scores covers a wide range of difficulty. This poses the problem that a student may do well indeed on a lot of easy items — items appropriate for a low grade — and thereby get a relatively high score, while some other student may know some easy items and some items at higher grade levels, and get the same relatively high score. Just getting a high grade-equivalent score does not mean that a student knows the material at the high grade. He may get that score from knowing lower level material very well. A fifth grade student who gets a grade-equivalent score of 9.0 may not at all be ready for ninth grade work. He may know nothing of the material in the sixth, seventh, and eighth grades that prepares him for the ninth. All he may have done is exceedingly good fifth grade work. But the naïve use of grade-equivalency scores in the way that the uninformed often use them will fail to recognize this possibility.

There is still more and worse. One way the naïve users of grade-equivalency scores like to proceed is to compare the grade-equivalent performances of an individual student in different subject matters. It is well known, however, that there are wide differences in the variability of performances of students in different subjects. For instance, in reading, students vary widely in any grade. Some will scarcely be able to read at all, while others read fluently. The variability within a class is huge. However, in arithmetic, the variability within a class is relatively small. Since there is little opportunity to learn arithmetic outside of school for most students, the pupils stay reasonably close together as they progress through the grades. Now, if you remember how grade-equivalent scores were determined, you will realize that a student in grade three might be much more likely to attain a high grade-equivalent score, say 8.2, in reading than in arithmetic. A grade-equivalent score of 6.0 in reading might be at only the seventy-fifth percentile for third graders, but a grade-equivalent score of 6.0 in arithmetic might be at the ninety-ninth percentile, just because the two subjects have such different variabilities within a grade. To give a concrete example, on the *Stanford Achievement Tests* at grade 5.2 a grade-equivalent score on Paragraph Meaning of 6.2 is at the seventy-fourth percentile, while a score on Arithmetic Computation of 6.2 is at the eighty-ninth percentile. Thus, no comparisons of grade-equivalent scores across subject-matters are interpretable.

Not only do grade-equivalent scores differ in variability from one subject to another, but they also differ in variability from one grade to another within the same subject. Generally, the variability is lowest in the lowest grades, when children are relatively uniform in beginning their education. In later grades, some have progressed much more than others, and the variability increases markedly. For instance, on the Paragraph Meaning Test of the Metropolitan Reading Test (1959 Edition) the spread of scores expressed as standard deviations increased from about 0.25 in the middle of grade 1 to 2.75 in grade 6 and above.

This causes a problem because a student who is at the same percentile score year after year appears to be at a lower grade-equivalent score each year if he is below the mean. If he is above the mean, the same percentile score translates into a higher grade-equivalent score each year. Grossly misleading interpretations based on this problem occur when, for instance, a school whose students average below the mean each year, but fall no further below the mean as time goes on, seems to have a lower and lower grade-equivalent score mean. By the naïve this might be interpreted to indicate that instruction was getting worse year by year. This kind of error was made, for example, in the *New York Times* of December 20, 1970, in reference to pupils in the New York City schools (Davis, 1972).

One of the most severe fallacies of using grade-equivalent scores is generated by their apparent meaningfulness. School personnel and lay people tend to speak of students' working "at grade level" and of getting the class or school up to grade level. They fail to recognize that the grade-equivalent score was based on a mean, and that there are always people below the mean, as well as above it. If, indeed, we were to get everyone in the country working "up to grade level," then grade level would just move up because it would, by definition, still be the mean score for students of a given grade. It makes no sense to strive for classes being entirely at or above grade level, and it is a cruelty to teachers and students to impose on them such a naïvely conceived set of goals. (Notice, the same faulty logic was called to our attention in connection with "getting all the students in a class up to the norm.")

One final fallacy in grade-equivalent score interpretations about which teachers should be aware results from the extrapolations that must be made in order for each test score to be given some grade-equivalent value. It turns out that in tests on the market this sometimes results in cases where getting a single additional item correct causes the grade-equivalent score for a student to increase by more than a whole year. For example, in the California Test Bureau's *Comprehensive Tests of Basic Skills* a score of 29 correct on Study Skills gives a grade equivalent of 7.6, i.e., the sixth month of the seventh grade. One more item correct, i.e., a score of 30, gives a grade equivalent of 9.2, i.e., the second month of the ninth grade. The learning that takes place in one year and six months can scarcely be represented by a single item, but the naïve use of grade-equivalent scores would lead the teacher into such interpretations. This is not true only of measures such as study skills. In Language Expression one additional item correct moves the grade equivalent from 7.3 to 8.9; one more item correct on Language Mechanics moves the grade equivalent from 8.0 to 9.9; and so on. This is a general problem associated with extrapolation to find grade equivalents for extreme test scores.

REVIEW OF FALLACIOUS INTERPRETATIONS OF GRADE-EQUIVALENT SCORES

Let us review some of the *fallacious* kinds of interpretations that the naïve might make in using grade-equivalency scores.

1. A grade-equivalent score for sixth grader Tim of 9.2 in reading means that he can read as well as ninth graders in the second month of the school year.
2. A grade-equivalent score for Tim of 9.2 in reading means that when a group of ninth graders in their second month were tested on ninth grade reading material they received scores equivalent to Tim's score.
3. A grade-equivalent score for Tim of 9.2 in reading means that Tim could well be put in with a class of ninth graders for material in which reading skills were important.
4. A grade-equivalent score for Tim of 9.2 in reading means that in a truly flexible school in which children worked at materials at their own level instead of being locked into classes, Tim would be put into the ninth grade in instruction on reading.
5. A grade-equivalent score of 9.2 in reading for Tim and of 7.3 in arithmetic means that in his reading Tim is nearly two years ahead of his performance in arithmetic.

6. Grade-equivalency scores of 9.2 in reading and 7.3 in arithmetic indicate that Tim is farther ahead of his group in reading than in arithmetic.
7. Since 30% of the students in Mr. Brown's fifth grade glass got grade-equivalency scores below 5.0, something needs to be done to improve the instruction in his class and perhaps in the instruction given to students before they reach Mr. Brown.
8. When Tim was tested in the fall of the sixth grade he received a grade-equivalent score of 9.2 in reading. Tested in the spring, he received a grade-equivalent score of only 8.0. That indicates that he lost a lot of his reading skill during the school year, and some effort should be expended to find out why and whether such losses can be expected to continue.
9. In Brown Elementary School in the inner city the mean grade-equivalent score in reading in grade 1 was 0.6. The mean increased each year until by the sixth grade it was up to 3.2. However, from being only 0.4 years behind at the first grade, the average student in Brown Elementary School was nearly three years behind by the time he had six years of instruction at Brown in reading. Obviously, the reading program at Brown is failing somehow since students, on the average, fall farther behind each year in spite of the claims by the teachers at Brown that they are doing everything they know how to do. An investigation is needed of the reading program, the teachers of reading, and perhaps the administration that would allow a condition such as this to exist.

Notice. All the above statements are false. They are *incorrect* interpretations of grade-equivalent scores. (They are, however, all too common.) You should be able to give at least one reason from your reading so far why each of them is wrong.

By this point, we hope you have concluded not to use grade-equivalent scores and not to let anyone else judge you or your work on the basis of these scores. However, you should not conclude that they are totally meaningless because sometimes there may be no other scores available in, for example, school permanent records. Grade-equivalent scores have the same kind of meaning, though not as clearly given, as percentiles. Someone who has a grade-equivalent score above his grade level can be concluded to have performed better than the average person tested at that grade level, and someone attaining a grade-equivalent score below his grade level performed less well than average. Unfortunately, you won't know how much better or worse than average from the grade-equivalent score unless you know the variability within that grade in that subject, but you will know something, even from as deceptive a bit of data as a grade-equivalent score.[11, 12]

---

[11]An audiotutorial is provided in *Exercises in Classroom Measurement* to clarify and emphasize the important considerations in avoiding misuse of grade-equivalent scores. It is number 18, entitled "Grade Equivalent Scores."

[12]In chapter 7 the manuals that test publishers provide for users were discussed, and it was noted that you should have some first-hand acquaintance with varied manuals so that you will be able to use them easily. The exercise to accomplish that was, however, being delayed until varieties of standardized test scores had been discussed. At this point in the instruction it is appropriate to turn in *Exercises in Classroom Measurement* to the audiotape exercise on "Use of Test Manuals and Norms," number 19, which will provide sufficient experience in the use of test manuals, norms, and varieties of scores that you will be proficient in their use at its conclusion.

IQ Scores

A kind of score that you will need to understand is the IQ score, even though it is not a general derived score applicable to any standardized test, as have been the scores previously discussed. IQ, of course, stands for intelligence quotient, and IQ scores are associated with aptitude tests. A little history may be illuminating here. Early in the twentieth century a French physician, Alfred Binet, had the problem of distinguishing between children who *could* not learn and children who *would* not learn. He approached it by creating and choosing tasks that are interesting to children and determining at what ages it becomes possible for children to complete each of these tasks. He then built a scale of tasks. Any child could do some of the simplest. But few, if any, children could do the hardest. The *mental age* (MA) of child was judged to be the age associated with the tasks between those he could do and those he could not do.

Later William Stern, in Germany, got the notion that in judging people's potential, it was not their mental age but their mental age in relation to their chronological age (CA) that was important. He suggested dividing mental age by chronological age to obtain a quotient that, when multiplied by 100, he called the Intelligence Quotient.

For many years IQ scores were obtained in that way. Eventually it was recognized that while chronological age keeps increasing each year, the increase in scores on the mental age tasks seemed to slow down or stop during adolescence. Thereafter, as people got older they got less intelligent according to IQ scores, though they did not seem to behave less intelligently. Other problems with the MA/CA quotient were also recognized, and some years ago a movement started toward a different way of calculating intelligence quotient scores. The earlier kind of IQ score was labeled the *ratio IQ* and the new kind is called the *deviation IQ*. Essentially all that was done in creating the new kind of IQ score was to decide that the average score for a given age was to be given the number 100, and the standard deviation of the scale was, quite arbitrarily, to be given the number 16. (Some tests use 15 as the s.d.) Thus a person who scores one standard deviation above the mean for his age is given a score of 116, the person two standard deviations above the average for his age is given the IQ score of 132, etc. Nearly all modern intelligence tests now use deviation IQs instead of ratio IQs.

PROBLEMS WITH IQ SCORES

In several ways IQ scores pose problems such that it might be better now if they, too, had never been invented. Four characteristics of IQ tests and scores make them far harder to interpret soundly than would seem to be the case. First, since IQ tests give one score that is supposed to reflect intelligence, the naïve or careless user of these scores might conclude that there existed one fundamental ability that was all-important. The evidence is clear that there are many different abilities, and they are far from perfectly correlated. In any IQ test many of these abilities may not be reflected. In fact, most intelligence tests reflect primarily one's vocabulary or verbal ability. For predicting how well a person will perform in school or otherwise, it is usually helpful to know something about other abilities, too, such as quantitative ability, spatial ability, and reasoning ability. Recent explorations suggest that even these categories of abilities may be too broad, and that there may be over 100 aptitude factors to be considered to get a complete picture of just cognitive aptitude, leaving out psychomotor aptitudes altogether. Thus, what any particular intelligence test score reflects about a person depends on what kinds of items are in that test, and most of them reflect only a narrow part of one's abilities.

A second problem is that somewhere in our folkways the idea appeared that one's IQ was a permanent, unchanging characteristic. However, different aptitudes do change as one ages; some increase while others decrease. Whether one's IQ score will change during his life depends partly on what skills are measured in the IQ test. Third, as with most test scores, the naïve person fails to realize the size of the standard error of measurement. With a standard deviation of 16 and high reliability, a characteristic of most IQ tests, the SEM would be about 5 points. Thus the third digit in an IQ score is not very meaningful—the IQ scale is too finely divided.

One last troublesome problem with IQ scores is that there are many IQ tests, but they are not parallel to each other. They include different kinds of content and proceed by a variety of techniques. Thus, no two tests may give the same result even though they both claim to measure IQ. In fact, they may be as far off as 10 or 12 IQ points on the average in certain score ranges (Lennon, undated). Putting this difference together with the standard error of measurement suggests that IQ scores for the same person that differ by as much as 20 points may come from two tests given on the same day without there being any important reason to question the results. Thus, IQs are not nearly as well measured as one might think on hearing the untrained school teacher contrast students with reported IQs of, for example, 120 and 140. Comments such as the rather common misconception that a minimum IQ of 110 is required for success in college become droll when one has some understanding of the nature of IQ scores.

Expectancy Tables

Now we have become familiar with various kinds of scores for standardized tests. With practice we should be able to deal with each of them easily, recognizing its virtues and its faults, and the extent of its meaning. However, test scores can be used in conjunction with other aids to make quite sound and useful inferences about people, and we should get acquainted with one of those aids that is becoming more common. That is the expectancy table.

Occasionally test publishers or researchers who work with tests will provide expectancy tables that make it easier for users to make practical use of the test scores. An expectancy table usually expresses the probability with which one can expect at least a given level of performance on a criterion from a given level of performance on a predictor. For instance, the fictitious expectancy table in figure 11-23 gives the probabilities of students with selected high school averages obtaining at least selected first-year college grade averages.

The probabilities can be obtained and tabled from procedures we have already learned about. We have learned that you make predictions from scores on one variable, like high school average grade, to another variable, like first-year college grade, by making a scatterplot of points corresponding to the two kinds of grades

First-Year College Average

F→ D→ C→ B→ A

		F→	D→	C→	B→	A
	A	100	99	84	60	20
High School	B	100	98	76	23	5
Average	C	100	92	53	16	1
	D	100	81	25	3	0

[Entries are probabilities without decimal points; →
means "equal to or higher," e.g., equal to F or higher.]

Figure 11–23
Expectancy Table A
(Fictitious Data)

for a number of individuals, as in figure 7-1 in chapter 7. You also learned that the prediction made for each predictor score is the mean of the criterion scores associated with it, and you learned that there is always a spread of criterion scores associated with each predictor score (unless the correlation is 1.00). Earlier in this chapter you became acquainted with the concept of *Standard Error of Measurement* (SEM), the measure of the degree of spread of observed scores around the true score for an individual. You might also think of SEM as being the standard deviation of observed scores you would get for any specific true score from a large number of individuals who had that score. Or you might think of SEM as the standard deviation of scores on a retest for any specific score on the first test—like predicting retest scores from scores on the first test.

Now, another standard deviation of errors is of interest when we predict performance on a different variable, instead of predicting performance on essentially the same variable. For reasons we won't go into here, this standard deviation of errors has a different name. It is called the *standard error of estimate*. The standard error of estimate is simply the standard deviation of estimates of a different variable, like college grade average, for every specific value on a predictor variable, like high school average grade. As usual with distributions of errors, we assume them to be normal, so that we can use the percentages under the normal curve that we have already learned.

To set up an expectancy table, we merely determine the standard error of estimate for our data, determine the mean criterion score for every predictor value, and use the normal curve percentages to tabulate the proportion of cases above any given criterion value associated with given predictor values. This is shown graphically in figure 11-24.

In that figure we have the ellipse representing the dots in a scatterplot of college average grades and high school average grades. Through the means of the vertical arrays of dots we have drawn a line representing the prediction of first-year college average we would make for each different high school average, just as was described in chapter 7 (see figure 7-2).[13] We have also shown in this figure the normal curve of college grades associated with a high school grade average of 2.0. From this curve

---

[13]An audiotutorial is provided in *Exercises in Classroom Measurement* to give you experience in making predictions and thinking with the standard error of measurement. It is number 20, entitled "Prediction."

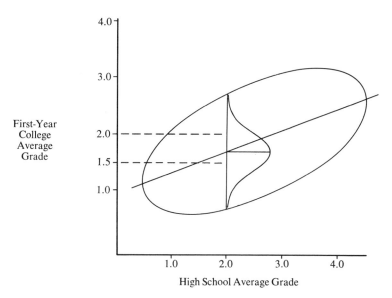

Figure 11–24
Development of an Expectancy Table
(Fictitious Data)

it can be seen that occasionally someone with a high school average of 2.0 will obtain a first-year college average grade as low as about 0.50 or as high as about 2.75, but most people with high school averages of 2.0 will get college averages of around 1.7 (for these hypothetical data). Using the normal curve percentages that we learned earlier in this chapter, we can see that about 16% of people with high school averages of 2.0 get college averages of 2.0 or higher. (The line from college average grade to the curve falls at about $+1.00\sigma$. About 16% in a normal curve fall above $+1.00\sigma$.) About 77% get college averages of 1.5 or higher. (The line from college grade of 1.5 falls at about -0.73σ, and about 77% in a normal curve fall above that point.) When percentages obtained this way are put into a table, we have an expectancy table like the one in figure 11-23.

Another way to proceed is to give for the selected high school averages the probabilities of achieving selected college averages, as in figure 11-25. Comparing

First-Year College Average

		F	D	C	B	A
	A	1	15	24	40	20
High School Average	B	2	22	53	18	5
	C	8	39	37	15	1
	D	19	56	22	3	

[Entries are probabilities without decimal points.]

Figure 11–25
Expectancy Table B
(Fictitious Data)

the two figures you will see that the entries in the cells of figure 11-23 are sums of the relevant entries in the rows of figure 11-25, i.e., the entry under C or better in figure 11-23, is the sum of the entries under C, B, and A of the corresponding row in figure 11-25 $(24+40+20=84)$.

These two ways of setting up expectancy tables, i.e., on the one hand for predictions of a specified grade level or higher and on the other hand for predictions of a specific level of grade, not including higher or lower grades, are easily confused. One clue is that the first kind always has high proportions for low criterion grades with lower and lower proportions for higher criterion grades. However, the only sound approach to using expectancy tables without making errors is to look at the captions or at the surrounding text to be sure that you know what has been tabulated.

Expectancy tables can be made up with "double entries" if there are two predictors. These, too, can have a variety of forms. An example of an uncommon form with real data appears in figure 11-26. This table gives the minimum combinations of

Minimum Scores for Males with Probabilities
of .50 of C (2.0) or Better Freshman Averages

FTGT	250	275	300	325	350	375	400	425
HSGPA	3.80	3.50	3.20	2.90	2.60	2.30	2.00	1.70

Figure 11–26
Double Entry Expectancy Table for
Florida State University
(Males, circa 1971)
[Prepared by Dr. F. J. King]

scores on the Florida *Twelfth Grade Testing Program* battery (Sum), FTGT, and High School Grade Point Average, HSGPA, that yield probabilities of at least 0.50 of a male entering freshman obtaining at least a C (2.0) average during his first year at Florida State University (circa 1971). The figure is read as follows. If a male applicant to the first year class has a FTGT as low as 250, he needs at least a HSGPA of 3.80 to have a 50-50 chance of obtaining a C (2.0) or better average during his first year at Florida State University. However, if he has a 275 on the FTGT, he needs only a 3.50 to have a probability of 0.50 of obtaining at least a C average. At the other extreme, if he has a poor record in high school (1.70) but is able to perform well on the tests (425) he may still expect to have at least a 50-50 chance of succeeding at the university.

There are a great variety of ways of presenting expectancy tables, and publishers should be encouraged to present data this way so that validity data will be more immediately useful. Therefore, it is important that teachers become familiar with the concept of expectancy tables, know how to use them, and ask for them at every appropriate opportunity.[14]

---

[14]An audiotutorial is provided in *Exercises in Classroom Measurement* to develop your understanding of and give practice in using expectancy tables. It is number 21, entitled "Expectancy Tables."

Summary

When a teacher has chosen and administered a standardized test, the resulting scores are initially raw scores (the number of correct answers) or formula scores (the number correct adjusted for guessing). These scores have little intrinsic meaning, but there are other derived scores that are more meaningful. The teacher must be able to think fluently about the various systems of derived scores that are widely used. These include percentiles, standard scores, z scores, T scores, stanines, percentile-band scores, grade-equivalent scores, and IQ scores.

Some of these kinds of scores are closely tied to the normal curve; others are not. Since a number of them are related to it, familiarity with the normal curve and its properties is important for the classroom teacher.

Some of these kinds of scores have certain advantages and other disadvantages. Others are primarily harmful ways of dealing with test information. The teacher needs to know the difficulties associated with some of the common kinds of scores, especially the grade-equivalent score and the IQ score. She also needs to know how to interpret sets of scores as they might be obtained from a test battery and displayed on a profile.

Expectancy tables are one way of presenting information about what test scores mean. They are not as common as they should be, but they are beginning to appear and will be more common if teachers understand them and demand them from test publishers.

References

Davis, F. B. Reporting test data in the media: Two case studies. *The Reading Teacher*, 1972, December, 305–10.

Diederich, P. B. *Short-cut statistics for teacher-made tests.* Princeton, N.J.: Educational Testing Service, 1960.

Lennon, R. T. A comparison of results of three intelligence tests, *Test service notebook number 11.* Yonkers-on-Hudson: World Book Company, undated.

Nunnally, J. C. *Psychometric theory.* New York: McGraw-Hill, 1967.

12

The Superintendent's Fallacy

Objectives

The objectives that you should have for this chapter are the development of the ability to:
1. Describe the *Superintendent's Fallacy*;
2. State situations in which the fallacy is to be expected;
3. Indicate sound procedures for preventing occurrence of the fallacy;
4. Recognize that the Superintendent's Fallacy is called the regression effect in technical discussions of research design.

Understanding the Superintendent's Fallacy

During this period in our society when the idea of accountability has been introduced into education, we cannot conclude a treatise on standardized testing without devoting a special section to the potential for misuse of these tests by naïve persons who think that because such tests are standardized they provide an easy route to accountability.

We have already pointed out the fact that standardized tests are seldom closely enough tied to any specific teacher's objectives to reveal appreciable improvement in achievement by her students in a year's time. We have also alerted you several times to the important difference between using norms to interpret the performance of individual students and using norms (school-mean norms) to interpret the performances of all the students in a class. There is another problem in the interpretation of standardized test scores that has been so prevalent in the past that it might be called the *superintendent's fallacy*. Teachers must understand it so that they can defend themselves against it (or, perhaps, take advantage of it).

To explain it, we must return to our scatterplots that are involved in studies of the degree of correlation between two variables. Remember, if there is less than a

172

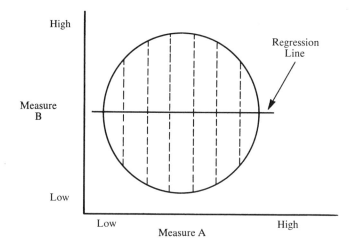

Figure 12–1
Regression Line with Zero Correlation

perfect correlation between two measures, let's call them A and B, the scatterplot will not be a straight 45 degree line from lower left to upper right. Instead the points will spread around the line. With zero correlation, the line through the mean of each column of dots in a scatterplot would be a straight horizontal line through the middle of a circle, as in figure 12-1. Also, the most likely score for any individual on measure B estimated from his score on measure A is the mean of the column associated with his score on A, i.e., the score on B projected over from the regression line. This indicates that with zero correlation, for every person we would predict the same score on B based on our knowledge of his score on A, i.e., we would predict the mean score on B for everyone because knowledge of A was of no help in predicting B. That is what zero correlation means.

Now suppose that we chose some "retarded" students, i.e., those who score low on A. If B was a test administered several days after A, and if A and B correlated zero, then we would find that the average score on B for these retarded pupils was the mean of B as in figure 12-2. Since the students were chosen for being low on A and since they score at the mean of B, one might be tempted to draw the conclusion that something had happened between A and B to raise the scores of the students. But nothing has happened at all — it is just a matter of there being zero correlation between A and B. In fact, if we had chosen a group high on A and tested them later with B, they would have scored at the mean on B, and we might have concluded erroneously that something had occurred in between tests A and B that impaired their performance. Nothing has happened except what is known as *regression to the mean.* To the extent that correlation is less than perfect, predictions from one variable to another are not as far from the mean on the second variable as they were on the first. In fact, the size of the correlation coefficient tells how much they will regress to the mean. If the correlation is .50, the predictions will only be half as far from the mean on the second variable as the initial measures were from the mean of the first variable.

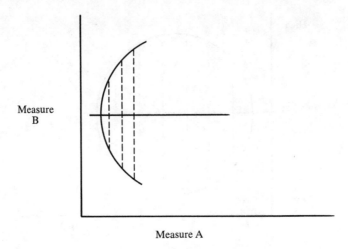

Figure 12–2
Regression to Mean of Low Group with Zero Correlation

To be more realistic, suppose that the correlation was indeed .50 instead of zero. Let's see what that would look like. The diagram of the scatterplot is in figure 12-3. Now we have an ellipse extending from lower left to upper right. As you can see, the best prediction of score on Measure B is no longer the mean of Measure B, except at one point — the mean of Measure A. For scores below the mean on A we predict scores below the mean on B, and for scores above the mean on A we predict scores above the mean on B.

Once again, suppose we choose some "retarded" students, i.e., those who score low on A. These are indicated by the solid bordered part of the ellipse. The rest of the students are enclosed by the dashed part of the ellipse. If we found the mean score on Measure A for the retarded group, it would be about point X. Now if we find the middle of the scores on B for the people who got score X on A, it will be about point Y on B. And if you measure the distance of Y below the mean on B and compare it with the distance to the left of the mean on A of point X, you will find that the retarded students seem to score, on the average, only half as far from the mean on B as they did from the mean on A. That is what happens when the correlation is .50. Again, one might be tempted to conclude that something had happened between administering A and B to raise the performances of the retarded students. If we *had* done something that we thought would raise their performances, we might be tempted to credit the improvement to whatever we did. However, what produced the increase was nothing more than regression to the mean. Our treatment would have had to cause the mean on B for our retarded group to be even closer to the mean for everyone on B, i.e., even higher than point Y, for us to have any reason to believe that the treatment had any useful effect.

Now the superintendent's fallacy occurs when a superintendent (or someone else) gives a pretest and a posttest that correlate less than perfectly, as they always do, and then concludes that whatever happened between the pretest and the posttest has helped the people below the pretest mean but has hurt the people above

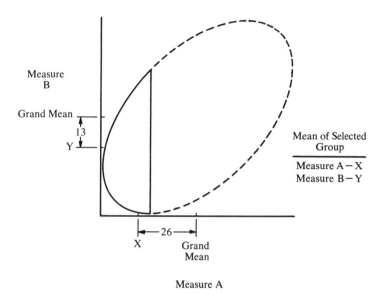

Figure 12–3
Regression to Mean of Low Group with Correlation of .50

the pretest mean. The superintendent may ease his mind by the thought that the "treatment" helped the weak ones, and the good ones who were hurt by it were still above the mean so that the gain outweighs the loss and we'll continue whatever treatment it was. (Remember, regression is back to the mean, not beyond it.) If the superintendent had a control group with no "treatment" at all, the weak students may have been "helped" just as much, and the good students "hurt" just as much. This would be a clear indication that the treatment had no effect at all — and, in fact, such a control group is what the careful experimenter will insist upon in order to avoid interpreting regression effects as treatment effects.

What does all this imply for the classroom teacher? First, if you ever hear about or see or are involved in a situation where an educational procedure seems to help the weak students while hurting the strong, you should immediately ask about the control group. If there was none, you should assume that all that has occurred is the regression due to imperfect correlation between pretest and posttest measures. It is a statistical artifact, not an indicator of an effective treatment.

Second, since school administrators and school boards are usually not sufficiently versed in measurement and research to know about the regression effect, the teacher should realize that if her performance is to be evaluated by pretesting and post-testing, she should try to avoid having to teach students who are selected because they score *well* on the pretest. The most likely thing to happen to them is regression to the mean, and any good teaching the teacher does will have to overcome the regression effect before the superintendent or the board will give her anything but blame! In fact, given the choice, the teacher should choose to work with the low scorers. There, if she does nothing, or if she does anything that is not harmful, the result will be improved scores (due to regression). If she does anything useful at all, it will have a positive effect in addition to the regression effect and make her look very good indeed.

These considerations are especially important because superintendents (and teachers) are so reluctant to use a control group when some new educational fad comes along. Instead everyone wants to put the new wrinkle in effect on all students. Teachers seldom think of trying their own ideas for improvements on one randomly-chosen class and continuing their usual practices on another in order to make a more valid comparison. When it comes to using tests to evaluate such casual experimentation, there is a high likelihood that someone will suggest pretesting and posttesting. Without a control group in that situation, the superintendent's fallacy, that is, the *regression effect*, can almost be guaranteed, especially since few educational innovations are ever found that make very large differences in performance. Teachers who have a basic introduction to the interpretation of standardized test scores should not fail to recognize this widespread fallacy when it occurs.[2]

---

[2]The regression effect is hard for many people to grasp, or even to believe. To provide additional examples and practice with it, an audiotutorial is included in *Exercises in Classroom Measurement*. It is number 22, entitled "Regression Effect."

Part Three

Introduction

Every classroom teacher must face the problem of evaluating the progress of her pupils toward mastery of what she is trying to teach them. In most schools, these evaluations will ultimately be in some form of grade or report. The process of producing evaluation reports on student progress is called *grading* or *marking*. The words seem to be used interchangeably.

Grading is a controversial issue. It probably always has been, and there is no reason to think that the controversy will end. Thus a teacher needs to have a sound understanding of grading to be in a position to deal with the controversy and to maintain her own integrity as she copes with an unavoidable and always difficult part of the profession of teaching. This book will attempt to give you the perspective you need.

One important kind of perspective is illustrated by the following often-repeated anecdote (Aikman, 1969).[1] It seems that a young lady wrote home from college to her parents:

> Dear Mother and Dad,
> Since I left for college I have been remiss in writing and I am sorry . . . I will bring you up to date now, but before you read on, please sit down. You are not to read any further unless you are sitting down. Okay?
> Well, then, I am getting along pretty well now. The skull fracture and concussion I got when I jumped out the window when the dormitory caught fire shortly after my arrival here is pretty well healed now. I only spent two weeks in the hospital, and I can see almost normally, and I only get those sick headaches once a day. Fortunately, my jump was witnessed by an attendant at the gas station near the dorm. He was the one who called the ambulance and the fire department. He also visited me in the hospital, and since I had nowhere to live because of the burnt-out dormitory, he was kind enough to invite me to share his apartment. It's really a basement room, but it's kind of cute. He is a very fine boy, and we have fallen deeply

---

[1]Reprinted with permission of *The Atlanta Constitution*.

Grading and Marking

in love and are planning to get married. We haven't got the exact date yet, but it will be before my pregnancy begins to show.

I know you will welcome him into our family with open arms. He is kind, and although not well educated, is ambitious. Although he is of a different race and religion than ours, I know your often-expressed tolerance will not permit you to be bothered by that.

Now that I have brought you up to date, I want to tell you there was no dormitory fire, I did not have a concussion or skull fracture. I was not in the hospital, I am not pregnant, I am not engaged, and there is no boy friend in my life.

However, I am getting a D in history and F in Science, and I want you to see those marks in their proper perspective.

Your loving daughter,

Obviously, we must do all we can as teachers to see to it that grades are used to reflect the achievement of academic objectives — not to evaluate the worth of the person as a person. But there are many other perspectives that the serious teacher must have on the grading problem, and there are good reasons for the teacher's having a solid comprehension of the issues.

Why Learn about Grading?

It is surprising that many teachers embark on their careers in the schools without ever having been taught anything about grading. This very important part of the teacher's task is often ignored in teacher training. Perhaps it is just taken for granted, or perhaps it seems too intractable to be taught. However, there are a number of specific considerations that justify extended examination of grading practices and procedures.

First, as we mentioned before, some form of grading is almost inescapable. Even if a particular teacher in a particular situation could escape the requirement of providing some form of feedback of information to the learner about his progress or to his parents or to the school administration, the teacher should know the implications of not grading. She should be able to evaluate whether some form of grading would be more sound than no evaluative feedback at all.

Second, giving grades soundly takes a lot of time and psychic energy. It is a large part of the teacher's function. It deserves an important position in her training.

Third, grading is a complicated problem. There are many pitfalls; erroneous practices abound; and the teacher cannot safely proceed on the assumption that what was done to her as a pupil is satisfactory for her to do to the students in her care. Good teachers will be trying to do a better job than was done for them as pupils, rather than simply carrying forward the mistakes of the past.

Fourth, there are many irrational ideas about grading that seem sound until they are considered in detail. To avoid some of these irrational notions, a teacher must learn to recognize what is wrong with them. The supporters of some of the irrationalities are highly vocal, visible, and emotional. They write books with catchy titles and sponsor annual nationwide conferences on grading — or against it. The teacher without a foundation of knowledge can easily be taken in by such "movements."

Fifth, there is little empirical research on grading. Although we have some well-established facts, there has been far too little study of such an important topic. Therefore, everyone seems to feel entitled to an opinion, and there are no data to refute most of them. The professional teacher should know that which is known, know what claims are subject to doubt, and have the foundation to reason about what empirical data might be expected to show.

Sixth, there are some useful technical procedures that assist in sound grading. The teacher should not be limited in the quality of her evaluations by lack of mastery of readily available techniques.

Seventh, and finally, faulty grading is potentially seriously detrimental to students. It can provide them with misleading information interfering with their learning process. It can provide misleading information for others who legitimately use school grades as part of their procedures in evaluating people. And it can mislead those who would study the instructional process to improve it or to hold it accountable to the society that supports it.

Goals for This Topic

We are going to study the main ideas about grading in the following pages. There are specific skills that a well-trained teacher should have in dealing with grading. You should be able to do everything that is listed in the objectives that follow when you have mastered the instruction on the topic. The list of objectives can be used effectively as a study guide or as a guide in reviewing the material before an examination. It may also be useful for the practicing teacher as a refresher before grading activities or discussions.

Behavioral Objectives for Instruction on Grading and Marking

The purpose of this unit is to teach the prospective teacher about grading and marking — the systems that have been tried and their shortcomings, the goals that should be sought, common errors that should be avoided, and procedures that may be helpful in making grades more effective.

A. Functions of Grading — You will be able to:
1. List five primary audiences with whom grades should be designed to communicate academic achievement;
2. List at least two functions other than communication that grades are sometimes asked to serve.
B. Processes of Grading — You will be able to:
1. List five different bases for forming comparisons that result in grades;
2. Describe the procedure of grading based on standards;
3. Discuss the virtues and flaws of grading based on standards;
4. Describe the procedure of grading based on comparisons with other students;
5. Discuss the virtues and flaws of grading based on comparisons with other students;
6. Describe the procedure of grading based on comparisons with aptitude;
7. Describe the virtues and flaws of grading based on comparisons with aptitude;
8. Describe the procedure of grading based on improvement;
9. Describe the virtues and flaws of grading based on improvement;
10. Describe the procedure of grading based on effort;
11. Describe the virtues and flaws of grading based on effort;
12. Describe the procedure of grading based on combinations of more than one kind of comparison;
13. Describe the virtues and flaws of grading based on combinations of more than one kind of comparison;
14. Describe the regression effect and its importance in grading;
15. Describe the problem of reliability of difference scores and its importance in grading;
16. Describe the "Jingle and Jangle fallacies" and their importance in grading;
17. Describe the concepts of over-achievement and under-achievement, their use in grading, and the problems associated with them.
C. Report Systems Resulting from the Process of Grading — You will be able to:
1. List at least eight common ways of presenting grades or evaluations;
2. For any of the common ways, describe at least two virtues;
3. For any of the common ways, describe at least two flaws or problems;
4. Describe the basic characteristics of grading on the basis of contracts with students;
5. Describe the research basis for contract grading.
D. Phenomena Concerning Grading — You will be able to:
1. Identify and describe at least eight relevant empirically derived conclusions from research about grading.
E. Fallacies in Grading — You will be able to:
1. Describe at least four common fallacies about grading practices.
F. Useful Technical Procedures in Grading — You will be able to:
1. Describe appropriate procedures to convert measurements to any numerical scale you desire;
2. Apply appropriate procedures to convert measurements to any numerical scale you desire:
   a. Calculate the mean of a set of measurements;
   b. Estimate the standard deviation of a set of measurements;
   c. Write and explain the conversion equation;
   d. Solve problems involving converting from one scale to another;
3. Describe appropriate procedures to combine measurements soundly into totals with the effective weighting you desire;
4. Apply appropriate procedures to combine measurements soundly into totals with the effective weighting you desire:
   a. Equalize the standard deviations;
   b. Apply the desired weights;
   c. Combine the weighted scores;
   d. Remember feasible alternative procedures;

     5. Describe appropriate procedures to adjust grades for differences in aptitude of different groups;

     6. Apply appropriate procedures to adjust grades for differences in aptitude of different groups:

         a. Determine the ability level of the group;

         b. Estimate the mean of the total group;

         c. Set the minimum score for each grade, A through D.

G. Faulty Grading Practices — You will be able to:

     1. List at least eight faulty grading practices, giving examples to clarify the faulty procedure and why it is judged to be unsound.

H. Complaints about Grading — You will be able to:

     1. List and discuss at least five common complaints about grades and grading.

I. Legal Aspects of Grading — You will be able to:

     1. Indicate the general current trend of courts' reactions to legal appeals concerning school grades. That is, the student should be able to describe the legal precedent in such cases;

     2. Describe the proper disposition of cheating situations;

     3. Describe the implications of recent laws and court cases for the grading activities of the classroom teacher.

13

Functions of Grading

Objectives

Study of this chapter should enable you to:
1. List five primary audiences with whom grades should be designed to communicate academic achievement;
2. List at least two functions other than communication that grades are sometimes asked to serve.

The Primary Function of Grading

The primary function of grading and marking is to communicate effectively to a variety of audiences or clienteles the degree of achievement of academic competence of individual students.

That statement is set out sharply at the beginning of the chapter because much of the difficulty about grading seems to come from misunderstandings about the primary function. Grading also has secondary functions — or at least secondary results or impacts. A very important one concerns motivation. In fact, much confusion about grading and whether grading is good or bad in schools centers on the motivational aspects of grades. Some people would abolish grades because they are too highly motivating, and others would use grades as punishments because grades are so motivating. Both sets of people are wrong. They are getting a secondary aspect of grading in the way of the primary function. Motivation should be handled in other ways; it can be supplied by a skilled teacher for most students without emphasizing grades. And it is unethical to use a low grade as a form of punishment because to do so is dishonest. The grade should be an accurate and meaningful portrayal in a summary form of the level to which a student has learned what he was being taught— the specific subject he was being taught, such as science or spelling, not deportment or promptness or conformity — and that communication should not be distorted by motivational or other considerations.

EFFECTIVE COMMUNICATION

When we say that grades should communicate effectively, we mean that they should inform the recipient about academic attainment in a school subject conveniently and with minimum error.

They should inform rather than conceal or confuse. But at the same time they must be concise without loss or waste of information. This is a difficult problem of balance and compromise. To inform completely would require reporting on a myriad of details, so much that no one would take the time to pore through it. Therefore, the detail must be summarized. Too great a condensation, into a mere statement of satisfactory or unsatisfactory or pass-fail, is often as inadequate as reporting in too great detail. The solution to this problem that has kept recurring over the ages, it seems, is a reporting scale for each subject with from 5 to 12 or 15 categories. The familiar example is letter grades of A to F, with perhaps pluses and minuses for some letters. It is not too surprising that this degree of discrimination keeps recurring as being satisfying. Psychologists find that this range of discriminations is about what the human mind can usually handle (Miller, 1956). This is perhaps why there are such divisions as 7 days in the week, 12 hours on the clock and months in a year, and many other groupings into 5 to 15 categories.

Not only should the number of categories be designed to be optimally useful, but we must be careful to keep the content of each grade clean. Among naïve teachers there is a great tendency to "try to consider everything" in the grade. As we will see later, this is self-defeating. It is about as useful as trying to have one gauge on the dashboard of an automobile with one needle summarizing all the different things one might want to know, such as how much gas is in the tank, how hot the engine is, what the oil pressure is, and what the tire pressures are. Looking at such a needle would tell us nothing useful because any single but important thing could be malfunctioning and be lost in the summary. The same happens when we try to include everything in a single grade for a course.

We must restrict the grade to the function of communicating one thing, a specific area of academic achievement — not academic achievement in some other course — or it becomes so misinterpretable as to be useless or worse. One great temptation seems to be to include consideration of the student's effectiveness in English or arithmetic in evaluation of his achievement in such courses as history, social studies, art, and music. Trying to emphasize to the student that English and arithmetic skills are not to be displayed just in classes having those names, but all through life, is a good idea. However, it is carried too far when it is allowed to distort the information function of grades in other areas of achievement.

We must avoid the temptation to try to use the subject-matter grade to change the student's character or personality. This error is evident in teachers who deduct points or grades for messy work, for tardiness in turning in assignments, for handwritten instead of typed reports. The most inexcusable distortion of grades of this kind is probably the giving of a grade of F for misconduct such as cheating. When a student has cheated, the outcome is that the teacher does not know the level of his academic achievement. True, he should be punished or corrected for his misbehavior, but for grades to communicate effectively about academic attainment, that punishment cannot consist of a distortion of the means of communication. The teacher must reevaluate the degree of attainment to get a reading of it without the influence of cheating, or no grade should be reported at all. The correction for cheating, however, should take some form other than altering the course grade.

VARIED AUDIENCES FOR GRADES

When we recognize that the primary function of grades is to communicate effectively, exercising that function soundly requires that we know the audiences with whom we are communicating. For grades, there are a number of important audiences and probably a host of incidental clients. The major audiences are six in number, i.e., pupils, parents, school administrators, employers, counselors, and other schools. All these groups need to be able to make sound interpretations of a pupil's grades in order to deal with him wisely.

Of course, the pupil wants to know how he performed, and the wise teacher knows that it is important that the pupil be informed of his evaluation. This information helps him to adjust his study schedule, choose a career, and decide what courses to take next if there are options.

His parents also want to know. They, too, are involved in guiding and planning the pupil's life. They want to be sure that he is treated fairly and that anything of importance is called to their attention promptly.

Counselors have an important function in assisting with educational and career planning of students. To do this effectively, they need to know the level to which the student has achieved competence in varied academic areas. From the general level of performance can be predicted future levels of academic performance, and from differences in performance in varied subjects, some pattern of the particular student's achievement may provide useful guidance for the future.

Employers have learned that the kind of academic achievements that are characteristic of a pupil in school may be reflected in his performance on the job. Not only does the general level of academic attainment, if measured well and recorded soundly in grades, indicate how effectively the person learns, i.e., how "bright" he is, but the employer may require specific skills, such as algebra, writing, spelling, typing, or speaking. The grades in specific courses may give him information he needs in making hiring decisions or decisions about what training will be needed on the job.

Other schools need and use grades because one's general level of academic performance in one setting is usually the best predictor of his general level of academic performance in a similar setting. Thus a school may predict academic performance from previous grades and decide whether to admit a student or not. Again, like the employer, the school may use grades to determine whether sufficiently high attainment of academic objectives has been met in specific areas. This, of course, is possible only if the grades have been given carefully so that they reflect specific academic attainments well, and do not include other irrelevant information.

The school administrator's need for grades has been left until last in this discussion because it is, perhaps, the most important. It is important for the teacher because the administration is the only audience that has a direct, significant, and unavoidable influence on the way grades are given. In other words, the teacher can ignore most of the other audiences in giving grades and not get into much trouble, but if she ignores the wishes of the principal or superintendent, she will hear about it. The principal and superintendent may have firmly fixed ideas about the form in which grades will be given, i.e., letter grades, numerical grades, or other types of grades. They may stipulate that there will be certain percents of various levels of grades. They may determine how often grades are given, on what basis they are given, and on and on. Their wishes are not to be ignored, no matter how wrong they seem to be. In that sense, they are the most important audience for grades.

The problem is that principals and superintendents usually are no better informed, and may be less well informed, about the grading process than teachers. The well-trained teacher, then, has the problem of trying tactfully to educate her principal and superintendent about the nuances of grading when the principal and superintendent think they already know all there is to know about the subject. Often there is no way out for the teacher but to make the best she can of a bad situation — trying to make her grades communicate academic achievement in specific subjects as effectively as she can given the constraints placed on her by her administrators.

One thing she can't escape taking into consideration, however, is the fact that the administration has the legitimate right to require a form of grading that provides a permanent summary record of the performance of each pupil. The administrator must be able to work effectively with parents who inquire how Johnny is doing or how Susie is doing in reading. To be effective she needs a convenient summary report that she can find quickly in a file, and that she can average with other grades if necessary. This limits, as we shall see, the kind of grade reporting procedures that are readily available for use.

Incidental Functions of Grading

We have stressed the primary function of grading, and will continue to do so, but we must be cognizant of some of the incidental functions or results of grading, if only to keep them in their place as incidental. One has been mentioned, that of motivation. There is no way to keep grades or other evaluative feedback from being motivating. Such feedback may enhance motivation by serving as positive reinforcement or reward, or it may decrease motivation if the grade is lower than was desired or expected, serving as negative reinforcement or punishment. This cannot be helped, but probably the effect should be kept as small as possible. The teacher must use other ways to reward or correct her pupils, and there are many. Psychologists use everything from candy and money, and tokens that may be exchanged for candy or money, to privileges such as cleaning the erasers or being a hall monitor, as rewards. There are so many possibilities for motivators that it is unnecessary to use grades deliberately for that purpose. However, there are not many alternatives to grades or some similar form of evalution to provide feedback about achievement. Thus it is essential to maintain that the motivational function of grades is incidental and must not be allowed to interfere with the communication function they serve.

Another incidental function that some people claim for grades is that of getting children adjusted to living in a competitive society. They argue that since our society is competitive, children must learn to live in that kind of society, and competition for grades is one way to teach them about it. If that is a sound argument, and not all would agree with it, the argument still does not justify deliberate distortion of the communication function of grades in order to achieve this goal. If children happen to learn something about how to get along in a competitive society during the process of receiving grades and evaluations, that may be all right. But that kind of learning can be achieved in many ways other than through grading, so grades should not be diverted from their main function to help achieve this incidental function.

A third incidental function of grades that occasionally appears in writings on the topic is that of keeping teachers honest. The idea is that with periodic grading and reporting, parents get a pretty good idea of what to expect from their children. If some teacher tries deliberately to hurt a child by giving him an undeservedly low grade, this will be noted by a parent, and a concerned parent will determine what is going on and get it corrected. So with periodic grading, no teacher can suddenly blackball a student, or, for that matter, suddenly favor a student to an extreme degree, without having to face documented criticism. An interesting situation of this type has occurred recently in a city school system that repeatedly passed a student with reports of normal progress until graduation from high school. At that time he found that he could not be employed because he read at the fifth grade level. He sued the state and the school system for fraud. At this writing the suit has not been settled (*Doe* v. *San Francisco Unified School District*).

Summary

In this chapter we have considered the primary and incidental functions of grading. The primary function is communication, not motivation, though many people get confused about this. The communication is about the degree of achievement of academic competence in a particular subject. Some people get confused about this also and think that the communication is about academic competence in general; that is, they think the grade should indicate how smart or how generally able a student is. But it is pointless and inefficient to use grades for that purpose. A relatively brief intelligence test will indicate that for us. The grade gives us specific information about a particular kind of competence, the kind that is taught in the subject for which the grade is given.

Since grades are supposed to communicate, they cannot be used to punish or reward or to attempt to change the pupil's personality. Also, they cannot attempt to communicate in too great detail, or no effective communication takes place. Too little detail has the same result. The compromise that is usually reached is a separate report for each subject in terms of a scale of 5 to 15 steps.

The audiences to whom we wish to communicate include pupils, parents, school administrators, employers, counselors, and other schools. Of these, the most important for the teacher is the school administrator.

Grades have incidental functions, and they must be kept incidental. The three major incidental functions that have been claimed for grades are motivation, teaching pupils to adjust to a competitive society, and keeping teachers honest.

References

Doe v. *San Francisco Unified School District*, No. 653 312 (Superior Court).

Miller, G. A. The magic number seven, plus or minus two: Some limits on our capacity for processing information. *Psychol. Review*, 1956, **63**, 81–97.

14

Processes of Grading

Objectives

The objectives of this chapter are that you should be able to:
1. List five different bases for forming comparisons that result in grades;
2. Describe the procedure of grading based on standards;
3. Describe the virtues and flaws of grading based on standards;
4. Describe the procedure of grading based on comparisons with other students;
5. Describe the virtues and flaws of grading based on comparisons with other students;
6. Describe the procedure of grading based on comparisons with aptitude;
7. Describe the virtues and flaws of grading based on comparisons with aptitude;
8. Describe the procedure of grading based on improvement;
9. Describe the virtues and flaws of grading based on improvement;
10. Describe the procedure of grading on the basis of effort;
11. Describe the virtues and flaws of grading based on effort;
12. Describe the procedure of grading based on combinations of more than one kind of comparison;
13. Describe the virtues and flaws of grading based on combinations of more than one kind of comparison;
14. Describe the regression effect and its importance in grading;
15. Describe the problem of reliability of difference scores and its importance in grading;
16. Describe the "Jingle and Jangle fallacies" and their importance in grading;
17. Describe the concepts of over-achievement and under-achievement, their use in grading, and the problems associated with them.

Comparisons Involved in the Process of Grading

Grading always is based on some kind of comparison. It is impossible to evaluate something in the abstract. The evaluation must always be in comparison with something. There are a number of widely used comparison bases for grading. Any teacher will probably base her grades on one of these. She should know what the advantages and disadvantages of each of them are so that she may choose as wisely as possible among them. None is without problems, but the problems associated with some are rather technical and not widely understood, and some of the problems may be more serious than others in a particular situation.

COMPARISONS WITH STANDARDS

One comparison basis a teacher can use is a set of standards of some kind. For instance, a typing teacher can say that to get a grade of A a student must be able to type 45 words per minute with no more than one erasure per page, for five pages. She might go on to specify whether the typewriter was manual or electric, and other limitations on the task. But what she has done is set a specified standard that does not depend on the performance of other students in the class, on how hard the student worked, on whether or not he was handicapped, or on how much he improved. The only issue is whether he has achieved the goal. Obviously, the goal was not set without knowledge of what could reasonably be expected, so in that sense the standard does depend on the performances of other students. But that is different from saying that the top 5% of the class will get A's regardless of how rapidly they type. In another course, a teacher could set her standards by making up an examination, and specifying that to get an A a student must get a specified percentage of the questions correct. In some courses, the standard would be expressed in terms of a product created or a rating of a performance, such as a dive or speech.

The virtues of using specified performance standards as the comparison basis for grading are several. One that has a lot of appeal is that all pupils can presumably obtain the best grade possible if they work hard enough and if the teacher is skilled enough. If the teacher improves her skill, more of her pupils should meet her standards and legitimately and defensibly get higher grades. That seems to be a highly desirable situation. Another virtue is that the teacher should be able to communicate clearly and effectively what her grades mean. Much of the fuzziness can sometimes be removed from communication about academic achievement through clear specification of the standards that result in various levels of grades. Finally, there are no deceptive or tricky technical problems with this comparison basis, such as we will find with some others.

There are drawbacks, however, and one is the problem of deciding what the standard shall be. Standards are not given; they are not "out there" waiting to be adopted. The teacher has to decide somehow what her standards will be and how to express them in a manner that is academically honest and satisfying. This requires considerable soul-searching. Set too high, many students will fail and few will succeed, and this may be cause for rebuke from parents and administrators. Set too low, other teachers will complain because of parental pressures on them to lower their standards correspondingly. In fact, standards must usually be set with the instructional milieu in mind. Standards appropriate for an ordinary school would not be appropriate for a school for the handicapped. But should the standards be raised for a school for the gifted? If they are, will the grades communicate meaningfully about the truly high academic attainments that the gifted sometimes achieve?

Besides the difficulty of setting standards, there is the problem that what seem to be fixed standards can sometimes shift up or down without the teacher's realizing that they are shifting. This is not so likely to happen with standards based on performances such as typing 45 words per minute as with standards based on getting a specified percentage of items correct on a test. The teacher can inadvertently make up tests with harder or easier items, and she is likely to do this even without realizing it if her teaching improves or if the ability of her students improves or declines. The classic illustration of shifting standards comes from the period of rapidly increasing enrollment pressures on colleges during the 1950s and 1960s. Numerous instances were documented in which the aptitude levels of entering first-year classes increased markedly, but the average first-year student's grades remained the same year after year. Faculty confronted with the data would claim that the aptitude test scores were faulty and that their grading standards had not changed, but other data clearly indicated the opposite. The teachers simply did not realize what they had been doing — adjusting to the level of students they were teaching, including raising their grading standards.

COMPARISONS WITH OTHER STUDENTS

A second comparison basis a teacher might use is deliberately to base her grades on how well a particular student performs compared to the other students in the class. This is what is usually meant by the term *grading on the curve* or *curve grading*. The curve that is meant by those expressions is, presumably, the normal curve, a bell-shaped curve often used in statistics because it has some useful properties. But the kind of curve used is not the significant issue. The significant thing is that a certain number or percent of the students in any class are to be given A's, another percent B's, and so on. Most college and many school grading systems are described this way in published information about their grading policies and practices.

The virtues of this comparison basis are that it is apparently readily understood by parents, students, and administrators, and that it doesn't require any soul-searching by teachers to determine what standards are appropriate. The standards appear to be given automatically, requiring no further thought. Some naïve teachers and administrators even think that curve grading automatically guarantees that all teachers are using the same standards.

The flaws are numerous. Students and teachers are likely to be upset when they have good classes or are effective instructors, but this can't be shown in their grades. No matter how well they perform, a certain percentage of students must fail, and no matter how little they learn, a certain percentage will get A's. This seems unreasonable and unfair.

Students are likely to take advantage of the system, if they think of it. In fact, there is the story about a small class at a large eastern graduate school who found that their instructor always graded on the curve. If she had five students in her class, she would give one A, one B, one C, one D, and one F. They discovered to their dismay that only five were enrolled. To avoid anyone getting the F, they agreed to pool their resources and pay a derelict from the street to enroll in the class and attend enough to get the F, a solution which worked out to the students' satisfaction and let the instructor follow her blind curve-grading practice.

The result of this kind of problem is that in practice there is a tendency for teachers' grades to be generous — the percent failing is smaller than the percent getting the highest level of grades, and the average grade is a B rather than a C. Every teacher convinces herself that her class is unusually good or her teaching is better than average, so she violates whatever curve she was supposed to follow. And administrators come to experts in measurement and ask, "What is the proper percentage of A's, B's, C's, D's, and F's?" Of course, there aren't any *proper* percentages. The setting of these percentages is just as arbitrary as the setting of absolute standards. It is less useful than the setting of absolute standards for the purpose of communicating about academic achievement because even when the percentages of A's, etc. are set, there is no communication of what the A means in terms of achievement. It means that the student who gets an A was among those at the upper level of achievement, but how high was the level? No one can say.

In fact, by setting specified percentages of the various levels of grades, one has insured that the standards, in an absolute sense, will fluctuate with the average ability of the class. When a class that is particularly able goes through, the standards are higher, and when a slow group comes through the standards automatically drop. This cannot be considered desirable in a procedure that is supposed to communicate effectively about academic achievement, although it may appeal to those who believe that the function of motivating students is more important than the function of communicating about achievement.

Unfortunately, teachers also need to be motivated, and as was mentioned above, there is little motivation for a teacher to improve her effectiveness if she knows that the grading system by its design prevents her increased skill from resulting in higher grades for her students. No matter how well she teaches there will still be the same number of F's and no increase in the number of A's if she follows the prespecified grade distribution plan. As we see, use of grades to provide motivation rather than to indicate achievement is becoming a bit of a problem. It will get worse as we go along!

COMPARISONS WITH APTITUDE

Some teachers would say that instead of just grading students by comparing them with whomever happens to be in the class with them, something more systematic should be done. They would choose to grade a student by comparing his achievement with his aptitude for that subject. A student who did not have much aptitude but still performed reasonably well would get a good grade, but one who had a lot of aptitude and still performed only reasonably well might even get a failing grade. This would seem to provide better motivation for all students, and it seems satisfying to those who want to emphasize the motivational function of grades. Presumably, a teacher who was able to get all students in her classes to achieve beyond what one might expect from their aptitudes could give all students high grades, and one whose students all did less well than expected could reasonably give all low grades. This, then, avoids one of the flaws in grading on a curve, and it provides motivation for teachers as well as students.

What are some of the problems with this system? An explanation of them will seem to involve straying from our main topic, but it must be done in order for you to understand the serious technical problems associated with grading on the basis of this kind of compromise. The first technical flaw concerns the regression effect, and to explain that we must first consider prediction and correlation. Here we go!

PREDICTION

When a teacher says she is going to grade students by comparing their performances with their aptitudes, though she may not realize it, essentially she is saying she is going to see what performance she would predict for the student from knowing how able he was. If his performance is higher than would be predicted, he will get a higher grade, and if lower than predicted, a lower grade. Presumably, if performance matches prediction, the grade would be an average grade, a C. What the teacher may not realize is that she cannot simply expect that the pupil with the lowest ability score will be likely to have an achievement score as far from the average on the achievement test as his aptitude score was below the average on aptitude. In fact, it is nearly inconceivable that the student with the lowest aptitude score will get an achievement score even lower than this aptitude test score, and thus obtain a grade below C. Likewise, it is nearly inconceivable that the highest scoring student on the aptitude test will get an achievement score even further above the achievement average and be eligible for a grade above C. We need to understand why this is so.

Predictions such as these are made on the basis of experience, if they are made well. The best way to use experience for this purpose is to compare the aptitudes and achievement of previous classes. The teacher might do something like administer an aptitude test to each student at the beginning of the year. Or perhaps the school routinely administers such tests at intervals during a student's school career as part of the school testing program. In that case the teacher might find the aptitude scores in the school files. She would probably proceed by plotting on graph paper the aptitude and achievement scores for one or more previous classes. She might prepare a graph, like that in figure 14-1, which has aptitude scores on the base line and achievement measures on the vertical axis. For each student, she locates the aptitude score and the achievement score and puts a dot at the juncture of these two values. Dots have been placed in figure 14-1 for a hypothetical group of students.

To turn this graph (called a *scatterplot* or *scattergram*) into predictions, for each score on the base line one obtains the average value of the associated scores on the vertical scale. These averages are then connected by the straight line that fits them best, having about equal numbers of means on either side of the line, as in figure 14-2. The usual name given to this line is *regression line,* which for now is just a name to be learned. The idea is that the best prediction for a person with aptitude at a given level is the mean of the achievements of a group of people who had that level of aptitude.

It turns out that not all groups of students will have scatterplots of achievement vs. aptitude that look like those in figures 14-1 and 14-2. We would expect to get ellipses of dots like those, but sometimes the plots may look more like circles, or

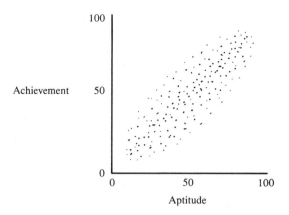

Figure 14–1
Scatterplot of Achievement vs. Aptitude

more like cigars or even pencils, as in figures 14-3 and 14-4. We need some way to describe the various shapes of dots because obviously there is a higher degree of relationship between aptitude and achievement in figure 14-4 than in 14-3. In figure 14-4 we can say with a great deal of assurance that a person with high aptitude will have high achievement, and vice versa. But in figure 14-3 we really can't be sure of saying anything about the level of achievement of anybody in the group on the basis of knowing his aptitude.

Statisticians have figured out a way of describing such varying plots by use of numbers. They call the numbers *correlation coefficients.* They describe the degree of correlation between the two sets of scores. Figure 14-4 represents two variables that are highly correlated. The numbers associated with figures 14-3 and 14-4 are zero and .98, respectively. Correlation values go from −1.00 to +1.00. A correlation of −1.00 indicates that as one score increases, the other decreases. A correlation of +1.00 indicates that the two scores increase and decrease together. A correlation of 0.00 (zero) indicates that as one goes up the other doesn't change,

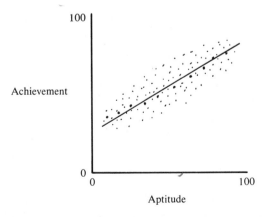

Figure 14–2
Scatterplot of Achievement vs. Aptitude
with Means and Best Fitting Line through Means

and as one goes down the other doesn't change. The value of correlation that one might expect between a test measuring aptitude and a test measuring achievement could reasonably be between .20 and .65 in the kind of school settings we are talking about now in connection with grading.[1]

REGRESSION EFFECT

Now let us examine the flaw in grading in relationship to aptitude that is called the *regression effect*. The regression effect occurs whenever the correlation between two variables is less than 1.00. In education that means always, since we never have correlations between our measures of 1.00. In figure 14-5 we have drawn a scatterplot for a relatively low correlation, about +.20. We have also drawn a line to separate off the lowest scoring 5% of the people on the horizontal dimension,

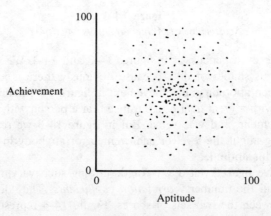

Figure 14–3
Scatterplot of Variables with Low Correlation

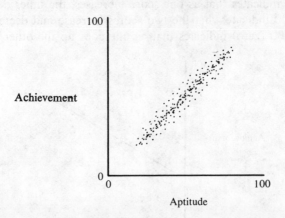

Figure 14–4
Scatterplot of Variables with High Correlation

---

[1]Four audiotutorials provided in *Exercises in Classroom Measurement* are relevant at this point. If they have not been done before, they may be helpful now. They are numbers 2, 3, 7, and 21 (in that order), entitled (2) "Frequency Distributions and Frequency Curves," (3) "Normal Curve, Mean, and Standard Deviation," (7) "Correlation," and (21) "Prediction."

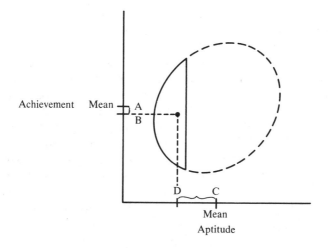

Figure 14–5
Regression Effect with Low Correlation

aptitude. We have indicated the mean score on the vertical dimension for these people with a large dot. This is the mean through which the regression line would tend to go.

Notice how near to the mean for the entire group of people on achievement (A) (vertical axis) is the mean predicted score (B) for those who scored in the lowest 5% on the aptitude dimension (horizontal axis). That is, notice how much shorter is the difference between A and B than the distance between C and D. The predicted achievement score for the lowest 5% of the group on aptitude (B) is closer to the mean on achievement (A) than is the average predictor score for that group of people (D) to the overall mean on aptitude (C). This phenomenon of predicted scores being closer to the mean than predictor scores when the correlation is not perfect (1.00) is the regression effect. It always happens with low correlations and, in fact, is synonymous with them.

If we had taken the top 5% on aptitude for our example, we would have found that their predicted scores would lie closer to the mean (be lower) in just the same manner. The only scores for which regression does not take place are those already at the mean. The predictions for those who are below the mean are, on the average, higher, and the predictions for those who are above the mean on the predictor are, on the average, lower.

Now let's consider what will happen if a teacher attempts to grade on the basis of students' achievements compared with their aptitudes. Since the correlation between achievement and aptitude is not 1.00 (and if it were 1.00 there would be no need to consider aptitude in grading), there is certain to be regression to the mean. It is absolutely inescapable since it means the same thing as imperfect correlation. Then, the students who were below the mean on aptitude will tend to appear to be overachievers. They won't score, on the average, as far below the mean on achievement as they scored on aptitude. This will be satisfying to the naïve teacher. So those pupils will get A's and B's. On the other hand, those who scored above the mean on aptitude will tend to get achievement scores less high above the mean due to regression. So their achievements will, on the average, appear to be lower than expected. This will be disappointing to the naïve teacher, and those pupils will tend to get D's and F's. But, aptitude and achievement are positively (though not perfectly) correlated. Therefore, in terms of competency and ability to perform the things being taught, those above the mean on aptitude tend to be more competent and should receive the higher grades to reflect that. At least, if we want grades to communicate effectively about academic attainment, those who are most competent should get the higher grades. So grading on the basis of a comparison of achievement with aptitude is bound to distort the communication by grades of academic attainment. Unfortunately, most teachers do not even conceive that a problem such as this exists when they glibly attempt in grading to take into consideration how "smart" each student is. (It should also be mentioned that some students may learn deliberately to score low on aptitude tests in order to get higher grades under this system.)[2]

RELIABILITY OF DIFFERENCE SCORES

The regression effect by itself should cause the informed teacher to avoid grading on the basis of how much aptitude, learning potential, intelligence, or IQ a student has. But there are some other technical problems with this kind of grading, too. One that most teachers do not know enough to consider is the fact that comparisons of two measures, such as aptitude and achievement, always result in *difference scores,* and difference scores are notoriously unreliable.

To explain that, let us talk about difference scores. Comparing aptitude with achievement implies that one obtains a score for an achievement measure, and one also obtains a score for measure of aptitude for that subject matter. The former might be from a teacher's test or a standardized achievement test or from a combination of tests, papers, projects, etc. The latter might be from an aptitude test in the specific subject or from grades in that subject in previous years of schooling.

The aptitude score is used to remove, i.e., to subtract, aptitude from achievement. The idea is this. Very able students achieve high levels with ease. Students with modest ability work as hard to reach modest levels of achievement. So we take away the aptitude score from each person's achievement presumably to make students more comparable in terms of effort for purposes of evaluation. This "taking away" is just another procedure for trying to do what we discussed before in terms of prediction, but it results in a difference score — the difference between two measurements.

Next let's consider *reliability.* Reliability in measurement implies consistency. To the extent that measures are reliable, they give the same results each time they are used on the same person, and if we have two tests that measure the same thing, they give the same results when applied to a group of people. The people's scores are in the same rank order on each of the tests. A yardstick is a reliable measure of length because every time you measure the height of a chair with it you get very nearly the same answer, and two different yardsticks applied to a group of chairs give heights that are in close agreement. The *amount* of food one eats is *not* a good

---

[2]An audiotutorial is provided in *Exercises in Classroom Measurement* to help you develop an understanding of this concept. If it has not already been done as part of the study of standardized testing, it may be helpful now. It is number 22, entitled "Regression Effect."

measure of his intake of calories because the *kind* of food differs from one time to another, and the number of calories won't be the same for the same amount of food each time.

Obviously we want measurements on which we base grades to be reliable. If we use tests of achievement, and if they are well-made and reasonably long, we can expect reliabilities in the range of .80 to .90 on a scale like the positive end of the scale for correlation where 1.00 is the maximum possible value. This is one good reason for using objective-test scores as the basis for grading.

However, it is the case that in most situations involving educational measurement, the reliability of a *difference* score is less than the reliabilities of the original measures. So comparing aptitude and achievement by subtracting his aptitude score from each pupil's achievement score results in dealing with relatively unreliable difference scores instead of with the more reliable original achievement test scores.

Let's see how this works. One formula for the reliability of difference scores is

$$r_{dd} = \frac{\bar{r} - r_{12}}{1 - r_{12}}$$

where

r_{dd} stands for reliability of difference scores,
$\bar{r}$ stands for the average reliability of the two measures, and
r_{12} stands for correlation between the two measures.

Now, we'd like to give grades on the basis of information with reliabilities at least near or, preferably, above 0.85. Good achievement tests have that kind of reliability coefficient. We might even expect our aptitude test to have reliability in the low 0.90s. Let's say that the reliability of the achievement measure is 0.85 and that of the aptitude measure is 0.91. Then $\bar{r}$, their average, is 0.88.

The correlation between the aptitude measure and the achievement measure has to be reasonably high or it is pointless to use the aptitude measure. That is, if the correlation between aptitude and achievement were near zero, then we might as well compare achievement scores with random numbers in giving out grades, and that is nonsense.

Let's see what happens if the correlation r_{12}, is reasonably high. Let's say it is .50.

Plugging into our formula, we have

$$r_{dd} = \frac{.88 - .50}{1.00 - .50} = \frac{.38}{.50} = .76$$

This is not a very acceptable degree of consistency for something as important as a grade in a subject-matter achievement that is going to be recorded in a permanent record, be used for counseling, and perhaps be used by employers in deciding about hiring and additional training.

To get higher reliability of the difference scores, we would have to have more reliable measures of achievement and aptitude so that $\bar{r}$ is greater, or else lower correlation between the two measures. It is not easy to get $\bar{r}$ higher. We have little control over the aptitude measure, presumably, and few give reliabilities greater than 0.91, anyway. We could make the achievement measure more reliable by doing such things as using more and better objective-test items, and adding more observations if they were highly reliable. But that is not easy. On the other hand, lowering the correlation between aptitude and achievement is not very palatable either because it does not make much sense to move further in the direction of comparing achievement with essentially random numbers in order to evaluate pupils to give them report-card marks. So the problems of difference scores and their unreliability make grading by comparing achievement with aptitude less attractive than it appears to be at first blush.[3]

JINGLE AND JANGLE FALLACIES

One element in this kind of comparison that the teacher must be aware of is a problem of test naming. In the measurement world, the problem is known as the *jangle fallacy*. The jangle fallacy refers to the fact that two tests with different names do not necessarily measure different things. Thus, one test called mathematics aptitude and another test called mathematics achievement may have in them essentially the same items or the same kinds of items. The correlation, r_{12}, in this case may be about as high as the reliability coefficient of either test, and the r_{dd} may drop to a very low value.

Another fallacy, the *jingle fallacy*, is that tests that have the same name measure the same thing. This fallacy might be troublesome in this context if the teacher were to decide to use a standardized test that had the name of her subject on it in order to get a more reliable measurement of achievement. The test with her subject's name might not at all measure the objectives she was teaching, and she would be grading on data of little relevancy. She would be a victim of the jingle fallacy.

OVER-ACHIEVEMENT AND UNDER-ACHIEVEMENT

Teachers who attempt to grade by comparing achievement with aptitude may think in terms of *over-achievement* and *under-achievement*. That is, they think that if a student achieves more than would be predicted from an aptitude test, he must be really trying and learning well and should be rewarded with a high grade. On the other hand, if he achieves less well than he is predicted to, it must be because he is lazy, is not working hard, or otherwise is undeserving, and the result is a low grade.

The concepts of over-achievement and under-achievement are treacherous. They, obviously, have the dangers of unreliable difference scores. However, they add a new problem, also. In dealing with comparing aptitude with achievement, we acted as though we had an aptitude test related to the achievement test. In fact, we were concerned that they might be so highly related that we would be throwing the baby out with the bath water. The two tests might be measuring the same thing so that differences between their scores would be only error, and thus the differences would represent the degree of unreliability inherent in error or in random numbers. In thinking about over-achievement, teachers are usually thinking not just about predicting a specific kind of achievement from a specifically related aptitude measure-

---

[3]An audiotutorial is provided in *Exercises in Classroom Measurement* to give examples and experience with this concept. It is number 17, entitled "Reliability of Difference Scores" and should be helpful at this point for readers who have not already studied Part 2 and encountered the same concept there.

ment. They are thinking of making the best predictions they can of achievement, using whatever prediction devices are available, and comparing actual achievement with those predictions.

From this point of view we need to recognize another fact about prediction. More than one predictor can be used at a time. Statisticians have provided us with procedures to combine predictors with the proper weights to make prediction as accurate as possible. Not just one or two, but ten or a dozen or a score of predictors can be combined. Theoretically, if enough predictors are combined, and if each is relevant but is not entirely duplicated by the others, prediction can be made exceedingly accurate — as accurate as the reliability of the thing predicted will permit. In such a case, differences between prediction and attainment represent only random error. Since over-achievement and under-achievement are merely observations of how much predictions differ from attainments, in such cases grades based on over-achievement and under-achievement represent only errors or random numbers. One could hardly justify grading on the basis of errors or random numbers!

But even when prediction is not so good, a sound argument can be made that if we went to the effort and found better predictors, there would be less over-achievement and under-achievement. So to grade on the basis of this is, in this sense, just grading on our inability to predict accurately — or perhaps grading on the basis of our laziness in not discovering or developing better prediction systems. This line of reasoning makes it difficult to justify grading on the basis of whether students achieve more or less than they would have been predicted to achieve.

IMPROVEMENT

Some teachers who want to get away from grading on the basis of comparisons with other students in the class decide to grade on the basis of each child's amount of improvement. To measure improvement, the usual procedure is to get a measure of initial status, a pretest, and then get another measure of final status, a posttest. The scores of the two are compared. Those who score higher on posttest than pretest get higher grades, and those who score lower on the posttest, or who improve the least, get the lower grades.

As soon as you read about that procedure your eyebrows should rise. Does this procedure seem familiar? It should. We are going to compare two sets of scores, posttest and pretest. What is the result? A set of difference scores. As soon as we detect *difference scores* what comes to mind? Unreliability! Differences between pretest and posttest scores on any specific subject are likely to be highly unreliable, less reliable than comparisons between aptitude and achievement because now we are talking about comparing sets of scores both of which were designed to be achievement measures of the same competencies.

Your eyebrows should stay elevated as you think further because in the same context in which you learned about difference scores you learned about regression. Is regression likely to occur in comparing pretest with posttest? Yes, to some extent it will occur — perhaps not to such a great extent as in comparing aptitude with achievement because the correlation between pretest and posttest of the same content would usually be higher than the correlation between aptitude and achievement. But what you gain in less regression effect, you tend to lose in lower reliability of difference scores. The same correlation that when high reduces regression, when high tends to reduce reliability of differences. So improvement would seem to be no better basis for grading than is a comparison of attainment with aptitude.

There is another problem with using improvement, also. It has been observed, and it can be proved mathematically to be the usual case, that there is a negative correlation between initial status and improvement. That is, the person who scores the highest on pretest is likely to show the least improvement, and the one who scores lowest initially is likely to show the greatest improvement (but not the greatest competence!). Thus, in grading on the basis of improvement one is likely to give the best grades to people other than those who know the most at the end of instruction and is likely to give lower grades to those who score quite well on the posttest. This is hardly a procedure one would choose if he wanted grades to communicate effectively about the degree of attainment of instructional objectives.

EFFORT

Still another group of teachers, particularly teachers of very young children, turn to comparisons of achievement with effort. (Note: We discussed subtle forms of grading on effort in the earlier section on Comparisons with Aptitude. See the paragraphs on *Reliability of Difference Scores* and on *Over-Achievement and Under-Achievement*.) They might look at two students who both achieved the objectives to a high degree and give a higher grade to the one who seemed to have worked the hardest to reach that level of performance. Somehow it seems to them less deserving for a student to learn easily than for him to learn with great difficulty. By the same token, a student who achieves only modestly but does not even seem to try obtains a lower grade than the modest attainer who appears to exert great effort for even the modest attainment.

Notice that this is quite unlike a coach picking out his first team. When performance is the basis on which evaluation will be made, one picks the performer who makes the difficult look easy — not the easy look difficult! And most anyone would rather have his tonsils removed by an adept surgeon who found such operations no problem than by a clumsy surgeon who had great difficulty getting the hang of it. You would rather have your airplane piloted by someone who could not see why anyone else found piloting hard to learn and have the airplane designed by engineers who thought aeronautical engineering classes were duck soup. So why would we want to give higher grades to students who found a certain level of school work difficult to attain rather than easy?

The teachers who grade this way when asked about it usually justify the practice on grounds of motivation. They feel that the struggling pupil who barely learns anything will no longer be motivated to try if he gets a low grade for what he does accomplish. And they feel that the pupil who achieves highly but at great effort requires greater reward to continue such effort than does the student who achieves similar levels with apparent ease. Obviously, such teachers have decided that for them the primary function of grading is not communicating level of achievement of academic objectives, but instead it is maintaining motivation at a high level. This certainly will not result in grades being meaningful to most of the audiences that need to use grades. Even the pupil is likely to be confused by such grading, and the bright pupil who is downgraded because he achieves easily is likely to be bitterly confused.

Let's analyze such a grading system to see what else we can determine about it. Since it depends heavily on measurements of effort, how are the measurements of effort usually made? There are no well-known measures of academic effort widely used in schools. For the most part, teachers attempt to judge degree of effort expended on the basis of their observations, reports to them from parents about how hard their children are studying, and other informal procedures. Ordinarily such measurements can be expected to be of very low quality. They may be invalid, but they most certainly are confused by different standards of what is great effort. Also, they are usually based on so few sound observations systematically collected and recorded that their reliability is low.

Furthermore, if a teacher grades primarily on effort it is possible that the highest grades will be given to students with low achievement, and the lowest grades will be given to those with high achievement. Or at least there may be a strong tendency in this direction. One really could not justify grades as representing academic achievement if such were the case.

COMBINATIONS OF GRADING BASES

Some teachers, seeking a satisfactory solution to the problem of finding a basis for making the comparisons that result in grades, choose to combine several bases. A combination of achievement and effort is common. That is, achievement is the primary basis, but adjustments are made on the basis of amount of effort expended. (In physical education or sports the adjustment would be reversed. The one who surpasses with ease would be given more credit than the one who surpasses with great difficulty.) Another combination that occurs is grading on the basis of whichever of achievement, effort, or improvement results in the highest grade. Any such combination method is bound to reduce the effectiveness of grades in communicating about academic achievement, and unless it is carefully explained, a combination system will be likely to fail to communicate effectively about anything at all. A much better procedure would be to report separately on each element, achievement, effort, and improvement, but this begins to develop into a cumbersome reporting system.

The primary reason for development of combination systems seems to be the fact that most teachers do not want to cause anguish to their pupils, and they want to avoid the pain that results from acknowledgment of low levels of achievement. It would be nice if it were possible for each pupil to achieve at a high level in at least something, so his entire report would not appear to be one of failure. Unfortunately, it may be impossible to find an area of effort in school in which some pupils can achieve satisfactorily — at least in about the same amount of time that others do. So the pain for the teacher often cannot be relieved by pointing to something the pupil can do well. She may be tempted then to give a higher grade than achievement would justify because the pupil tried hard or at least did improve.

Bias of the Author

In view of various advantages and disadvantages of the comparison bases for giving grades that have been examined above, it may be useful for the author to indicate his bias. No solution is perfect, but it does seem that grading on the basis of preset fixed standards may promote effective communication about academic accomplishments more than any of the other procedures. Admittedly it is difficult to fix standards, and the standards may have to be adjusted after experience with them. Also, the standards have to be set with some idea in mind of what people can reasonably be expected to accomplish — they depend in that sense on what the group does. But the standards can be described. One way to describe them is to base them on objective test scores and to let the test, itself, describe the standards. Another way is to list objectives and state what proportion of them must be satisfactorily performed to obtain various grades. Stated this way, standards do not fluctuate inadvertently, but they can be modified when appropriate and with some degree of precision. Thus this comparison basis seems to be the only feasible method of those studied that will reduce misinterpretation and maintain a semblance of effective communication about academic achievement.

This procedure tends to remove from consideration the motivational consequences of having one's accomplishment evaluated. The solution to this problem seems to be to maintain motivation in other ways. It is true that grades have a motivational side effect, but direct attacks on motivation should be as effective as the side effects of grading, and the direct approach should be emphasized.

It is important if you base grades on comparisons with standards that extra effort also be exerted to clarify the fact that academic achievement is not the same as personal worth. Just because a first grader can't write his name, pronounce the vowels, name the colors, and cut with scissors does not mean that he is no good. This point must be emphasized again and again when dealing with grades.

15

Report Systems Resulting from the Process of Grading

Objectives

As a result of reading this chapter you should be able to:
1. List at least eight common ways of presenting grades or evaluations;
2. For any of the common ways, describe at least two virtues;
3. For any of the common ways, describe at least two flaws or problems;
4. Describe the basic characteristics of grading on the basis of contracts with students;
5. Describe the research basis for contract grading.

Grading Systems

Grades are usually reported on some kind of a form, often called a report card though not necessarily in the form of a card. The various characteristics on which each student is to be graded are often listed, and some form of entry is made for each characteristic at each grading period. There is a variety of kinds of grades or entries, as well as a variety of kinds of forms. We will examine the most frequent kinds of grade-reporting systems next.

LETTER GRADES, A TO F

The most common grade symbol for a subject, such as English, music, art, or social studies, is a letter grade, with A being the highest grade and F being the lowest, and the letters B, C, and D falling in between. The letter E, for some reason, is seldom used. It may be that the letter F is the first letter in the word failure, and no similar common word starts with the letter E. (This system was used in 68% of American high schools in 1972.) Often the five-level scale represented by the letters A, B, C, D, and F is added to by using + and − symbols between some of the letters. A+ is not used very much. A−, B+, B−, C+, C−, and D+, and even D−, are widely used. Rarely seen are F+ and F−, though it would make as much sense from a measurement point of view to use A+, F+ and F− as to use any of the other pluses and minuses. If only the five letters are used, the scale has only five points, and in most kinds of judgments people can make more discriminations accurately than just five. If the common pluses and minuses are used, seven or eight more levels are added, making a total of 12 to 13 steps in the scale. That is somewhere near the optimal level for human discriminations. More steps than that tend to be superfluous. That is, people cannot consistently make the necessarily fine distinctions to choose which level applies, so little is gained by having even more levels in the scale.

Sets of letters could be used other than A through F. Tomasson[1] has suggested that different letters could be used for different kinds of courses. For example, in men's contact sport classes the letters could be HIS:

H Highest level of performance
I Intermediate level of performance
S So-So level of performance.

In standard academic courses, it has been suggested that better attitudes might result if the letters were LOVE, as

L Lovely work
O Outstanding work
V Voluble, but lacking substance
E Encouragement needed.

However, no widespread movement toward such systems is evident. The letters A through F seem to be the common coin of the realm.

What are the virtues of an A to F scale? First, it permits there to be maintained a convenient summary record of pupil performance. Remember we noted among the clienteles for grades that the one group who could most readily influence the form of the grading system was the administrators. Their primary need is for a set of records on each pupil which can be easily kept, easily referred to and evaluated, and reported when appropriate. Letter grades suit those requirements rather well, much better than some of the other possibilities we will discuss, such as letters to parents.

A second virtue of the A to F scale is that there is no confusion in the United States about which is the good end. One could think that A meant awful and F meant fine, but no one does. Later we will consider a numerical scale from 1 to 5 which has many of the virtues of the A to F scale, but has the problem that at some schools 1 is the good score and at others 5 is the good score.

The third virtue is one we mentioned earlier, the A to F scale has near the optimal number of levels. Somewhere in the range of 5 to 15 seems to be the optimal level for human judges, the level between a point where too much information is lost and a point where additional levels add confusion without adding useful information (Miller, 1956). The A to F scale can have as few as five categories or can easily be increased with plus and minus signs to any number of levels up to 15. So it fits human judgment capabilities quite well.

The letter grade scale is not without flaws, however. One complaint about letter grades is that they do not clearly indicate what the student can do. In fact, they are

[1]Used as modified with permission of the author and the American Sociological Association. From *The American Sociologist*, 1972, **7**, p. 8.

usually defined in schools on a "curve" basis, i.e., A's go to the highest scoring or best performing students in the group, no matter how good or poor their performance is. Sometimes a specific percent who can or must get each letter grade is defined by the school administration. This effectively prevents the letter grades from indicating what each student who obtains a given grade can do.

A second flaw is that the meaning of letter grades fluctuates from course to course, from teacher to teacher in the same course, from one school to another, or from one time period to another. That is, different teachers have different grading standards, and teachers placed in different settings change their grading standards. They often do it unwittingly, without recognizing that they are doing it. This was discussed in greater detail earlier when we considered using other students as the comparison basis for grading.

A third flaw in A to F grades is that one common administrative procedure with grades is to average them in order to get an overall evaluation of performance. Letters can't be averaged without first converting them to numbers. If grades were given in the form of numbers in the first place, averaging would be easier, and fewer mistakes would be made.

NUMERICAL GRADES, MAXIMUM = 100

Let us examine some of the widely used numerical systems. Very common in the past (16% of American high schools in 1972) has been what is often called the *percentage* system. It is called that because the maximum value is 100 just as the maximum in many uses of percentage is 100. However, the vague relationship to percents ends there, so the name *percentage* is inappropriate and misleading.

Scales whose top value is 100 come in a wide variety of forms. Usually some coordination is provided between the number and letter grades. For example, sometimes a simple transformation such as the following is prescribed:
  90-100 = A, 80-89 = B, 70-79 = C, 60-69 = D, Below 60 = F.
Other common prescriptions are:
  92-100 = A, 85-91 = B, 78-84 = C, 72-77 = D, and Below 72 = F.
  91-100 = A, 86-90 = B, 81-85 = C, 75-80 = D, and Below 75 = F.
Usually the level set for failure is quite high, probably a heritage from practices of the U.S. Civil Service Commission, which years ago set passing scores as 75 on their examinations. However, one case has come to our attention in a law school in which 55 was the highest score reported, the professors having judged that no student knew more than 55% of all there was to know about any field of law. It is not known what score was passing in that system. Sometimes in addition to having prescriptions for the letters, there are scores designated to correspond to pluses and minuses. For example, 95-100 might be A+, 90-94 = A, 85-89 = B+, 80-84 = B, and so on.

The virtues of a numerical scale like this are in many respects similar to those of letter grades. First, they provide a convenient summary record for administrators. Second, they are more convenient than letter grades because the numbers can be averaged directly without any transformation to a different scale. Third, there is no confusion about which end of the scale is high. The large numbers are better than the small in all scales in which the maximum value is 100.

There are several flaws in the 100-point grading system. First, there is the confusion with percentages, already noted. Second, the 100-point scale is too fine. Humans can't distinguish, for instance, between an 86 and 87. They can't make 25 clear distinctions between 75 and 100, or 30 between 70 and 100, and it is too much to ask them to. When they try to make such refined judgments, they open themselves to the possibility that someone will demand that they justify giving one performance a score of 91 and another a score of 92, and that is nearly impossible to do. Third, most of the scale is seldom used. Rarely are values below 50 on the 100-point scale given as grades, and when they are given it is usually not a reflection of academic attainment but some form of punishment or discipline which should *never* be incorporated in a student's grades on academic attainments.

A fourth flaw in the 100-point scale is that, like the letter-grade system, it does not reveal what the student can do. Only if standards in terms of subject-matter achievements are specified for each number on the scale can this system avoid being tied to something like comparisons with other students. A pretense can be made by having the number of test items or other scores generated during the instruction total to 100, but that is a deceptive approach unless done very carefully so that the various elements are weighted in accordance with their importance. We will consider the problems of weighting performances later.

The last flaw, a common one in grading systems, is that the meaning varies from teacher to teacher, course to course, and so on, as with letter grades. The system only appears to have common meaning, except perhaps in a few cases where meticulous and sound measurement techniques have been used to insure comparability.

NUMERICAL GRADES, FROM 1 TO 5

A system sometimes used (3% of American high schools in 1972) for reporting grades is the set of numbers from 1 to 5. In 1972 this was the most popular way of reporting *cumulative high school average* grade. (Second most common was letters A to F, and third was a 100-point system.) Varieties of this scale using numbers like 1 to 5 are scales ranging from 1 to 4 or 0 to 4. Sometimes certain numbers are not used, e.g., A might be 5, B = 4, C = 3, and D and F both = 1.

A marking system like this has similar properties to the A to F scale, with two very significant differences. First, the numbers from 1 to 5 or 0 to 4 are easily averaged, and there is no need to convert them to some other system. Remember, letters must be converted to numbers before they can be averaged, and then the average must be reconverted to letters unless two scales are going to be used, one for marks and the other for averages of marks. Converting a 3.52 back to a mark on the A to F system poses a problem. Is it an A, a B, an A−, a B+, or what? This problem does not arise if the letters A through F are never used.

Second, a disadvantage of the 1 to 5 or 0 to 4 system is that no one knows without being specifically informed which grade is high. In some cases the larger the number the better the performance, and 4 (or 5) is equivalent to A. In other schools the *lower* the number, the better the performance. They usually use the 1 to 5 system, and 1 is equivalent to A, as though 1 indicated first in the class.

This system has the virtues of providing a convenient summary record, and being near the optimum blend of information transmitted with convenience in use. It is perhaps a little on the coarse side, but not bad. It does not lend itself to being made finer with plus and minus signs, but occasionally a school simply uses numbers from 1 to 15 or 1 to 10 instead of 1 to 5 in order to get a finer scale. This is not a bad idea, but it is not very common.

The flaws are familiar to us. In addition to the confusion about ends of the scale, the meaning of the numbers varies from one instructor to another, and so on. Also, this scale does not indicate directly what the student can do. More often it merely indicates his performance relative to his classmates. Finally, it has the flaw that people are more used to the A to F scale. In fact, a common question about a numerical scale like this is "Which end is A?"

Reasonable conversions between the A to F system, the 100-point system, and the 1 to 5 system can be made. For example, the letter grade of A corresponds to between 90.8 and 92.3, to between 3.53 and 4.51 on systems in which 4 or 5 is high, and to 1.43 on the 1 to 5 systems with 1 high. This suggests that these systems are similar enough to be nearly interchangeable in function. If one is to choose among them it should be to avoid a particular flaw or to obtain a particular virtue important in the local situation.

PASS-FAIL GRADES

A grade-reporting nomenclature that has had some recent favor (less than 2% of American high schools in 1972) but now seems to be fading again is the two-value system. It is often called Pass-Fail grading. Only two grades are used, one to indicate success and the other, failure. The advocates of this system claim that it allows students to broaden their backgrounds and take courses outside their field of special interest. The use of the system seems to have originated in colleges where a physics student might want to take a course in art, just to increase his general knowledge, but not to attempt to compete with students who intended to become artists. Or an art student might take a course in physics out of curiosity, which is encouraged, but not to compete for grades with potential scientists. The reduction of pressure for grades supposedly would make such excursions into knowledge more pleasant and more frequent, and this is considered desirable in a liberal arts curriculum.

The virtues of such a system are that the grades are convenient to record, provide a convenient summary record, and if scored as numbers, such as 0 and 1, instead of letters such as P and F, or S and U, are easily averaged. Also, it might be considered a virtue that graders have fewer discriminations to make. No decisions between A's, B's, and C's are necessary.

The flaws in the Pass-Fail marking system which are leading to its abandonment are numerous. First, it does not provide a very good summary record. The basic problem is that it provides too little information. One reason for its loss of popularity in colleges is that for students whose grade record is important for continuing in graduate school or getting a desirable position, students with many A's on their records are favored over those who only have P's. P, after all, could be no more than a D, and from the point of view of an employer or graduate school, it is better to bet on known A's than on just possible A's. Parents who see just a P are likely to ask for additional information on just how good the performance was. Legislators and school boards are likely to ask administrators for finer discriminations, also.

A second flaw is that it is confusing to try to combine Pass-Fail grades with grades given on other scales in order to obtain an average. Fail is not much of a problem. It simply corresponds with the lowest grade on another scale, i.e., F, or 75, or 0.

But what value do we give P? There is no sound solution. It does not make sense to just leave out Pass-Fail grades, because the Fail end is important and is no problem to average.

A third flaw is that students, themselves, don't get enough feedback from this reporting system. They need to know for their career and other planning whether they are doing well or just barely passing in particular courses. For that matter, they need to know at midterm whether they are borderline passing or clearly above any danger point. If records are kept on a more refined scale at midterm, why should the information be thrown away when grades are given?

Research on Pass-Fail grading has revealed some other flaws. To continue our sequence, a fourth flaw is that in use of Pass-Fail grading it has been found that students tend to settle for the minimum work that is required to pass, when with only a little more effort they might have accomplished more. Thus other grading systems have a greater incidental motivational effect that some teachers desire. Research at the high school level indicates that students graded on a Pass-Fail basis achieve at a lower level and have poorer attitudes toward the subject which is taught on a Pass-Fail basis.

Research also indicates that the Pass-Fail option at the college level does not result in broadening of students' curricula. They tend to take about the same subjects whether they use the Pass-Fail option or not. So the major claim of the advocates of this system is not supported by research.

Finally, a fifth flaw is that what usually happens to a two-point grading system like Pass-Fail is that dissatisfaction with only two points causes a third point to be added, something like "Honors." Now we have a three-point system, Honors-Pass-Fail. Further experience leads to further dissatisfaction, and the scale is modified by inserting plus and minus signs. Now we have Honors +, Honors −, Pass +, Pass −, and Fail. Believe it or not, we are back to a five-point scale, which we could just as well call A, B, C, D, and F, or 4, 3, 2, 1, and 0, or 1, 2, 3, 4, and 5.

CHECKLISTS

All the above grading systems have shared the fault that they do not say what the student can do or what he typically does. In that respect, they do not provide as much information as some users want. One form of an attempt to provide more specific information, and to include information on students that is not a legitimate part of an academic grade, such as deportment, attitude, willingness, attentiveness, promptness, etc., is a checklist. Usually checklists are added to grades on one of the other systems to provide additional information. The checklist is a list of statements to each of which the teacher reacts by checking its presence or degree. The virtues of the checklist as a supplement are that the checklist seems easy to use and it seems to add information.

There are several flaws. If the checklist were to be used as the only form of grade, and if it were to supply information on specific performances, it would have the problem of requiring many judgments of many statements. This is a very difficult and time-consuming task for a teacher if it is to be done in a worthwhile manner. If the list is shortened, the desired specificity of information is lost. If the teacher does not exert herself at the task for each pupil, the apparent information in the checklist is worthless.

If the checklist is only to supplement grades reported in another system, it still has some problems. First, the checklist results cannot easily be averaged with the other grades to form a convenient summary record. Second, it is not easy to develop good checklists. Psychologists have spent years of research on developing sound procedures by which humans can make and record judgments. Checklists and rating scales are procedures they have studied, and they can tell you of many problems in developing good checklists and many kinds of errors that will still be made in using the best of them. There are such things as the fact that if an entire checklist is filled out for a single pupil before the next pupil is considered, there will be a *halo* effect. The general impression of the student will influence ratings of what are supposed to be separate characteristics. The psychologist would recommend that all pupils be rated on one characteristic, and then the next characteristic be considered for each pupil, to avoid or reduce the halo effect. But that is just too much to demand of a teacher's time. There are other well-known errors and problems in developing and using checklists that are often ignored in school settings to the detriment of the value of the checklists. So what appears to the naïve person to be a simple and convenient procedure is really a complex and demanding problem in design and use.

A third problem with checklists is that the very detail that is desired is often overdone. Checklists have the habit of promptly becoming too long. Statements that overlap or are redundant get added, and nothing gets taken away. Soon the task is so onerous that the teacher becomes careless in doing it. Now, instead of adding information, the checklist adds misinformation or confusion. On the other hand, if the checklist is kept very short, then it adds so little as to be not worth the trouble. Finding the happy balance, and maintaining it, is one of the flaws in the use of the checklist as a supplement to grading. If you happen to be in a school that uses checklists or is contemplating their introduction, be sure to become informed about their sound development and use. (A suitable, though not simple, reference would be Guilford, 1954, 263-98.)

PARENT CONFERENCES

In order to increase the communication between parents and teachers about the pupils, one procedure sometimes tried is to replace the report card with its grades by conferences between the teachers and the parents. This would seem to increase the detailed communication from the teacher and also to permit reaction from the parent and thus clarification of the meaning of the grades. It would seem to be much more versatile, letting the teacher tell what the child can do, letting her compare him with other pupils, describe his effort, his achievement compared to his aptitude, and so on, as appropriate. It would help the teacher to understand problems individual pupils may be having in school also. These are important virtues, many of which cannot be gained in other ways. Another virtue claimed by some is that such conferences help to get the parents involved in the functions and operations of the schools. This is considered to be very important, and not easy to achieve in other ways.

The parent conference has many problems, though. In fact, there are so many that it is seldom used as a replacement for grades on some kind of report form. (It is widely considered a desirable supplement, of course.) What are some of the flaws in the parent conference as a grading and reporting system?

First, the parent conference leaves no convenient summary record. In fact, it sacrifices all the other audiences for grades. The pupil, himself, is usually not included in the conference. Other teachers don't know what was communicated in the conference. The information is not later available to potential employers, to counselors, or to other schools.

Second, it has been found that conferences take a lot of time. In fact, they take so much time that using that system requires either hiring additional faculty or else expecting the teachers to work evenings and weekends to make up for the time taken by the conferences. One device is to have conferences less frequently than every six weeks, or whatever term is used for usual report cards. But, of course, that in turn reduces the level of communication, and increased communication is what is sought by the conference system.

A third problem, often not recognized until too late, is that conferences may be exceedingly inconvenient for parents. Parents may work during the daytime, so any conferences would require their being absent from their jobs or the teacher's working on conferences in the evening after the usual school day. Many parents in rural areas simply don't have the transportation to get to the school for a conference. The teacher must then drive to the home or transport the parent to the school for the conference.

A fourth problem is that the conference system tends to disrupt the teaching schedule. The teacher must program her time carefully, indeed, to fit a conference of unknown duration into her school day at 10:30 A.M. when a parent is available. It is even worse if the parent just shows up unexpectedly and asks to have his periodic conference right now!

Fifth, experience has shown that some parents just won't participate in such conferences. Usually when the procedure is first instituted it is an apparent success; 60% to 70% of the parents participate. After the first year or so, however, it is likely that the parents of the weaker students realize that these conferences aren't much fun. All they hear about is their children's problems. They are less and less likely to come back for more. The parents of the very able students also may drop out because they don't learn anything new at the conference. Their children have always done well and will continue to do well, so why bother to go hear that? In fact, if the conferences are left up to the parents to arrange, it is more than likely that after the first year there will be no conferences — and now we have no communication instead of improved communication between the school and the parents.

LETTERS TO PARENTS

Since parent conferences tend to break down for the reasons indicated above, an alternative that is not so demanding of parents is sometimes tried. This is the practice of having teachers write a letter to each parent about each pupil instead of simply filling out grades on a report card. The idea is to improve communication, still, but to see to it that lack of interest of parents or simple inconvenience does not incapacitate the communication system. Communication is only one way, but at least there is less probability that communication will disintegrate entirely than is the case with parent conferences.

The virtues of the use of letters to parents are that it seems more feasible to report on each student in terms of what is particularly important for that student, and the teacher is more free to include various comparison bases, including what the student can do, how well he performs compared to others, compared to his effort, and his aptitude. The letter seems more personal than a report card, but it seems more likely to survive than a parent conference system.

The flaws in the use of letters in place of report cards with grades include the fact that there is no convenient summary record for administrative purposes, and all the other clients are completely without information. The letters don't go to employers, to other schools, or even to the pupil, himself, in most cases.

Also, it has been found that teachers do not usually write very well. If they are left to write letters to each parent about each child several times a year, some rather bad writing goes out from the school. Even statements that may damage the school or cause it legal difficulties may be made. So, the principal often has to review each letter before it goes out. Obviously, this is a tremendous burden on the principal, but the alternative is antagonism from the community or even the need for a school lawyer to be retained.

When teachers are restricted in their writing of the letters, or when they have so many to write that it becomes burdensome, they tend to resort to stereotyped comments, often designed to be unrevealing rather than to communicate fully and effectively. Teachers might even develop several form letters to be sent to parents of students who are all performing at about the same level. But this is little more than a checklist, and a checklist is more economical if that is what is to be done.

Economy is an important factor with the letter-to-parents system. Writing all those letters, even when they are all about the same, takes a lot of time. And it requires more secretarial help than most schools are accustomed to having. So new burdens and expenses are added, and, unless it is well done, the system may add little to less expensive and time-consuming systems.

SELF-EVALUATION PARAGRAPHS

A grading procedure that is sometimes tried is having students write evaluations of themselves that they take home to their parents. This reduces the time and effort that the teacher must spend on grading and marking, and it may help students to learn to be responsibly self-critical and self-guiding. Adults, to be effective, must learn to evaluate themselves and to correct their behavior when it is not effective. Pupil self-evaluations may help this learning to take place, it is argued. Certainly if the procedure does help students to learn self-scrutiny and to learn from their mistakes without an outside agency correcting them, there is virtue in using self-evaluation in place of grades.

What are some of the flaws of such a procedure? First, it leaves no convenient summary record for administrative purposes and for clients other than students and parents. Second, there is little basis for comparability between students. For some purposes, such comparability is an important feature of a grading system. Third, this kind of grading really requires that the teacher help the student to learn a new set of skills. It is not something that students can just be told to do. In fact, it is not something that children in the early grades can even be expected to learn to do. So one problem is that it is not feasible with young children. Fifth, students may not know or recognize what is important to consider in their self-evaluations. What they think is important may seem trivial to the teacher who looks into the future of the child. Sixth, students may be too severe on themselves. They may also be too lenient, but we will discuss later some empirical evidence that indicates that adults, at least, tend to grade themselves lower than the teacher would grade them. Finally, since the teacher must help the students to learn and grow in their self-evaluation skills, and must probably monitor the self-evaluations to keep them from becoming frivolous, the procedure may take more instead of less time for the teacher.

SAMPLES OF STUDENT WORK

Many of the grading systems discussed earlier have been criticized because they did not reveal what the student can do. Someone has suggested that the way to satisfy that need is to have the students take home a sample of their work so that their parents can, indeed, see what they are able to do. This would be in lieu of grades.

The virtue of the procedure would be that it shows what the student can do, and the parent can evaluate the product. The teacher would not have the responsibility of evaluating it with a grade. It would also tend to orient education toward learning that resulted in products that students produce, and some people think that there is too little of this in current education.

There are a number of glaring faults with the procedure as a general replacement for grades. First, there is no convenient summary record. The principal's office cannot reasonably keep samples of student work, and, indeed, if it did it would have to arrange for duplicates to be made of the work samples that the children took home, a thought that boggles the mind. Second, even if the students took their work home, the parents would be very likely to inquire as to how good it was. "Is this what should be expected of a child in Susie's grade?" a parent might ask of the drawing she brought home, or of the tin cup that Johnny made in manual arts. If that happens, then the teacher has not avoided the problem of evaluation. She must still grade, as well as send work samples home, and her load has been increased rather than lightened.

A third problem is deciding what to send home. Shall a product be sent home for each different part of the curriculum in which a child is involved at a particular time? Or shall one be selected to represent all the various parts of the curriculum? In either case, what does one choose to send? The best? The worst? The average, if that can be defined? Or the easiest to send? In fact, a fourth problem is that for some parts of the curriculum there is nothing to send. What does one send in music? In citizenship, if that is taught? In physical education? In speech? If nothing can be sent, how does one communicate even to parents about degree of academic achievement in a subject? These problems lead to the fifth, that making these decisions, and arranging for the products to get home, and taking care of the inquiries that are generated by them involve so much teacher time that special provisions for staffing must be made if such a scheme is to be attempted as a replacement for some kind of course grading system.

DUAL OR MULTIPLE SYSTEMS

Some schools adopt dual or multiple grading systems in order to obtain the advantages of more than one and reduce disadvantages by making up with one system for failings of another. One common dual system is to have grades in subject matter and also a checklist for such things as conduct, effort, attendance, and personality traits or work habits. This provides for the convenient summary record of evaluated academic performance, but also provides a place for reporting things that otherwise might be allowed to distort the communication of academic achievement. Sometimes a different reporting system will be used for the checklist than for the academic grades, for example, grades on an A to F scale but checklist items indicated only as satisfactory or unsatisfactory.

Another common dual system is to have one grade based on a comparison with a set of standards, and another grade based on another comparison base, such as performance compared with aptitude, or performance compared with fellow students. In such a system it might be reported that Susie reads with 90% comprehension books written for the second grade, but since Susie is in the fifth grade, this is a very low level of performance compared with her classmates. One mark, comparing her reading with her ability, might be A, and the other, comparing her with her classmates, might be D.

The virtues of multiple systems, if they are well designed and carried out, are the transmission of more information. The way of reporting on performance can be adapted to the kind of performance. While letter grades may be appropriate for performance in history, a mark on a checklist indicating "always" may be more appropriate for reporting on whether a pupil gets her work done on time, and a report of the number of times she was tardy in arriving at school may be more appropriate for that information than a letter grade or a mark on a checklist.

The flaws of a multiple system are that it is hard to assemble a convenient summary of all the information in the system. This may be handled by merely summarizing the academic grades, and attaching a report of anything outstanding in the rest of the report, such as frequent illnesses, inability to get along with other students, etc. Also, such a reporting scheme may take more time than the use of a single system. This may be worth the sacrifice if teachers are less frustrated by having the medium better fit the message. A third problem is that it is often difficult to judge such a variety of things independently, and it may be difficult for a parent or other recipient of grades to comprehend how Susie could get both an A and a D in reading. Some study has indicated that it is even difficult for teachers to report such disparate grades for one student in one subject. There tends to be a high positive correlation between reports for the same student using different comparison bases — so high that in practice this idea tends to produce redundant information, and is perhaps not worth the effort.

CONTRACT GRADING

In some circles there has come into vogue a type of grading called *contract grading*. The essence of it seems to be that the student and the teacher negotiate a set of tasks the student will do in order to obtain a certain grade. This is the contract. If the student fulfills it, he gets the grade.

It would be simple to describe contract grading if only one pattern was based on this theme. But in any group of college students it seems that one can find past experience with as many different kinds of contracting procedures as there are students. Each teacher who tries it seems to invent her own unique system. Some systems require the student to set the contract, say for a B. If he does enough for an A, he still gets only a B, but if he only does enough for a C, he fails. Others would simply give him all the time he needs to get his B, regardless (theoretically) of how long it takes. Some would let him complete his contract whenever he is able to, and if he finishes early, give him free time or some other pleasant experience for his success. Other teachers feel uncomfortable about free time, and just set up another contract, so there is no benefit to a student (from the student's point of view) to prompt completion. He sees it as a task without end, and not something to complete with dispatch.

Some teachers base their contracts merely on such things as level of test performance. For example, a contract to get 90% of the test items correct would yield an A, but a contract for only 85% would yield a B. Others contract on volume of work, such as ten book reports is an A, but only seven is a B. Then there is the problem of the level of quality of each of the book reports. Does the teacher say ten "satisfactory" reports? If so, how is "satisfactory" judged? On a letter grade basis? If so, we have some kind of dual system. The variations on the theme go on and on, and no one procedure seems to be particularly common or general.

It would be nice if we could say that the contracting idea was the result of sound research that indicated that this was a superior way to evaluate performance. Unfortunately, not only is there no sound research on contract grading, but the writer has been able to unearth very little published research of *any* degree of quality, good or bad, on this procedure (Lloyd, 1971; Poppen & Thompson, 1971; Taylor, 1971). Contract grading thus has all the appearance of an educational fad. How transitory it will be cannot be said at this time. If one could state the virtues of contract grading and the flaws, it would be easier to evaluate. But the virtues and flaws of each different blend of various aspects of the general idea would have to be evaluated, and as yet no one has listed all the kinds of contract systems, or provided a taxonomy for them. Perhaps it will never be done, if the fad disappears soon. As with any such procedures, it can be seen now that some teachers and some students like it and some don't, and some like some forms of it but not others, but little else about contract grading can be said with any degree of authority.

Summary

We have examined and attempted to evaluate a number of different possibilities for reporting of students' performances in order to communicate effectively about academic achievement to the various audiences who are interested in such reports. One of the purposes of doing this is to save school teachers and school systems the anguish of reinventing the wheel, so to speak. Probably no teacher who serves for very many years or in very many different schools escapes the experience of having the grade reporting system of her school criticized, and having it suggested that they change to some better reporting form. The classic description of what happens when this is diligently tried appears in a book by William Wrinkle entitled *Improving Marking and Reporting Practices in Elementary and Secondary Schools*. A teacher should try to obtain in a library this now out-of-print book and profit from the author's experiences.

The fact that people do not have a sound background in the problem when they develop new systems is illustrated almost daily. A report, for example, appeared on page 59 of the February 18, 1974, issue of *TIME*. The heading of the story is *The Dallas Monster*. The first paragraph of the story says:

"When a student comes home with a B, it doesn't really communicate anything to the parent," says Dallas School Superintendent Nolan Estes. That could be true, but the "report cards" that the younger pupils in the Dallas Independent School District are coming home with this winter may well have completely eliminated any communication between home and school. The latest educational innovation, imposed upon Dallas parents and children for the first time this fall, is an 8½-in. by 14-in. number-filled sheet that looks more like a page from a company audit than a report card. To assist them in deciphering the report, which is used for kindergarten through third grade, pupils' parents are supplied with a 32-page booklet called *Your Child Starts School* and a 28-page manual with the remarkable title *Terminal Behavioral Objectives for Continuous Progression Modules in Early Childhood Education*. Says School Board Member James Jennings, who labeled the whole package a "monster": "Seventy percent of the parents will never raise the lid on a cover with a title like that."[2]

The story continues and ends with a note that a freelance writer has been hired by the Dallas Schools to write another supplementary pamphlet to explain the explanation, but after three months he is only halfway through his project because he is having difficulty understanding the manual. The problems of the report form obviously have not yet been solved!

References

Guilford, J. P. *Psychometric methods.* (2nd ed.) New York: McGraw-Hill, 1954, Chapter 11, 263–98.

Lloyd, K. E. Contingency management in university courses. *Educ. Technol.* 1971, April, 18–23.

Miller, G. A. The magic number seven, plus or minus two: Some limits on our capacity for processing information. *Psychol. Review*, 1956, **63**, 81–97.

Poppen, W. A. & Thompson, C. L. The effect of grade contracts on student performance. *J. educ. Res.,* 1971, **64**, 420–24.

Taylor, H. Student reaction to the grade contract. *J. educ. Res.,* 1971, **64**, 311–14.

The Dallas Monster. *Time*, 1974, February 18, p. 59.

Wrinkle, W. *Improving marking and reporting practices in elementary and secondary schools.* New York: Holt, Rinehart and Winston, 1947.

---

[2]Reprinted by permission from *TIME*, The Weekly Newsmagazine; Copyright Time Inc.

16

Phenomena Concerning Grading

Objective

Study of this chapter should enable you to:

Identify and describe at least eight relevant empirically derived conclusions from research about grading.

Dearth of Research about Grading

There are many controversial aspects about grading and marking. We have already examined the different views about the comparison bases that are to be used in determining grades and the views about the form in which grades are to be reported. In subsequent chapters we will examine other varied points of view about grading. In the presence of all of these controversies, you would think that a large body of sound and substantial research would develop that would resolve the controversies or at least clarify them. Oddly, this has not happened with respect to grading. Considering how significant the activity of grading is, the paucity of research is striking. And much of what we know from research that bears on grading was derived from efforts to understand other phenomena. In this chapter we will consider what is known about grading from research. Some of the findings are based on large bodies of data carefully analyzed by a variety of researchers over a period of years. Others are based on only single studies and are much less well substantiated. We will consider the former first.

Well-supported Research Findings

Only about four pieces of knowledge about grading relevant for school teachers are based on multiple studies over many years. Two of them come from studies that were not primarily of the grading process.

GRADING STANDARDS VARY

One of the thoroughly studied aspects of grading is the question of whether, given the same paper, different teachers would give it the same grade or whether the same teacher on different occasions would give it the same grade. The most frequently cited studies are by Starch in the early 1900s. In a variety of subjects he and his associate found that in marking copies of the same paper, a hundred or more teachers would give grades all the way from failing to highest honors. This happened not only in less rigorous subjects such as English and history, but also in topics like geometry. These findings brought essay examinations for grading purposes into disrepute and promoted the early objective testing movement.

Similar findings continue to be reported right up to the present time. Probably any college that studies it will find markedly different proportions of letter grades from different departments, and this cannot ordinarily be attributed to different levels of student quality. The grade seems to be more dependent on the personality of the instructor or the tradition of the department than on the achievement of the students in the subject matter. Though they seem to be reported less frequently, it is likely that the same phenomenon can easily be found in any school at any level that studies the pattern of grades given to its students. So, it seems to be well established that no clear standards based on wide agreement are available for grading of student achievements in school projects.

PASS-FAIL GRADING FAILS TO MEET ITS PURPOSE

You should remember that initially the idea of pass-fail grading was that students would take a broader variety of courses and thus get a more liberal education if they did not have to compete for grades with students majoring in the specific areas of those other courses. Art students might safely study physics or chemistry without having to compete for grades with future physicists and chemists, for example.

Study of the course-taking patterns of college students given the pass-fail option indicates that they do not take any broader patterns of courses than their peers who do not take advantage of that option. They are more likely to use the pass-fail option to lighten their load during a particular quarter or to avoid a low grade in a course reputed to be difficult. These studies have been done recently, and usually have to be located in the files on individual campuses rather than in the published research literature, but the nature of the usual finding from such study seems to be rather clear by now. The implications for pass-fail grading in schools are not clear, but this form of grading was adopted in schools in imitation of colleges. That it fails to meet its purpose in colleges may be relevant to schools. Further, one study at the high school level (Gatta, 1973) indicates that students in chemistry graded on a pass-fail basis achieve at a lower level and have less favorable attitudes toward chemistry than students graded conventionally.

BOYS GET LOWER GRADES THAN GIRLS

A finding that comes from studies that were not designed to find out about grading, in particular, is the striking phenomenon of a bias against males in grading. Most of the data come from research on the prediction of grades, for example, the prediction of first-year college grades from high school grades and test scores for the purpose of college admission decisions. The regular finding, reported since the late 1930s at least, is that girls get higher grades for the same predictor values than do boys. In fact, some studies have evaluated not only aptitude but also achievement by means of test scores and have contrasted those scores with the grades given by teachers. The finding is the same. For a given level of aptitude and achievement as measured by tests, the girls will get a noticeably higher grade on the average. This seems to occur in all kinds of courses, not just those in which females might be expected to excel.

The reason for girls' receiving higher grades has not been established. One wag has said that it is because girls are graded on the curves. No doubt that wag was a man. More likely, our culture for many years relegated to girls and women the roles of docility and submissiveness. A busy teacher often finds it difficult to avoid rewarding these traits in a grading system. In fact, these traits may be judged by some to reflect an important part of learning that test scores fail to include. Whatever the reason for their higher grades, and the justification or lack thereof, the phenomenon is prevalent — grades are biased in favor of girls when compared with their academic achievement or potential as measured in other ways.

GRADES ARE NOT THE ONLY MOTIVATION

As we noted earlier, some people think of motivation as an important function of grading. In fact, we argued that motivation was only an incidental function of grading, and it should not be allowed to distort the primary function — the communication of academic accomplishment. We also noted at that time the abundance of evidence, largely from study of behavior modification, operant conditioning, and counseling, that human beings can be motivated by a wide variety of things. Candy has been used so often that mentioning it is trite. Tokens, like poker chips, that can be cashed in for privileges, like dusting the erasers or going to the library or being a hall monitor, are widely used. Simply putting an empty children's plastic swimming pool in the corner of a room and letting children be in it as a reward has proven effective. Counselors use a smile or the encouraging "Uh-huh," or "Yes, go on." One of the gags college students pull on their instructors is to modify the teacher's behavior by having everyone smile or pretend to pay special attention whenever she stands up, sits down, or some other specific behavior. Often the frequency of the selected behavior can be significantly and noticeably increased by the reward system that the pupils put into effect. There is no doubt that there are many motivators other than grades and that they are very effective, though the knowledge has not come to us from studies of grading practices.

Research Findings from Limited Studies

There are a few findings that have been reported only once or perhaps twice, but in no substantial and related series of studies. They are worth noting because they are about all we know from the empirical studies of grading that have been reported in the literature. We won't spend much time on them because, until their generality is established, they provide only clues. Occasionally they seem to conflict, and that is not surprising to an experienced researcher who happens across isolated findings. Usually we won't know why the conflict exists until much more study has been done. Perhaps it is only a difference in methodology, or a random fluke. Or maybe it is something fundamental.

One study has been found which indicates that among college students who are asked what grade they think they deserve and what grades they think their fellow students deserve, individual students think they deserve B or better, but they think some of their fellows deserve lower grades than B. This suggests that some students overestimate the quality of their performance and competence.

Another study, however, finds that when adult students are asked what grade they deserve, i.e., to grade themselves, and when these grades are compared with the grades the teacher would give them, the students give themselves lower grades than the teacher would assign. This suggests that some students may be too severe in their self-evaluation.

In another area, some study indicates that if parents are given their choice between having letter grades for their children's reports or having letters from the teacher, they will prefer the letter grades.

Some study of the reports teachers tend to write about students when they use written letters to parents indicates that the teachers tend to use innocuous statements instead of clearly revealing comments. It is as though the teachers fear putting their evaluations down in black and white. If this is true, then the written letters are failing to communicate about academic accomplishment — almost deliberately. And the grading system that uses written letters filled with innocuous statements fails in the fundamental purpose of grading, the communication of information about academic achievement of individual students.

There has been limited study of grading of advantaged and disadvantaged black and white students. At least one study (McCandless et al., 1972) has been reported with rather interesting findings. Apparently the grading of the disadvantaged and the blacks differs from the grading of the advantaged and the whites even when they are all in the same classrooms. In this study it was reported that grades were more highly related to aptitude test scores than to achievement test scores considering all students taken together, a rather discouraging phenomenon in some respects. It was also found that, for the disadvantaged, teachers' grades were more closely related to achievement test scores than they were for the advantaged. That is, the teachers seemed to be grading the disadvantaged on their achievement as revealed in tests, but this was not true for the advantaged. In fact, there was essentially no relationship between grades and achievement for advantaged white boys or girls, but for the disadvantaged black boys and girls the relationship was quite large. The authors of the study speculated that teachers may mark the advantaged and white children according to how well socialized they are according to the teachers' standards, but mark the poor and particularly the black poor more according to their objective performance.

In terms of actual level of grades given to these students, the study reported that disadvantaged black boys got the lowest average grades (2.0 on a scale in which A is 4.0), and the white girls (advantaged and disadvantaged) got the highest grades

(2.75). There are a myriad of other details in the study, and it opens a whole area for research if we are to have a sound empirical foundation for making generalizations about grading in the schools.

References

Gatta, L. A. An analysis of the pass-fail grading system as compared to the conventional grading system in high school chemistry. *J. Res. Science Teaching,* 1973, **10,** 3–12.

McCandless, B. R., Roberts, A., & Starnes, T. Teachers' marks, achievement test scores, and aptitude relations with respect to social class, race, and sex. *J. educ. Psychol.,* 1972, **63,** 153–59.

17

Fallacies in Grading

Objective

As a result of the study of this chapter you should be able to:

Describe at least four common fallacies about grading practices.

When a topic as important and ubiquitous as grading and marking is so little studied by formal research, it is inevitable that teachers will grasp at straws as they try to solve their grading problems. Sometimes the straws take on the appearance of respected truths, even though they are entirely unfounded and largely unevaluated. And sometimes just a careful logical analysis reveals that these apparent truths are not sound. They are fallacies. Several fallacious ideas about grading are so common that they need to be taken up specifically as one tries to develop competence in this part of the job of teaching. We will take up five fallacies in connection with grading in this chapter.

Fallacy A: There Is One Correct Way to Grade

The naïve teacher or school administrator may often be heard discussing the correct way to give grades to pupils as though there were a correct procedure and all others were somehow incorrect. By now you know too much to accept that idea. You know that there are a variety of possible comparison bases for grades and a variety of possible ways to report student progress. So there is no single correct way to grade. Many reasonably sound, though different, procedures can be developed from the possibilities available and new ones that may be created.

Unfortunately, administrators of educational institutions may be as naïve as untrained teachers when it comes to grading. Yet they may specify the grading policy of their school, and they may do it without adequate thought. In fact, they are likely to adopt blindly the system that they are most used to, or that they have heard touted most recently. This poses a problem for the informed teacher who may recognize clearly the weaknesses of the particular system adopted or may note the confusion that results from teachers' deviating from the specified system in different ways without anyone's seeming to care.

Teachers should have a major voice in the grading system that is to be used in the institution in which they teach. That is, informed teachers should have a major voice. Undoubtedly there are many teachers who are almost totally uninformed about grading problems and issues. That may be why administrators don't typically take the teachers into consideration when adopting or changing a grading practice. Even informed teachers may not agree on the system to adopt because of the many reasonable possibilities available.

Teacher trainees are likely to find that the grading practices in the school in which they first teach are not very effective, considering what they have learned about grading and marking from an experience such as you have been provided. They will wonder how the grading practices can be changed. It seems clear that for a major change to occur in most schools, considerable groundwork must be laid. An informed group of teachers and administrators must be developed so that whatever change is made is as sensible as possible rather than just a move to the newest fad. Whatever practice is to be adopted, it would be a tragedy if the move toward improvement just went over the same ground that has already been tried years before in search for a better grading and reporting system. In particular, the move should not be made without a careful consideration of Wrinkle's book on improving grading practices referred to in chapter 15. No school in the present or future should repeat the process of learning what Wrinkle found out so long ago.

Fallacy B: The Meaning of Grades Is Clear and Standards Are Available

Often the audiences for grades are much more prone to this fallacy than are the teachers who give the grades. In fact, it is the experience of most teachers to be upset at grading time by the difficulty in making the decisions involved. The most difficult is probably that of determining what level of performance deserves each level of grade. The ranking of the performance by the students is often not so hard as deciding where the division is between A and B, and whether any performance is so bad as to deserve an F. The standards just are not readily available or agreed upon, and each teacher is largely left to herself to decide what reasonable standards are. With that much variability left in the grading system, it is no wonder that the meaning of grades is not clear. Even the bases for giving grades are often left up to the teacher, and when that is the case, the user of the grades has only limited clues as to what they mean.

In particular, there still prevails in some circles the fallacy that there is something inherently meaningful about certain numbers, such as 75%. Some people can still be found who believe that a score below 75% is failing. This, as you know by now, is clearly nonsense, but the fallacy is sufficiently widespread as occasionally to be a nuisance. It may be being replaced now by a similar fallacy in connnection with mastery learning that seems to center on 80%. One often finds statements that mastery will be demonstrated by satisfactory performance on 80% of the objectives, or performance of each objective 80% of the time, as though there were something especially significant about 80%. Careful study would probably indicate that other levels of performance are quite reasonable, but that as the level demanded is raised, disproportionately large amounts of instruction and practice time are required to reach the required levels. Somewhere there has to be a compromise between the degree of perfection to be required and the amount of time to be consumed on a particular learning task. One would want his parachute packer to reach a criterion of 100% mastery on all trials, no matter how long it took him to reach that criterion, but for some other tasks one would be willing to settle for much less. Discussions of the relationship between level of standards, amount of time to be spent on reaching that level, and importance of the task are almost nonexistent in the literature of grading and marking.

Fallacy C: Grades Are Inherently Unreliable

A statement often found in textbooks of previous decades is that grades are unreliable. These statements are probably based on the studies of disagreements among graders of the same paper that we have mentioned earlier. However, it is not true that grades are inherently unreliable. It is only true that some common practices may result in unreliable grades.

Grades don't need to be based on single papers judged in a global way by a single rater or judge. That is the kind of material that results in unreliability. However, if several papers were collected from each pupil, and if they were graded independently by different competent teachers, and if the average of those grades was used as the evaluation of the pupil, there is abundant evidence to indicate that the evaluation would have a substantial degree of reliability. Thus, grades are not *inherently* unreliable. In fact, if grades are based on objective test scores, and if there are a number of tests with a number of well-written items, and if these tests results are combined into a grade by an objective procedure, then the resulting set of grades will probably be slightly more reliable than the most reliable of the tests. And that may be reliable, indeed.

To go further, if grades are averaged across courses, even though the grades in the individual courses may not be very reliable due to faulty grading practices, the average over a number of courses may again be quite reliable. After all, a grade average is almost always based on a number of observations by relatively independent judges. The fact that such averages are, indeed, reliable is illustrated by their regularly being the best predictors of future grade averages. They almost always will predict future grades better than the most reliable tests that can be conveniently used, as is witnessed by years of research on predicting first-year grades in college from high school average grades and admissions tests scores. So it is fallacious to damn grades as being, by their nature, unreliable.

Fallacy D: The Normal Curve Is a Fundamental Concept in Grading

The fallacy that is prevalent here is that there is a correct percent of various levels of grades "under the normal curve." Measurement specialists are often asked by teachers and administrators what is the correct percent of A's under the normal curve. That is a meaningless question, as you know by now. There is no theoretical, mathematical, or empirical evidence to indicate that the normal curve has anything to do with grading. Some curve shape other than the normal curve could as easily be invoked. Any decision about the percents of any levels of grades is fundamentally arbitrary, though hopefully based on good judgment tempered by experience.

Now, sometimes one decides to use the normal curve in thinking about grading because it is a useful and helpful model. It makes some kinds of manipulations easier or more reasonable. In the next chapter we will deal with one use of the normal curve in grading in which it is helpful as a model. But the choice there of using the normal curve was arbitrary, as it always is in grading situations.

Remember, if anyone asks you questions like what is the correct percentage of A's or F's under the normal curve or whether there should be more A's than F's or whether a particular letter grade should be a standard deviation wide or only half a standard deviation wide or whether there should be more high grades for young children than for high school students, or in remedial than regular classes — if they ask any such questions they are either asking simply for an opinion, or they are ignorant of the fact that such questions cannot be answered in terms of what "should" be. Nothing about the normal curve will help tell them what should be because its use in grading, if it is used at all, is arbitrary, not based on a sound logical or empirical relationship.

Fallacy E: Gaps in Distributions Indicate Divisions between Grades

The last of our common fallacies occurs as an attempt to find another reed to lean on when the normal curve has been taken away. The idea in this fallacy is that students of different levels of achievement tend to group themselves automatically into clusters, and that these clusters show up in test scores. By placing the divisions between grades, such as A, B, and C, at the naturally occurring divisions between clusters of scores, then, one has fallaciously graded according to the natural divisions of quality.

As an example, consider figure 17-1. It depicts a hypothetical situation in which the scores for a 40-item test taken by 30 pupils are represented. A teacher who attempted to solve her problem of which grades are A's, B's, etc. might be tempted to decide that the top three scores should be given A's, the next seven should be given B's, the next eleven C's, the next six D's, and the last three F's. She would be making her divisions at the convenient places in the distribution where the frequencies were zero, e.g., scores of 37, 33, 28, and 23. This is sometimes called grading on the basis of *gaps in the distribution* of scores.

This is a fallacy because those gaps in distributions are purely accidental. There is no reason to presume that a clustering of students into levels of A, B, C, D, and F, or any other set of marks, occurs. No one provides those gaps. They are happenstances. In fact, no measurement specialist of superb qualifications could use the material from classroom tests built by teachers to produce such gaps. To produce deliberately a gap in a distribution where an expert wants it requires large numbers

Figure 17–1

*Example of Use of Gaps in
Distribution for Grading*

Scores	Frequencies
40	
39	1
38	2
37	
36	2
35	3
34	2
33	
32	4
31	4
30	2
29	1
28	
27	1
26	2
25	1
24	2
23	
22	1
21	2
	30　　Total

of highly intercorrelated test items, all of precisely specified difficulty level. In educational testing of any kind this is nearly an impossible demand. In achievement testing, where the difficulty levels of items depend heavily on exactly what the teacher has taught, and how and when it was taught, the production of gaps at specified places is impossible. So to set the standards for various levels of grades on such whimsy is a fallacy.

Now, it should be noted, however, that if a gap in a distribution occurs near the place where a teacher on other bases thinks a division between marks should occur, there is an advantage in using the gap as the dividing point. If the gap is where the division is made, there is no one to argue that if he had only had one more point he would have gotten a higher grade. It is nice to avoid such arguments. The student who sees that one more point would have raised his grade, and who notices that he was the only student at that score, so it would not change things very much to give him a higher grade, can have a lot of appeal to the teacher who really has no firm idea of why she set her standards the way she did. It is hard to turn down such arguments, but they always lead to lowered standards. It is more *convenient* to use the points in the distribution of scores where there are fewest scores — the gaps — as the divisions between marks, than to use other points and deal with students' appeals. But this is an argument of convenience, not an argument that there is something educationally and statistically sound underlying such choices of division points.

18

Useful Technical Practices in Grading

Objectives

Careful study of this chapter should enable you to:

1. Describe appropriate procedures to convert measurements to any numerical scale you desire;
2. Apply appropriate procedures to convert measurements to any numerical scale you desire:
   a. Calculate the mean of a set of measurements;
   b. Estimate the standard deviation of a set of measurements;
   c. Write and explain the conversion equation;
   d. Solve problems involving converting from one scale to another;
3. Describe appropriate procedures to combine measurements soundly into totals with the effective weighting you desire;
4. Apply appropriate procedures to combine measurements soundly into totals with the effective weighting you desire:
   a. Equalize the standard deviations;
   b. Apply the desired weights;
   c. Combine the weighted scores;
   d. Remember feasible alternative procedures;
5. Describe appropriate procedures to adjust grades for differences in aptitude of different groups;
6. Apply appropriate procedures to adjust grades for differences in aptitude of different groups:
   a. Determine the ability level of the group;
   b. Estimate the mean of the total group;
   c. Set the minimum score for each grade, A through D.

Some Problems in Grading

When a teacher has determined the basis on which she is going to give grades, has adopted a set of marks and a reporting form, has alerted herself to the common phenomena in grading and the common fallacies, she still has some problems in giving grades the way she wants to. Three of those problems are the following. First, she will usually have a set of numbers, such as sums of scores in different tests for each student, that she must convert to the scale of the set of marks she has adopted. She wants to make the scale conversion so that the students stay in the same order and the same relative distances apart. Below we will describe a technical procedure to accomplish this. The same procedure could be used to convert grades from a percent scale to a 4, 3, 2, 1, 0 scale or to a 15-point scale or to any scale she chooses.

A second problem she faces is combining different elements or observations of a student into a single score soundly. The problem enters when the teacher thinks that some elements or observations are more important than others. For example, she may think the final exam is more important than the quizzes, but a project's importance lies between those two. How does she make the total score that she converts to a grade reflect those unequal weights? It is not as simple, usually, as just adding the scores together. It is not even as simple as just multiplying the final exam scores by 3, the project by 2, and leaving the quiz scores unchanged as the three parts are added together. We will learn here a procedure for insuring that the various elements do, indeed, get the effective weights that the teacher desires.

The third problem is to be sure that a procedure such as homogeneous ability grouping does not distort the grading scale to such a degree that the grades lose much of their meaning. Somehow grades must be given to different groups of students so that the grading standards do not fluctuate entirely with the talent of the students. Otherwise no audience for the grades can figure out what they mean, and the audiences are likely to reach the conclusion that grades are meaningless. You will learn here a relatively simple procedure that will assist with maintaining standards.

Converting Scores from One Scale to Another

When you consider the problem of taking a set of scores that might come from adding together each student's results from three or four tests and putting them on a 100-point scale, perhaps for grading purposes, at first glance it may seem to be a trivial problem. You might be tempted to convert each score to a percent of the total score, for instance. But if the 100-point scale is to be one on which the average performance is represented by the number 75, which is sometimes specified, the problem is no longer trivial. The average of all the percentage scores on the tests may not be 75. Then what do you do so that the highest score is 100, but the average is 75? The solution to that problem is not obvious. However, the problem can be handled easily with a few tools that we will now develop.

THE MEAN OR AVERAGE

First, we need the concept of the mean or average, and we need to be sure that everyone understands the same thing by that term. It is simply the result of summing all the scores in a group of scores and dividing that sum by the total number of scores. Thus the mean of the scores 46, 62, 38, and 54 is 50. That is obtained by adding $46 + 62 + 38 + 54$ to the sum of 200. That sum is divided by 4, because there were four scores, and the quotient is 50. There is nothing really new about that idea. We need it in order to be able to convert to a new scale in which someone has told us what the mean is to be.

The second idea we need may be newer. It concerns the spread of numbers in a scale. If we had added together each student's scores on three tests and had to convert the results to a scale in which the mean was 75 and the highest score was 100, we might have all of the students' sums clustered closely together. Suppose all of their scores when converted to percentages ranged between 80% correct and 90% correct. We could find the mean percent correct, perhaps 85%, and change every score of 85% to a score of 75 in order to get the prescribed mean on the new scale, but how do we arrange so that a percent score of 90 becomes a score on the new scale of 100, which is prescribed for the highest score, and so that the other scores are spaced properly in between? To do that effectively we have to have a useful way to represent the spread of scores. The most useful representation is a statistic called the standard deviation, and next we will learn how to estimate it.

THE STANDARD DEVIATION

Standard Deviation is an impressive name for a simple concept. It is the name for a useful way of describing the spread of values in a set of measurements such as scores. You will see how it is useful in a minute. First, let us see how we estimate it.

We mentioned earlier that a set of scores in one of our examples ranged between 80% correct and 90%. We use that range of scores, which is 10% in this example, to estimate the standard deviation. For our purposes we will estimate standard deviations by finding the range, i.e., subtracting the lowest score from the highest score, and dividing that range by a number, which we will label k. The size of k depends on how many scores we are dealing with. For classroom-sized groups of about 30 scores, we divide the range by the number 4 to estimate the standard deviation. For very large groups, like 400-500, we would divide by 6. For about 100, we would divide by 5. The correct divisors for various sized groups appear in table 18-1.

Table 18–1
Divisors for Estimating Standard Deviation from Range

Number	k
4	2
9	3
27	4
98	5
444	6

You should memorize that table to avoid having to look up the values in it. Whatever you do, be sure that you remember two of the k values, 4 for classroom-sized groups and 6 for very large groups.

Sometimes you will have to deal with groups of scores that fall between the sizes of 4, 9, 27, and 444. Two procedures are useful in handling such cases. One is simply to use the k value for the number closest to the number you have. If you have 7 scores for which you wish to estimate the standard deviation, you should use the k for 9 since 7 is closer to 9 than to 4. The other procedure that can be used is to divide by an intermediate fractional k value. For seven scores you might divide by a k of 2.5 or 2.6. That will give you a little better estimate of the standard deviation, but it will require a more difficult division. Since we are only estimating anyway, it may not be worthwhile. Obviously, there is a more complicated formula for computing standard deviations, one that will give you the values we are only estimating. It is to be found in statistics textbooks. However, it is sufficiently complicated that it is unlikely that any but the most devoted teacher would ever use it, so we will not present it here.

Now that we know how to estimate the standard deviation, how do we use it and the mean to solve our problem of converting scores from one scale to another? Here is the beauty of it. We use a simple formula to do the job on each score, and the result should be just about what we want. The formula is

$$\text{New Score} = \frac{\text{New s.d.}}{\text{Old s.d.}} (\text{Deviation}) + \text{New Mean}$$

In that formula, *s.d.* stands for standard deviation, and *Deviation* means how much the score differs (deviates) from the mean of the old set of scores that is being converted.

Let's look at an example to clarify the use of the formula. Suppose we have these scores that turn out to range between 80% correct and 90% correct, and we are supposed to convert them to a scale on which the mean is 75 and the highest score is 100. Let's say that there are 30 scores, as there might be in a common-sized classroom. The first step would be to compute the mean of these scores by adding them all together, and dividing by 30, the number of scores. Earlier we used 85% as the mean, and let's understand that we obtained that value by dividing the sum of all the scores by the number of scores.

The second step is to estimate the standard deviation. We found the range to be 10%, i.e., 90% − 80%. We divide that range by 4, since we have 30 pupils, and the appropriate k for 30 is 4. The standard deviation for our old distribution of scores, then, is $10/4 = 2.5$.

Now we want the new mean to be 75, and the spread to reach as high as 100. If the mean is in the middle, as it most often will be, then the spread will go as far below the mean as above it. It is asked to go 25 points above $(100 - 75)$, so we might expect it also to go 25 points below. The range on the new scale is then asked to be a total of 50 points. To estimate the new s.d., we divide 50 by 4, parallel to the operation we used to estimate the s.d. on the old scale, and find the new s.d. to be 12.5.

Now we can put most of our formula together. We have the old mean, the new mean, the old s.d., and the new s.d. We also need for every pupil the difference between his score and the old mean. For instance if Susie got 87% correct, her deviation is 2, i.e., 87% − 85% = 2. If Bill got 81% correct, his deviation is −4, 81% − 85% resulting in negative 4. It is important to pay attention to the positive and negative signs at this step. Anyone scoring below the mean deviates negatively, and anyone scoring above the mean deviates in the positive direction.

Let's put Susie's scores into the formula .

$$\text{New score} = \frac{12.5}{2.5} \, (2) \, + \, 75.$$

To solve that, divide 12.5 by 2.5, resulting in 5. Multiply 5 times 2, resulting in 10. Add 10 to 75, and Susie's score on the new scale is 85. Similarly, Bill's score on the new scale would be 5 times −4, which equals −20. Added to 75, that equals 55, which is Bill's new score. (Remember that adding a negative number to a positive number is the same as subtracting that number from the positive number, and multiplying a positive number by a negative number always yields a negative number.)

If we knew who had scored 90% we would find her score on the new scale. It would be 5 times (90 − 85) + 75, which would be 5 times 5, or 25, plus 75, equaling 100. We see that the top of our new scale does go to 100, just as it was required to do.

To develop the skill of converting scores from one scale to another fluently, you should practice on a variety of problems. You can make up problems of your own and then have one of your classmates check your work. (Notice, scores don't have to be in percents to use this procedure. They can be any kinds of numbers.) One important thing you may not have noted is that to use this technique, it is not enough simply to describe the new scale by the highest possible score, e.g., by saying that A is 4.0. You need to know what the mean is, and the mean on a 4.0 scale is often not really 2.0. It is more often 2.3 or 2.5, since most teachers are lenient. Sometimes you may have to make an intelligent guess as to what the mean on the new scale should be, or you may have to try out one or two different means for the new scale to get results that satisfy the demands of the situation.[1]

Combining Scores with Weights

When a teacher tells her class that she is going to give grades on the report card in a subject according to how well the students perform on several tasks, and that she is going to give more importance to some tasks than to others, the students can reasonably expect that to score high on the more important tasks will have greater effect on their grades than to score high on less important tasks. It might seem that one could give twice the weight to the final exam as to the score on a project, or give twice the weight to performance in playing badminton as to knowledge of the rules and history of badminton, by simply multiplying by two the final exam or the rating of performance in playing. But that is not necessarily true.

The key element in weighting variables that are to be combined is the spread of their values, and you have just learned that this spread is measured by a statistic called the standard deviation. You must account for the standard deviations of the

---

[1]Programmed instruction is provided in *Exercises in Classroom Measurement* to develop competence in converting scores from one scale to another. It is number 23, entitled "Converting Scores to a Scale with a Desired Mean and Standard Deviation."

variables to be combined if you are going to give the different variables the weights that are specified. (Notice, the means of the variables are irrelevant when it comes to weighting. The variable with the largest mean does not necessarily have the largest weight. In fact, if its standard deviation is the smallest, it will have the smallest weight when the scores are simply added together.)

Let us take the badminton grade as an example. Suppose that the teacher has a class of 12 students for badminton. She teaches them the techniques of playing the game and also teaches them something of the rules, the history, and the relationships among badminton, tennis, and squash. She has them perform certain basic strokes, such as the serve, and has them play against her, and she rates them on those performances. She also has a 40-item multiple-choice test on rules, history, and relationships with other games. Let's suppose that the scores on the two measures, performance and knowledge, are as in figure 18-1.

Figure 18–1
Scores on Knowledge and Performance —
Unweighted

Pupil	Performance	Knowledge
A	7	32
B	8	21
C	8	24
D	6	35
E	6	37
F	7	27
G	6	36
H	8	25
I	7	31
J	7	33
K	7	26
L	7	32

If the teacher has told these students that the Performance score is going to have twice the weight of the Knowledge score, then the highest scoring students on the Performance test (B, C, and H) should expect to get the highest grades in the course — or at least not the lowest grades in the course. And the lowest scoring students on Performance (D, E, and G) should not expect to get the highest grades in the course. Let's see what happens if the teacher simply multiplies the Performance scores by two and adds them to the Knowledge scores (see figure 18-2).

As you can see, B and C, who got high scores on the performance test have the lowest scores on the composite, and H is among the lowest. However, E and G, who got low scores on the performance test, get high scores on the composite, and D is tied for being next to them at the top. This is not at all what was promised when the teacher said she would weight performance more heavily than knowledge. Instead of the best performers' getting the highest composite scores, the students who had the highest knowledge scores, D, E, and G, got the highest composite scores. The error that produced this result is that the teacher failed to take into consideration the standard deviations of the initial scores before she weighted them and combined them. Let us see what she should have done.

Figure 18–2
*Scores on Knowledge and Performance —
Incorrect Weighting*

Performance		Knowledge	2P + K
A	7 × 2 = 14	32	46
B	8 × 2 = 16	21	37
C	8 × 2 = 16	24	40
D	6 × 2 = 12	35	47
E	6 × 2 = 12	37	49
F	7 × 2 = 14	27	41
G	6 × 2 = 12	36	48
H	8 × 2 = 16	25	41
I	7 × 2 = 14	31	45
J	7 × 2 = 14	33	47
K	7 × 2 = 14	26	40
L	7 × 2 = 14	32	46

To combine scores correctly with specified weights, the first step is to estimate the standard deviations of the scores that are to be combined. We have learned how to do this. We find the range of each score and divide it by a k value according to the number of scores. In this case we have 12 scores so we can use the k value of 3. (To be more precise, we could use 3.2 for k, but it is hardly worth the trouble.) The range of the performance scores is $(8 - 6)$ or 2, and the range of the knowledge scores is $(37 - 21)$ or 16. Dividing each of those by 3 we get the standard deviation of the performance scores as ⅔ and the standard deviation of the knowledge scores as 5⅓. Now to equalize the effects of the standard deviations, we should multiply the performance scores by a number that will make their standard deviation equal to that of the knowledge scores. Multiplying ⅔ by 8 makes the standard deviations equal, i.e., 5⅓ is the same as 16/3, and ⅔ times 8 is also 16/3. Technically, what we have done is to choose the largest standard deviation as the one to which we were going to equalize the other, and we have divided the largest by the smallest to find our multiplier, i.e., 5⅓ ÷ ⅔ = 8. (Remember, to divide fractions, you invert the divisor and proceed as in multiplication. Thus, we first convert 5⅓ to 16/3, by multiplying 3 × 5 and adding 1. That is, 5 is the same as 15 thirds, and we had 5 plus one more third, making 16 thirds. Inverting 2/3 gives 3/2. Now 16/3 × 3/2 is easily solved because the 3's cancel out, leaving 16/2, which is 8.)

To achieve the weights the teacher specified, we have to do some more adjusting. Multiplying the performance scores by 8 equalizes the standard deviations and gives the two sets of scores equal weights. But the teacher said she wanted to give performance twice the weight of knowledge. So she has to multiply the equalized performance scores by 2, again. That is the same as multiplying the adjustment factor of 8 × 2, for a total adjustment of 16. So to get what the teacher wants in this case, she should multiply the performance scores by 16 and add them to the knowledge scores. Let's see whether that results in the high scorers on performance receiving the highest total scores (see figure 18-3).

Now, B, C, and H who had the highest performance scores do, indeed, have the highest composite scores, and D, E, and G do have the lowest composite scores. It won't always turn out that the lowest two or three on the variable given the greatest

Figure 18–3

*Scores on Knowledge and Performance —
Correct Weighting*

	Performance × 16	Knowledge	Composite
A	7 × 16 = 112	32	144
B	8 × 16 = 128	21	149
C	8 × 16 = 128	24	152
D	6 × 16 = 96	35	131
E	6 × 16 = 96	37	133
F	7 × 16 = 112	27	139
G	6 × 16 = 96	36	132
H	8 × 16 = 128	25	153
I	7 × 16 = 112	31	143
J	7 × 16 = 112	33	145
K	7 × 16 = 112	26	138
L	7 × 16 = 112	32	144

weight are lowest on the composite, and vice versa. But if the effective weights are what the teacher tells the students they will be, the tendency should be that way, and certainly not the opposite of that way, which is what we observed when we did not take s.d.'s into account.[2]

When a teacher is first introduced to the operations that are required to give the elements to be included in a grade the weights she says they will have, she is often surprised. It seems like a lot of work — certainly more work than she meant to get into. She may be tempted to ignore all these technical refinements, and just go ahead and simply multiply by two in order to give twice the weight, ignoring standard deviations. But that is dishonest. Even if the pupils don't realize that they are being mistreated, it is still dishonest. It is not possible to advocate or support or defend dishonesty in education, whether we are dealing with pupils, parents, or others. So the teacher with integrity cannot take the easy way out.

She can do one of three things. She can just not say anything about the weights she will give the various components, and let them fall as they will. That is a rather ignorant way to proceed, but ignorance is slightly more defensible or less reprehensible than dishonesty. Or she can use a weighting procedure that takes standard deviations into account. (And really, proper weighting takes even more into account, but the additional refinements don't usually make the huge differences that neglecting s.d.'s makes.) Or she can use another available procedure. That is to make her measures that are to receive greater weight proportionately longer.

At least with tests, the standard deviation often seems to be nearly proportional to test length, so a test that is twice as long will often have about twice as large a standard deviation. One test can be given two or three times more weight than another, to a reasonable approximation, by having two or three times as many items in it as in the other test. That does not always work out, but the teacher can check on it by estimating the standard deviations and comparing them. That technique is not much help when combining a test with a rating of a speech, a drawing,

---

[2]Programmed instruction is provided in *Exercises in Classroom Measurement* to develop fluency in combining scores with specified weights. It is number 24, entitled "Combining Scores with Weights."

or some other product, because the s.d.'s of the scores from ratings and other nontest evaluations may behave quite differently with lengthening.

Before concluding this discussion, we should point out one more thing. The scale that results from combining scores with weights is a totally arbitrary scale, and it has no meaning of its own. In our example, for instance, the scores came out ranging from 131 to 153. If a teacher wanted to convert them to a scale with a mean of 2.5 and a standard deviation of 0.7, like the common 4.0 = A scale, she would use the procedures we have already learned to do that. For example, she would estimate the standard deviation of the composite scores by the usual method. That is, $153 - 131 = 22$. That divided by 3 (since we have 12 pupils) is $7\frac{1}{3}$. She would compute the mean by adding all the scores and dividing by 12. The result of doing that is 141.9, or approximately 142. Now to convert scales we use the formula

$$\text{New score} = \frac{0.7}{7.3}(\text{Deviation}) + 2.5$$

or

$$\text{New score} = 0.10\ (\text{Deviation}) + 2.5$$

Converting the highest score, 153, which deviates $+11$ from the mean of 142, we get

$$\text{New score} = .10\ (+11) + 2.5 \text{ or } 1.1 + 2.5 = 3.6$$

If we really wanted the highest composite score to get a value on the new scale of 4.0, and that was more important than having a new scale with a s.d. of 0.7, we could enlarge the s.d. of the new scale. The reader should verify that if we let its s.d. be 0.9 instead of 0.7, we would get a score on the new scale of about 3.9 for a composite of 153.

Adjusting Grades for Differences in Aptitude Levels

As we noted much earlier, in chapter 14 when we discussed grading on the basis of comparisons with other students, it is sometimes difficult for a teacher to maintain the meaningfulness of her grades if the level of ability of the students she teaches fluctuates markedly. When she happens to get a class which is unusually dull, how can she determine how much lower grades she should give them, on the average, so that her standards will not lower just because the class is not very sharp? On the other hand, when an unusually bright group goes through, how can she determine just how high her grades can be to reflect properly their attainment, without overdoing it or not giving them enough credit? For that matter, if she teaches multiple sections of the same course, and if the students have been grouped into different levels of ability, how can she avoid giving A's in the low ability group for work that would not be worth even B's or C's if it was performed by the high group? The teacher needs help with this problem if her grades are going to communicate meaningfully about academic achievement.

There are several procedures that can be used. Sometimes the teacher can just use the same examinations for the various groups, and base grades on them, using the same cutoff scores regardless of the group. However, there is always the possibility that some students will obtain an advantage by finding out what the questions on the exam are. So this is not a very desirable procedure.

The teacher could build equivalent forms of her examinations, so that approximately the same score would result for each student no matter which exam he took. Then different, but equivalent, examinations could be used during different terms. That, however, requires a lot of sophisticated examination building. Complicated procedures for equating the scores from different tests or sets of scores can be used, but they usually are so cumbersome as to require a computer for any typical number of students.

A procedure that is feasible for use by the classroom teacher gives satisfactory results in many school situations. This procedure assumes that the marking system in use is one in which an A is represented by the number 4.0 and an F by zero. It makes no assumption about the width of the band of scores given to each grade, though as you are learning how to use it we will think in terms of having about 5% of A's and F's, 20% of B's and D's, and 50% C's.

The procedure starts from the notion that if all the students involved in the course were to be combined across all the homogeneous groups, or across all the years that present some bright groups and some dull groups, the resulting total group would have a distribution of scores that was statistically *normal*. That is a reasonable starting point since many things that are determined by a large number of factors, such as people's heights, weights, and test scores, are often approximately normally distributed.

The procedure assumes that the teacher wants a set of grades such that there are more high grades in the able group and fewer high grades in the low ability group, and correspondingly, there are fewer low grades in the high ability group, and so on. If the teacher does not think that is the way things should be, she should not use this method. However, if grades are to communicate meaningfully about academic achievement, it does seem reasonable to suppose that low ability groups are highly likely to have, on the average, lower achievement than higher ability groups given the same amount of study time and about the same teaching procedures. A reflection of that belief is what the method is designed to produce in a set of grades.

The method proceeds by using the data from the subgroup of students that is available to estimate the mean score for the total group; that is, the mean for all the sections that might be taught, or all the classes that might take the course over the years. Then minimum score levels are set for the various grades providing for the proportions of each letter grade one would expect in the total group. Finally grades are assigned based on those minimum score levels.

To go through the procedure in more detail, the first step is to find for the available group of students their average stanine score on a standardized ability test that all of them have taken. For instance, if all of the children in a grade have taken the *Otis-Lennon Mental Ability Test*, their mean score in terms of nationally normed stanine scores for their grade is obtained. This is a measure of the average aptitude of the group. If all of them have not taken the same test, or if scores for nearly all of them cannot be found, one cannot estimate the average ability of the group this way. (Notice, you cannot soundly average stanine scores from different ability tests for this purpose.) What you can do if suitable test scores are not available is use average grades in previous courses or years as an estimator. In this case you would calculate the mean grade-point average.

When the indicator of the average aptitude of the subgroup has been calculated, one then estimates from it and table 18-2 what part of the total group is represented by the subgroup. The estimate is in terms of fifths of the total group. In table 18-2 it can be seen that if the mean stanine is about 7.8, we estimate we are dealing with the upper one-fifth or 20% of the total group. If the mean grade-point average in prior work is only about 1.5, or D+, we estimate we are dealing with a subgroup that is in the next to the bottom fifth, between the twentieth and fortieth percentiles of the total group's disribuion.

Table 18–2

Determining the Ability Level of Students in a Subgroup

Subgroup Level	Mean GPA	Mean Stanine
Upper Fifth	3.4	7.8
Second Fifth	2.5	6.0
Middle Fifth	2.0	5.0
Fourth Fifth	1.5	4.0
Lower Fifth	.6	2.2

The next thing we need to do is to calculate the mean and estimate the standard deviation of our subgroup on the variable on the basis of which grades are to be given. It is likely that the variable will be a combination of scores with weights as described in the previous section.

Then we use the mean of our group and its standard deviation to estimate what the mean of the total group would be if we had similar data on everyone. We do this using the information in table 18-3. Those entries show by how much and in what direction we should modify our subgroup's mean to estimate the total group's mean. For example, if we find that our group appears to be the upper 20% of the total group, we subtract six-tenths of a standard deviation from our group's mean to estimate the total group's mean.

Table 18–3

Estimating the Mean of the Total Group

Ability Level	Add to the Subgroup Mean
Upper Fifth	− .6 s.d.
Second Fifth	− .3 s.d.
Middle Fifth	no change
Fourth Fifth	+ .3 s.d.
Lower Fifth	+ .6 s.d.

Now we can set the minimum score levels for each letter grade in terms of the total group, as though they were all here. Our group will get more of the higher grades and fewer of the lower grades if its mean is above the total group's mean, and vice versa. If we are willing to assume that the grades for the total group would be normally distributed, we can set the cutoff scores based on the normal curve. We simply determine what proportion of the grades should be A's, for instance, and locate the distance from the mean on a normal curve that cuts off that proportion of the curve. Above a point 1.7 standard deviations from the mean fall 5% of the cases in a normal curve, so the cutoff for A's is the score 1.7 s.d.'s from the mean in the positive direction. If we set the cutoff point for B's at plus 0.7 s.d.'s, 20% of total group would get B's. Setting the lower cutoff for C's at minus 0.7 s.d.'s from the mean allows for 50% of the total group to get C's, and a lower cutoff for D's at minus 1.7 s.d.'s provides for 20% D's and 5% F's. If you want some other percentages of grades, the normal curve table found in any statistics textbook can be used to set the cutoffs you want. (You may need the help of someone who has taken a course in statistics to use the normal curve table to do this properly, but it is simple once the operation of the table is understood.)

Now your cutoff points have been determined based on the total group's estimated performance. For your group you will use the same cutoff points, but if your group is expected in general to be above the mean, more than the total group's percentage of grades will be A's, and fewer will be F's, which is what you desired when you used this procedure to adjust the distribution of grades for aptitude level.

Let's do an example for clarification. Suppose that we have a class of 30 students in World History. We think they are an above average group, but to be sure we look up their stanine scores on the standardized ability test that our school has every student take. We average these scores, and suppose that we find that the average stanine for these 30 pupils is 6.5. We look that value up in table 18-2 and find that we could reasonably think of these students as being like the second fifth from the top of a complete group of students at this grade level. They are above average, clearly. Now we find the mean and standard deviation of our group, by methods we have already learned. Suppose that the mean score turns out to be 24, and the standard deviation is estimated to be 4. (This might occur, for instance, if the range of scores were 16. We would divide by 4, since the number of students was 30, and the result would be a standard deviation of 4.)

Next we estimate the mean of the total group, by subtracting from the mean of 24 for our group the value 0.3 s.d., as found in the second line of table 18-3. Three-tenths of 4 is 1.2, so we estimate the total group's mean to be 22.8.

Using the percents of A's, B's, C's, D's, and F's that we described earlier, we set the cutoff point for each letter grade. The lowest score to receive a grade of A is 1.7 s.d. above the total group mean of 22.8; that is, a score of $22.8 + (1.7 \times 4)$. This is $22.8 + 6.8$, which is a score of 29.6. Since we don't have fractional scores, the lowest actual score to receive an A is 30. The lowest score to receive a grade of B is 0.7 s.d. above the total group mean. This is $22.8 + (.7 \times 4)$ which equals 25.6. Again, since there are no fractional scores, the lowest score that actually gets a grade of B is 26. Working the same way, the lowest score to get a grade of C is $22.8 - (.7 \times 4)$ or 20, the lowest to receive a grade of D is 16, and any score below 16 gets a grade of F.

We went through this procedure in order to maintain somewhat consistent grading standards. We found that this group of students was above average and deserved slightly higher average grades, presuming that they would achieve more highly than average due to the typical positive correlation between aptitude and achievement. They got higher average grades from this procedure because their mean was higher than the estimated mean for the total group. For practice and to convince yourself that a group of lower aptitude would actually receive fewer A's, redo the same problem but assume that the group was below average—had an average stanine on the aptitude measure of only 3.0.[3]

Using such a procedure with successive groups of students, or across groups of homogeneously grouped students, will certainly help to make grades communicate more effectively the academic achievement of students. In high schools in which different students take different subjects, use of such a procedure could serve to make more meaningful grades in different areas. A procedure such as this deserves much wider application than it has had if we really want grades to serve their various audiences by reflecting soundly what students know and can do with things they learn in school.

---

[3]Programmed instruction is provided in *Exercises in Classroom Measurement* to develop competence in making these adjustments to grades. It is number 25, entitled "Adjusting Grades for Differences in Aptitude Levels."

19

Faulty Grading Practices

Objective

Study of this chapter will enable you to:

List at least eight faulty grading practices, giving examples to clarify each faulty procedure and why it is judged to be unsound.

Common Practices That Have No Worthwhile Advantages

In previous chapters you have learned about several faulty grading practices, such as using gaps in distributions to set standards and relying on the normal curve to determine your standards. You have also learned about the advantages and disadvantages of grading on various bases. There are also a number of errors commonly made in grading that really have no advantages in terms of making grades useful or meaningful as communications. These faulty practices are based on three different kinds of confusion, (1) confusion about the role of controlled observation in grading, (2) confusion about the objectives of the instruction, and (3) confusion about the role and effect of grading.

Confusion about the Role of Controlled Observation

It is probably time that we specified one of the secrets to good grading, to grading that is consistent, i.e., reliable, and has potential for validity, i.e., for being highly correlated with the students' actual achievements. The secret is that reliable and valid grades must be based on large numbers of controlled observations. By controlled observations we mean examinations of the students' performances that are done carefully so that we know what they mean. We want to be able to compare soundly between students in terms of those observations. And we want to be able to compare students this year with students of other years on the basis of those observations. An example of sound observations would be having each student walk at normal speed down a six feet long 2″ x 4″ board and counting how often each student lost his balance and touched the ground. Another controlled observation would be to have each student give a two-minute speech he had prepared and to count the number of times he said "uh." Obviously, the usual teacher-made or standardized test is a highly controlled form of observation. In fact, it is such a good example that for the rest of this chapter we will speak of tests instead of controlled observations. But if yours is a subject that uses kinds of controlled observations other than tests extensively, you can make an appropriate substitution for the word test.

There are about six different common ways that grading goes wrong due to confusion about the proper role of tests in grading. We will discuss each of them briefly.

USING CARELESSLY BUILT TESTS

Some teachers have not developed professional competency in building tests. They carelessly slap together a few items just before a quiz or examination, and they give grades based partly or wholly on such tests, without ever considering the quality of the individual items, the reliability of the test, and so on. This is not conducive to making grades meaningful.

Carelessly built tests may only conceal what is truly grading on essentially random behavior. Controlled observations are observations whose characteristics have been studied and perfected so that we have a good understanding of how they behave and what they mean. An airplane pilot would not be willing to look at the size of a toy balloon to tell him how high he was above the ground. He knows that the balloon gets bigger as his plane gets higher, but he does not know how many feet produce what increase in size and how to translate that into feet above the ground. Instead he relies on a carefully calibrated and checked altimeter. It works on the same principle as the balloon but provides a *controlled* observation. The teacher who relies on casually built and unchecked tests is like the pilot who looks at a toy balloon to see whether he should cut his motor because his plane is on the ground!

USING NO TESTS OR CONTROLLED OBSERVATIONS

Worse than using poorly built and unchecked tests is the practice of grading with no tests or controlled observations at all. While such a practice is more common in college than at lower levels, and most common in graduate school, it does not reflect even minimally good practice. Such grades are likely to be based on general impressions, glibness of speech, politeness, and other characteristics which may be totally unrelated, or even negatively related to achievement of the academic objectives of the instruction. Some form of controlled observation—tests, checklists, observation schedules, projects, and so forth—is essential to sound grading.

USING ONLY ONE TEST

Some teachers let their evaluations of students wait until everything else has been done. Then they find that they do not have time to build and give three or four carefully constructed tests or measures prior to assigning a grade. Many experts in instruction and curriculum design, however, would suggest that the first thing to do in planning instruction is to think about, and perhaps draft, the examinations for a course or unit — maybe even before the instruction is designed. That way the instruction can be designed to prepare students for the tests or exercises that represent the desired outcomes. At least, it is certainly not a sound practice to base grades on only one test. One long test, say a final examination, is better than one short test, but even a long test does not avoid the problem of a particular student's being indisposed on a particular day or the problem of a particular set of items working against an individual student. So the sound practice is to use several controlled observations of each student, properly combined, to determine a grade.

USING TOO MANY TESTS

The urge to evaluate carefully can be carried to the other extreme, that of giving so many tests that there is really little time left for instruction. Teachers have been known to obtain every available standardized test on their subject and give all of them to their students in the misguided belief that this would prepare them well in the subject. Other teachers test every day, at least with a brief quiz. That procedure is not without merit, but it tends to encroach heavily on time that might better be otherwise spent. Such testing is usually good for pacing the students, if they need help in keeping up, but it is not especially good for evaluation, partly because the quality of so many tests is hard to monitor. The use of repeated tests over every objective in a program designed for mastery learning is likely to involve a great deal of testing and will require elaborate procedures to maintain the quality of the tests and keep the records of student progress. Without careful expert planning and unusual financial and staff support, such an effort can become merely a faulty grading practice.

DESIGNING A COURSE TO FIT
AN AVAILABLE TEST

Occasionally a teacher may be tempted to try to solve her course planning and evaluation problems by letting someone else do it for her. She might, in such a case, choose a widely-used standardized achievement test in her subject, examine its items, and plan her course to cover the proper responses to those items. That would commonly be called *teaching to the test*. Or she might not be so flagrantly dependent on the decisions of someone else, and she might merely try to cover the same content that was included in the standardized test, not necessarily the answers to that test's specific questions. Neither of these procedures is sound. Teaching to the test is bad practice because the idea of those who constructed the test was to sample one or two of the many possible items in each of many aspects of the course to evaluate whether the student had learned a lot more than just the answer to those particular items. Teaching only the answers to the questions causes the test to give a false reading of the degree of achievement of the student and will, obviously, result in a loss of meaning in a grade based on such a test score.

Teaching to the objectives or content covered by a standardized test is also faulty. Constructors of standardized tests approach their problem of having tests widely appropriate for many schools across the country by making the tests very broad in coverage. They don't expect anyone to know all the answers or to have covered all the topics touched on by the test's items. That would be far too much to try to crowd into any one course. Having such wide coverage is necessary if the test is to sell to enough different schools to be profitable, but it makes it somewhat inappropriate for any one school or teacher.

The sound practice is for the teacher to design her course to fit the needs of the students, school, and community in which she is situated. Then, if she wants information from a standardized test, she should pick one that covers the same topics, as nearly as she can find among the available tests. But she should not alter her teaching or content, then, to fit the test she chooses. That is getting the cart before the horse— or the test before the course, one might say. Neither is effective.

CHANGING THE DIFFICULTY OF TESTS DURING THE COURSE

Controlled observations are used in grading to produce grades that communicate effectively about academic achievement. They only incidentally influence motivation. Some teachers are tempted to pervert the sound use of grades and tests to emphasize motivation at the expense of measurement. One way that is sometimes done is by manipulating the difficulty level of tests during a course. Sometimes the teacher may decide to give a really hard midterm examination or set of quizzes so that the students will be prepared for a much harder final examination than she really intends to use. Hopefully they then do unexpectedly well on the final. Other teachers may decide on equally valid grounds to give very easy midterms or quizzes so that the students have success experiences and remain interested, even though the final examination will be much harder when they get to it.

Both of these procedures are faulty in terms of sound grading. The sound procedure is to inform the students as well and truly as possible about the standards they are expected to meet. Ideally, then, the midterms or quizzes before the final should be representative samples from the same pool of items from which the examinations that influence grades will be drawn. Then there will be no surprises, either pleasant or unpleasant. This will be most likely to result in the soundest measures of academic achievement.

Confusion about Objectives of the Course

For grades and marks to communicate achievement, they must be kept free from distortion by other characteristics of the students. Sometimes teachers attempt to make the subject matter course marks perform functions such as building character in students, or modifying their personalities. Unless these aspects are specifically stated and recognized objectives of the course, and effort is made to provide instruction and experiences that will help students to reach these objectives, letting extraneous aspects influence grades will decrease their meaningfulness.

GRADING ON CHARACTER TRAITS

Although schools are interested in students developing sound character traits, such goals are not always specifically included and provided for in the instruction in subjects such as geography, spelling, arithmetic, and reading. When they are not specifically taught and stated as goals in such courses, they should not be allowed to alter the grades that represent academic competence. Thus it is faulty practice to lower a student's grade because he is often tardy or absent, because he turns in papers late, because his work is not neat, or because he seldom participates in class. If these things cause him to achieve less well than other students in the actual objectives of the course, they will also be reflected in the tests that determine grades. To introduce them again as punishment only distorts the meaning of the grades. It is just plain wrong then to deduct points from students' papers or projects because they are turned in late or to lower the grade for a paper by one letter grade because it is late or to give extra points for a project's being turned in early, or to let neatness of work result in higher grades than those of other students who have learned as much. There are teachers everywhere making this error, and it is little wonder that as a result they and everyone else complain about the lack of meaning of grades! Instead of influencing the course grade, such character traits should be reported separately in terms of grades or other reports on attendance, tardiness, neatness, etc.

GRADING ON EXTRA WORK

Another kind of confusion about the objectives of the instruction appears when the teacher arranges for students who are not doing well on the tests and other controlled observations to do an "extra project" in order to enhance their grades. Sometimes a student will ask if he can do an extra assignment to bring up an otherwise low grade. If such an assignment can be designed so that it will improve performance on the measures used to evaluate academic attainment, it is a sound kind of remediation. The result will be represented in his scores and needs no extra credit. However, if a student gets a higher grade merely because he has done extra work, but does not perform more satisfactorily on the usual measures as the result, then the meaning of the grade has been distorted. A grade should not ordinarily be designed to reflect amount of work done — it should reflect level of knowledge or skill developed. We saw earlier that grading on the basis of effort was not very satisfactory. That kind of grading should not be subtly reintroduced in the form of extra projects not directly designed to improve performance on the measures of the course objectives.

USING GRADES TO KEEP DISCIPLINE

It is necessary to keep discipline in a classroom. The attempts to learn of those who want to learn cannot be allowed to be frustrated by misbehavior of others. Sometimes the teacher is tempted to use the most potent weapon she can find in order to solve the discipline problem so that instruction and learning can take place. If she decides that the best weapon at her disposal is the students' grades, she will have distorted the meaning of grades from their primary function. They will no longer communicate effectively individual students' academic attainments. This cannot be accepted. It is a faulty grading practice. The discipline problem must be solved, but not at the expense of destroying communication with all of the audiences who depend on grades to reflect academic attainment. It is bad practice, then, to do such things as give zero or F to students who misbehave. (The concept of *zero for the day,* or a *red F,* a threat sometimes used in schools, is a faulty one. It should not be condoned. Nor should any similar idea of using grades as punishments or as weapons be permitted or suggested.)

Confusions about the Role and Effect of Grades

Grades are supposed to provide information. They are supposed to tell students, teachers, and parents about student strengths and weaknesses so that weaknesses can be overcome and so that students can emphasize and take advantage of their strengths. Other people, such as guidance counselors, employers, other teachers, and other schools, should also be able to trust grades as guides to helping or to using the talents of students. Two practices sometimes occur to impair the effectiveness of grades for their proper role of providing sound information and feedback.

AVOIDING DISCRIMINATION

Because some kind teachers realize that some students will find it painful to receive low grades, and other students may flaunt their success if given high grades, there is a temptation to give everyone the same grade. Avoiding discrimination between the different levels of accomplishment of different students would seem to circumvent the problem of students who are hurt by or complain about low grades. Occasionally a teacher will be tempted to give all C's, or in physical education to give C's to all but the students who are participating in athletics, or some similar practice. This is faulty grading, ordinarily, because it is most unusual for genuine evaluations of groups of students to find everyone uniformly mediocre. Avoiding discrimination by giving the same grade to everyone is really a dereliction of one of the teacher's professional responsibilities, unless sound observations do, indeed, indicate an amazing uniformity. If there are observable differences in levels of performance, the students deserve to know about them, and so do the other clienteles that make use of grade information.

PERFECTIONISM

Another form of failing to provide reasonable information results from the attitude that since no student knows all there is to know about a subject, no student deserves an A. This kind of nonsensical attitude is probably not often found below the college or graduate school level, but occasionally in such places as law schools teachers have been known to try to grade on whether a student knew all there was to know about a certain branch of the law. Of course, it would be impossible to verify that anyone did know all that there was to know about anything, so the uninformed professor feels justified in giving no A grades. After all, no one can prove that he deserved an A, and giving no A's makes it look like the professor has high standards. Clearly, any grade average that includes grades of that kind is going to be distorted downward, and thus is going to become less meaningful than it should be. That is faulty grading. By the same token, the argument that no student who attends could fail to learn anything at all, so there should be no F's, is just as faulty.

Now a recognition must be made of one form of grading that, if used, might result in no grades of certain levels, or even all grades of the same level. Suppose instruction is carefully developed with specific objectives, preset reasonable standards, and tests designed to evaluate mastery of those objectives at those standards. Then if all students master everything, a school may decide that such performance results in A grades for all the students. By the same token, if none reaches mastery, some other grade, even F, may symbolize that situation. That kind of arrangement is sometimes called *mastery learning,* or *criterion-referenced* learning, instruction, and testing.

Notice, however, that if the school defines the grade of C as average performance, and if everyone meets the standards, then logically it follows that everyone should get a grade of C, even though all have accomplished all that was required. Giving C's for master performances is going to be very confusing to the users of grades, and those kinds of grades cannot reasonably be averaged in with other grades, say those that indicate by an A the best performances in a group. Such combinations of differently conceived elements would be like trying to average the number of hours spent in class in one subject with the number of pages assigned in a text in another subject to indicate how much students were learning or studying. It simply does not make sense, even though both are expressed in numbers and obtained by counting. Once again we see that developing and operating a sound grading procedure in a school is no simple task. It requires the development of a philosophy or point of view about grades, what they are to indicate, and how they are going to indicate it for the entire school, and an agreement by all concerned to use grades the same way. Without that, it is indeed hard to ascertain what sensible thing or idea grades can convey. And without that it is only by knowing the idiosyncrasies of each teacher that the viewer of a grade report can decipher the various meanings. Averaging together elements developed on the basis of various teachers' whims about grading practices sums to nonsense.

20

Evaluation of Common Complaints about Grading

Objective

As a result of study of this chapter you should be able to:

List and discuss at least five common complaints about grades and grading.

Complaints about Grading

If one tries to examine all that has been written about grading and is currently in the magazines and journals, he finds that there is a massive amount of material. A high proportion of the writing expresses complaints about grading and grades. The same complaints seem to be repeated over and over again, year after year, by one writer after another. Oddly, the complaints are rarely, if ever, supported by data, research, or figures or statistics of any kind. They are mostly vague feelings or reports of specific incidents. The complaints can be categorized, and it turns out that they fall into only a relatively few groups. In this chapter we will consider separately each different kind of complaint, evaluating whether it is a sound or helpful complaint, whether it is necessarily true of grades or only of faulty grades, and what can be done to develop grading systems that are more satisfactory. Often what will be said will be review of earlier discussions, but this way of looking at the problems may put them into a new light and may help the teacher to defend her grading practices soundly when they, or grades in general, come under attack.

Grades Are Illogical, Easily Abused, and Subjective

Complaints that grades are illogical, easily abused, and subjective are grouped together because they are rather vague, tell us little that will help us to improve grading, and may reflect faulty practices instead of sound grading systems.

There is no need for grades and grading to be illogical. We have discussed many practices and procedures in earlier chapters that, when used, can insure that grades are logical.

There is no need for grades to be abused or to be used to abuse students. We decried such practices in several earlier discussions. No one who insists that grades shall not be distorted from their primary function will permit them to be used abusively.

The complaint that grades are subjective is not very helpful because a subjective element is part of any conceivable system of evaluation or feedback. Even the decision to evaluate or provide feedback at all is a subjective one. Somewhere in any system, one or more persons has to use judgment in making decisions. One would hope that the judgment was sound, and teachers are trained to be professionals so that they will be able to make such decisions as soundly as they can be made. If sound judgment were not required, it would not be necessary to educate teachers.

However, the degree of subjectivity in grading can vary, and it should be minimized. Grades based on large numbers of controlled observations, as we have noted, will tend to reduce unnecessary subjectivity. The basis for grading will not be vague. Sound tests can help yield grades with a high degree of objectivity in that all students with the same measurements get the same grades. (There is still a subjective element in the construction of the tests, though.)

Subjectivity can be reduced to a greater degree in some courses than others. It can be brought to a low level in spelling compared to art, in arithmetic compared to speech, in auto mechanics compared to physical education. Sometimes you can't use written tests effectively, or even tests based on performances of a constant task. In boxing, someone must decide from watching the sparring of two students whether one has mastered the skills of dodging and counterpunching. It requires judgment because it is nearly impossible to provide a constant problem identical from one student to another. But where identical problems can be used to reduce subjectivity, they should be, and the complaint about the subjectivity of grades will be brought to an irreducible minimum.

Grades Fail to Communicate Meaningfully

We have learned many ways that grades can be spoiled by inept teachers so that their meaning is reduced or destroyed; so this is a valid complaint about faulty grading procedures. But it is not a sound objection to well-designed grades that emphasize the primary communication function and avoid being fouled up by incidental functions, carelessness, and unsound practices. Let's review quickly some of the most common actions that reduce meaning in grades.

First, teachers are likely, if not careful, to confuse other elements with subject-matter competence in their students. We must not grade on the basis of personality, likeableness, promptness, conformity, and so on; we must restrict subject grades to reflections of subject accomplishment.

Second, teachers may use poor tests that don't reflect the instructional objectives and thus base their grades on inadequate measures of subject accomplishment.

Third, teachers may not set communicable standards for their grades. As a result, the audiences that use the grades cannot understand what those grades mean. Or, teachers who give grades according to the performance of the students in the class may not adjust for differences in average ability of classes. Either of these failures will reduce the meaning of the grades, and most of the users will not even recognize what the problem is. All the user will know is that the grades don't seem to indicate very consistently what they pretend to indicate. The user will sense that a B in spelling for one student doesn't mean the same thing as a B in spelling for another. And that is what is meant by grades' failing to communicate meaningfully.

A fourth way we have considered that grades can be given whose meaning may not be very sensible to the lay person is to use tricky comparison bases, such as growth or improvement, achievement compared with aptitude, or effort. These comparison bases have such subtle complications that only expert users who knew exactly how the grades were given could soundly extract their meaning. The general user, such as the student, the parent, the employer, or the school administrator, will find that grades based on such kinds of comparisons seem to be inconsistent from student to student, and they will be described as meaningless.

Grades Are Inconsistent — Among Teachers, Subjects, and Schools

This is a more specific complaint about lack of meaning of grades. It says that Miss Jones' grade of A isn't the same as Mr. Brown's grade of A, even though they both teach eighth grade English in the same school. It also says that in Roosevelt Elementary School the average grade in music is much higher than the average grade in arithmetic, and since the school does not select its students for being good in music or bad in arithmetic, this does not make sense. And it says that if you go to Technical High School, it is harder to get good grades in mathematics than if you go to General High School, or if you go to school at University High you really have to be smart to get good grades, but if you go to City High, it is much easier.

This complaint is certainly true of grades as they are usually given. It has been documented in various forms many times in many different settings. Probably nearly any school in existence would find by rather simple analyses that grades in some subjects average higher, year after year, than grades in other subjects. There is no way to justify this logically. Any subject can be made as hard or as easy as any teacher wants to, or is willing to, make it. The instruction can be adjusted to be more or less thorough, or the standards used in the controlled observations on which grades are based can be adjusted. Arguments that mathematics is just naturally harder than history, or that social studies is just naturally easier than physics, just won't stand critical scrutiny. One subject yields lower or higher grades than another because the graders arrange for that to be so, and for no other reason. And as long as the graders are allowed to cause such inconsistencies or are not taught how to avoid them, the complaint that grades are inconsistent will continue to be valid. No teacher who has absorbed what has been presented thus far in this book will have any sound reason for producing inconsistent grades. The trick is to get all the other teachers to agree on a consistent set of procedures. That is, perhaps, too much to hope for, but those of us who know better can reduce to a minimum our contribution to inconsistency.

Grades Are Too Motivating

Some writers complain that grades are too motivating. They argue that students work only for grades, instead of being interested in learning for its own sake. Some seem to think that the fact that grades are given is what produces cheating. Others suggest that highly motivated students take courses in which they can expect high grades rather than taking a broader curriculum or taking courses that would be more useful or appropriate to their needs. Occasionally a writer complains that the system of giving grades overemphasizes competition at the expense of cooperation.

The unfortunate thing about these complaints is that while they are directed at grades, they would apply to any procedure that provides evaluative feedback. If we did not provide the feedback in the form of grades but changed to some other form, then that form of feedback would get the same criticism. So the only way out is not to provide evaluative feedback at all. But any student of learning knows that the process of learning is dramatically impeded by preventing the learner from having knowledge of the results of his efforts. Some form of evaluative feedback is absolutely indispensable for efficient learning. It is not reasonable to expect a schooling system to handicap itself by deliberately choosing not to use one of the most effective devices for instruction, telling students how they have performed after their efforts.

Any kind of evaluative feedback may result in too intense motivation among some students. However, there are also complaints that in spite of grading, some pupils are altogether too little motivated to be effective students in our schools. The complainers can hardly have it both ways — that grades are too motivating and that they are not adequately motivating. It appears that this group of complainers are merely seeking a scapegoat, and grades and marks have been the handy candidate.

Another point of view regarding motivation that should be considered is that of the group who ask the school to teach students to survive and prosper in a competitive society. They would hardly be satisfied if the schools abandoned grades in order to de-emphasize competition.

Finally, we should remember once more that while grades do have a motivating effect on at least some students, this is not the primary function of grades. To throw away the primary function because of the kind of complaints we have reviewed here would be foolish, indeed.

Grades Overreward Memorization

A complaint that may sometimes be appropriate but not in a sound grading system is that the grades give too much emphasis to memorization and too little emphasis to other mental processes or skills. Of course, in the hands of the inept teacher grades can be based on observations of only elementary skills, or of one kind of skill, at the expense of others. But no competent teacher would do that. So the complaint is not about grades, really, but about teachers who are incompetent in the skills of making sound controlled observations on which to give the grades. Those skills can be learned and should be learned and practiced by every teacher. When that takes place, this complaint about grades will have no merit whatsoever.

Grades Are Used to Punish Students

A legitimate complaint about the way some naïve teachers use grades is that the grade becomes a weapon or instrument of vengeance or punishment, rather than a measure of competence. We have already noted a number of times that this is a faulty grading practice. So when grades are used this way, the complaint is legitimate, but the informed teacher will never use them that way. So the complaint is really about poor teaching rather than about grading, itself.

Grades Become Symbols of Personal Worth

The final kind of complaint that you can find in the literature about grading is that grades sometimes come to be thought of as indications of the worth or value of the person, rather than indications of particular academic competencies he has or has not developed to specified degrees. This kind of thinking was illustrated at the beginning of part 3. It is unfortunate, and should be avoided, but grades don't produce this kind of thinking, and any other evaluative feedback system would have the same complaint lodged against it. Getting rid of grades by replacing them with some other feedback system would not satisfy these writers, and getting rid of all feedback would not satisfy anyone who wanted any degree of efficiency in instruction. So about the best that can be done about this complaint is frequently to remind the users of the grades that they don't indicate the value of the person. High grades don't mean someone is better or more valuable or more honorable than if he had received low grades. It is a hard lesson to learn and to remember, so it will bear much repetition.

21

Legal Aspects of Grading

Objectives

Careful study of this chapter should enable you to:
1. Indicate the general current trend of courts' reactions to legal appeals concerning school grades. That is, you should be able to describe the legal precedent in such cases;
2. Describe the proper disposition of cheating situations;
3. Describe the implications of recent laws and court cases for the grading activities of the classroom teacher.

The Importance of Sound Grades

Over the years, the courts in the United States have tended to avoid becoming involved in issues associated with school and college grading. Usually they have refused to intercede between the student and the teacher at all. Lately, however, there appears to be a trend toward more active intervention by the courts and to more frequent recourse to courts by students and parents. For example, each year now there are many cases involving problems of racial integration in all of its aspects.

Among many people there is the assertion, and perhaps belief, that a high school education, or even a college degree, is necessary if one is to obtain employment that will permit a satisfying experience. Thus, unfairly to deprive a student of a satisfactory grade or a diploma is to deprive him of some part of his livelihood. The legal recourse is to sue for adjustment of the grade, reinstatement of the privilege, or perhaps for recovery of the resulting damages. If the deprivation is major, the courts will take the matter seriously.

For example, in 1967 Marsha Goldwyn was a senior at Flushing High School in New York (*Goldwyn* v. *Allen*). She took the Regent's Examination in History on 25 January. Near the end of the examination a proctor saw her referring to a piece of scrap paper containing notes on both sides. He confiscated the paper and took Marsha and the paper to the acting principal at the end of the examination. Marsha said she had prepared the notes for herself during the first half hour of the exam period. The principal then asked her simply to copy the notes for him. After twenty minutes she had not copied one-fourth of them. After further questioning, she admitted to cheating and signed a written statement to that effect. However, the next day she repudiated the confession. The acting principal then sent a letter to the Department of Education reporting her cheating. Her credit was cancelled in that examination, and she was suspended from taking any other Regents' Examinations.

In New York State the Regents' Examinations are important. Their results can have an impact on further schooling, earnings, and so on. Thus, the court regarded the cancellation of her score and the suspension of her right to further examinations as a major sanction. This being the case, the issue was whether Marsha had been given due process. By due process is meant, basically, a fair, impartial hearing in which both sides are allowed to present evidence, and perhaps to cross-examine opposing witnesses, and be represented by an attorney who is expert in such matters.

After Marsha's privileges had been suspended and her score cancelled, her lawyer protested the lack of a hearing for Marsha before such severe actions had been taken. The Board of Education of New York City held a conference then, but the board did not permit Marsha to have her lawyer there. Her lawyer advised her not to attend either. At that meeting, the assistant superintendent concurred in the acting principal's action revoking her privileges.

The court ruled in this case that the Department of Education violated Marsha's rights by acting on the letter of the acting principal and imposing sanctions without a hearing of the student, aided by her lawyer. However, the court restricted its ruling to Regents' Examinations that have such serious ramifications. It did not intend for the ruling to cover all tests given in the schools.

That is an example of a situation in which the student was deprived of a satisfactory evaluation unfairly. On the other hand, to give satisfactory grades when learning has not taken place and to promote students through graduation who cannot perform skills for the development of which the schools are responsible may also result in a person's being unemployable. If the school has not exerted reasonable diligence and effort to inform the student and his parents of the lack of progress (presumably by such mechanisms as low grades), then the school may be held at fault, and subject to the payment of damages.

An example of this kind of case is one in California filed in 1972 *(Doe v. San Francisco Unified School District)* in which a graduate of the San Francisco Public Schools claims to have been of average intelligence, a regular attender of school, and not a disciplinary problem. The mother was assured throughout her son's attendance in school that he was making normal progress and did not need special help. However, the suit claims that the schools defrauded the student and his parents because upon graduation from high school he could read at only the fifth grade level, which has interfered with his employment. The parents are suing for one million dollars representing a lifetime's reduced earnings due to failure of the school, as well as punitive damages to make sure that school never does this again.

Since more school-related cases are being considered by the courts, and the impact of education on one's life and one's earnings is being recognized as of value, it is worth our while to examine the general trends that can be inferred from recent court decisions.

Courts Tend Not to Interfere with Academic Evaluations

In general, the courts have decided many times and set a precedent that they will not try to substitute their judgment about a student's academic performance for the judgment of the teacher. However, this assumes that the academic evaluations are not capricious, arbitrary, malicious, or in bad faith. If there is any claim that the evaluations are contaminated by such behavior, the courts will review the issue, have a hearing, and perhaps demand a reevaluation. It may seem unfortunate, but the court cannot be relied on to intercede even when the grading practice is obviously wrong, if it is applied to everyone without caprice, malice, or bad faith. An example is a case in New York City.

Melvin Lesser was a high school student in Brooklyn (*Lesser* v. *Board of Education of New York City*). He was encouraged to participate in a scholarship program designed for the top 10% of the entering high school class. He was a good enough student to win a Regents' Scholarship, and he was a good school citizen, according to school records. However, in this special program, Melvin got only an 84.3 high school average, and Brooklyn College required an 85 average for admission. Melvin's mother, Mollie Lesser, went to court asking that special adjustment be made to Melvin's average to reflect the fact that his grades were in advanced-scholarship types of courses. Adjustments in such things were not without precedent since in a previous period the passing scores in New York's Regents' Examination had been revised downward after complaints that the tests were too difficult.

The court ruled that the procedure used by the high school and the college to evaluate Melvin's performance was faulty and that an adjustment should be made to the high school average to reflect the advanced track Melvin was encouraged by the school to enter. As you know from chapters in this book, that was an educationally sound ruling. The grades should have been adjusted for the aptitude level of the students by a procedure similar to the one you have learned.

However, the school appealed the case to a higher court. At that hearing it was pointed out that there were 170 other students whose averages were between 84.3 and 85.0 who were also denied admission to Brooklyn College. Thus the court ruled that the Board of Education was not being arbitrary, and the court would not substitute its judgment for that of the Board of Education. In other words, as long as the school is *consistently* wrong, the court won't interfere. The court said, ". . . , a court should refrain from interjecting its views within those delicate areas of school administration which relate to the eligibility of applicants and the determination of marking standards, unless a clear abuse of statutory authority or a practice of discrimination or gross error has been shown."

This theme appears regularly through cases involving testing, grading, marking, and related matters during the current century. (See, for example, *West* v. *Board of Trustees* and *Dehaan* v. *Brandeis University*.) For the teacher this means that it is even more important that her grading practices be sound because the parents don't even have a way to appeal to the courts to get an unsound procedure changed, as long as it is used consistently, without caprice, malice, or arbitrariness, and does not discriminate against minority groups unfairly. On the other hand, it also suggests that as far as the courts are concerned, the schools need not be sound, and teachers' grading practices can be seriously faulty. What the teacher or· the schools cannot do is be irresponsible in the sense of capriciousness, arbitrariness, or malice.

An example of bad faith or malice is the case of a student named Connelly who claimed that a professor in medicine had decided to give him a grade of F in a course regardless of the quality of his work (*Connelly* v. *University of Vermont and State Agricultural College*). This grade would result in his dismissal from the medical school. The judge indicated that faculty alone are skilled in matters of scholarship and should be free from interference from the judiciary. However, since the plaintiff felt that the institution acted arbitrarily, capriciously, or in bad faith, he was entitled to have that issue tried before the court. If he convinced the court, the court would order the university to give a fair and impartial hearing on the dismissal. Notice, however, the judge did not try to decide what grade the student should have received. He merely said that the university should attend to that fairly and impartially.

Similar caprice was displayed in California by a faculty which refused to instruct a teacher trainee named Henry E. Miller many years ago (*Miller* v. *Daily*, 1902). It seems that the faculty thought he was taking too long with his studies. The California Supreme Court examined the student's record and found no failing marks. He had not yet passed practice teaching, however. The court found that the faculty had declared his performance unsatisfactory and denied him a diploma prematurely, and thus abused their discretion and exceeded their power. The court ordered him reinstated as a student. In Colorado that same year, however, a student named Steinhauer protested that the faculty had asked him unusual and unwarranted questions in an examination (*Steinhauer* v. *Arkins*). The court there upheld the authority of the faculty to evaluate students. A few lears later (1908) in Nebraska a court denied its ability to fix a student's grade when there was conflicting testimony, even after the court had the lady's examination papers scrutinized by experts during the course of the hearing (*State ex rel. Nelson* v. *Lincoln Medical College*). The court ordered that Mrs. Nelson be granted her degree in medicine, and the judge denounced the professors' autocratic right to fix examination grades and indicated that an appeal procedure was needed for students.

In the case of *People ex rel. Cecil* v. *Bellevue Hospital,* the plaintiff, Cecil, was arbitrarily refused permission to present himself for examination and to receive his degree. The Court of Appeals ordered that the degree be granted. In *Keller* v. *Hewitt,* Keller applied for a certificate to teach grammar school. She met all the requirements, but the board refused the certificate. The court ordered that the certificate be granted. Such arbitrariness as this apparently cannot be defended.

Time Is a Weapon for Both Parties

The teacher needs to realize that in disputes with students over grades and related matters, such as promotion and graduation, time is one of the weapons that both parties use. Pursuits of claims in courts take a lot of time and effort from all parties involved. Students may take advantage of this in an effort to get schools to modify their decisions. A settlement with the student can avoid the tremendous burden on the school staff and budget of going to court. Hundreds of hours are taken up in meetings with attorneys, gathering evidence, locating witnesses, planning a case, and just plain waiting around in hallways and courtrooms. No school provides for this in its budget and staffing. So a court case is a tremendous extra burden, one to be avoided except for a major benefit. A student may then threaten a court case in order to get a favorable settlement without going to court. Of course, if the student makes such a threat idly, without intending to go through with it, this is a crime called *barratry,* and on conviction is also punished.

On the other hand, students expect and like to proceed through school with their classmates. It is not necessary that they proceed on the basis of their age. A case in Glen Cove, New York, in 1967, indicated that the board of education can provide rules and regulations for promotion from grade to grade based not on age but on training, knowledge, and ability (*Pittman* v. *Board of Education of Glen Cove City School District*). So the school can suspend a student, expel him, or refuse to promote him at the usual time, and this is not attractive to a student. To avoid a long interruption in schooling, a student may be willing to be reasonable in his demands on the school.

An example of how long things can drag out is that of Royal Anne Carter in a dispute with the University of North Carolina (*In re Carter*). She was accused of cheating in May of 1961, and suspended from the university. In 1964 she was still getting orders from the courts of that state to get the university to proceed with rehearings of her case to decide whether the charges against her were true or whether she should be reinstated as a student. The court finally had to order the university to carry out the rehearing with reasonable promptness. It is obvious from the record of proceedings that for Miss Carter after three years no promptness could be soon enough! Of course, even longer delays are evident in cases involving school integration, but that is not particularly relevant to a discussion of legal aspects of grading and marking.

Cheating Is a Disciplinary Matter, Not an Academic Matter

The courts have pretty consistently taken the view that cheating behavior, even though it is on examinations that determine grades, is not an academic problem but a disciplinary problem. The remedy for cheating is not to give a grade of F. In Colorado in 1966 a student was accused of cheating in English but cleared by the student discipline committee for lack of evidence (Sandman, 1971). The English teacher then failed her. The student filed suit to get her grade changed from F to B. The case was settled out of court, but it suggests that a teacher is unwise to try to get even with a student for cheating by lowering the grade. This would probably be regarded as capricious, arbitrary, or malicious behavior if it ever went to trial.

The appropriate remedy seems to be to have a full disciplinary hearing, granting the student due process. The student should be present, allowed to present evidence, allowed to question the witnesses, and should be represented by a lawyer if he chooses to. In any case, the evidence of cheating should be solid. Just suspicion of cheating or circumstances that look like cheating might have taken place will not do. We have already cited Marsha Goldwyn's case in New York City. There the court ruled that she should have had a hearing with due process in the case of an accusation of cheating on the Regents' Examinations, but the court said this did not necessarily apply to other examinations. The point at issue was how severe the penalty for cheating was. Perhaps not all cases deserve a hearing with due process. In a case at the University of Illinois Medical School in 1956, Patricia Bluett was accused of turning in, as her own, examination papers written by a Dr. Wong (*People ex rel. Bluett* v. *Board of Trustees of University of Illinois*). She was suspended in May of 1953 but was not even told why until June 1954. At that time she appeared with her attorney before the Committee on Policy and Discipline. No witnesses were heard, and no evidence other than Miss Bluett's denial of the charges was heard. However, after the meeting the committee changed her sentence from suspension to expulsion. The court upheld the action, indicating that formal hearings were not necessary before expulsion. So it is not clear that due process is necessary, but it seems reasonable to provide it, and a formal hearing giving the student every right to defend himself seems the wise thing to do.

That the evidence of cheating should be solid is indicated by Royal Anne Carter's case and by the case of Kathleen Ryan. We already noted that Miss Carter's problem was with the University of North Carolina (*In re Carter*). She was charged with cheating on a Latin I make-up quiz. To be precise she was accused of not taking the quiz specifically made up for her by her Latin instructor, John Catlin. The honor council of that university found her guilty and suspended her. After repeated appeals to university authorities without avail, she appealed to the courts. Judge Clark held that all of the evidence offered failed to indicate that she was anything but innocent. Therefore he ordered her case to be reheard.

The case of Miss Kathleen Ryan happened many years ago (*Ryan* v. *Board of Education*). In 1927 she was charged with cheating in an American History final examination in a Eureka, Kansas high school. It was the day before commencement. The instructor found a paper in Kathleen's possession containing notes on American History. A rule forbade having notes, so she was told to stop her work and was denied credit in the course. Since the course was required for graduation, that meant she could not graduate with her class.

Kathleen admitted that the notes were hers, but she claimed that they got on her desk accidentally. The were folded up in a blotter that was under her ink bottle. The teacher, herself, was in doubt that Kathleen had ever looked at the notes and had avoided using the word "cheat" with regard to the situation.

The school board met hastily. It was told that Kathleen had a disposition to cheat, that she had used other students' notes on other occasions, and that she had wandering eyes. It decided that she would not be allowed to graduate. Kathleen appealed to the superintendent. He had Kathleen reexamined. She made a passing grade on the reexamination, but meanwhile the faculty protested and threatened to resign if Kathleen was allowed to graduate. The board met again hurriedly and voted to deny her graduation. In all this, Kathleen was not heard and was not represented by counsel. On hearing the case the district court decided Kathleen should have her credits and be given her diploma.

Evaluations Based on Race Are Not Permissible

It should no longer have to be said that grades, tests, and so on must be impartial. In particular, the courts have no patience with schemes, whether simple or sophisticated, that deny equal opportunity to black students or those of other races. The law books are full of cases concerning this, but perhaps the best illustration is the case brought by Hobson against the schools of Washington, D.C. (*Hobson* v. *Hansen*). The protest was against the tracking system that resulted in most of the black students being placed in the lower tracks. Tracking was based on test scores, but since the tests had been developed and standardized on middle-class white students, according to the courts, and since they resulted in extensive resegregation within schools and reduced education for the blacks, the practice was ordered discontinued.

The courts seem to indicate that if properly developed instruments that are not racially biased are used for a sound educational purpose, they will be permitted, even if they do not provide an even balance among races. However, any suspicion that bias is operating alerts the courts' antennae, and they will strike violators.

School Records May Be Open to the Public

Some states have enacted laws that public records must be available to the public. In New Jersey the law is known as the *Right to Know* law. In Florida it is called the *Government in the Sunshine* law. School records are likely to be regarded as public records under such laws, and such records, including test scores and grades, must be made available to members of the public who want to see them. In New Jersey in 1973 an appeals court ruled that under the *Right to Know* law a citizen did not have to show any personal or particular interest in the material in order to require that it be made available to him to inspect, copy, or purchase a copy (*Citizens for Better Schools* v. *Board of Education of City of Camden*). In that case it was a request of a citizen's group for the reading scores by school and by grade within school for the years 1968 to 1970, along with the national norms for each grade. The school board, supported by a ruling by the New Jersey Commissioner of Education, wanted to present only the data by region and by grade without identifying the particular grades within schools, but the court ruled that this did not meet the requirement of the law.

The possibility of public scrutiny of all of a teacher's records suggests more strongly, perhaps, than anything else we have examined that teachers should be able to defend their grading practices. They should know what they are doing and why, and they should keep records so that they will not be found capricious or arbitrary in their practices. As it was put by a court in Texas in 1973, only when there is a clear and convincing showing that an official acted in an arbitrary and capricious manner will the federal courts interfere with exercise of discretionary power of university officials to determine fitness of a student to continue his studies (*Keys* v. *Sawyer*). The teacher should be ready to demonstrate that her practices were not capricious or arbitrary, but were carefully studied out and decided upon with full knowledge of the available alternatives and their advantages and limitations, and she should be able to show that she applied her chosen principles evenly and fairly to all her students.

Potential Future Developments

One cannot, of course, predict what cases may come before the courts in the future, or how the courts will decide them. However, one very important case in the field of business and industry may have significant ramifications for education. It is the now famous case of *Griggs* v. *Duke Power Company,* decided in 1971, by the U.S. Supreme Court. In this case Willie S. Griggs and several other black employees of the Duke Power Company's Dan River (North Carolina) Steam Station in a class action protested the conditions that similarly situated blacks must meet to be employed by or to transfer within the station. Until 1965 all blacks were hired into the Labor Division, which was largely janitorial work and the lowest paid division of the plant. The problem was that starting in 1965 a high school education and satisfactory scores on tests of intelligence and mechanical comprehension were required for transfer to all divisions other than labor, even though white employees who had not graduated from high school but were hired before the time of the high school education requirement continued to perform satisfactorily and achieve promotions in those other departments. The blacks did not have high school educations and could not meet the cutoff scores on the tests. The cutoffs were set at the national high school graduates' average.

There is much of interest in the ramifications of this case through its appeals on the way to the Supreme Court. The significant part for us here is the decision by the Supreme Court that to be acceptable as employment tools, requirements such as test scores and high school graduation must have a manifest relationship to the employment in question. In our terms, the grades or scores must be *valid* for the job. While this decision was made in the context of integration and the Civil Rights Act, it makes sense for employment in general. The opinion of the Supreme Court as stated by Chief Justice Burger was that Congress requires, ". . . removal of artificial, arbitrary, and unnecessary barriers to employment when the barriers operate invidiously to discriminate on the basis of racial or other impermissible classification." It would be sensible to remove such barriers when they discriminate against anyone.

It would not be farfetched for litigation to arise questioning whether high school grades really reflect what students had learned, if high school grades are to be used in employment. And if high school grades in relevant subjects are often found not to be related to job performance, certainly some question is going to be raised about the professional skill of the teachers who gave such grades. Of course, that kind of question is already being raised in another context in the case of *Doe* v. *San Francisco.*

Another case, which may be of interest for the future, concerns not just the grade but the quality of the instruction in a college course. Mrs. Illene Ianniello filed suit in 1975 against the University of Bridgeport complaining that the university did not provide the course described in the catalog and that she did not learn anything in the course, though she received a grade of A. The course was "Methods and Materials in Teaching Basic Business Subjects," and she claims that class periods were spent in reading to the students pamphlets and other materials already distributed to the class. The only requirement of the course was to hand in one book report, she claims. Mrs. Ianniello is suing for $470 as payment for tuition, expenses, and time lost from her job. The university's Vice President for Academic Affairs, Warren Carrier, claims that Mrs. Ianniello was mistaken in thinking that the catalog was a promise of exactly what the course would contain and argues that the courts don't have the capacity to determine whether students have learned from their courses or whether they just disliked the professor. Cases like this suggest that in the future not only must slipshod grading practices be corrected, but also that care must be taken to provide sound instructional settings and to provide evidence to support that such was the case.

Taken together these cases are probably a healthy sign that slipshod practices in teaching and grading that are important to students are going to have to be straightened out. With the tools you have developed in studying this unit on grading and marking, you should be well prepared for giving grades and evaluations to your students that will meet the tests of being systematic, carefully planned, and valid indicators of academic achievement.

References

Citizens for Better Schools v. *Board of Education of City of Camden*, 308 A 2nd 35, 124 NJ Super. 523.

Connelly v. *University of Vermont and State Agricultural College*, 244 F Supp. 156.

Dehaan v. *Brandeis University*, 150 F. Supp. 626.

Doe v. *San Francisco Unified School District*, No. 653 312 (Superior Ct.).

Goldwyn v. *Allen*, 281 NYS 2d. 899.

Griggs v. *Duke Power Co.* 401 US 424, 91 S Ct. 849, 28 L.E. 2d 158.

Hobson v. *Hansen*, 269 F Supp. 401, aff'd sub. nom. *Smuck* v. *Hobson*, 408 F 2d 175.

In re Carter, 262 NC 360, 137 SE 2d 150.

Keller v. *Hewitt*, 109 Cal 146, 41 Pac 871.

Keys v. *Sawyer*, 353 F Supp. 936.

Lesser v. *Board of Education of New York City*, 232 NYS 2d. 151, 239 NYS 2d 776.

Miller v. *Daily*, 68 P. 1029.

People ex rel. Bluett v. *Board of Trustees of University of Illinois*, 134 NE 2d. 636.

People ex rel. Cecil v. *Bellevue Hospital*, 60 Hun 107, 14 NY Supp. 490, 128 NY 621, 28 NE 253.

Pittman v. *Board of Education of Glen Cove City School District*, 287 NYS 2d 551.

Ryan v. *Board of Education*, 124 Kan. 89, 257 Pac 945.

Sandman, P. M. *Students and the Law*. New York: Collier, 1971, p. 109.

State ex rel. Nelson v. *Lincoln Medical College*, 81 Neb. 533, 116 N.W. 294.

Steinhauer v. *Arkins*, 18 Colo. App. 49, 69 Pac. 1075.

West v. *Board of Trustees of Miami University*, 41 Ohio App. 367, 181 NE 144.

22

Practice in Evaluating a Grading Procedure

To help review what you have learned about grading and marking practices, it may be useful to try to evaluate a serious, though novel, proposal for grading in college classes. The following was made by a college level teacher of physical education at a major state university. The proposal was presented to the community in which the university is located. You should be able to consider it and evaluate it critically, pointing out any features which are sound and any which are unsound in a grading system that is designed to perform well the primary function of grades.

This is the proposal, outlined in six specific statements.

1. No student will fail due to grades.
2. By means of state and national standardized examinations minimal scores for passing each course will be set.
3. During each grade (freshman, sophomore, etc.) it will be mandatory that a given percent of those taking any course fail it.
4. Those who fail a course must retake the course or take a different course until they pass the cutoffs required for the grade they are in.
5. Each year the cutoff is to be lowered so that 5% fewer are required to fail.
6. Each state is to decide on the maximum number of years that will be allowed to its students before graduation. The same limit on time will apply to all colleges and universities of the state.

Part Four

Introduction

Wasted Testing

In many modern schools, testing is a great waste of money. By that it is not meant or implied that tests and testing should be abandoned. But the administration, scoring, and filing of test results that are not fully used is embarrassingly common. Some tests, of course, are administered that should not be. They may be inappropriate for the purpose or may just be of such poor quality that they should really not even be on the market. This topic is fully discussed in part 2. Our concern here is that even sound, carefully selected tests are wasted if their results are not brought to bear on educational decisions. Far too often elaborate school testing programs are developed, and the principal use of the results is simply to enter them on each student's cumulative record and ignore them otherwise. When that takes place, all the time involved in test selection, administration, scoring, entering on the record, and filing represents money down the drain. That is not the way things should be, and for us to prevent that from occurring, teachers need to know what test results should be used for, and how to use them wisely. That is the subject of this unit of instruction.

Uses of Test Results

Testing can be used for five major purposes in modern schools. We will consider each of the five in detail in the subsequent pages. They are:

1. Organizing instruction,
2. Placing students into appropriate instruction,
3. Providing feedback during instruction,
4. Improving memory and application of what is learned, and
5. Modifying instruction and evaluating modifications of instruction.

Using Tests to
Improve Instruction

The use of tests for some of these purposes is rather straightforward common sense. In other cases there are complex ramifications; traditional practices appear now to be incorrect, and the teacher must know what she is doing to avoid continuing the mistakes of the past. In still other cases, what seems simple may be harmful to the teacher and her career, as well as to the field of education. New ideas that have not been thought through very well may have surface appeal to a school board. Without well-informed counterarguments from school staff, they may be adopted with destructive results.

Some of the ideas that we will present are probably sound and appropriate for use on small segments of the curriculum that deserve special effort, but they would not be feasible for the total curriculum unless done by a separate organization supported by the government or a foundation.

Some of the ideas we will present have never been tried. They have been culled from the very scattered literature on using tests. They are presented here because they seem worth trying.

Some of the ideas are rather new developments or discoveries about learning that are related to things like tests and items. They are introduced here because they may become important in the near future, and a teacher who has had formal instruction in using tests wisely should have a reasonably current knowledge of their status. She should also, of course, direct some of her professional reading in the future to the journals that present such findings so that she may remain current.

Goals for This Topic

We are going to discuss in detail the use of tests for the five purposes in the subsequent chapters. Teachers should have specific skills and knowledges about test use to be effective in taking full advantage of this professional tool. The specific skills she should master are listed as behavioral objectives for this topic. You should be able to do everything that is listed in these objectives when you have mastered the instruction on the topic. The list of objectives can be used effectively as a study guide or as a guide in reviewing the material before an examination. It may also be useful for the practicing teacher as a refresher before planning to use tests, participating in the development of a testing program, choosing tests for a particular purpose, or planning, developing, or modifying a part of her instructional activities.

Behavioral Objectives for Using Tests to Improve Instruction

The purpose of this unit of instruction is to teach the prospective teacher how to use standardized and teacher-made tests to improve classroom instructional planning and practice.

A. Use of Tests to Improve Instruction — You should be able to:
 1. List five general areas in which test results can be used to improve instruction.
B. Organization of Instruction — You should be able to:
 1. State the general principle involved in using tests to improve instruction;
 2. Describe and illustrate a *table of specifications;*
 3. Demonstrate how a *table of specifications* reveals what should be added to or deleted from instruction;
 4. Describe the nature of an instructional hierarchy;
 5. Describe the procedure of using tests to verify a proposed hierarchy;
 6. Recognize the degree to which hierarchical instruction in school subjects is now available;
 7. Describe a procedure for using tests to involve parents in curriculum planning;
 8. Recognize the role of tests in determining student motivation.
C. Placement — You should be able to:
 1. Describe a procedure for using standardized normative achievement tests for determining:
  a. the general level of the class;
  b. weaknesses of individual students in broad areas;
  c. weaknesses of the whole class in broad areas;
 2. Describe newly developed published materials for placing students with respect to behavioral objectives;
 3. List at least seven of the ten important aspects of a sound diagnostic and remedial procedure;
 4. Describe and evaluate the state of the art in currently available diagnostic instruments;
 5. Describe the procedure and requirements of diagnosis by comparing achievement with aptitude. Include:
  a. standardization on a common group;
  b. jangle fallacy;
  c. requirement of large differences;
 6. Describe a relatively simple procedure for diagnosis of some kinds of problems;
 7. List four functions of using tests during remediation;
 8. Describe and evaluate the current status of the effectiveness of remediation;
 9. Summarize arguments for and against homogeneous grouping;
 10. Evaluate the evidence on the arguments related to homogeneous grouping;
 11. Describe and illustrate the main aspects of an aptitude-treatment interaction;
 12. Describe the status of current ATI research as related to subjects taught in elementary schools;

13. Describe the use of item scores to locate a student in an instructional hierarchy;
14. Contrast the views of learning theorists and measurement theorists on the number of items per objective required in placement tests for a learning hierarchy;
15. Describe the general attitude of courts toward use of tests for placement;
16. Describe the attitude of the court in *Hobson* v. *Hansen* toward use of tests for tracking in Washington, D.C.;
17. Describe the legal aspects of using tests for placement into special education.

D. Providing Feedback — You should be able to:
1. State the relationship between feedback and efficient learning;
2. Describe the delay-retention effect and its implications for teachers;
3. Describe the effects of kind and quality of feedback on learning;
4. Discuss the designing of items to enhance feedback's effect;
5. Describe item analysis in class and how it can enhance feedback.

E. Aiding Memory and Application — You should be able to:
1. Describe a technique to enhance memory for what is learned, and the writing of items for that technique;
2. Describe the use of adjunct questions to aid retention of what is read;
3. Describe the implications for teachers of research on the use of adjunct questions.

F. Evaluation — You should be able to:
1. Describe a feasible and effective procedure for evaluating effectiveness of classroom instruction;
2. Discuss the difference between evaluation of the effectiveness of sequential and nonsequential instruction;
3. List three other procedures for assisting in the evaluation of instruction in the classroom;
4. Describe three elements to be included in any evaluation of instruction which contrasts different classes;
5. Illustrate with an example the result of leaving out any of the needed elements in evaluation of instruction across classes;
6. Describe the status of performance tests for teachers as a way of evaluating quality of instruction.

23

Using Tests
to Organize Instruction

Objectives

As a result of study of this chapter, you should be able to:

1. State the general principle involved in using tests to improve instruction;
2. Describe and illustrate a *table of specifications;*
3. Demonstrate how a *table of specifications* reveals what should be added to or deleted from instruction;
4. Describe the nature of an instructional hierarchy;
5. Describe the procedure of using tests to verify a proposed hierarchy;
6. Recognize the degree to which hierarchical instruction in school subjects is now available;
7. Describe a procedure for using tests to involve parents in curriculum planning;
8. Recognize the role of tests in determining student motivation.

The Basic Principle

There is a basic principle involved in taking advantage of testing to improve the organization of instruction. It is that the curriculum and the tests that are used to ascertain whether students are learning it must be coordinated for instruction to be most effective. An instructional program is weakened if the tests do not reflect the instruction or the objectives that the instruction is supposed to accomplish. Put the other way around, the effectiveness of tests to ascertain whether or to what degree students have learned what they are supposed to learn is lessened if the instruction is not relevant to what is being tested. These two parts of instruction have to work together. In this chapter we will examine some of the ways such coordination can usefully be accomplished.

Coordination of the Table of Specifications with Instruction

TABLE OF SPECIFICATIONS

Tests which are soundly constructed are built to meet specifications, just as a house is built according to a plan. The plan for a test is called its *table of specifications*. It is a table because traditionally the plan for a test includes two dimensions, the test's content and the behaviors that are observed in connection with the content. These two dimensions are laid out as the columns and rows of a two-way table. An example appears in figure 23-1. This might be the table for a test on the first lesson in a course in introductory Spanish. The content of the course is listed down the left side of the table. It indicates that some vocabulary words will be learned, of course. There will be some work on pronunciation and speaking the language. Some specifics will be covered, like dealing with negatives and questions, and some of the formal aspects of language as it applies to Spanish will be started, i.e., the first conjugation of verbs.

Across the top of the table are listed the ways performance on the content will be observed. As you will note, an *etc.* at the right-hand margin indicates that there are

Content	Pro-nounce	Substi-tute Word	Negative Reply	Give Correct Article	Translate (Written)	Etc.
Vocabulary Words		1			1	
Vowel Sounds						
Sounds of c, d, h						
Linkage						
Questions			2		1	
Present Indica-tive of first conjuga-tion					1	
Use of Subject Pronouns		2			1	
Genders				2	1	
Plurals		2		2	1	
Definite Articles		2		2	1	
Negatives			2		1	
TOTAL	0	7	4	6	8	

Figure 23–1
Table of Specifications for Spanish, Lesson One

additional ways that we will observe, and the chart could readily be extended for several more categories. Also, at the extreme right would appear a column for totals of the rows, just as there is a row at the bottom for totals of the columns.

The numbers in the table indicate how many points will be counted in the test for each cell, i.e., each conjunction of a content and a behavior. Since this is to be a test in which the students respond on paper with a pencil, there are no items or points in the column for "Pronounce." The table thus indicates that this aspect of performance must either be evaluated some other way, or it is of no importance. By the same token, there are no entries for the row "Vowel Sounds" indicating that this kind of content must be tested in some other way (presumably an oral examination of each individual student). Under "Translate" there are points on many different kinds of content. Presumably the students will be required to write a translation of a written paragraph, and one point will be given for satisfactory use of vocabulary, one for satisfactorily dealing with questions, and so on for a total of eight points on the translation.

If the entire test were included in the table as presented in figure 23-1, there would be a total of 25 points, eight of them being on the translation. However, in actual practice there would probably be additional columns, such as one for translation from oral presentation and another for changing from singular to plural. To keep the test within 25 points, some cells would have to be reduced in weight or left out altogether. These are the decisions that a teacher makes as she designs a test soundly.

RELATIONSHIP BETWEEN TABLE OF
SPECIFICATIONS AND CURRICULUM

Obviously from the comments above, the table of specifications puts down in concrete terms just what is really important in the instruction given to a particular group of students. In theory, all may agree that pronunciation and skill in speaking a foreign language are important. However, the tables of specifications for the tests in a language course might consistently have empty cells dealing with this behavior. If there is no other kind of test with specifications that do include this behavior, then regardless of what is said in theory, the course is not giving any substantial weight to skill in speaking the language. Similarly, if the tests of a certain course typically have large proportions of their points on written translation, then reading and translating are being given great weight — even though the teacher may only give all those points to translation because it is easy and convenient to do so. A careful teacher may decide that even though it is easy to accumulate points on translation, that skill is not so overwhelmingly important. So she may decide deliberately not to take advantage of all the easily accumulated points on translation in order to give proper emphasis to other skills. This is soundly coordinating the testing with the curriculum.

In tables of specifications for other kinds of courses, one often finds behaviors like applies, analyzes, synthesizes, and evaluates. One might speak of these as higher order abilities or achievements, contrasting them with such behaviors as describes, lists, and recognizes. The presence of these higher order competencies in a table of specifications for a test reflects the fact that the teacher intends to develop these kinds of skills. If she does intend that, she should have items in her tests that attempt to demand those skills. One function of the table of specifications, then, is to remind her that she needs to develop items that call for more than the lower levels of learning.

At the same time, if the students are to have a reasonable chance at getting such items correct (or to put it differently, if the items are to be at a sound difficulty level), the instruction may have to be modified to develop those skills. One of the glaring examples seems to be the behavior of applying knowledge. Most instructors in elementary and secondary schools would have as part of their goals the application of the knowledge and skills their students develop in their classes. All too often the instructors give inadequate emphasis and practice to the applications. The students begin to think of school as "book learning," and they lose interest. If the instructor puts application items in a test, the students often fail them miserably. What must take place in soundly designed instruction is for training in applications to take place *and* for applications items to appear on the tests in proper proportion to their desired emphasis in the course. This is the way that tests are used to improve the organization of instruction.

Now it may turn out that when a behavior like application or analysis or synthesis is put into a table of specifications, the teacher decides that she does not want to develop one or more of those skills in her students in this particular course, for example, in introductory Spanish. Then she deliberately leaves out that behavior, knowing what she is doing. If there is some kind of instruction that does *not* appear in her table of specifications, such as skill in speaking a language, and she does not provide for other sound measurement of achievement of that skill, she should also remove it from her instruction. If she comes across test items from another teacher or a book publisher and attempts to fit them into her table of specifications, those that do not fit well should be discarded, or else her table and her instruction should be modified so that they do fit soundly.

Ideally the tables of specifications for the tests for a course and the instruction for that course should be developed together, one enhancing the other. The tables of specifications will then indicate to anyone — the students, the teachers, the administrators, the parents — what is seriously taught in the course.

It is perhaps worth noting briefly at this point that there is currently a large group of educators who think in terms of "behavioral objectives" as guides for their instruction and testing. A behavioral objective is little more than a statement of the behavior and the content represented by each cell of a table of specifications. For example, the upper left cell of the table in figure 23-1 is stated as a behavioral objective: *The student will be able to pronounce correctly the words in the vocabulary list for lesson one.* Once that is recognized, all the comments above about tables of specifications are readily translated into the language of those who prefer to think of behavioral objectives.

Coordination of Tests with Levels of an Instructional Hierarchy

INSTRUCTIONAL HIERARCHIES

Some people who develop instruction or theorize about instructional development suggest that often it is sound to think of the steps in an instructional process as being a hierarchy. There is an ultimate objective, but before that can be learned subordinate objectives or prior steps must be learned, and before they can be learned, there are still prior learnings that must be developed. Eventually in the process one comes to the place where everyone who is to be instructed in a group can be shown to have learned everything before a certain step. Instruction starts at the step after those *entry behaviors*. If the instruction is individualized, for each student one determines the entry behaviors that are available for that student and starts instruction with the next behavior that must be learned. As each step is learned, the subsequent step is introduced until ultimately the final objective is accomplished. In a true hierarchy there is only one best order in which to learn things. That is implied by the word hierarchy. Any deviation from that order is inefficient. If a step is left out, the rest of the hierarchy cannot be learned because there is a missing link.

While it is not easy to demonstrate that a learning sequence is truly hierarchical, the idea of a hierarchy is illustrated in figure 23-2. This is a sequence of steps required for learning to deal effectively with the scores from standardized tests. The final objective is given at the top of the figure. The last step before the final objective is then stated (number 20). Next is the step that comes before the next-to-last step. The process continues down to the step of putting scores into rank order. It is assumed that no student who approached this instruction will have to be taught anything prior to that, such as how to add.

Figure 23–2

A Learning Hierarchy

Unit Objective: Given a graph of the normal curve, and a specific instance of any of the types of scores listed below, the student will be able to locate the position of the test score within the normal distribution, and convert the score to any of the other scores, (1) raw scores, (2) percentiles, (3) z scores, (4) T scores, (5) stanines.

20. Given one of the stanine scores on the normal curve, the student will convert the stanine into the appropriate z score, T score, and percentile.
19. Given a graph of the normal curve with the stanines marked off, the student will write in the percent of cases within each stanine area.
18. Given the normal curve with the mean and standard deviations marked off, the student will be able to mark off the stanines.
17. Given the normal curve with the mean and standard deviations marked off, the student will convert T scores to z scores and percentiles.
16. Given the normal curve with the mean and standard deviatons marked off, the student will locate the T scores along the baseline.
15. Given the normal curve with the mean and z scores marked off, the student will write in the percentile equivalents along the baseline of the curve for any desired z score.
14. Given the normal curve with the mean and standard deviations marked off, the student will write in the percentile equivalents for the mean and the standard deviations.
13. Given the normal curve with the mean and standard deviations marked off, the student will write in the percentile equivalents along the baseline of the curve.
12. Given a frequency distribution, the student will compute the percentile equivalent of each raw score.

11. Given a graph of the normal curve with the mean and standard deviations drawn in, the student will write in the percentage of scores contained within each standard deviation unit.
10. Given the values of the mean and standard deviation for a set of normally distributed scores, the student will construct a normal curve to fit these data.
9. Given a graph of a normal curve with the mean and its value shown, and given the values for the range, indicate the location and values of the standard deviations.
8. Given a picture of the normal curve and value for the mean, locate the mean on the normal curve.
7. Given a list of raw scores, the student will compute the standard deviations (plus and minus three) by dividing the range by the appropriate number.
6. Given a list of scores in rank order, the student will compute the range.
5. Given a plot of test scores on a two-way graph, the student will draw a line indicating the curve of the distribution.
4. Given a frequency distribution of test scores, the student will plot the scores on a two-way graph.
3. Given a list of test scores in rank order, the student will construct a frequency distribution.
2. Given a list of scores, the student will compute the mean.
1. Given a list of test scores, the student will place them in rank order.

Tests can be used to help organize a curriculum that is hierarchical by helping the curriculum developers decide what the hierarchy is and whether a sound hierarchy has been discovered. White (1974) provides the most clear description of what is required to develop and demonstrate a hierarchy. He uses tests to clarify whether any step in the hierarchy could be divided into separate skills that should be separate steps. That is, he wants to find out whether students can do one part of the step without being able to do the other. If so, there are two separate steps; if not, there is only one step at that point. He also uses test questions imbedded in programmed instruction to determine whether the remaining separate steps are really hierarchical, i.e., in an order that could not be reversed. Sometimes he goes through several cycles of teaching and testing before being satisfied with the hierarchy. Thus, in developing a hierarchy, testing is used to determine what the separate steps are, what their order should be, and whether there is, indeed, a hierarchy at all.

With all this discussion of hierarchical instruction, it is important to note that very few instructional hierarchies for practical use have yet been discovered. In an earlier paper, White (1973) stated, "These flaws [in research design] mean that no meaningful quantitative conclusion has been reached about the validity of even one step in any hierarchy."

In private conversations White has indicated that he believes there may be hierarchies among intellectual skills, such things as dividing fractions, for example. (He described his research developing a clear one in his 1974 paper.) But one cannot yet point to extensive parts of any subject matter that have been laid out in carefully validated hierarchies. A lot of effort currently is being devoted to this approach, and if such hierarchies are even developed, their existence will be verified by tests, and tests will be used to place students at the proper level in them. We will return to the placement problem later.

Involving Parents in Curriculum Planning

Some educators advocate community participation in deciding what is taught to the children of the community. (See, for example, Esbensen, 1973.) They would like to see active discussions among parents and school officials and teachers, mutually determining the content of the curriculum, the objectives of the school, and the behaviors that the school should develop in the pupils. They might join in deciding the areas in which other parts of the community, such as the home and the church, should take the major responsibility. The school cannot do it all, of course, and some modern data suggest that the school makes a relatively modest contribution to the efforts of other parts of society. Some areas, such as religion and morals, are usually recognized as the province of the home and church, with the school being specifically directed to avoid the topics or treat them most carefully, as in the case of religion.

One of the real problems in obtaining community participation in determining the school's curriculum is trying to communicate to the parents the various possibilities that the school could consider. For example, should the school include training in woodworking? Some parents may think that with the high price of furniture, training in woodworking might be a good idea for all pupils. However, the school may indicate that with the time that can reasonably be allotted to woodworking for all students, all that can be accomplished is that each student will have made a drawer divider for silverware or a simple bookshelf and will have learned at a beginner's level how to use ten tools, not including a lathe. The parents may decide that this kind of training is not worth it for all pupils.

By the same token, one might ask whether the school should train the students in civics? Some parents, again, might think that with our government being in as bad shape as it is (and there are always some parents who think that things are in bad shape in the government), more civics is needed. However, when the school indicates the kinds of things students can do in government after the civics training that can be offered, again parents may doubt that it is worthwhile. The same illustrations can be made for any school subject — spelling, composition, literature, history, geography, reading, arithmetic, and so on down the list.

It is relatively easy to show what the outcome of the woodworking training will be for most students. How does one show what the outcome of civics, literature, history, reading, and other similar relatively abstract courses will be? There are many possibilities, but one of these that comes readily to hand (but should not be overemphasized because of its availability) is to indicate to parents what kinds of questions students can answer on the topic. That is, parents should be shown the test questions that are used in evaluating mastery or success in the subject and which questions most students get correct after training along with which questions many students still get wrong.

USING TESTS TO INDICATE TO PARENTS
WHAT IS BEING LEARNED

In order to make sound and full use of test results to communicate with parents about the school's curriculum and to get their participation in deciding on what the curriculum should be, it is necessary to do more than just send the children's tests home to the parents. First, some precaution has to be taken so that the tests and items that are shown to the parents don't simply become specific things that the parents make sure that their children know for subsequent tests. No one who is informed about testing would suggest that sound evaluation of instruction takes place when all the instruction amounts to is the learning of answers to specific test items. The test items are ordinarily thought of as being representative samples of similar items that the student would answer correctly or incorrectly. So using tests this way implies that there will be large pools of items. Those sent home to parents from time to time will be only a few of the many possibilities that may occur in subsequent tests. If the pools are large enough, there is no need to send home only the results on "retired" items — items that will not appear in future tests. The odds of any student getting a future test composed largely of items he has been coached on specifically should be so small as to be unimportant.

Second, it is probably not a very efficient practice simply to send test papers home. The items on them may not be placed in sensible groups so that the implications of success and failure on them comes through to the parents. The school should probably regroup the items into sensible categories, by skills or by objectives, so that parents can see at a glance which skills or objectives are being mastered or failed.

Third, it is not very revealing to parents just to see what their own children did as they try to assist in determining the curriculum. Some form of summary over classes, or perhaps several recent years, is much more helpful. A number of possible arrangements can be developed. One, for an illustration, is suggested in figure 23-3. There items on a hypothetical test have been grouped under categories that a teacher thought would help parents see the picture. (Obviously, there could be many more categories. Those listed are merely suggestive.) Then the performances of each of a number of students are indicated by a + sign for correct and a 0 for incorrect. Usually there would be many more students, but the four shown here serve to illustrate the procedure. At a glance it can be seen that there seems to be a weakness in performance on vocabulary items. The parents could then turn to the items themselves and decide whether they thought vocabulary skills on those kinds of items

Items

Pupil	Reading Comprehension				Vocabulary				Work Attack Skill		
	1	13	15	21	3	7	17	19	5	13	22
Mary	+	+	+	+	0	+	0	0	+	0	+
Susie	+	0	0	0	+	0	0	0	+	0	0
Billy	+	+	0	0	0	0	0	0	+	+	0
Tom	+	+	+	+	+	0	0	+	+	+	+

Figure 23–3
Using Tests to Inform Parents
about the Curriculum

were important for students like these. If so, the instruction needs improvement. If not, perhaps other changes should be made, including the possibility of dropping the skill from the training of students at this level.

If many students are to be involved, it might be easier to enter for each item the proportion of students who get the item correct, or the proportion of correct responses to all the items in a particular category. This, however, involves a computational burden that can become sizable, and it may not communicate so effectively to parents as plusses and zeros.

The procedure above is appropriate for tests that are developed in the schools. Some testing agencies provide tables similar to this for their commercial tests as one of the services they sell to schools. The purchase of such a service may be a sound investment for a school that finds the content of the commercial test is very close to the curriculum of the school.

There is an important thing to remain aware of in the use of feedback from the school to parents for the purpose of involving the parents in the school's curriculum development. To use feedback for this implies that parents do have a voice in determining what the school shall teach. Presumably the school invites parents to participate in order to obtain the parents' support. This should increase the motivation of the students as well as the facilities and opportunities that can be made available to the students and the community. It will do more harm than good if the school seems to invite parent participation and then ignores it or disputes the parents' recommendations. Some schools seem to be run like kingdoms ruled by the principal or superintendent. Those schools will not want to use techniques like this to invite parent participation in determining something as important as what the children shall be taught.

Using Tests to Direct Student Effort

Test questions have an important effect on the nature of the real curriculum of the school, as opposed perhaps to the stated curriculum, due to a fundamental psychological principle of learning. Organisms learn to do that which is rewarded. If there is no reward, the organism is less likely to perform. The psychologists say that the response is extinguished. It is like putting out a fire by removing the fuel.

For most students, getting items correct on tests has a reward function. The topics on which there are no questions will tend not to be learned because there is no reward for good performance on them. In other words, students learn that on which they are, or expect to be, tested. They tend not to learn that on which they are not, or expect not to be, tested. Thus, regardless of what we say about the curriculum, it is the tests and other forms of evaluation of student performance that really determine what the effective curriculum is.

This means several things to those who would use tests to improve instruction. One thing is that each student's performance on every important objective must be evaluated somehow. Often it will be by a test of some kind, but it might be by means of some other kind of observation of a performance, such as giving a speech, writing a story, serving a tennis ball, or running a mile. A second, and more far-reaching, meaning is that whoever controls the tests and evaluations in a school really controls the curriculum. If you want to control what is learned, get control of the tests — not the textbooks, the choice of teachers, the size of the class, the syllabus of the course, or any of the other things that curriculum developers talk about. If a classroom teacher's tests do not agree with the curriculum as spelled out for the instruction, what will be learned will agree with what is tested, not what is in the curriculum. In this sense tests have a fundamental role to play in improving instruction by their impact on the effective curriculum.

Summary

Tests are used in a number of different ways to assist in the organization of instruction. Ideally, when instruction is being planned, the tests that are part of that instruction are also planned. The plan for a test consists of a table of specifications or a list of behavioral objectives on the basis of which test items will be written and assembled. The table of specifications helps to assure that no important objective of instruction will accidentally be left out or unevaluated. It also helps monitor the relative emphasis that is given to various topics and skills.

In hierarchical instruction tests have several important roles. They are used to determine whether a hierarchy exists at all, and if so, the nature of its precise form. Once a hierarchy is isolated, tests can be used to determine whether the instruction is mastered, and if not, at what level an individual student needs to start his next bit of instruction. Unfortunately, not many hierarchies of consequence have yet been demonstrated to exist in usual school instruction.

Tests can also be used to communicate with parents the content of the curriculum and to get them to assist in deciding what shall be included and with what degree of emphasis. Showing parents the kinds of items that students tend to get right and wrong after instruction helps the parents to see what the school is doing.

Finally, the organization of instruction must provide for student motivation. Tests are motivating for students. It is rewarding for most students to get test questions correct. For this reason, the tests may be the most important factor in deciding what the real curriculum is.

References

Esbensen, T. Family-designed learning: Accountability as customer satisfaction. *Phi Delta Kappan*, 1973, **54**, 465–68.

White, R. T. Research into learning hierarchies. *Rev. educ. Res.*, 1973, **43**, 371.

White, R. T. The validation of a learning hierarchy. *Amer. educ. Res. Journal*, 1974, **11**, 121–36.

24

Using Tests to Place Students in Optimum Instruction

Objectives

As a result of study of this chapter you should be able to:

1. Describe a procedure for using standardized normative achievement tests for determining:
   a. the general level of the class;
   b. weaknesses of individual students in broad areas;
   c. weaknesses of the whole class in broad areas;
2. Describe newly developed published materials for placing students with respect to behavioral objectives;
3. List at least seven of the ten important aspects of a sound diagnostic and remedial procedure;
4. Describe and evaluate the state of the art in currently available diagnostic instruments;
5. Describe the procedure and requirements of diagnosis by comparing achievement with aptitude. Include:
   a. standardization on a common group;
   b. jangle fallacy;
   c. requirement of large differences;
6. Describe a relatively simple procedure for diagnosis of some kinds of problems;
7. List four functions of using tests during remediation;
8. Describe and evaluate the current status of the effectiveness of remediation;
9. Summarize arguments for and against homogeneous grouping;
10. Evaluate the evidence on the arguments related to homogeneous grouping;
11. Describe and illustrate the main aspects of an aptitude-treatment interaction;
12. Describe the status of current ATI research as related to subjects taught in elementary schools;

13. Describe the use of item scores to locate a student in an instructional hierarchy.
14. Contrast the views of learning theorists and measurement theorists on the number of items per objective required in placement tests for a learning hierarchy;
15. Describe the general attitude of courts toward use of tests for placement;
16. Describe the attitude of the court in *Hobson* v. *Hansen* toward use of tests for tracking in Washington, D.C.;
17. Describe the legal aspects of using tests for placement into special education.

The Meaning of *Placement*

There are at least two common uses of the word *placement* in education. One is to refer to the process of finding jobs or work situations for students during summers, after graduation, or as part of supervised work experience in connection with their schooling. The other meaning of *placement* is the one we are interested in here. That is placing students into instruction at the most profitable place or level. We don't want the students to undergo large amounts of instruction about things they already know or can do, nor do we want to skip them ahead so far that the new material is unnecessarily difficult due to what has been left out. We want to place them into instruction optimally.

Finding Out What Students Have and Have Not Learned

Finding out what is wrong that is impeding learning is a kind of placement called diagnosis, which we will take up a little bit later. Right now we want to see how tests can be used to improve instruction by helping us to place at the proper level students who are learning normally.

In the previous chapter we mentioned that tests can be used to find out what step in a hierarchy students have reached, if a hierarchy is known for a unit of instruction. We will return to this idea later in this chapter. Suppose that no hierarchy is available. Then one can use a layout of the items that different students get right and wrong, such as in figure 23-3, in another way. Earlier we introduced such a chart as a way to work with parents in deciding what elements should be retained or deleted from a curriculum. Now we are assuming that the curriculum decisions have been made and that we are satisfied with them. We want to know now what Mary, Susie, Billy, and Tom need to study next. By looking across the row for each student we can spot his or her weaknesses. Mary and Tom, in that figure, need to work on vocabulary, but they don't seem to need more work on reading comprehension. Billy also needs work on vocabulary, and Susie needs help on everything. It looks like the whole group needs work on vocabulary, so group instruction on that seems like a good idea, but there is no point in taking group time for reading comprehension since it would be inefficient for Mary and Tom.

Remember that such a chart would ordinarily include more groups of items than the three shown in figure 23-3, and it would include all the students in a group rather than just the four used here for illustration.

It is important to keep in mind another aspect of such a chart. If you are looking for areas in which the whole group needs work, a relatively few items can give good information if everyone tends to get all of them right or wrong. However, for individual students if there are only a few items, they provide us with no more than clues. We would want to test Billy further in vocabulary before we decided that he definitely needed a lot more work on it because we ordinarily can put very little faith in only four questions when making a decision about an individual student.

The layout in figure 23-3 can help tell us what needs to be tested further or what areas need careful scrutiny by the teacher. Sometimes she can provide that further scrutiny by operations other than formal tests. She might want to give Tom and Mary something new to read and have them tell her what it says in order to verify that their reading comprehension was as good as the test indicated. She might want to listen to Susie read aloud some new material to verify that her word attack skills were really deficient. In general, teachers should beware of making interpretations for individual students on the basis of small numbers of items, but performance on only a few items of a given kind can provide useful clues as to where to look further.

FINDING OUT WHAT OBJECTIVES STUDENTS HAVE MASTERED

Finding out what students have learned and finding out what objectives they have mastered are not very different ideas, but the two approaches to teaching are sometimes thought of separately. The procedures available for the two may be different enough that they should be treated separately. One important reason to take up placement according to objectives mastered is that there are a number of newly developed commercial services available to teachers that can be of great help in this process. Traditional achievement survey tests, or tests that teachers make up on their own, are useful for deciding what students have learned. But for those teachers who orient their teaching toward behavioral objectives, several organizations have compiled large numbers of objectives in various subjects at various levels of school and have items for sale that measure those objectives.

For instance, the Institute for Educational Research, Downers Grove, Illinois[1] sells at modest prices sets of objectives and items in language arts, science, mathematics, and social studies. These include a total of 4,595 objectives and 27,259 items, including some in the affective domain. They are available at the primary, intermediate, junior high and high school level, and are sold at the cost of reproduction and handling. The development of the pool was made possible by a United States government grant. This governmental project can save an individual school or teacher all the cost of developing the objectives and the items for them.

Another agency, the Instructional Objectives Exchange (IOX), of the UCLA Graduate School of Education, also has a pool of objectives, and it has associated tests. Some of the topics of their pool overlap the Institute for Educational Research's pool, but for many topics, such as business education, home economics, industrial arts, physical education, and others, there is no overlap. Their pool contains about 50 sets of cognitive and affective objectives. These are also sold

---

[1]The institute is located at 1400 Maple Avenue, Downers Grove, Illinois 60515 (Phone: [312] 971-2040).

very reasonably, about $8.00 for a set of objectives and sample items on a topic such as junior high mathematics containing over 250 objectives and over 500 items.

The Instructional Objectives Exchange also distributes brief criterion-referenced tests keyed to objectives. The tests are on preprinted spirit masters, so that the school can run off 250 to 300 copies of each test. The tests are short, taking only five to ten minutes and consisting of only five or ten items. The tests are sold in sets, each set containing about 40 tests. For each set there is an alternate form of each test. So a school could pick out an area such as American Government, grades 10 to 12, and buy the spirit masters for 37 tests on objectives within that topic for a reasonable price. If it wanted both forms for pretesting and posttesting, it might buy both for slightly less than twice the cost of a single set. The school would then run off the number of copies of each test that it wanted to use. A manual is available for each set describing the objective being tested, the instructions to the student, and the scoring procedure.

Through these two agencies a school or teacher can perhaps save a great deal of effort in developing tests to determine whether students have mastered each of the objectives that is a designated part of the school's curriculum. The teacher would, of course, have to obtain the set of objectives and items she wanted, and evaluate the objectives as to their agreement with her objectives. She would select those that agreed, and using the associated items set up tests or buy spirit masters for tests that would function for her in the manner described in the previous section, with a layout of successes and failures as in figure 23-3. The difference would be that instead of a name for a group of items at the head of each column, she would have an objective. Otherwise the procedure and the precautions are the same.

For those who want even more help, the Westinghouse Learning Corporation, Iowa City, Iowa,[2] offers still more in a service they call "School Curriculum Objective-Referenced Evaluation" or "SCORE." This organization has all the objectives mentioned above from the Institute for Educational Research and the Instructional Objectives Exchange, plus the objectives from Project PLAN, a pool of over 8,000 objectives and 20,000 items. They are also adding objectives written by local school districts. You can select the objectives you want from their catalog or add your own to their pool, and they will create and print the tests required to measure those objectives. They indicate that a typical test from them would include from 70 to 180 questions; it is not clear from their advertising how many items there would be for each objective. They will also score the tests for you after you have administered them, and they will produce score reports for you within ten days. They will do this at whatever intervals you want, apparently, from every 6 or 9 weeks to once or twice a year. The prices undoubtedly vary with the services rendered. Experience with SCORE is not widespread yet. The initial announcement of the service was made in July of 1973.

Another organization, Educational Testing Service,[3] not only has pools of objectives and items, this time adding to the others the National Assessment of Educational Progress exercises, but also offers specialists who will come to your school to design and conduct teacher-training programs in assessment. They also offer assistance in designing and conducting studies that will help schools develop con-

---

[2]Westinghouse Learning Corporation's address is P.O. Box 30, Iowa City, Iowa 52240.
[3]The Educational Testing Service is located in Princeton, New Jersey 08540.

clusions about mastery of objectives from performances on existing standardized testing programs. This service was announced in the organization's newsletter, *ETS Developments,* in fall of 1973, so again experience with it has not been widespread.

Some schools, and even whole states, have embarked on programs of developing objectives for all school subjects, and items for all those objectives. They, apparently, were not aware of the large number of services of this kind that are available at much less cost commercially. Certainly no more should anyone start to reinvent this wheel without being fully informed about the wheels that have already been invented!

Diagnosing Students' Learning Difficulties

Earlier we postponed consideration of how one would use tests to diagnose what problems were inhibiting a student's further learning, as opposed to merely finding out what he had learned so far, and what should be undertaken next. Now we will turn to the diagnostic use of tests in analyzing learning difficulties among normal children. We add the phrase "among normal children" so that we will not have to embark on a whole new field, that of dealing with those students who are so educationally handicapped that they must be put into special classes or programs. The handicap may be a physical one, such as poor vision, poor hearing, poor coordination or psychomotor or perceptual development, or it may be less obvious. But if it is severe enough to be best handled by special education, we are not going to discuss it here. Our problem is that of the usual classroom teacher, trying to find out what is hanging Johnny or Susie up that can be remedied within the regular classroom.

ANALOGY TO MEDICINE

To get a proper perspective on this, let us consider where we found the term *diagnosis* for this kind of problem. Obviously, it was from the field of medicine. When one is having a difficulty, such as with a very sore forearm that is swollen and blue and painful to use, after a short time he is likely to seek the help of an expert. The expert, a medical doctor, is likely to ask about the onset of the problem. That is, he will ask how the arm got hurt. Perhaps it was a fall. It is possible that the patient won't know how it happened.

Before the doctor can very successfully provide a remedy for the performance disability, the sore arm, he needs to diagnose what is wrong with it. The standard diagnostic procedure is an X-ray of the bones. If one is broken, the remedy is pretty standard, too. It will be putting the arm into a plaster cast for about three weeks or so. After the three weeks, there will be another three or four weeks of regular hot baths for the limb and exercise to restore the muscles that atrophied from disuse. Then after a gradual increase in use, after six months to a year the arm will be as good as new — the performance disability will have been remedied. There will be no difference between that arm and the other arm, or between that arm and the arms of similar people who do not have broken arms.

This is the process of diagnosing and remedying a physical disability, and that is the model we would like to follow with learning disabilities. We would like to be able to give a diagnostic test of some kind, find out what the problem is, be able to prescribe a specific remedy, and tell how much to apply, for how long, with what side effects, and how to treat the side effects. We would like to be able to say on what proportion of the people the treatment would be successful (nearly 100% for broken arms) and on what kind of people it might be unsuccessful (for broken arms, the very old, those with calcium problems, and perhaps others that trained physicians are aware of). We would also like to know how long the remedy would last (for broken bones it lasts permanently, but not for cancers of some types).

Notice that no doctor would ordinarily have all his patients take a diagnostic test — a complete set of bone X-rays. Only for an unusual malady, such as glaucoma or high blood pressure, would a diagnostic test be routinely given. Then it would be given only to selected patients — patients over a certain age, perhaps — and then only if the test was simple to do, inexpensive, and quickly accomplished. Notice that schools don't even require that every pupil have a blood evaluation every year — relatively simple tests that are quite revealing and take little of the pupil's time. But oddly enough, you do find teachers and schools giving to every pupil diagnostic tests in certain subjects. It is as though they all had disabilities that were to be discovered, or as though there were severe disabilities that were easily treated, if recognized, that deserved such extensive diagnostic work. One has reason to suspect that something has gone wrong when the idea of diagnosis and remediation is carried over from medicine to education. We will sense more of that as we go along. First, let us look at some of the modern educational diagnostic procedures that are available.

SOME DIAGNOSTIC INSTRUMENTS

There are a great number of tests that are published with the phrase "diagnostic" in their title or that are recommended for use in diagnosis of learning problems. A development for illustration here is the *Stanford Diagnostic Reading Test,* published in 1966. As the introductory announcement says, "A child who can't read is hurt. He is hurt every day when he walks into class and faces the frustration and confusion of failure. You know that each child is different. The best way you can help him is to find out what his individual reading problems are. The *Stanford Diagnostic Reading Test* can help you find out." Doesn't that sound like the doctor's X-ray for the broken arm?

This test comes in two levels. At the lower level, suitable for second to fourth grade, there are seven subtests. Each takes about fifteen minutes to half an hour, for a total of two and a half to three hours of administration time, roughly half of a school day.

The publisher offers a special scoring and reporting service for Level II of the test (grades 4 to 8) which analyzes each pupil's pattern of scores on the various parts of the test and then groups the pupils into one of 11 possible groups who have similar learning problems. For each of these groups there is a description of the characteristics of the group. Then there are a number of suggestions for instruction that will, presumably, remedy the weaknesses of pupils with those characteristics.

Another diagnostic device from another publisher takes a slightly different course. The *Prescriptive Mathematics Inventory,* published in 1971, is based on the procedure of teaching students to master specified behavioral objectives. The test author analyzed all the most widely used mathematics textbooks in the United States and listed the objectives they covered. He found that there were a total of 345 objectives in grades 4 through 8. For each objective he wrote a test item. He also listed for each text the pages that presented the material on that objective. The procedure in using the *Prescriptive Mathematics Inventory* is to see which items each student got wrong. These represent objectives he has not mastered, so he is referred to the appropriate pages of his textbook to go back and restudy that material. Of course, sometimes more than one student may need to restudy the same material, so groups can be formed that work together. Or perhaps the whole class can learn together points that many of them missed.

Still a different approach is that of the *Individualized Mathematics Program,* published by the Educational and Industrial Testing Service of San Diego. This program claims to follow the fundamental procedure of individualized instruction, i.e., assess the progress of each student, diagnose his difficulty, and prescribe appropriate instruction. The program includes pretests, objectives, instructional material (MATH-PAKs), and posttests. For Level C, grades 8-9, there are 64 objectives. A criterion-referenced test (TABS-IMP) is given before instruction. On a student progress chart, the teacher indicates from those test results which objectives have and have not been mastered. Then for each objective that has not been mastered, one of the 64 MATH-PAKs is assigned. The MATH-PAK also contains more specific pretest material to determine precisely the student's difficulty. It contains lessons, problems, and answers for the student. Finally, in the MATH-PAK for an objective there is a posttest so the student can evaluate whether he has mastered the objective.

Other modern diagnostic procedures for classroom use are available, and more will be made available in the near future. There are a *Prescriptive Reading Inventory* and a *Stanford Diagnostic Arithmetic Test* parallel to the tests we have described above. Obviously, there is no reason that a teacher cannot develop her own diagnostic tests, as well. For one thing, diagnostic tests like those we have described above do not depend on the collection of normative data, i.e., data on the performance of large representative samples of students on the test or the items. That is not really relevant to the function of diagnosis. The teacher merely wants to know whether the students can do certain kinds of operations, perhaps chosen because they represent previously specified objectives of her instruction. By the pattern above, if a student cannot get the item correct on a certain objective, the teacher has him restudy the relevant part of his textbook, or better (Block and Tierney, 1974) study a special treatment of the material, or perhaps go over the kind of instruction that has already been done in cases where study has not been from a text, as for example, in beginning reading.

APPROACHES TO THE USE OF INSTRUMENTS

The essence of the kind of diagnosis we have been considering has been the use of a *post*test to determine where deficiencies or learning difficulties are located. There are other possibilities.

DIAGNOSIS BY COMPARING ACHIEVEMENT WITH APTITUDE

We have considered placing students by giving them a pretest to determine what they should learn next (perhaps called a placement test), or giving students who are obviously having difficulty a posttest (diagnostic) to see what is causing their trouble.

However, some would approach diagnosis by comparing a student's achievement with his aptitude to see whether he is learning as fast as he might be expected to learn. A follow-up diagnostic test might then be used with those who aren't learning "up to capacity."

Standardization on a common group. A problem with this approach is that many teachers do not realize the serious demands on the instruments that are required for this purpose. One is that the aptitude and achievement tests that are to be contrasted must have been normed on the same population. Otherwise to find that Johnny is at the fifty-third percentile on aptitude but only the forty-first percentile on achievement may reflect the differences in the norms groups for the tests not Johnny's achievement in relation to his aptitude. Experts recommend that it is not enough just to say that both sets of norms are "national norms." Different publishers have different populations that they call "national." The two tests must have been normed on the same groups of students, at the same time, in the same norming operation for comparisons as delicate as these to be made soundly. Not a great many sets of tests have been normed in this way, but each of the major publishers of tests seems to have something available, such as the SCAT aptitude and STEP achievement tests of the Cooperative Test Service of Educational Testing Service. But the teacher *cannot* do something as simple as look up each child's national percentile on whatever aptitude test happens to be on his record and compare that evaluation with his national percentile on achievement. From that she cannot make a sound evaluation of whether there is a learning problem that needs diagnosis.

Jangle fallacy. Another problem that must be contended with in comparing aptitude and achievement is the jangle fallacy. This fallacy is the belief that because tests have different titles they measure different things. It is particularly important in comparing aptitude and achievement because in many subjects an aptitude test and an achievement test may contain items that are basically the same. It is reported that one investigator took the items from a mathematics aptitude test and a mathematics achievement test and scrambled them. He then asked experts in measurement and in mathematics to sort them back into aptitude items and achievement items. The result was utter failure. Now if the items on the two kinds of tests are so nearly the same, how can one expect to find differences between scores except due to random errors of measurement? How foolish to interpret such differences as indications of learning difficulties and then to try to diagnose what the difficulties are!

Even though a test may be supposedly a test of general aptitude, many of the items may be essentially arithmetic or mathematical items, so the jangle fallacy may creep into the problem to some extent — enough to hide real differences between "aptitude" and "achievement." The problem of distinguishing between these two abstract concepts is so fraught with difficulties that in February of 1973 a conference was held in California involving many of the greatest names in educational measurement to try to disentangle the two ideas. By the end of the conference (Green, 1974) some experts were still saying that there is no real difference, while others were demonstrating how to tell that there is a real difference.

Large differences needed. A third problem with comparing aptitude with achievement is that only quite large differences between scores on the two are interpretable.

This is true even when tests have been standardized on a common population and when it has been determined that the items in the aptitude and achievement tests are sufficiently different to cause one to believe that they are measuring different things. The reason that only large differences are interpretable is the problem of reliability, or to look at the other side of the coin, error of measurement.

We call a test that gives the same score for an individual each time he is measured with it highly reliable. A test that gives inconsistent results, high one time and low the next, is unreliable. It is inconsistent. For a rough analogy, in a recipe that calls for a pinch of salt, different cooks will put in different amounts of salt, depending on how big their fingers are, and what they think a pinch is. When someone wants to be precise about the amount, he specifies something like ⅛ teaspoon in order to get consistent results. Teaspoons are much more reliable measures than pinches. There is less error of measurement in using teaspoons than pinches. That is the same idea we are talking about when we demand that school measurements be reliable. They should behave more like teaspoons than like pinches. (Actually, it is hard to get educational measurements to be even as reliable as pinches, when you get right down to it. So we need them to be as reliable as we can reasonably get them.)

We can get a measure of the degree of unreliability of educational measurements by describing how much error they involve. The concept here is called the *standard error of measurement.* Suppose we were to have a hundred students in a cooking school each take 10 pinches of salt, and put each pinch onto a separate bit of waxed paper. We could then measure the separate pinches very accurately in a special set of teaspoon measures to see how much they differed from each other. We could find the average amount in a pinch, say ⅛ teaspoon. Then if we took all those pinches that were smaller than average but closest to average until we had included the largest two-thirds of the small pinches, we might come to one that had only 3/32 of a teaspoon of salt. The difference between ⅛ (or 4/32) and 3/32 teaspoons would be defined as the standard error of measurement of pinches of salt. In this hypothetical illustration, the standard error of measurement would be 1/32 of a teaspoon.

This standard error of measurement is an arbitrary convention that helps us describe the amount of error in measurements. In general, plus (or minus) one standard error of measurement from a score includes about one-third of the values one might get from repeated measures of the same thing. Plus *and* minus one standard error of measurement includes approximately two-thirds of the measurements we would get by repeatedly measuring the same thing. Sometimes in engineering the values of quantities like the thickness of steel plate or the amount of resistance of a resistor in a radio are expressed in numbers like 500 ± 10, which means that the thickness or resistance is 500, within 10, two-thirds of the time.[4]

Now careful and informed users of educational test scores don't interpret two scores as being different from each other unless they differ by much more than the standard error of measurement. In fact the usual rule is that if tests have been standardized on the same population, then to see if two scores really can be described as

---

[4]For further instruction on this concept, see chapter 11. There is also an audiotutorial provided in *Exercises in Classroom Measurement* that develops facility in understanding and using this idea. It is number 14, entitled "Standard Error of Measurement and Confidence Intervals." If you have not already done so, you may want to do the following audiotutorials: (2) "Frequency Distributions and Frequency Curves," (3) "Normal Curve, Mean, and Standard Deviation," (7) "Correlation," and (10) "Percents under the Normal Curve" to develop skills required for efficient use of audiotutorial number 14.

different we subtract one standard error of measurement from the higher score and add one standard error of measurement to the lower score. If the result for the higher test is still above that for the lower test, we are willing to say that the higher score is really likely to be above the lower score. If when the standard errors of measurement are taken into consideration the lower test's result is at or above the higher test's result, we conclude that the apparent differences in the two scores may merely be the result of imperfect measurement, i.e., of random wobble or error in the scores.

That argument is hard to follow without a picture, so let us use one. Suppose that we have given a reading aptitude test to a student and have also given him a reading achievement test. We have looked at the two tests to assure ourselves that they are not both using the same kind of items or procedures with the student, i.e., we are not committing the jangle fallacy. And we have ascertained that the two tests were normed together on a common population so that we aren't going to be fooled by differences in samples or populations.

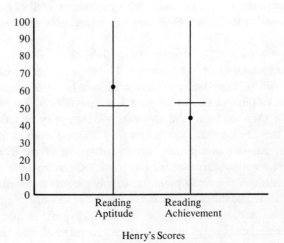

Reading Aptitude   Reading Achievement

Henry's Scores

Figure 24–1

*Use of Standard Error of Measurement
in Determining Whether Test Scores Are Really Different*

We look in the test manual for each test, a booklet which describes the test, tells how to administer the test, how to score it, and so on, and find the standard error of measurement for the test for pupils like the one we are studying (say second grade boys). It is likely that our two tests will have different standard errors of measurement, but that will cause no problem. Now we draw a graph, as in figure 24–1, which has the score scale on the left (each of the tests must have the same score scale for sensible interpretations to follow) and a vertical line representing each of the two tests. On each of the vertical lines there is a dot representing the student's score on that measure. For our illustration let us use Henry's scores. On the left is the line for reading aptitude and on the right the line for reading achievement. Let us say that the common score scale is percentiles for second grade boys, the percentile score being the score at or below which a given percent of the students in the norm group scored.

We want to use the standard error of measurement to determine whether Henry's aptitude score differs from his achievement score far enough for us to be confident that his true achievement really is different from his true aptitude. To do this, we must find the percentiles that go with scores one standard error of measurement above his low score and one standard error below his high score. In our illustration, let's say Henry got a lower score in achievement, the forty-fifth percentile, and a higher score in aptitude, the sixty-second percentile. We are really asking whether he is an underachiever and whether further diagnostic testing is in order to see what is handicapping him in reading.

We add one standard error of measurement to Henry's lowest raw score and look that value up in the norms table for achievement. Let us say that the result is a percentile value of 54. We then subtract one standard error of measurement from his score on aptitude, and look that value up in the norms table to see what percent of students in the norms group fell at or below that score. Let us say that the result is 52%, so that score is at the fifty-second percentile. Now we mark those points on the graph with bars, and check to see whether the bar for the higher score (aptitude here) is indeed higher than the bar for the lower score (here achievement). It turns out that this is not the case. Even though Henry scored at the sixty-second percentile on aptitude and at the forty-fifth percentile on achievement, there is sufficient error of measurement in the two test scores that we cannot be at all sure that tested again the scores might not come out in the opposite order. The sound conclusion is that pending further information, we judge Henry's aptitude for reading and achievement in reading to be at approximately the same level.

To people who are not sophisticated in use of test scores, it may seem remarkable that we would conclude that a score of the sixty-second percentile on one test was not detectably different from a score on another test at the forty-fifth percentile. But that is the way the educational measurement world really is. Our measures are not usually more reliable than this. Especially if someone is near the middle of his group on performance, the standard error of measurement is very wide in terms of percentiles. In those cases it takes a very large difference for us to be able to conclude safely that two scores are really different.

There is another way to look at this problem of comparing scores. Instead of seeing how much error there is in each of the individual scores, we look at their difference as a new score and ask how reliable is this *difference score*. The degree of reliability of a difference score is influenced not only by the reliability of the two measures considered separately, but by the degree to which scores on one measure tend to go up or down along with scores on the other measure. Difference scores based on highly reliable measures tend to be more reliable than difference scores based on less reliable measures, other things being equal. However, the more scores on one measure tend to rise or fall with scores on the other measure, the less reliable are differences between those scores, other things being equal. Since aptitude and achievement are usually substantially correlated with each other, difference scores contrasting aptitude and achievement suffer in reliability. That is, only large difference scores can be trusted.[5]

---

[5]An audiotutorial is provided in *Exercises in Classroom Measurement* entitled "Reliability of Difference Scores." It is number 17. If you have not already done it, you may need to do number 7, "Correlation," and its prerequisites, before starting on 17.

Knowing these problems in comparing scores on different measures in order to reach diagnostic conclusions puts quite a damper on the use of comparisons of this sort except, of course, for the ignorant. And it is really not very easy to learn enough to deal with these problems properly. The problems are sufficiently complex that the experts are still coming out with new technical treatises for each other trying to work out useful, statistically sound solutions for such comparisons (Cronbach et al., 1972, Chapter 5).

After that highly technical tangle, it may seem like dropping from the sublime to the ridiculous, but a very useful procedure in trying to find out what a child's learning difficulty is consists of a simple thing used by our predecessors when they taught algebra and geometry. Instead of giving diagnostic tests, trying to compare aptitude with achievement, using prescriptive inventories, and all that, our predecessors simply had their pupils go to the blackboard and work problems aloud. When a pupil got a problem wrong, they could see where he got off the track and perhaps diagnose right then and there why the error was occurring. One might have said, "Henry, you simply have not memorized the Pythagorean Theorem, and until you do, you will have trouble with problems like this. Now you go back to your seat and memorize that. In half an hour I am going to have you write it on the board and give you another problem to solve using it." On the other hand, the teacher might have suddenly realized that the problem given to Henry was not entirely clear, and he could not be expected to work it.

Modern teachers can use the same kind of procedure profitably with their tests as they try to improve instruction. When a student is having trouble with a particular kind of item, the teacher can have him solve it aloud, and try from that to diagnose what the cause is and what kind of instruction will remedy it. This is using tests to improve instruction by placing students into the proper instruction by diagnosis just as surely as is the elaborate use of standardized diagnostic tests. The modern teacher, like her predecessor, may also use this technique to improve her test items, but that is really a different topic.

Using Tests during Remediation

This would not be a sound and adequate treatment of using tests to improve instruction via diagnosis and remediation of learning problems if we did not spend some time on the remediation part of the procedure. We will turn to that now. First, let us consider how tests might be used to help with the remedial process, assuming that a sound remedy for the specified problem exists and is known.

We will not ordinarily be thinking of standardized, commercial tests at this point but of the tests that a teacher might make up. During the process of remediation, a teacher can make effective use of frequent tests for about four different functions. First, her tests can help the student to understand what she expects of him. The golf pro will try to explain to a pupil who has trouble because he "slices" the ball (makes it curve sharply to the right in mid-air) about "hitting the ball from the inside out." That may or may not make much sense. So the pro will have the pupil put a golf ball on the ground, and then she will stick two tees in the ground showing the pupil the path she wants the club to take as it goes through the ball. She'll then ask the pupil to hit the ball with a swing that touches both of the tees. To the pupil's surprise if he does it, his ball will fly beautifully straight, or perhaps even curve left instead of right. He may exclaim. "Oh, now I see what you mean by inside out!" That is using a test to clarify what is expected. Of course, the clever teacher can do the same sort of thing in other subjects, from word attack skills to balancing equations.

The teacher's tests during remediation can serve another purpose, that of improving the diagnosis. We noted earlier that the first clues to a student's problems may come from a very few items on a commercial survey test or on one of the teacher's tests. Further questions would be needed to pin down the specific problem. These further tests may be constructed and given for ascertaining whether particular things are problems at various points during remediation. The golf instructor may notice during the practice session that not only does the student swing from outside in, but perhaps he does that because his right elbow gets too far from the body during the down swing. She might use another test, placing a handkerchief under the right armpit and having the student swing, to test that idea. If the handkerchief drops to the ground, the diagnosis may be improved and a new remedy worked on.

A third use of frequent tests during remediation is to give the student the satisfaction of partial success during the process. It is rewarding and reassuring to the student to be able to do some part of the process right, even though he cannot master the final objective yet. Tests, properly designed, can provide that kind of encouragement.

Finally, we have to determine when the remedy is complete so we can move on. The doctor may have to take the cast off and take another X-ray to see how the healing is progressing and whether recasting for additional treatment of the broken arm is necessary. Henry's teacher told him that in half an hour she was going to give him another problem using the Pythagorean Theorem to see if he had mastered it. These are all ways that tests can be used to improve instruction during the remedial phase.

PROBLEMS WITH USE OF COMMERCIAL DIAGNOSTIC TESTS

Remember that with the medical doctor's diagnosis of the broken bone, he was able to specify the proper remediation (treatment), the length of treatment, the probability of success, and the kinds of people for whom the probabilities were different, i.e., for whom might the treatment not be effective or take longer? This is the area in which most commercial and teacher-made diagnostic tests fall short. While it might give us some comfort to know that a patient's problem can be diagnosed as muscular distrophy and there is no remedy for it, if that was all we could expect from doctors for all kinds of maladies, we would not continue to use doctors very much. Our interest in medical doctors is not just that they can tell us what is wrong, but that for them knowing what is wrong is the same as knowing the cure in a great many cases.

By contrast, most diagnostic tests in education over the years have not even suggested remedies. It is only recently that test publishers have taken on the task of providing not only test scores but also telling us even as much as what pages of common texts cover the troublesome points or what kinds of instruction might be useful for pupils with these problems.

Unfortunately, none of our diagnostic tests at present goes on to describe a treatment *and* how long it should be applied, how often it should be conducted (how many hours per day, how many problems, how many practice swings of the golf club), what the probability is that after the specified treatment the problem will be corrected, for what kinds of pupils the treatment might be ineffective, and whether the treatment will last. A difficult assignment for a graduate student in education is that of taking any diagnostic test of his choice and finding evidence that any treatment can be shown to remedy the learning problem associated with any pattern of low scores in a specified, reasonable amount of time, eliminating that problem from causing any future difficulty for that child. The usual outcome of such an exercise is a paper that criticizes the technical quality of the diagnostic measure and criticizes the technical adequacy of any research on possibly related remedial procedures. But it is nearly impossible to find situations in which diagnostic tests and remedial procedures are coordinated, as they must be to be effective, and which show that remediation is effective in the long term. In fact, evidence of short-term remedies for most learning difficulties of normal children is not easy to find.

PROBLEMS WITH REMEDIATION

Perhaps one of the problems is that we just do not know much about how to remedy the learning difficulties of normal children. There has been a great deal of research effort on this topic lately associated with remedying the problems of the disadvantaged child who is otherwise normal. Some findings are beginning to emerge.

We are beginning to find that some things thought to be necessary for successful instruction really are not necessary. The Council for Basic Education compared successful and unsuccessful reading programs in 1971 and found out that very small classes are not necessary. Of four schools judged as successful in teaching reading, class sizes ranged from 22 to 29 per teacher.

Preschool training of the pupils is not a factor in success. Almost all of the children in three of the four schools had not had preschool experience.

Outstanding teachers were not found to be important. The teachers in the successful schools seemed to be above average but not strikingly so.

Ethnic identification did not seem to be important. One of the four leaders in the programs was from a minority group, and many of the teachers did not represent the ethnic background of the community.

Homogeneous grouping was not clearly a factor. Three of the schools used it, but one did not.

Physical plant was not the secret. Two of the schools were noticeably old, and all of them were of the egg-crate type (*Report on School Staffing*, 1971).

We are also beginning to find that most efforts to compensate for educational disadvantages are not successful, and that even those which claim to be successful usually cannot substantiate their claim. The American Institutes for Research in the Behavioral Sciences in 1971 reviewed over 1200 reports of evaluations of compensatory programs to form a list of successful ones. Success was defined as:

1. producing gains in achievement greater than the gains of their more advantaged counterparts,
2. resulting in a rate of gain that was maintained until the disadvantaged actually caught up,
3. having been successful on a representative sample of at least thirty children, and
4. having the achievement gains measured by some reliable testing instrument.

These seem to be reasonable requirements as we think of our medical analogy.

Out of the over 1200 reports that were studied, these criteria narrowed the contenders down to 500 possibilities. Of these, 326 agreed to participate in the search for successful programs by providing data to AIR. And of those 326, 10 were actually found to be successful when subjected to in-depth analysis. It is not, then, surprising that experienced researchers are skeptical when hearing of successful remedial programs for students with learning difficulties! But one begins to wonder at the popularity of diagnostic tests that presumably lead one to the proper remedy for such problems. (*Report on Educational Research,* 1971)

It is not as though a lot of effort has not been expended on trying to help children with learning problems. A review of the literature on summer compensatory programs for the disadvantaged covering all published references and those available through ERIC yielded 18 studies, none of which showed clearly that achievement gains were greater than would be achieved without the program or that the gains persisted through time. These research results are the result of the government's spending $174 million dollars on 2½ million children per year over a period from 1966 to 1970 (Austin et al., 1972).

The fact that large amounts of money per student are being expended on such remedial programs is perhaps best illustrated by one program reported in the Bronx. There $42,863 were reported to the New York Legislature as being spent on 25 seventh to ninth grade students, or about $1700 per student. The report states that these students were severely retarded in reading and mathematics. After this expenditure, the report indicates that the students gained more than the one-year gain that can be expected of the average child, but the report does not indicate that the gain was maintained afterwards, nor that there was a control procedure to assure that the gain was not just an apparent gain. The appearance of a gain could result from lack of perfect correlation between the test that was used to select these seriously retarded students and the test that was used to evaluate their gains, i.e., the regression effect[6] (University of The State of New York, 1971–72).

The problem of poorly conducted research permeates the literature on remediation of learning problems. The ineptitude of researchers in this area is so gross and so widespread that if you hear of a successful remedial effort, you should first of all question whether the study indicating its success was sound. Until that has been established, it is of no interest to read what factors might have produced the apparent result. You might almost rely on the maxim that for the research currently being reported, if remediation is shown to be effective for normal children, most likely it is a case of poor research.

Tracking or Homogeneous Grouping

So far in presenting ideas about using tests to place students in instruction, we have taken up placing students according to what they have already learned and what they haven't yet learned, placing them according to what objectives they have mastered, and placing them according to what their particular difficulties or problems are.

---

[6]An audiotutorial is provided in *Exercises in Classroom Measurement* to explain the regression effect. It is number 22 and is entitled "Regression Effect." A prerequisite for understanding number 22 is previous completion of number 7, "Correlation," and number 3, "Normal Curve, Mean and Standard Deviation."

Now let us turn to a different but common type of placement, that of grouping students by their ability to learn or their estimated rate of learning. In some schools this is called ability grouping, in some it is called tracking, in some it is called homogeneous grouping, and it probably has a number of other names. The underlying idea in each case is to group together the fast learners, to put into another group the slow learners, and perhaps to have several intermediate groups according to how fast they are expected to learn.

This procedure has come under careful scrutiny recently because it is related to the integration-segregation issue, as we shall see. Historically, ability grouping came into prominence in the 1920s, after the development of standardized ability tests. There was a decline in its popularity in the 1930s and 1940s, but interest increased in the 1950s with the country's renewed interest in academic achievement. In the 1970s the practice seems to have been increasing in popularity, and it seems to have been increasing in prevalence as the grade level of students increases.

There is an interesting contrast between the points of view of those who advocate homogeneous grouping and those who are opposed to the practice (Esposito, 1973). The arguments of the advocates of homogeneous grouping are these:

1. It takes individual differences into account by letting pupils of similar ability progress at their own rates, and it offers them teaching methods and materials suited to their ability levels.
2. With homogeneous groups of students, more individual attention from teachers is possible.
3. In homogeneous groups, pupils are challenged to do their best in their own groups, and this provides more appropriate levels of competition for the various kinds of students.
4. Teachers find it easier to teach a group of students whose talents are about equally great than a group with very mixed degrees of talent.
5. In heterogeneous groups there is a tendency to teach to the average or below average student, ignoring the delay this imposes on the above average student.

The arguments of the advocates of heterogeneous grouping, i.e., of having a complete mixture of levels of student aptitude in each group of students, are:

1. Homogeneous grouping is undemocratic. It places a stigma on the students in the lower groups, and it gives an inflated sense of worth to those in the faster groups.
2. Adult life is not ability grouped. Therefore, ability grouping is detrimental to students because it does not give all children experience in working with all levels of ability.
3. Pupils of less ability may learn more effectively and otherwise profit from working with pupils of more ability.
4. It is not possible to achieve truly homogeneous groups, anyway, since our measures are not that good.
5. In homogeneous grouping, teachers may assume that the pupils in a single group are more homogeneous than they really are, and thus might impede individual students from revealing their talents.

If you compare these two sets of arguments in terms of their total orientations, it seems clear that the advocates of homogeneous grouping are emphasizing the instructional advantages of that procedure, while the advocates of heterogeneous grouping are trying to avoid harm to the personalities as well as to the instruction of the slower students that might be associated with homogeneous grouping.

It should be possible to evaluate data on students in the two kinds of grouping, heterogeneous and homogeneous, to see whether one point of view is more sound than the other. One might ask, "Do students who are taught in homogeneous groups out-perform those in heterogeneous groups?" Or, even prior to that, one might ask, "Is the instruction in homogeneous groups clearly different from one group to another and from that in heterogeneous groups?" If that is not the case, then one could not reasonably expect differences in performance to appear.

The research described by Esposito (1973) on differences found in instruction between schools grouped in the two ways indicates that no clear differences generally exist. Apparently, teachers do about the same things regardless of the kind of grouping in their schools. It is not surprising to find, then, that there is no clear support in student performance data for superior performance by students who have been taught in classes in which students have been grouped by ability. Thus, there is not much evidence to support the contentions of those who suggest that it is advantageous to group students by ability.

What about the advocates of heterogeneous grouping? If their claims are sound you might expect to find that the slow groups would tend to contain disproportionate numbers of minority and disadvantaged children. Studies of this question indicate that, indeed, this is the case. So, apparently from the analyses of the studies that have been done, there is little reason to believe that homogeneous grouping is a sound educational practice, and substantial reason to believe that its only result is to harm some students. Apparently tests are not going to be useful to improve instruction by sorting students into homogeneous groups unless, perhaps, something more effective is done with the groups that have been sorted. Esposito (1973, p. 177), after reviewing the evidence and arguments, concludes that the present status and predicted trends with respect to homogeneous grouping suggest that professionals in government and education should eliminate the practice. We will find later that court cases on the issue point in the same direction.

Placement According to Particular Student Characteristics

APTITUDE-TREATMENT INTERACTION

One approach to trying to improve teaching is to look for the best teaching method or style. Many, if not most, rating instruments for use by students to evaluate the teaching effectiveness of their faculty are based around some person's or group's idea of what the best kind of faculty member would be or how he or she would behave. However, it is just as sound at our present state of knowledge to assume that there are a variety of effective ways to teach. What is effective for one student may not be effective for another. A sound procedure might then be to sort students out according to their characteristics and to adapt the teaching approach to those characteristics. The name commonly given to this approach is *Aptitude-Treatment Interactions*. It would be sounder to call them *Trait-Treatment Interactions* because the characteristics of students that are important may not be just their aptitudes. But the name is now 10 or 15 years old, so we will probably have to learn to live with the misnomer. In our case, the treatments to which the name refers will be different approaches to instruction. And the term *interaction* gets in there to indicate that different treatments are differentially effective for students with certain characteristics. Since aptitude-treatment interaction is such a long and cumbersome phrase, it is common to abbreviate it by the letters ATI.

To clarify, consider this example. A few years ago, the Navy was interested in training computer programmers in large numbers. It was found that to learn to be a computer programmer, an enlisted man in the Navy had to have a lot of mathematical aptitude. There were not enough men with that level of aptitude to go around to all the jobs that required it. Someone concerned with the problem noticed that all the instruction about computer programming seemed to involve solving difficult mathematical problems, complicated formulas, or other exercises dealing with many numbers. The reason was probably because these kinds of examples are very neat. Also, the people who were already in the field of computer programming tended to have gotten into that field out of mathematics or statistics. So those examples were natural choices for them to use as teachers.

However, there is no intrinsic reason that computer programming instruction has to deal with mathematical problems for its examples. So, it was thought that if an instructional program (a treatment) were developed that did not rely on mathematics for examples, then students without very high mathematical aptitude might be able to learn to be computer programmers. Such an instructional treatment was developed, and it turned out that success in it was essentially unrelated to one's mathematical aptitude. That being the case, one could give men who were interested in computer training a mathematical aptitude test. Those who scored high on it could be put into the traditional training in computer programming. Those who scored low on it could be put into the new program in which success was independent of one's mathematical aptitude. Both groups could learn to be good computer programmers, and we have a case of a clear aptitude-treatment interaction. The aptitude is that for mathematics. The treatments are (1) training based on mathematics and (2) training independent of mathematics. And the interaction is the fact that if you put the right people in the right kind of training, you get more better-trained programmers than if you used either kind of training alone or sorted people at random into the two kinds of training.

Notice in the illustration that a test was used to improve instruction by placing students into the proper kind of instruction. It was not the level of instruction or the pace of instruction in this example. To return to our previous discussion of homogeneous grouping for a moment, that would be an instance of an ATI that did not work. There we attempted to sort people according to their rate of learning, to provide different instruction for the different rates, and thereby to have all of them learn better than they otherwise would have. Perhaps due to the fact that there usually were not really different treatments for the different groups, or perhaps for other reasons, the bulk of the evidence indicates that the students do not learn more for having been sorted on learning rate. This is just one of many attempts to find ATIs that have been unsuccessful. Not many such attempts so far have yielded ATIs of importance that can be relied on to work in about the same way in one situation after another.

An attempt to use aptitude-treatment interactions intuitively is that of sorting students according to their responsiveness to certain teachers. Pupils who are strongly motivated toward athletics and outdoor activities might be taught mathematics by a teacher who shared those interests, while pupils more interested in reading and indoor and less vigorous activities might be taught mathematics by a teacher who was similarly interested. The question would be whether both groups learned more mathematics than if they had been assigned to the teachers at random or in the reverse pattern. (There is no evidence that we know of that this ATI works, either.)

Other possibilities are that treatments could be devised that compensate for weaknesses common among students. For instance, a group of students who seem unable to organize their study might be taught in a situation that was highly organized by the teacher. Other students might learn better without the interference of the teacher. Or treatments could be devised that depend on the strengths of students. One treatment of a subject might depend heavily on memory ability and be effective with, say, music students who have to do a great deal of memorization to develop concert repertoires and who thus develop this skill to a high degree. Another treatment for the same topic might depend on other abilities, say those of developing concepts and being able to classify things into them. Our earlier consideration of remedial instruction was a form of ATI. There students were grouped according to their need to have some defect or the other remedied, in the hope (perhaps largely vain) that once the remedy had been applied, their performance would be as high as students without the defect.

Since there has evolved an abundance of research activity in this area, and there is still promise that ATIs which will be useful in schools will be found, let us see how tests should be used to place students into treatments. The first requirement is that you have a criterion measure of performance that will be applied to each of the groups of students. The same criterion measure must be applied to each. This implies that you have the same objectives for each group, but that you are going to achieve them in different ways. For example, you might have a common examination in spelling that you will apply to two groups of students. One may be taught to spell through use of group social activities, like spelldowns, and the other might be taught by practice in memorizing. But both are to learn to perform on the same final test of spelling competence. It will not be satisfactory if the criterion is to be teacher's grade in spelling and the teachers grade on different bases or using different standards! The same criterion must be applied to all the various treatments. Often to be certain that this is the case, a test whose scores represent the desired attainments of the instruction will serve as the common criterion.

Once we have settled on the common criterion for the various treatments, we need, of course, to arrange so that instruction by means of the different treatments can be provided for different students. We are assuming here that we want to put into practice in our school an ATI that has already been demonstrated as being useful. (In this discussion we will not attempt to describe how research should be conducted to find effective ATIs.) The research on which we are relying should also tell us what kind of a placement test should be used to tell which students should be put into each group. Our problem is to find for our use the test score that will decide for each student into which group he should be placed. This does require a modest empirical investigation. It is done as follows.

First, all students are given the test that is to be used for placing students into treatments. Then, ignoring their scores students are placed at random into the different treatments. After the instruction has taken place, all of the students are given the common criterion test to see how well they can perform what they have been taught. Then a scatterplot, like the one in figure 24-2, is drawn. A scatterplot, you remember, is a diagram in which for each of many students a dot is placed on the diagram at the juncture of a pair of test scores for that person. For instance, in figure 24-2, the *x* labeled Bill represents Bill's score on the placement test (the horizontal axis) of 7 and his score on the criterion (vertical axis) of 10. In that scattergram we have used *o*'s to represent the students who were put into one treatment, which we will call Treatment I. We have used *x*'s to indicate the scores of students who were put into Treatment II. The solid black line which goes from lower left to upper right of the scattergram goes through approximately the mean or average score on the vertical axis for all of the *x*'s with any given score on the horizontal axis. It actually goes as close to all of the means as any straight line can go, if it is drawn properly. The dashed line does the same for the *o*'s, going as close as it can to the average criterion score of all of the *o*'s for a given score on the predictor.

Our cutoff score for placement is simply found from this scattergram by locating the point where the solid line and the dashed line cross each other. We then determine what score on the placement test corresponds to that point. In this illustration, we have drawn a dotted line down to the horizontal axis, and we see that the cutoff score is 29. Anyone in the future who scores above 29 is placed into Treatment II, since above that point the mean criterion score (the solid line) is higher for II than for I (the dashed line). Future students who score below 29 on the placement test are placed in Treatment I since below that score the dashed line is always higher than the solid line.

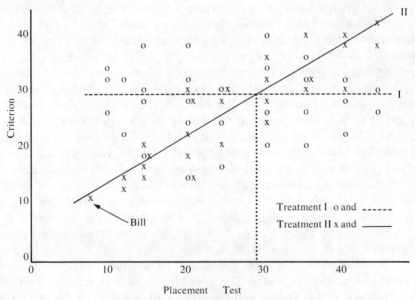

Figure 24–2
Placing Students into Instructional Groups
Based on Aptitude-Treatment Interactions

If the two lines do not cross, then we do not have an effective ATI. If the research indicated that we should have found one, something has gone wrong. Maybe our treatments don't correspond well enough to those used in the research, or our placement test or criterion test is not sufficiently like those used in the research. Or, of course, we may just have a fluke, and if we do the study again we will find that it comes out the way we thought it would.

We took the time here to illustrate this ATI approach not because there are many well-known ATIs that teachers can use at present but, more importantly, because teachers should realize that this is really the underlying concept involved when they consider the topics we discussed earlier under the heading of remediation and of homogeneous grouping, and, for that matter, any use of tests for placement purposes. We are always using tests in placement in order to sort students into groups that will be treated differently because we have reason to believe that more satisfactory results on some common criterion will thereby result. Thus, in placement we are always looking for ATI effects, whether we realize it or not. This clarifies for us what we must do to ascertain whether placement and differential treatment are effective, and it clarifies for us how tests are useful in this instructional effort.

You might say that we don't always have a common criterion in placement — that we place some students into a general education program and some into a college preparatory program, and those programs have different criteria. However, the counterargument is that you have simply moved the criterion away from academic or school attainment to the more ultimate criterion of success in life. You decided to place some students into one curriculum and others into a different curriculum because placing them all into the same curriculum would waste too much of the lives of those unsuited for a given curriculum.

Again, you might say that all you wanted to do in placement was to get the student started at the right level of instruction, above the level he had mastered but below the level that would overwhelm him. Again, unless you think that starting him at a lower level would bore him, you are saying that review would be useless in improving performance. That is rarely true of anything in education. Review nearly always will enhance performance — but sometimes not enough to be worth the time and effort. Now you have simply changed the criterion from level of performance to a combination of level of performance and economy of time and investment. It is inescapable. Placement is a matter of finding useful interactions between scores on a placement measure and different ways of teaching students when measured against some common criterion.

USING TESTS TO INDICATE LEVEL OF MASTERY IN A HIERARCHY

Before we leave the use of tests in placement we should remind you that in the early pages of this part, in chapter 23, we discussed using tests in organizing a curriculum by coordinating the tests with levels of an instructional hierarchy. There we pointed out that those who think in terms of instructional hierarchies usually think of using tests to place students in the hierarchy.

Obviously, to be efficient in teaching a hierarchical unit of instruction, it is important to be able to determine at which step to start. It is also important to be able to ascertain when each step is mastered so that a student can proceed promptly to the next step, but no step will be left unlearned. Tests can be helpful in determining which steps have been mastered. In fact, those who argue in support of developing instructional hierarchies lean heavily on tests to aid in instruction. Many brief tests are used, with at least one test for each step, and with multiple tests for students who may not have mastered the step the first time they are tested on it.

What kind of tests should be used for this purpose is a matter of some disagreement. The theorists who specialize in instructional development suggest that tests with very few items can be used quite satisfactorily. They talk about two-item or three-item tests as being adequate. In fact, it is conceivable that some of them might even settle for a single question on an objective. The instructional theorists realize that if there are to be tests at every step of the hierarchy, there will be a great deal of testing. So unless the tests are very short, a lot of time will be consumed just verifying that the steps have been mastered.

Results from a test with a single item for each objective in a hierarchy might look like the hypothetical illustration in figure 24-3. There we have data from a place-

Figure 24–3
Using a Test to Locate a Student's Level in a
Learning Hierarchy

			Placement Test			
Item	Bill	Susie	Mary	John	Michael	Ann
1	+	+	+	+	+	+
2	+	+	+	+	+	+
3	+	0	+	+	+	+
4	+	0	+	+	+	+
5	0	0	+	+	+	+
6	0	0	+	+	0	+
7	0	0	+	+	0	+
8	0	0	+	+	0	+
9	0	0	+	0	0	+
10	0	0	+	0	0	+
11	0	0	+	0	0	+
12	0	0	+	0	0	+
13	0	0	0	0	0	+
14	0	0	0	0	0	+
15	0	0	0	0	0	+
16	0	0	0	0	0	+
17	0	0	0	0	0	0
18	0	0	0	0	0	0

ment test for six students. The test has 18 items, one for each hierarchical objective, with item 18 asking the students to perform the final objective. If all is as it should be, notice that there will be a pattern to the +'s and 0's in the table. No student ever gets another + after he or she once gets a 0. That is, once a student gets an item wrong, he gets all the subsequent items wrong. That is what is implied by a hierarchy. Now single-item measures might be effective if they give results in this pattern because in a sense each item supplements each of the others. One item per step in the hierarchy might be effective if results have this clear pattern. It probably is unlikely that this pattern will ever occur, of course, if objective items are used that might be answered correctly by guessing. And this pattern cannot be expected if there is not a true hierarchy.

Measurement theorists are not nearly so optimistic as learning theorists about the quality of most educational measurements. Even the most generous recommendations that they make are for tests of a minimum of seven or eight items. And they only recommend such short tests when certain conditions prevail, such as the condition that the instruction is known to be very effective so most students will pass each test that they take. Otherwise longer tests are necessary in order not to make too many serious mistakes in deciding whether mastery has been attained. After all, if a student is mistakenly determined to be a master of a step, and he goes on into further instruction, he is doomed to ultimate failure because a link in the chain has been left out. Unless there are frequent checks on mastery so failure is caught promptly, the decision about mastery is quite important and not to be decided upon hurriedly. Which group of theorists is most nearly correct is still a matter for debate.

Legal Aspects of Placement

Since the 1954 *Brown* v. *Board of Education* decision of the U.S. Supreme Court that state-imposed segregation of public schools is unconstitutional, it is no longer feasible for a school system to place students in instructional programs without attending to the implications of such placement for minority students. The problem is that often the members of minority groups get lower scores on the placement tests and get assigned disproportionately to certain of the homogeneous groups. This is a form of resegregation within the school. If such resegregation tends to result in the students in different groups receiving different kinds of education, the placement operation is especially pernicious. Let us see what we can reasonably conclude from examining some of the court decisions about such matters in recent years. You must remember, of course, that what is decided in one court is not necessarily binding on courts in other jurisdictions. Yet, what has been decided in one place may be influential in determining court decisions in later cases, so it is worth our while to see what patterns and precedents now exist.

PLACEMENT IS ACCEPTABLE IF NOT BASED ON RACE

Courts in several jurisdictions have indicated that placement, per se, is not illegal. The issue seems to be whether the placement is based on or highly associated with minority or racial status. For example, in a case in South Carolina in 1966 the court specified in its decision that discrimination by accelerated or slow sections is permissible. Only racial discrimination is to be eliminated. In a case in New York in 1967 the court ruled that the board of education has the power to provide rules and regulations for promotion from grade to grade, based not on age but on training, knowledge, and ability. In this case, a six-year-old boy was demoted from first grade to kindergarten after scoring only 2 points out of 102 possible on a test requiring first-grade work. The court ruled that demotion in such a case was not arbitrary, capricious, or unreasonable, and therefore the school's action was not overruled by the court.

Perhaps the most interesting case concerning placement is that of *Hobson* v. *Hansen* (1967) tried in the U.S. District Court in Washington, D.C., in 1967, and affirmed on appeal to the U.S. Circuit Court of Appeals (as *Smuck* v. *Hobson*) in 1969. In this case, Mr. Hobson, a black, complained that the tracking system in Washington's schools was unfair to blacks because aptitude tests were important in deciding which children would be placed in which tracks, and aptitude tests discriminated against blacks because the tests were

> standardized primarily on white middle-class children. Since these tests do not relate to the Negro and disadvantaged child, track assignment based on such tests relegates Negro and disadvantaged children to the lower tracks from which, because of the reduced curricula and the absence of adequate remedial and compensatory education, as well as continued inappropriate testing, the chance of escape is remote.

It is interesting to notice in the court's opinion that although both achievement and aptitude tests were used in placement into the tracks, the complaint does not question the achievement tests, their relevance, or their standardization, but only the aptitude tests. This, of course, seems rather odd to those of us acquainted with the jangle fallacy.

It is also interesting to notice that the court emphasizes the idea that aptitude tests should measure "innate ability" and should measure it without error in order to be used in such important decisions as placement in various curricula in school. Thus the court says,

> There is ample evidence, already examined, that for disadvantaged children aptitude tests are inappropriate for obtaining accurate information about innate abilities.

At another point, it says,

> While government may classify persons and thereby effect disparities in treatment, those included within or excluded from the respective classes should be those for whom the inclusion or exclusion is appropriate; otherwise the classification risks becoming wholly irrational and thus unconstitutionally discriminatory.

As the court presumably was aware, no responsible expert in the field of measurement claims to know how to measure innate abilities or how to measure anything psychological or educational without appreciable error. The court was probably intending to say that instruments that were systematically biased against particular groups would introduce so much error in a specific direction that they could not be tolerated. And it was demanding evidence that aptitude tests are sound measures of learning potential for all the students on which they are used. For example, in one place the court says the school system could, "conduct an empirical study of the predictive validity of the aptitude tests it uses." The court goes on to state, "The District has not made any empirical studies of this sort, . . ."

The court indicated that sound tracking is appropriate. It says,

> At the outset it should be made clear that what is at issue here is not whether defendants are entitled to provide different kinds of students with different kinds of

education. Although the equal protection clause is, of course, concerned with classifications which result in disparity of treatment, not all classifications resulting in disparity are unconstitutional. If classification is reasonably related to the purposes of the government activity involved and is rationally carried out, the fact that persons are thereby treated differently does not necessarily offend.

However, the court insists that in a tracking program, the remedial and compensatory education used for the lowest track be effective. It states,

Moreover, any system of ability grouping which, through failure to include and implement the concept of compensatory education for the disadvantaged child or otherwise, fails in fact to bring the great majority of children into the mainstream of public education denies the children excluded equal educational opportunity and thus encounters the constitutional bar.

In the case of the Washington, D.C. schools, the court found that the remedial and compensatory education programs in existence were inadequate. In their operation, the disadvantaged student consigned to the lower track tended simply to get the lesser education, not the push to a higher level of achievement. The court asks,

... how a student given a steady diet of simplified materials can keep up, let alone catch up, with children his own age who are proceeding in a higher curriculum at a faster pace and with a more complex subject matter content.

That is, indeed, a good question for those who would propose using homogeneous ability grouping in the schools — especially if there is any tendency for minority groups or the disadvantaged to be assigned to lower tracks, as will usually be the case. As the court noted,

... tracking translates ability into educational opportunity ... when the school system undertakes this responsibility it incurs the obligation of living up to its promise to the student that placement in a lower track will not simply be a shunting off from the mainstream of education, but rather will be an effective mechanism for bringing the student up to his true potential.

As a result of considering the tracking system in the schools of Washington, D.C., the court ordered the school district to submit a plan on October 2, 1967, that would, among other things, abolish the track system and would,

include compensatory education sufficient at least to overcome the detriment of segregation and thus provide, as nearly as possible, equal educational opportunity to all school children.

As we have seen, to develop a plan that will accomplish this is to do something that had never been done before in the history of carefully researched education in this country, or perhaps any other. One wonders what could have been presented on that day in 1967 if the case had not been appealed.

It should perhaps be noted that though the appeals court affirmed the *Hobson* v. *Hansen* decision, the effect of the appeals court's ruling was to water down the impact of the earlier decision markedly. For example, the appeals court stated that the district court's decree that the track system should be abolished referred to the track system as it existed at the time of the decree. Since that plan had been modified by the time of the appeal, the appeals court determined that the decree had been followed. In the appeals court's opinion, the decree permits full scope for ability grouping other than the earlier tracking system.

The appeals court apparently was not prepared to accept the precise wording of the requirement of the district court that certain kinds of tests could not be used in ability grouping. The appellants wanted freedom for the newly elected board of education to function, and the appeals court took the position that with its interpretation that freedom was not hampered by the district court ruling. (Smuck was a member of a newly elected board of education.) This may seem like the appeals court stretched a point, and, indeed, one judge argued that the holding of the district court was not affirmed as written but only as construed by four members of the appeals court.

The result of all of this is less than perfect clarity, but it seems sound to conclude that a homogeneous-grouping plan that resegregates and cannot be justified on sound educational grounds will be rather easily challenged in court.

TESTS MAY BE USED IN ELEMENTARY SCHOOLS

The use of tests at all is an issue that may be part of many cases. However, a case in Louisiana decided by the U.S. Court of Appeals in 1973 specifically ruled that tests were permissible in elementary schools.

APTITUDE, ACHIEVEMENT, AND PERSONALITY MEASURES MAY BE USED

Some people would suggest that students should be placed in school just based on their age. As we have seen above, in several cases test scores were used and found acceptable. Those seemed to be achievement tests, however. In a case in Georgia in 1964 the court ruled that aptitude tests were appropriate if they were not applied solely to blacks. In another case in Georgia in 1963 it was ruled that aptitude tests and personality interviews could not be used if they were applied only to blacks, which suggests that they would be acceptable if applied uniformly. A similar ruling was made in Virginia in 1962. Probably a close perusal of cases concerning integration would find this same pattern in many states and jurisdictions. It seems clear that the courts are not averse to placement, or to the use of measures of various kinds, as long as they are used without regard to race. An exception might be in the *Hobson* v. *Hansen* kind of dispute in which aptitude, but not achievement, tests were criticized in terms of their content, their norming, and their inaccuracy. We will turn next to some additional exceptions.

TESTS MUST BE VALID IF THEIR USE IN PLACEMENT RESULTS IN GROUPING BY RACE

The first exception may not really be an exception in the formal sense. The issue is the same one that came up in the *Hobson* v. *Hansen* case, but perhaps we can phrase it more appropriately from the point of view of what we know about measurement. We know that we cannot make tests that measure perfectly without error, and we know that it is unsound to think about tests as measures of innate abilities.

If we stop to think about it, for the purposes of placement it does not matter what group of people tests are normed on. They would not need to have norms at all for effective use in placement.[7] And we agree that to place students into an inferior track and there to give them inferior education is unsound and unfair. What, then, must a placement test demonstrate to be usable without segregating students *primarily* on the basis of race?

The answer is familiar to us. The placement test must be an effective part of an ATI. It must sort people into educational treatments (or tracks) in such a manner that the educational outcome is maximized for each of the groups. The procedure is depicted in figure 24-2 and described in the related paragraphs. The only problem is we don't know what kinds of ATIs will work yet. In most of the important kinds of placement that might result in litigation, we don't know how to proceed. Would that it were now possible to produce what the judge demanded in *Hobson* v. *Hansen,* a plan for compensatory education sufficient to overcome the detriment of segregation!

ASSIGNMENT TO SPECIAL EDUCATION MUST BE UNBIASED

The other exception to approval of use of various measures as long as they are not based on race takes us slightly afield from dealing with normal children, but it is too important to be ignored. Woefully ignorant test users have used tests to remove minority groups from regular classrooms based on those groups' employment of a language other than standard English in their ordinary nonschool communication.

A case in southern California filed in 1970 provides an example. There nine Mexican-American students protested that they were given the Stanford-Binet and the Wechsler Intelligence Tests in the English language, and as a result of their scores were placed in classes for the mentally retarded. After retesting in their native language, many of them no longer scored as retarded. Here the test did not discriminate in a biased manner — but the use of it did when knowledge and fluency in the language were more important determiners of the test score than was the characteristic which the test was designed to measure.

This abuse was so flagrant that before the case even got to trial, a number of requirements were placed on the schools by the court. Among them was that all children whose primary home language was other than English be tested both in their primary language and in English. Also the schools agreed to use only tests and sections of tests that did not depend on vocabulary, general information, and other similar unfair verbal questions.

As a result of such retesting, it is said that close to 10,000 students in California have been returned to regular classrooms! Similar cases have been filed in Massachusetts and Arizona.

It is a shame that ordinary teachers typically don't know enough about testing, or care enough, to see that a stop is put to such practices before they involve tens

---

[7] We rejected placement by contrasting achievement with aptitude because of its many complications. Placing students into a level in a hierarchy, according to what they have mastered, according to whether they are above or below a cutoff in an aptitude-treatment interaction, or even into homogeneous groups, is appropriately done on the basis of raw scores. Thus norms are unnecessary and irrelevant; even bad norms are not harmful for these purposes when raw scores are used.

of thousands of mistreated students. Perhaps with the increased attention of parents and resort to courts, at least the worst misuses of tests in placement will be rooted out.

Summary

To summarize our consideration of the use of tests to place students in instruction that is optimum for them, we have considered many ideas, from the very simple to the very complex. At the simple extreme, tests can be used by examining students' responses to individual items or small groups of items on common topics or items based on similar behaviors. From this we can obtain clues about what the student has adequately learned or still needs to learn or practice. Students can be asked to work test questions aloud for the teacher to obtain some insight into what instruction is still needed. These uses of tests and items have been with us for a long time, without much formal study. They seem to be helpful.

At the more complex level — the use of tests for diagnosis and remediation, for tracking, or for capitalizing on aptitude-treatment interactions — more extensive formal research has been conducted. The results are disappointing, not because of the tests, their quality, or their manner of use, but because we have not been able to isolate and demonstrate effective treatments and remedies and the kinds of students for whom they are effective. When research has clarified the kinds of treatments that are effective and for whom, it appears that we will have fairly well-developed ways of using tests for sorting students into the proper treatments. Some issues such as how many items there should be in short tests of mastery of specific objectives are still being contested and explored.

Unfortunately, the impatient use of tests without full consideration for some of the outcomes of using them carelessly has resulted in such improper placement of some students that issues that should have been avoided by school personnel have been settled by the courts. The placement of students into ability groups must be prepared to meet exceedingly severe standards if it is to survive court test, it appears, and the placing of students into special schools for the mentally retarded on the basis of faulty testing can be and has been successfully challenged. Reasonably sophisticated teachers and school personnel should no longer make the kinds of mistakes that have brought about such litigation in the past.

References

Austin, G. R., Rogers, B. G., & Walbesser, H. H. The effectiveness of summer compensatory education: A review of the research. *Rev. educ. Res.*, 1972, **42**, 171-81.

Block, J. H. & Tierney, M. L. An exploration of two correction procedures used in mastery learning approaches to instruction. *J. educ. Psychol.*, 1974, **66**, 962-67.

Cronbach, L. J., Gleser, G. C., Nanda, H., & Rajaratnam, N. *The dependability of behavioral measurements.* New York: Wiley, 1972.

Esposito, D. Homogeneous and heterogeneous ability grouping: Principal findings and implications for evaluating and designing more effective educational environments. *Rev. educ. Res.*, 1973, **43**, 163-79.

Green, D. R. *The aptitude-achievement distinction.* New York: McGraw-Hill, 1974.

Hobson v. *Hansen.* DDC. 1967. 269 F. Supp. 401.

Report on Educational Research. Washington: Capitol Publications, 1971, October 27, pp. 6-8.

Report on School Staffing. Washington: Capitol Publications, 1971, December 15, p. 10.

Smuck v. *Hobson.* 401 F2d. 175.

University of the State of New York. *1971-72 Urban Education Report.* Albany, N.Y.: Office of Public Information, New York State Education Department.

25

Using Tests to Provide Feedback during Instruction

Objectives

Study of this chapter should enable you to:
1. State the relationship between feedback and efficient learning;
2. Describe the delay-retention effect and its implications for teachers;
3. Describe the effects of kind and quality of feedback on learning;
4. Discuss the designing of items to enhance feedback's effect;
5. Describe item analysis in class and how it can enhance feedback.

Reinforcement and Learning

For about 100 years, scholars in universities and laboratories have studied formally how it is that organisms learn. Probably the most significant thing that they have learned is the importance of reward (or *reinforcement*, as they call it) in making learning efficient. Learning is speeded up dramatically when the experimenter suddenly starts rewarding the organism for doing the desired performance. The desired performance begins to disappear when the reward is no longer offered. One of the important aspects of providing the reward for much of the learning of animals is how quickly it is presented after the performance. The quicker the reward, the faster the learning takes place.

It has been too easy to assume that the same applies to school learning of human organisms. However, research during recent years indicates that it is doubtful that the importance of immediate reward holds true for much of the learning that takes place in schools, especially the learning from tests. The reward or reinforcement from tests can be considered to be the knowledge of results — finding out whether an answer is correct. It can be thought of as feedback, sort of analogous to the principle widely used in electronics of taking some of the output of a device and putting it back into the input to improve the performance of the device. Knowledge of the correctness of responses in learning helps improve the performance in a rather similar way. The issue, then, is how quickly to insert the feedback.

Delay-Retention Effect

Brackbill (1962) seems to have done the studies that alerted us to the fact that what is true about immediate reinforcement for correct response for animal learning is *not* true for human learning of meaningful materials like school instruction. We emphasize the *NOT* because it is often very hard for people who have heard of the animal studies to realize what we are stating. To say it again, it is *not* the most effective practice in human learning of school instruction to provide reinforcement immediately. It is more effective to delay the reinforcement if one wants the greatest retention of the learning. Brackbill labeled this the "delay-retention effect." That is, delay of reinforcement enhances retention.

By delaying reinforcement we mean that instead of telling the pupil immediately after he answers a question whether he got it right or wrong, as might be done if he took the test on a computer terminal, it is better to wait until, say, 20 minutes after the test before telling him the correct answers. It is even better to wait at least 24 hours before providing the feedback. This kind of result has been found by several investigators, using students of different levels and varied content such as knowledge of English words and knowledge of subject matter to which the students have never before been exposed.

So far only a relatively few different levels of delay have been studied formally. Delays of seconds have been studied, as well as delays of minutes and delays of a day. Also only one retention period has been studied, that of one week. The common finding across the studies is that after seven days better scores are obtained on the learning if the reinforcement, in terms of knowing whether individual items were right or wrong, is given after a delay instead of immediately. The longer the delay, up to the longest delay studied, the better the retention score.

If certain conditions of the experiment are changed, the general conclusion has to be modified to a modest extent. For instance, if the students are given a multiple-choice test immediately after the learning session, their retention is improved (even though they are not told how well they performed on that test). Also, the greatest effect from delaying the reinforcement appears if the retention test is of the brief-essay form, i.e., a form in which the examinee has to create a response instead of merely choosing among alternatives.

Important in understanding the delay-retention effect is the finding that the effect is reduced when clues are provided during reinforcement. That is to say, when the correct answers are given, some help is provided so that students can remember why those answers are correct. Such help might be merely a discussion of why the incorrect answers are incorrect. Or it might be some memory trick for coming up with the right answer. If that is done during the reinforcement given, say, right at the end of the test, the retention after seven days will be about the same as if the reinforcement were delayed for a longer period, say 24 hours. This suggests that the secret to the delay-retention effect may be that after 24 hours or so when students go back to the test items they pay attention to the entire items instead of just to the response they chose and the one that is keyed correct. As a result they develop fuller understanding. But when knowledge of results comes immediately, they may not pay as much attention to the entire set of concepts involved, and they may learn only superficially what the correct answer should have been.

At any rate, the advice for the teacher about using tests to improve instruction by providing feedback is fairly clear, and not entirely what one would expect. First, a teacher should not go over the items in the test right after the students have taken the test. She should wait at least 24 hours if possible. Second, when she does go over the items, she shouldn't just read off the key, but instead discuss the items showing why the keyed answer is correct and the other answers are wrong, providing memory clues where possible to help students remember the correct answers in the future. It is especially important to have the discussion of items if the delay is short, and retention can be improved even further by having a multiple-choice test immediately after instruction.

This delaying of reinforcement or feedback will not be liked by the students, to judge from the writer's experience. Students want to know right now how they did. But the research data at present seem to indicate that what the students want, as is so often the case, is not what is best for them. However, we say that the research data seem to indicate this conclusion because even though the findings have appeared several times from several different researchers, they still deserve much more exploration before we adopt them on a large scale. The laboratory is not the classroom, and isolated studies of specific instruction are not necessarily the same as general studies of applying specific procedures such as this to all aspects of the instruction of all children. Maybe the same conclusion will be reached in larger scale studies, but maybe it will not. That remains to be seen.

Quality of Feedback

Other study of feedback to students has indicated that the quality of the information given back to the student influences his learning. Above we indicated that it is more effective in yielding improved retention if students are told what is wrong with various alternatives in a multiple-choice question than if they are merely told whether they got the item right or are told their total score. Other study with essay tests has indicated the same kind of result. When students merely receive their scores on the essay, they do not learn as much and improve as much as when the instructor or grader puts his comments directly on the page so that the student can see what he has done wrong (Page, 1958). Of course, putting in all of those comments takes a teacher a long time, and it is not easy work. In all probability, this is one of the reasons why many children find it difficult to learn to write effectively. They have never had a teacher who was allotted enough time so that for each of her students she could give this kind of quality feedback. But we know that it is important, whether or not our school systems are willing to afford it.

Publishers of commercial tests have recognized the importance of having more feedback than just a score. Some of them provide a service that lists for each student which items he got right and wrong. This is necessary because most machine-scored answer sheets do not indicate the wrong responses on the answer sheet itself. That would slow down the scoring process intolerably for large-scale scoring operations.

But the separate reports of item performance for each student are often available to schools that want them. That level of feedback, though not as effective as discussion of why an alternative is wrong, may still be useful in promoting learning and retention.

Kind of Feedback and Kind of Student

There is some indication in the research literature on feedback and its effect that different kinds of students profit from different kinds of feedback. By different kinds of students, we refer to a characteristic of students called their tendency to be "inner-controlled" vs. "externally-controlled." The inner-controlled student would tend to set his own goals and be rewarded when he met them or disappointed when he did not, regardless of what any other person might think. The externally-controlled student, in contrast, tends to work for the praise of other people.

By different kinds of feedback in this line of research is meant feedback that is related to the student's expectations of level of performance versus feedback that is not tied to his level of expected performance. In the former case, the feedback might be of the form that since the student only expected to do C work, but really did B work, the teacher is pleasantly surprised and the performance is very good! The student should keep up the good work. In the latter case, the feedback for B work would merely indicate that it was good, and above average, and the feedback would be the same whether the student expected to do A work or C work, or even F work.

The research findings, from limited study as yet, are that when students were given comments based on their expectations, their grades on the next exam in the course were 8 points higher than the grades of the students whose comments were not based on their expectations (78.3 vs. 70.4). In addition to that general effect of having grades based on expectations, the greater the degree of external control the more later test scores were enhanced by having comments based on expectations. The researcher who did this study thinks that the reason for the finding is that the externally-controlled student works hard to perform well because it will enhance the view that others have of him.

This kind of finding is interesting and opens a whole new arena of study of the effect of feedback on learning. We don't know much about it yet or, for that matter, whether the finding cited above will occur for any students other than the college physics students used in the study which reported it (Hammer, 1972).

Instruction Centered on Feedback from Testing

The use of feedback from testing to enhance instruction is being attached such importance in some circles that the instruction in some courses is based largely on feedback. Thus, one procedure widely used in teaching introductory psychology at the college level depends heavily on having students respond to large numbers of items, followed by explanations of why their answers are right or wrong.

In the way the system is organized, advanced students are used as tutors for beginning students. Each tutor has his pupil answer aloud large numbers of written brief-answer items while being timed. The pupil is encouraged to answer as rapidly as possible, as well as corectly. After each timed oral test, the tutor clarifies, explains the material, and corrects the mistakes. Then a new timed trial begins on more items. When a criterion level of performance has been reached, the pupil tackles new sets of items on another topic in the same manner. The progress of each student toward each objective of the instruction is displayed graphically, since it seems to be the case that graphic displays of progress in instruction are enhancing for the learning of students of all ages. This is about the ultimate in using tests to enhance instruction by providing feedback during instruction.

Test Construction and Feedback

If we are going to use our tests deliberately to improve instruction by providing feedback, we may want to sacrifice some of their potential for good measurement in order to get more useful feedback. One important way to do that is to write our objective-test items so that common errors have the opportunity to appear. In multiple-choice items, that means that one or more of the distractors (wrong answers) for an item is a common error that students who don't know the material make. In true-false items, it may mean that a common error, perhaps an "old-wives tale" that ignorant or uninformed people think is true, is presented for the student to evaluate as true or false. In some fields, such as the social sciences (and tests and measurement), there are a great many misconceptions that have to be "stamped out" and replaced by sound understanding that leads to different, sometimes opposite, answers.

One way to find these common errors is to give questions as brief-essay or completion items to see what kinds of wrong answers are common among the pupils to be taught. For future groups of students, those wrong answers become distractors in objective-test items.

The reason that we indicated that we would give up some measurement accuracy in order to make full use of feedback to improve learning is that items constructed in the way we have just described will tend to be hard items unless the teaching is superb and the students are all highly motivated. That is to say, experience indicates that in spite of a teacher's best efforts some students will still choose the common misconceptions as their answers. That means that the proportion who get the item correct is relatively low, and for good measurement that is a bad condition. For sound measurement, no item should be gotten right by less than half of the students. In fact, there is no good reason from a measurement point of view for having multiple-choice test items that fewer than 60% of the examinees get correct (assuming that there are a maximum of five alternatives per item). Items encouraging common mistakes will often be too hard for optimum performance as measures, then. However, we may be willing to use them to get the beneficial effects of the feedback that occurs when we can tell the students one more time why their choice of the common error is faulty. One way around this problem may be to use such items in quizzes or relatively unimportant tests, when measurement is not as significant as instruction, but to leave such items out of major examinations when measurement for evaluation is emphasized.

ITEM ANALYSIS IN CLASS

A technique that teachers skilled in the techniques of test development use is called item analysis. In item analysis, each item of a test is subjected to scrutiny to determine if the students' responses to the item indicate that it is of a reasonable degree of difficulty. The item is also examined to see whether it will contribute to sound measurement of whatever the rest of the items of the test measure. Items that do not show these two properties are examined carefully to see whether they can be rewritten so that their characteristics will be improved when they are administered to a subsequent group of students.

Item analysis can be quickly and easily done on a high-speed computer, and it can be done by the individual classroom teacher working by herself. It can also be done in the classroom working with the students. The procedure is simple. The tests are first of all scored. Then it is necessary to find out how difficult each item was, i.e., what proportion of the students got it correct. This is done by handing out to the students the test papers with the students' answers. The teacher calls off *Item one* and says what the keyed response is. All the students with that response marked on their papers raise their hands. The teacher notes that number on a piece of paper, or on the chalkboard, beside the number of the item. She does this for each item in turn. At the conclusion, each of these numbers is divided by the number of pupils who took the test, and the results are the proportions getting each item correct, or the item difficulty levels. These are sometimes called *item p values* or simply *p's*. As we noted above, it is desirable for *p's* to be above 0.50, and usually above 0.60, but rarely as high as 0.90, for optimum measurement.

The knowledgeable teacher will carry her item analysis further than this. She will find out to what extent each alternative response was chosen more often by the students who did the best on the test. To do this, she first of all has to get the distribution of test scores. This is done by calling off the various possible scores and having students raise their hands if they got a score that has just been called out. These counts are recorded. The teacher then divides this distribution in half, and all the tests or answer sheets with scores above the middle are passed to one side of the room; all those with scores below the middle are passed to the other side.

The papers above the middle are called the High (or Upper) group, and those below the middle are called the Low group. A teller is appointed among the students holding papers of each group. The teller's function will be seen below.

The teacher then makes a table for an item, like this:

Alternative	1	2	3	4	5	Omit	Total
H							
Item 1							
L							

She then calls out, "Response 1, High Group?" The teller for the high group counts the number of hands raised by the high group showing that their papers have response one marked. The teacher writes that number in the table in the row for H and the column for 1. She then calls out, "Low Group?" The teller for the low group tells her how many hands in his group indicate that response number one was chosen. This is entered just below the previous entry, in the L row. The process is continued for the remaining responses and for papers on which the item was not answered (Omits), if there are such. The rows are totaled to be certain that all the papers are accounted for. Then the next item is treated the same way. This process can be followed for every item in a test, or, to save time, it can be used only for the difficult items.

The purpose of all of this for the teacher is to improve her test items — to find out which ones are working well and which ones are not, to locate the difficulties in the items, and to eliminate incorrect alternatives that are avoided by the Low group while being chosen by the Highs. But just as important a function of item analysis when done in class this way is the capitalization on the students' interest in test results to teach them the concepts that are giving them trouble.

For instance, if more of the Low group than the High group choose the response that the teacher has keyed as correct, obviously something is wrong. It may be the way the item is written, or it may be a genuine misunderstanding among the students who otherwise know the most and get the highest overall scores. Either way, if it is detected during the item analysis and discussed with the students then and there, not only does the teacher learn how to improve the item but also the students get a good review and, perhaps, reinstruction at a time when they are highly motivated to learn. There is probably no situation in which students are more highly motivated to learn than when they are seeing how they have performed on a classroom test. The teacher who uses this procedure usually has to terminate the discussion before all of the students are satisfied, they are so interested. The students who want to ask about items that only a few missed can often be handled best on an individual basis, rather than using class time. However, great progress can often be made for many students on important topics by item analyzing the more difficult items at this level of detail using the whole class as participants.[1]

Summary

In this chapter we have presented a number of ways that instruction can be improved through the use of tests to provide information to students about the level of their performance, i.e., feedback. We have noted that feedback about performance on individual test items is most enhancing of retention when it is delayed at least 24 hours. We also found that retention can be enhanced by giving a multiple-choice test immediately after the instruction. We have seen that it is important to give feedback that has been designed or arranged to be helpful — at least more helpful than just knowing one's test score. Students learn more efficiently if they are told what they are doing wrong and how to do it right. For some students, feedback is more effective if it is based on their personality characteristics, especially the characteristic of being other-directed.

[1]An audiotutorial is provided in *Exercises in Classroom Measurement* to develop understanding and competence in this kind of item analysis. It is number 5, entitled "Item Analysis for Traditional (Norm-Referenced) Tests." If you have not done this as part of your study of Part 1 of the textbook, you may find it helpful now.

Feedback is such an effective instructional device that in some college level instruction, particularly in psychology (a field in which the processes by which organisms learn is a very important topic of study), whole courses are sometimes taught around the process of test taking and receiving of feedback about performance on each individual item.

Effective feedback can be enhanced by careful design of test items — by designing items so that they invite important problems to be clarified during feedback — and by analyzing the individual test items in class with the participation of the students. This capitalizes on the intense motivation that many students have at the time when they receive results about their test performance.

References

Brackbill, Y. & Kappy, M. S. Delay of reinforcement and retention. *J. comp. & physiol. Psychol.*, 1962, **55**, 14–18.

Hammer, B. Grade expectations, differential teacher comments, and student performance. *J. educ. Psychol.*, 1972, **63**, 454–58.

Page, E. B. Teacher comments and student performance: A seventy-four classroom experiment in school motivation. *J. educ. Psychol.*, 1958, **49**, 173–81.

26

Using Tests to Aid Memory and Application

Objectives

Study of this chapter should permit you to:
1. Describe a technique to enhance memory for what is learned, and the writing of items for that technique;
2. Describe the use of adjunct questions to aid retention of what is read;
3. Describe the implications for teachers of research on the use of adjunct questions.

That Which Is Used Is Best Remembered

In the previous chapter we discussed some ways that testing can be used to help students learn and remember what we are trying to teach them. There we emphasized the function of feedback in aiding retention of learned material. In this chapter we are going to present two additional ways of using tests to improve learning and application of what is learned that do not depend primarily on feedback. We treat remembering and applying together because the first technique we will discuss is based on the relationship between the two.

The connection between use and memory is stated in the heading of this section — that which is used is best remembered. If you want a person to remember what he has learned, a very effective procedure is to start him right out using it and to make sure he uses it often. This technique will be recognized immediately by any arithmetic teacher, but it might seem foreign to the social studies teacher. The arithmetic teacher is likely to follow any period of instruction with a period during which students try to apply what they have learned to problems stated by the teacher. The retention of advanced mathematics concepts, like analytic geometry or calculus, is not very good when they are taught to ordinary people who may not have genuine applications for those concepts until years after they are learned. The mathematician,

314

physicist, or engineer, who puts the ideas to use immediately, ends up years later with a much better memory for and fluency with those concepts. How much worse yet would those concepts be remembered by nonusers if they did not at least do some problems involving the operations just after they were presented?

So a sound principle in instruction is to emphasize material that will be useful and will be used often. To follow this principle, the instructor must select material to be taught that is widely applicable. He must also help the student to realize that he should expect to use what he is being taught. And the instructor must often help the student to learn to recognize the situations in which the material can be used. This, of course, is much easier in some subjects than in others. The English teacher might be rather taxed in analyzing what topics in literature should be chosen for their usefulness and wide applicability, for example — and so might the teachers of art and music. But where applicability is more readily apparent, it is inefficient to fail to take advantage of it. Often the applications that can be provided depend largely on the imaginativeness of the teacher.

A coordinate principle is that the test items used by a teacher who is trying to enhance memory and application of what is learned should be parallel to her instruction; that is, the test items should concern material that is widely applicable. Specifically, items should not emphasize rare phenomena, unusual situations, special cases, or trivia. Some teachers are prone to use such material in their tests because it seems to them that items based on it will surely tell which students have thoroughly learned the textbook. But that is a faulty notion. A basic question to be asked of any test item is "Is this worth knowing?" One might even go so far as to ask "Will it be important two years from now that each student can answer this question?" If the item concerns widely applicable knowledge or skill, the answer will most likely be yes. If the answer is no or doubtful, perhaps the item deserves no place in the test.

Not only should the test items emphasize widely applicable knowledge or skill, but items should provide practice in recognizing appropriate applications. This is one way the teacher can help students learn to use knowledge. The teacher can also use such items to verify that she has not neglected to provide adequate instruction on recognizing applications. The social studies teacher can have a lot of fun using items to help students recognize the relevance of what they are learning to the problems of inflation and depression, to the problems of separation of powers of the federal government, and to the problems of making a small club function to the mutual advantage and pleasure of all the members. If the students can't recognize how parliamentary procedure can be used effectively by a small club after instruction and practice, then the instruction has probably not been effective in promoting retention and application of parliamentary procedure.

Third, of course, is that test items should provide a variety of situations in which the learning can be applied. The teacher's illustrations can provide a variety of situations, but her test items can enlarge the variety while at the same time providing evaluative feedback for her and for her students.

APPLICATION ITEMS

Items that emphasize applications of interest to students are not the usual test items. Application items don't simply take a sentence out of the text, insert the word *not*, and ask the student whether the statement is true or false. What they do is to invent a situation likely to be of interest to the student in which a principle or skill or concept can be applied. They pose this situation and ask the student to respond with an appropriate reaction to the situation. In arithmetic, you could simply ask a student to add and multiply various combinations of numbers. That would not be an application. But now suppose that we pose the problem that the student is to figure out how many board feet of 2″ x 6″ joists will be needed for the floor of an outdoor utility shed with dimensions of 10′ by 10′ and with three joists inside a box frame of joist material. That is an application item involving the same kinds of numerical operations (plus some instruction on what is meant by "board feet").

At another level, an application item might be that the principal of a school has decided to consider using part of the budget next year to have each third grader take a diagnostic reading test. She wants the teachers to help her choose the test. What is the most important suggestion a teacher can make so that the money will be spent most wisely? Alternative answers might be:

1. Ask professors at a nearby university to recommend an appropriate test.
2. Choose only among tests that have clear evidence that treatments based on the diagnoses do remedy the defects located, and that the remedies last at least one year.
3. See what neighboring schools are using for diagnostic reading tests.
4. Use the *Mental Measurements Yearbook* to locate possible tests.

You can see that writing applications items is not easy. They tend to be long items because a problem must be posed. The teacher must know her subject well to be sure that she can specify clearly the best answer and to be able to introduce interesting and plausible distractors for students who don't know the correct answers. But once a teacher has practiced writing such items, it gets to be fun. It must be remembered, of course, that not all items in a test should be applications items since much of what pupils are to learn in most courses is terminology and fairly simple concepts and relationships. The mastery of these must be verified, and rather direct items are appropriate. However, to enhance retention over long periods, some applications items should be used so that students will learn to expect that in the tests they must be able to apply what they have learned as well as to recite it.

Another important facet to use of applications items should be noted. The teacher who starts introducing such items is highly likely to find that they prove to be too hard for her students. Why? Because she has not been teaching them how to apply what they have learned. The solution, of course, is to teach students how to apply their new knowledge and skill. The items thus reinforce sound instruction, and that is just as it should be with good classroom tests.

Using Testlike Events to Aid Memory

Until now we have been presenting ideas about using tests to enhance learning, memory, and usefulness of what has been learned. Now we are going to digress to introduce a topic that has been receiving a great amount of attention among psychologists concerned with learning of written prose material; that is, the use of questions inserted in the material. They are questions just like test questions, but they are meant to help the reader, rather than to measure or evaluate him. Thus we might call them *testlike* events. The researchers choose to call them *adjunct questions*. It turns out that adjunct questions have rather interesting effects on retention, and they have properties that one might not anticipate.

The typical research project might ask students to read a part of a book that they had not seen before — a section that might take the average reader about 15 minutes. Some subjects in the experiment would find that after about every 350 words there would be a question concerning what they had just read. Other subjects would find that with about the same frequency there appeared questions about what they were going to read next. Some experiments would provide the answers to the questions when the questions were presented. Other experiments would not provide the answers. After the reading, at any time from immediately to as long as two weeks later, a test would be given. It would include some of the questions that had been read during the reading of the text and other questions that had not been seen before but that were on the same topics.

Now the interesting results concern whether having the inserted questions enables people to perform better on the test that comes sometime after the reading, and whether questions about what one *has read* have different effects than questions about what one *is going to read*. It turns out that the inserted questions tend to enhance retention. But the questions about what one *is going to read* improve one's memory of the answers to those specific questions (and sometimes seem to depress one's ability to answer questions he has not seen before). The questions about what one *has just read* tend to enhance his ability to answer all the questions, especially noticeably those he has not seen before. Furthermore, questions about what one has just read tend to be most beneficial if the answers are not given. Questions about what one is going to read work best if their answers are given. Thus, in the laboratory it seems clear that testlike events inserted in reading can improve one's ability to answer questions about what one has read after a period of at least several weeks.

The size of the effect in many studies is roughly 10%. That is, one gets about 10% more questions correct on the retention test if he has had adjunct questions inserted after his reading. One study found that if the readers were just firmly told to read carefully because they would be tested sometime later concerning what they remembered, there was about the same amount of improvement.

Studies have shown that if questions are given about what one has read and the answers are not given, it takes longer for the student to read the material. In fact, it takes about as much more time as is consumed when subjects have been told to read carefully because they will be tested later.

These findings lead one to believe that the adjunct questions accomplish their effect by increasing the attention that the students pay to what they are reading. That increased attention requires more reading time. One possible advantage of the adjunct questions over telling people to read more carefully is that the questions serve as frequent reminders, while the instructions to read carefully may soon wear off.

Current studies of this phenomenon (called *mathemagenic* behavior) are trying to discover whether adjunct questions work differently for different kinds of people, i.e., people who are motivated vs. those who are not, people who get high grades vs.

people who do not, people in grade school vs. people in college (they work for both), and so on. But one study suggests that we be cautious before adopting the principle of inserting items in reading passages in general textbooks. Hiller (1974) compared the procedure of having questions inserted in a text with (1) telling students to read and study but not make notes or underline, or (2) telling students to underline, make notes, or do anything else they usually did during study. He allowed plenty of time to study as carefully as one might want to study. He found that the inserted questions did *not* increase either immediate retention or performance after two weeks. Thus the author cautions against expecting favorable results from inserted questions in usual classroom study. Furthermore, he points out that if questions *after* reading prove to be more helpful, we have no readily available procedure at present to prevent students from looking ahead so that those questions then become questions *before* reading, and possibly depressing on retention.

Clearly much more work is going to be needed before we will understand the function of inserted questions well enough to use them wisely. The work is proceeding rapidly in several laboratories, so there is hope that in the near future the issues will be resolved clearly enough for practical application. Meanwhile, it is an interesting laboratory use of testlike events to enhance retention of prose reading.

Summary

In this chapter we have continued our presentation of ideas related to using tests to help students remember what they have learned. In particular this chapter emphasized the value of having items on tests that require the student to apply his knowledge or skill. Employing what we have learned is an effective way to increase its retention, so we ask our test items to provide this kind of practice. This requires a different kind of item writing, taxing but interesting, and it also is likely to change the way we teach. Otherwise the students often will find our application items too difficult. The changed teaching will help students to recognize situations in which they can apply what they have learned. It will also help them develop the skill of applying their knowledge to practical problems. It will probably be better teaching from more points of view than simply improving students' ability to remember what they have learned.

We also considered here a recent development in the study of retention of what one has learned from reading of prose, such as textbooks. That development is the idea of inserting testlike items into the text at rather frequent intervals. Such questions tend to enhance memory of what one has learned, but it makes a difference whether the questions are inserted before one reads the material or after one has already read it. The best technique appears to be to insert the questions after one has already read the material. However, most of the findings in this regard come from laboratory studies in which students are not permitted to read ahead, to skim, to make notes, underline, and review before the test as they would outside the laboratory. When inserted questions are compared with realistic student procedures for study, or simply with passive reading when plenty of time is given for rereading and thinking about what one has read, the inserted questions do not seem to enhance memory (according to one study). Thus, further research will be required on this idea before we know how to apply it in practical instructional settings.

References

Hiller, J. R. Learning from prose text: Effects of readability level, inserted question difficulty, and individual differences. *J. educ. Psychol.,* 1974, **66,** 202–211.

27

Using Tests to Modify Instruction and to Evaluate Modifications of Instruction

Objectives

After study of this chapter, you should be able to:
1. Describe a feasible and effective procedure for evaluating effectiveness of classroom instruction;
2. Discuss the difference between evaluation of the effectiveness of sequential and nonsequential instruction;
3. List three other procedures for assisting in the evaluation of instruction in the classroom;
4. Describe three elements to be included in any evaluation of instruction that contrasts different classes;
5. Illustrate with an example the result of leaving out any of the needed elements in evaluation of instruction across classes;
6. Describe the status of performance tests for teachers as a way of evaluating quality of instruction.

Evaluating Instruction and Its Modifications within the Classroom

The final use of tests in improving instruction that we are going to study is their use to modify instruction and to evaluate modifications of instruction. Many of the ideas about using tests to modify instruction have been introduced in other contexts already in this book. Actually, we have talked about modifying instruction several times because it was an alternate procedure to modifying tests, or because it was appropriate for increasing retention of what was learned. Or it might have been necessary for placement to be effective, or inherent in organizing instruction. Or perhaps instruction was modified when tests were used to provide feedback. At this point we will try to bring those ideas together in a general framework.

Any good teacher must be concerned about how effective her teaching is, about which parts of her efforts are working better and which worse, and about how to improve the parts that are less effective. That is part of what it means to be a professional teacher, not just a group baby-sitter. The obvious procedure for studying this with tests is probably the most feasible and effective for use in the classroom. That is to *pretest* the students over the material of concern, *posttest* them when they have been exposed to the instruction that is to be provided on that material, and then to test them at some later time for *retention* or memory of what they were to have learned. This testing should be considered separately from testing that is done to evaluate the students for grading or other purposes, although conceivably the results may be taken into account for those purposes. But we are not talking here about midterms, final examinations, and such. Rather we are talking about rather specific and detailed tests designed to reveal to the instructor information she wants about the effectiveness of her instruction.

The instruction may take many forms. It may be lectures, demonstrations, textbook reading, excursions to the zoo, listening to classical (or other) music, and so on, through all the possibilities. The teacher may not do the instruction, but merely arrange for it, as in programmed instruction, computerized instruction, or library work. But whatever instruction is provided can be checked up on by means of *pretest, posttest,* and *retention test.* That instruction which is weak can then be modified and rechecked in the same manner. Obviously, the instructional procedures that are most effective in producing improved posttest and retention-test scores are to be favored, providing they are not prohibitive in cost or infeasible for other reasons.

EXAMPLE INVOLVING SEQUENTIAL LEARNING

In cases of instruction that has been found to be hierarchical, or that at least seems to have sequential properties, it may be possible to pretest, posttest, and retention test with relatively few items to determine how well the instruction is working and where its weak points are. The procedure would be to write one or two good items for each of the key parts of the sequence or perhaps for each objective in the hierarchy or at equally spaced intervals through the hierarchy. These questions would be given as a pretest to determine where the students stand in the hierarchy, or what parts of the sequence they have mastered, before instruction starts. This can also verify that the instruction starts at a level low enough to include all the students; that is, the first item in the test should be gotten correct by everyone — maybe even the first two items just to be sure. If most of the pretest items are gotten correct by most of the students, it suggests that the material does not need to be taught, but perhaps only reviewed, or maybe left out altogether. (We are assuming here that the test items are subjectively scored, i.e., completion, brief-essay, or similar items in which there is little chance of a student getting the item right by guessing.)

The pattern of results we are looking for appears in the upper part of figure 27-1, in the section labeled *pretest.* A plus sign there indicates a correct response, and a zero indicates an incorrect response. Our test has 10 items, one for each of 10 critical steps in a learning hierarchy or sequence. It can be seen that the average performance on the pretest for these six illustrative students is two items correct, and everyone got the first item correct. This encourages us to believe we are starting at a level which they have all reached.

Now after we have taught the material, we expect a different pattern of test results. If we have not given the students the answers to the pretest questions (and there is no good reason to give them for this kind of a test), we can expect relatively little improvement at posttest time due to their previous experience with the questions.

Figure 27–1

*Using Tests to Modify Instruction and
to Evaluate Modifications*

Pretest

Item	Bill	Susie	Mary	John	Michael	Ann	Average
1	+	+	+	+	+	+	
2	+	0	0	+	+	0	
3	0	+	0	+	0	0	
4	0	0	0	0	0	0	
5	0	0	0	0	0	0	2.0
6	0	0	0	0	0	0	
7	0	0	0	0	0	0	
8	0	0	0	0	0	0	
9	0	0	0	0	0	0	
10	0	0	0	0	0	0	

Posttest

Item	Bill	Susie	Mary	John	Michael	Ann	Average
1	+	+	+	+	+	+	
2	+	+	+	+	+	+	
3	+	+	+	+	+	+	
4	+	+	+	+	+	+	
5	+	+	+	+	+	+	8.2
6	+	+	+	+	+	+	
7	+	+	+	+	0	+	
8	0	+	0	+	+	+	
9	0	0	0	+	+	+	
10	0	0	0	+	0	0	

Retest

Item	Bill	Susie	Mary	John	Michael	Ann	Average
1	+	+	+	+	+	+	
2	+	+	+	+	0	+	
3	+	+	+	+	+	+	
4	+	+	+	+	+	+	
5	0	0	+	+	+	+	6.3
6	+	0	+	+	+	+	
7	0	0	+	+	0	0	
8	0	0	0	+	+	0	
9	0	0	0	+	0	0	
10	0	0	0	+	0	0	

If there is reason to believe that there might be improvement from previously seeing the specific questions, we should prepare twice as many items as we need for the pretest, and at each level of the sequence we should assign one-half of the items at random to the pretest and the other half at random to the posttest. The tests would then be as parallel as random tests can provide. On looking at results of an appropriately designed posttest given at the conclusion of instruction, we would like to see the kind of results shown in the posttest section figure 27-1. To be realistic, we have not shown all +'s in that section. In fact, we have shown a cropping up of 0's at about the level of items 9 and 10 to illustrate an idea we will take up just below. But the pattern is now for a much more satisfactory performance, with the mean being at 8.2 instead of 2.0, indicating that the instruction has accomplished a lot.

Finally, after several weeks we give a retention test. In this case, we must provide a different set of items than was used in the posttest. It is almost always unreasonable to assume that posttest items will be so forgotten that they will not influence retention-test performance when the retention test is given after an interval of only weeks or a few months. (This may imply that initially three times as many items will have to be prepared as will be needed for any one test and that they will have to be assigned randomly within objective or subtopic to three different test forms.) There will almost always be a reduction in performance on retest, as illustrated in the retest part of figure 27-1. However, sometimes the reduction will be much worse than displayed here. The mean may fall all the way back to the pretest level. That would indicate instruction that was not properly designed to provide for retention. The instruction should be modified to aid retention and the modified instruction evaluated again, in such a case.

In the posttest section of figure 27-1 we showed a sudden drop in performance at items 9 and 10. That suggests that the instruction was effective until it reached those topics (assuming that there was sufficient time for instruction so that those last topics were not slighted due to time pressures). Our clue tells us to look at the topics that those items represent, especially item 9 in sequential instruction and to improve the instruction of those topics. Then the instructional procedure should be evaluated again. When the +'s turn to 0's in sequential or hierarchical instruction we have an indication of where the trouble is, though it may take a lot of insight and ingenuity to detect specifically what is wrong and what must be done to make it right. That is where the teacher earns the stars in her crown!

Notice that we have been discussing all of this as though we had used items in which there was little chance of getting the correct answer by guessing. If we use objectively scored items in which the student chooses his response from among a small number offered, there is an appreciable chance that he could choose the correct answer without knowing the topic or possessing the skill. To be reasonably sure that he is not getting credit for good guesses, we simply have to use more than one item per topic or objective. Probably we should use at least about six items per topic, but the minimum number one can get away with depends on a variety of factors too complex to introduce here.

NONSEQUENTIAL LEARNING

When learning is nonsequential, the pretest-posttest-retention test idea is still sound. However, it is not as neat as with sequential learning. With nonsequential material even using completion and brief-essay types of items we cannot expect a neat pattern of correct responses followed by wrong responses with a rather clear break between them. We have to evaluate each topic separately. To be reasonably sound in deciding that each topic has been mastered, we would have to include a substantial number of items for each topic, say 6 to 10 at a minimum. An alternative, of course, is to try to make an overall evaluation, using only one or two items per topic or objective but drawing our conclusions only about total score performance. When one has a set of pretest and posttest results that reveals that the lowest score on posttest was higher than the highest score on pretest, it is unquestionably clear that effective learning has taken place. This would be even more emphatic if a later retention test revealed that much of the increased achievement was maintained over an extended period. Results like that are achievable, especially if the test items are designed to reflect mastery of what is being taught. This implies that items should be written with the intention that students who have not had the instruction will get them wrong, but students who have profited from the instruction will get them correct. Such items, naturally, will not concern concepts or skills that many people master without the specific instruction under consideration. They won't be the kinds of items that people get right by being experienced test takers or by just being generally intelligent. But, remember, they should not concern trivia, either.[1]

OTHER USEFUL IDEAS

We have discussed earlier several procedures that can assist in using tests to modify instruction and to evaluate modifications within the individual classroom. We will remind the reader of these here.

First, when we discussed diagnosis of learning difficulties we mentioned having students work problems or answer items aloud, revealing their thinking or their procedure as they reached a choice among responses. As well as assisting in diagnosis of students' learning problems, this procedure should tip the instructor off to useful ways to modify and improve her instruction. She should be thinking about how she could help future students to avoid the kinds of procedures and the kinds of reasoning that are leading these pupils into error. After she has modified her instruction and used it on students, the same procedure of having problems worked aloud can let her check informally on whether those errors that she tried to prevent have been stamped out effectively.

When we were discussing using feedback from tests, we mentioned that one useful procedure was to analyze test items in class having the students participate by showing their hands for various counts and having student monitors do the counting. One of the virtues mentioned there was the fact that students could discuss the items that many got wrong or that failed to discriminate between successful and unsuccessful students. They learn from the instruction, and the teacher learns how to improve items, how to present material more effectively so that certain kinds of errors no longer occur. After modifying her instruction according to her best idea of how to improve it, later item analysis in class with other

---

[1]Further discussion of construction of tests and items to serve particular purposes is contained in Part 1 of this text.

students can indicate to her whether her modification has been successful. In a sense, the teacher's goal should be to decrease the effectiveness of her items by virtue of improved teaching. (Not, however, simply by teaching that certain responses are wrong to particular items.)

Also when we discussed using tests to provide feedback, we presented the idea of using items that permit common errors to be made. This serves to emphasize to students that those common errors will no longer be tolerated. Items of this kind can be used effectively to see whether carefully planned instruction has, indeed, stamped out the errors. Some old wives' tales and ideas based on superficial analysis are most difficult to eradicate, just like it is hard to stop saying that the sun sinks into the West. Effective education has to change the way people think about such issues, it has to verify that the change has taken place, and it has to verify that the educational procedures in use result in such change or that new procedures are tried until we find methods that do work. Inviting the error to happen if it will is one way to help evaluate how well our methods are succeeding.

Evaluating Instruction and Its Modification across Classrooms

The prospective teacher might wonder why she should be concerned about evaluations of instruction that could be made comparing her class with other classes. After all, that is research or something, not teaching, and her business is helping students to learn efficiently. However, recent interest on the part of people, legislators, and others who control schools by controlling their budgets has centered on something called *accountability*. They are beginning to ask whether there is waste in schools, whether schools are as effective and efficient as they might be, which schools are most efficient and which least, and how the least effective can be improved. To evaluate such issues, they become interested in the relative performances of students taught in one school versus those taught in another, the relative performances of students taught by different teachers, or taught in open vs. traditional classes, in ungraded vs. graded primary schools, and so on. If a teacher finds that her class is about to be included in such study, she should insist that the study be conducted without glaring mistakes in methodology that would evaluate her teaching performance unfairly. Certain unsound practices are well enough recognized by experts that they should never again occur. Unfortunately, however, many evaluation studies and accountability studies are conducted by people who are not experts and experienced in the area. Therefore, it becomes necessary for the teacher to know at least some of the rudiments of such research so that she can protect herself against abuse by incompetent investigators (who, incidentally, may have the best of intentions).

There are many technical aspects to studies evaluating schools. We are only going to discuss one. It is so glaring and so important that one wonders how so many studies could have been done, and continue to be done, ignoring it. This one is a relatively simple idea: there are three essential aspects of evaluating the quality of instruction. First, you must take into account the input. Second, you must account for the output. And finally, but most often neglected, you must account for the treatment itself. (Some might call it the *throughput*.)

By *input,* we are referring to description of what the conditions are like before the treatment (instruction) is applied. This includes what the students are like. Also, what resources are available for supporting the instruction? For example, we would want to know the socioeconomic level of the students, their average ability, and their range of abilities. We would want to know their age and range of ages, their sex, their scores on achievement tests related to the topic under study, and so on, through a list of variables that might influence output regardless of what is done in instruction. We would also want to know such things as the pupil-teacher ratio and the availability of teaching interns. We would want to take into consideration the quality of the school's physical plant, the laboratories, the surrounding environment, the air-conditioning in the South and the heating in the North. We would want to allow for interruptions due to weather, holidays, strikes, or similar disruptive influences, and on through other series of variables that might influence output regardless of the instruction.

By *output,* we mean to include specifically measures of the performances of students. These might be scores on achievement tests, but they might include other kinds of performances such as in art or music, attendance in institutions of higher learning, grades in the next course, being elected for student office, athletic performance, prompt employability, and so on. Whenever possible all the kinds of goals that the instruction had for the students should be evaluated because instruction may be more effective for some goals than others. Or it may be more effective for some goals for certain students, but for other goals for other students. We should also evaluate side effects, such as harm done to other instruction or improved social skills.

By *treatment, instruction,* or *throughput,* we mean measurement and description of precisely what is done to the students, or perhaps better, for the students. What goes on in the classroom? What goes on in other places if instruction is organized to take place outside of, as well as in, the classroom? Does what is described as the method of instruction really occur? An example you are now familiar with is that of homogeneous grouping in which we found that advocates of homogeneous grouping often support it because it presumably lets groups of different learning speed be treated differently. But study of what takes place in classes for different groups indicates that either there is little or no difference in the instruction methods, or else, as in the Washington, D.C. schools at the time of the *Hobson* v. *Hansen* court case, a different set of educational goals is provided for the lower tracks.

The treatment is clearly the hardest of the triad to evaluate. Over many years there have been attempts to develop measures of what goes on in classrooms, but there is little general satisfaction with the measures that have been developed. To get satisfactory measures or evaluations it is often necessary for an observer to be in the classroom during instruction, and there is the danger that this will change the nature of what takes place. Students can be asked about the instruction, but their observations are not necessarily sound nor reflective of the important aspects of what is taking place. This remains a very difficult, unsolved problem — but, at least some very rough evaluations can be made of gross aspects. In Washington, D.C., it could be determined whether different tracks were indeed being taught the same things but by different methods according to the track a student was in, and whether students were being taught in the lower tracks in such a manner that before too long they were improved to the extent that they could be returned to the "mainstream" tracks. When not even such gross evaluations are included in evaluation studies, the conclusions are likely to be monstrous, as we shall see in several examples a little later.

ILLUSTRATIONS OF ERRORS MADE BY IGNORING ONE OR MORE ELEMENTS

Some illustrations of things that have actually happened when evaluations have left out one or more of the three elements may bring home the points we are trying to make.

STUDYING ONLY INPUT

The classical example of studying only input is the typical "self-study" done for an accrediting association. In such studies the final report will contain hundreds of pages on input reporting the budget, the physical plant, the library resources, the number of maintenance people, and the plans for the future of these resources, but it will spend only a few pages at most on reports of actual observations or measurements of what takes place in individual classrooms. There may or may not be any lengthy attention paid to the measured or counted performances of students after they have passed through the school. Often the attention paid to output is slight or nonexistent. As a result, those who know what goes on in the school may wonder that it can retain its accreditation. But they don't realize that evaluations of input, which seem to satisfy accrediting associations, don't concern what goes on in the classroom or what students can do, and a high level of input does not necessarily indicate a high quality of instruction.

STUDYING ONLY OUTPUT

Many kinds of mistakes can be made when only output is considered. Some of them can have important effects on individual teachers as in the case of Mrs. Norma Scheelhaase (*Scheelhaase* v. *Woodbury Central Community School District*). Mrs. Scheelhaase had been a grade school teacher in Woodbury Central Community School District in Iowa for 10 years in 1970. The scholastic program of her school was being criticized in 1970 by the North Central Examining Committee and by the North Central Association. The school was on the unapproved list of the Iowa Department of Public Instruction.

A new school superintendent was appointed, Mr. W. B. Devine, a man of many years experience in school administration. Mr. Devine took a number of remedial steps to improve the scholastic program of the school. He visited Mrs. Scheelhaase's English class and observed her methods and her relationship with the class. Afterwards he advised her that her work was unsatisfactory. A month later he notified her of the fact that she was going to be terminated at the end of the year. This was permissible since there is no law providing tenure for teachers in Iowa. He followed all the legal requirements in terminating Mrs. Scheelhaase, including hearings and appeals. She was told during these proceedings that the reason for her termination was the low scores of her pupils on the Iowa Tests of Basic Skills (ITBS) and the Iowa Tests of Educational Development (ITED).

She took the issue of her termination after such long service to court in 1972, arguing that her civil rights were violated. Additional reasons for her termination were offered at that time, but the court refused to consider them since they were not given to her during the earlier hearings or made part of the letter notifying her of termination.

The district court ruled in Mrs. Scheelhaase's favor, ordering that she be reinstated and paid $13,644 damages. It stated, "A teacher's professional competence cannot be determined solely on the basis of her students' achievement on the ITBS and the ITED, especially where the students maintain normal educational growth rates." (The superintendent of her school had testified that the test results showed normal achievement.)

However, the school district appealed the case to a higher court. The appeals court decided on November 28, 1973, to reverse the decision of the lower court and to dismiss the case. Rehearings were denied. The appeals court made this decision on the basis that the district court did not have jurisdiction since the case was not really a civil rights issue, nor was there a legitimate question of whether Mrs. Scheelhaase had been granted due process. The court pointed out that since there was no tenure law, the school board could dismiss any teacher for any reason or no reason at all, subject to any contract between the board and the teacher. It also refused to consider such matters as the competence of teachers and how it might be measured, these not being "matters of constitutional dimensions." In a concurring opinion, one judge pointed out that, while the superintendent may have been wrong to use the test results as the sole basis for evaluating the competence of Mrs. Scheelhaase, his conclusion was not an unreasoned one. It was not arbitrary or capricious. And that is the test on which the issue was judged.

Thus, although we know that more should have been considered in using test scores to evaluate a teacher's competence than was used here, we also know that legally there is now a precedent for misusing test scores in this way. It is only through teachers' and teacher groups' knowing that this is an unsound and improper use of test scores that such matters can be settled soundly before they get to court. The courts are only concerned with whether the administration tried, in good faith and without caprice, to reach a sound conclusion. In the absence of evidence or convincing argument to the contrary, misinterpretation of data will appear to the court to be soundly reasoned conclusion. The unsound and unfair judgment of the teacher will be allowed to stand as within the discretion of the school administration.

A different kind of error occurred when an attempt was made to evaluate the relative quality of various colleges by examining the rates of attendance in graduate schools and rates of obtaining the doctorate degree for the graduates of each of the colleges. A pecking order of colleges was established that many people accepted as sound. Then further investigation took into account the ability levels of the entering students at these colleges. It found that the ability levels of the students closely corresponded to the measures of the college's output. That is, those colleges that took in bright students turned out students who went on with graduate work and got advanced degrees. When that factor was taken into account, a different set of colleges were recognized as being superior in what they did for their students. The first study, which ignored input, merely indicated that some colleges do well at selecting students who will later be successful. The second study, which studied both input and output, located the colleges that are effective at something other than just choosing students wisely. It remains to be determined what the important differences in treatment are between the two kinds of colleges, however.

IGNORING TREATMENT

Although the study just mentioned ignored treatment and still provided useful evaluative information, there are good examples in which that approach leads to grossly erroneous conclusions. The procedure of *performance contracting* provides startlingly clear illustrations.

In performance contracting, usually a profit-making company contracts with a school district to take over some of the instruction of the district's pupils. Usually the instruction is of reading or mathematics. Often the pupils chosen for this special arrangement are the disadvantaged. The company may or may not use local teachers. It usually emphasizes the addition of hardware, paraprofessional personnel, and perhaps *contingency management* (perhaps called *behavior modification, operant conditioning,* or *Skinnerian conditioning*) as an instructional technique. Often nationally standardized tests are used as pretest and posttest measures, and the company is paid according to increases in posttest over pretest performance. If the students' scores do not increase sufficiently, there may be a penalty clause requiring the company to pay the school for failure. Usually there will be an arrangement in which losses in scores by some students deduct from the payment provided from other students' gains. When this procedure was first introduced it seemed to have much promise for improving instruction by using the best of instructional methods and business management methods, coupled with the profit motive. The initial studies seemed to indicate great effectiveness and potential for revamping American education.

However, those studies did not pay enough attention to a number of factors, such as the regression effect, the appropriateness of the standardized tests for the school's objectives, and the difficulties of measuring change. More important, they did not provide for study of what actually went on in the classrooms. Eventually scandals occurred in places like Texarkana where it was discovered that the students were being taught the answers to the questions on the tests that were to be used in determining how much the contractors would be paid.

One especially clear study was done by faculty members of the University of Indiana. They gave a reading test to seventh and eighth graders in a rural Indiana junior high school. After four weeks they retested the same students, without providing any instruction whatsoever on reading. However, a control group of students was told on the retest that they were being retested to see how much they had learned since the last testing. The experimental group was told that rewards would be given for the best improvement. The rewards included transistor radios, Indiana University sweatshirts, and candy bars (Tuinman et al., 1972).

The results clearly favored the experimental group so much that a typical performance contract would have yielded a payment of about $3,000 — for nothing! All that had been done was to provide a different kind of motivation for the posttest. Students then got higher scores without having improved their reading skills at all. Notice that even though we had measures of input and output, we would have been deceived seriously in this study by not evaluating the treatment. Incidentally, it is perhaps worth noting here that a large-scale study of the effectiveness of performance contracting for aiding the disadvantaged, costing $6,000,000, involving 25,000 students, and using 6 different performance-contracting companies, yielded results that have been interpreted by research experts as being uniformly unsuccessful. The performance-contracting procedure had no detectable effect on student learning (Page, 1972).

Another example of the disastrous kinds of conclusions that can come from ignoring treatment — failing to observe and record what actually happens — comes from a real study of differentiated staffing. In this instance, just by happenstance, a certain set of schools were involved in two studies of differentiated staffing. One agency was studying the problems associated with implementing differentiated staffing. A different agency was studying the effects of differentiated staffing on student achievement. The second study reached the conclusion that there was no difference between the achievement gains in differentiated staffing compared with conventional staffing. At the same time, the study of problems involved in introducing differentiated staffing showed that no differentiated staffing had actually occurred in those schools where it was supposed to have occurred. Actual observations of classes showed that nothing different took place in the classes supposedly using differentiated staffing from what took place in classes that were staffed conventionally. So the appraisal of the effectiveness of differentiated staffing was an evaluation of an event that never took place (Charters, 1973). It is no wonder that the conclusion was that there was no difference! This is the kind of monstrosity that can occur with evaluation research that does not take into account all three aspects: input, treatment (*throughput*), and output.

Performance Tests for Teachers

One final way in which tests might be used to improve instruction and to evaluate modifications of instruction is that of using teachers' test performances to evaluate the quality of the teachers. Perhaps only the best qualified could be allowed to teach without supervision, and those who failed to meet the standard set could take further instruction in teaching. This might be a way to improve instruction via tests. If that kind of testing could be done, then one might feel that he did not have to evaluate what happened in the classroom. He could take the position that different kinds of instruction work for different kinds of students and situations, and the good teacher is the one who is versatile in using a variety of methods when they are most appropriate. The improvement in instruction that resulted from modifying the quality of the instructors could be evaluated, using the teachers' test scores as indicators of the quality of their instruction.

This kind of an idea has been tried out in a very limited way. One study deliberately set out to develop performance tests for teachers. Specific objectives that were to be reached by instruction were laid out. A variety of materials for teaching the objectives was prepared. Pretests and posttests of students' achievement of those objectives were carefully prepared. The plan was for an instructor to be given the objectives and the resource materials well in advance of her taking the test. She was to be told to devise a sequence of instruction that would reach the objectives. Then she was actually to teach the objectives, using any procedures she wanted to. After a specified period of instruction time (about 10 hours over a two-week period), the students would be tested to see how effective the teaching had been.

The researchers developed such performance tests in three subject areas, social science research methods, basic power supplies, and automotive carburetion. They then tried out the procedure to see how well it would work. They reasoned that their test ought to be at least good enough to distinguish between trained, experienced teachers and people off the street. So in a research study they compared trained social science teachers with college students who had completed two years of college majoring or minoring in social science but with no teacher training. They compared trained teachers of auto mechanics who had taught for at least two years with mechanics from garages and auto agency service departments who had no teacher training experience. And they compared electronics teachers who had teaching credentials and at least two years of teaching experience with television repairmen and workers in electronics industries who had no teacher training or experience (Popham, 1971).

Unfortunately, the results of the study were that no appreciable differences appeared between the performances of students taught by trained vs. untrained teachers. The obvious conclusion is that this very careful attempt to develop a measure of teacher effectiveness failed. That suggests that it may be very difficult to develop such measures, indeed. On the other hand, the researchers point out that an alternative explanation could be that typical trained and experienced teachers are not any better than lay people at bringing about specified behavior changes in students. A study in which instructors were specifically trained to produce prespecified changes in student behavior indicated that such trained teachers do produce greater changes in their students on performance tests like those described above than do teachers who have not been trained to produce specified changes in students' behaviors. So maybe in this case testing of teachers will improve instruction by improving the kind of instruction that we give to the teachers of the future!

Summary

In this chapter we have considered two frames of reference for using tests to evaluate instruction and its modifications. One was the individual classroom; the other involved comparisons between classrooms or comparisons among larger units.

Within a classroom we can use such procedures as the pretest-posttest-retention test model. We can also do such things as have the students answer questions or work problems aloud, have the students participate in analysis of the items, and have the students answer questions that invite common errors to verify that they have been sufficiently eradicated.

Across classrooms, evaluations of instruction are quite complex, but a basic consideration is that all three major aspects of the teaching situation be included in any study: input, treatment, and output. The most difficult to include is treatment, i.e., just what occurs in the classroom? Is it different from classroom to classroom when it is supposed to be, and the same when it is not supposed to be different? Does what takes place in the classroom agree with what it described as taking place there when administrators discuss the classroom procedures of their schools? We do not have generally accepted, effective ways of measuring or describing the significant aspects of what takes place in instruction, so efforts to deal with treatments adequately are at a primitive level.

Since it is difficult to measure and describe the process of instruction, it has been suggested that performance tests of teacher competence be used as overall measures of quality of instruction. Either such tests are very difficult to develop, or else what is typically taught to teachers about the educational process does not enable them to help children learn any more effectively than lay people help children to learn. The process of trying to develop such tests may have its greatest impact in changing the way we teach teachers. That is one more example of how testing can improve instruction.

References

Charters, W. W., Jr. & Jones, J. E. On the risk of appraising nonevents in program evaluation. *Educ. Researcher*, 1973, **2**, 5–7.

Page, E. B. How we *all* failed in performance contracting. *Educ. Psychologist*, 1972, **9**, 40–42.

Popham, W. J. Performance tests of teaching proficiency: Rationale development, and validation. *Amer. educ. Res. Journal*, 1971, **8**, 105–17.

Scheelhaase, v. *Woodbury Central Community School District*. 349 F. Supp. 988, rev. 488 F 2d. 237 (1972–74).

Tuinman, J. J., Farr, R., & Blanton, B. E. Increases in test scores as a function of material rewards. *J. educ. Meas.*, 1972, **9**, 215–23.

Part Five

Introduction

The measurement of attitudes is a little different from the measurement of abilities and achievements that has been described in the previous parts of this volume. Abilities and achievements are in the *cognitive* domain, and attitudes are in the *affective* domain. When we measure an attitude we want to know how a student feels, instead of what he can do. Interests and personality traits are also in the affective domain, but while no one would seriously suggest that a teacher construct her own personality or interest tests, it is sometimes seriously suggested that teachers construct their own attitude measures. The reason may be that there is a greater likelihood of success for a teacher to develop a sound attitude measure. Also, attitude measures are probably more useful to the teacher than personality or interest measures.

It must be recognized, however, that the development of sound attitude measures is no simple matter. In fact, as you will see, once she knows what she is getting into, only a teacher with unusual resources would attempt to develop an attitude measure without expert assistance. Since it is important to know what effects curriculum changes have on students' attitudes, teachers need to know enough about attitude measurement to be aware of the pitfalls and the steps that are necessary in creating sound measuring instruments.

Opinion measurement is much like attitude measurement. It, too, is important. It seems simple, but is not. Teachers are, or should be, interested in the opinions of their students. Thus, they should know how opinions are soundly measured, and how representative samples of students are chosen so that the measurements of the opinions of a group are not biased in unknown ways. The fundamentals of attitude and opinion measurement will be presented in this part of the book.

28

Measurement of Attitudes

Objectives

As a result of study of this chapter, you should be able to:

1. Explain what an attitude is;
2. Discuss reasons for and against having the development of attitudes as instructional objectives;
3. Discuss reasons for and against the measurement of pupil attitudes;
4. Describe a procedure for developing an attitude scale;
5. Describe the characteristics of good and poor attitude items;
6. Describe the important qualities of a good attitude measure;
7. Describe procedures which will reduce "faking" when attitudes are measured;
8. Indicate how the quality of an attitude measure is evaluated;
9. Describe at least one way of estimating an attitude without asking pupils for their opinions;
10. Describe the measurement of opinions and its relationship to the measurement of attitudes;
11. List four resources or references for locating existing attitude measures.

What Is an Attitude?

Attitudes have been a subject of study over a period of years. As a result, there have been many and varied definitions of what an attitude is. One that seems to tap the essence of the idea, and which we will use here, is that an attitude is a consistency among responses to particular stimuli or objects. For example, a favorable attitude toward studying mathematics might be represented by consistent positive reactions to such things as statements about mathematics, doing puzzles involving numbers, learning tricks with numbers, solving arithmetic problems, learning the logic of

335

mathematics, taking additional mathematics courses, belonging to a mathematics club, and planning to major in college in a field requiring mathematics such as engineering, physics, chemistry, or statistics. The consistent response to things involving numbers or mathematics is labeled an attitude.

Attitudes are descriptions of how people feel or typically react instead of descriptions of what they know or can do. Thus attitudes are considered descriptions of *affect*, i.e., feeling, as opposed to aptitudes and achievements that are considered to be descriptions of *cognition*, i.e., knowing. Other affective characteristics that are sometimes measured are interests, temperament traits, and personality traits of various kinds. Temperament traits and personality traits are measured by psychologists as they try to help or study people, especially people who are behaving abnormally. Measurement of such characteristics is so difficult and so often done unsoundly, even by experts, that teachers are ill-advised to involve themselves in such measurements. Interest measurement is nearly as tricky, though sometimes guidance counselors in schools may develop sufficient understanding and skill to avoid being dangerous to students when measuring and interpreting interests. Attitude measurement is also very complicated, but there is great interest among some educators in the area so we will discuss it at some length here.

Should Attitudes Be Objectives of School Instruction?

It is not a clearly decided matter that attitudes should be deliberately taught in the schools. There are some attitudes about which there would be little objection. For instance, most people would agree that the schools should try to develop attitudes of good citizenship in students. Probably the attitude of treating others with honesty would be acceptable to all parents and educators. However, some parents would probably like for the schools to develop in their pupils a positive attitude toward competition, while others would want the schools to develop a positive attitude toward cooperation. The two are somewhat incompatible. Some parents would want their children to be taught to value conservative approaches to life, and others would want their children to be taught to value a liberal point of view. Some might want their children to develop positive values toward school and continuing their educations. Others might not want their children to develop such positive values toward school that they continued into college, graduate school, and generally a prolonged and expensive educational career. They might prefer for their children to value the world of work and vocations so that they soon became self-supporting. Other examples could, of course, be mentioned, but the point here is that even if we were agreed that attitudes were important objectives of instruction, we might have to poll our communities to find out which attitudes were generally acceptable so we would not be teaching something that the parents of many of our pupils would reject.

Not all parents, or even educators, agree that attitudes should be deliberate objectives of instruction. Some take a strong stand that the development of attitudes is the most important part of education and that what the school accomplishes in attitude formation is more important than what it teaches students to understand and be able to perform. Others argue equally strongly that the development of attitudes is no business of the school. They claim the home, the church, and other agencies outside of the school are the proper places for attitudes to be developed. They would argue that the school should teach the things that society can agree on as sound and useful for everyone and that different parents will want different attitudes instilled in their children. The school should not interfere and try to pre-empt this important part of the child's development. (Of course, still others argue that both knowledge and attitudes are important objectives.) So we cannot argue that, since it is their business to develop attitudes and to be sure that they have been developed, therefore all teachers should know how to measure attitudes.

If we were to accept the point of view that attitudes were the *primary* objectives of education, our reasoning would lead us into some interesting problems. We know that the typical students are going to develop along directions in which they expect to be evaluated. Part 3 of this book argues that students should be evaluated in terms of the instructional objectives. It follows, then, that if we want attitudes to be our primary goals, we should test and grade students so that high test scores and high grades reflect acceptable attitudes more than appropriate knowledge and skills. In other words, a student with the attitude we desired to create would get a high grade in spite of the fact that he knew little about the subject and could do few of the things we might have also tried to teach him to be able to do. His attitude was the primary goal, and his grade was based on the primary goal.

To complicate things further, there are people who try to escape some of the problems of attitude measurement (which we will examine later) by deciding to define attitude as what a student responds on an attitude questionnaire. (Others would define it as including what he would *do*. What he will say on a questionnaire and what he will do are not necessarily the same, as research has shown [LaPiere, 1934], so the easy way out is to define attitude as what is easy to measure.) Now, if our primary objective is to develop desirable attitudes, and our definition of attitude is what a student indicates on an attitude questionnaire, then all a student has to do to get a high grade is to answer the questionnaire items in the way the teacher prefers them to be answered. Many students might opt for credit by examination in such a system!

But there is still another problem. Suppose that one of the attitudes we try to develop is that of personal integrity. Now what if a child is able to learn all we could ask her to know about English, but hates it? If she has integrity, she will answer the attitude questionnaire about English in a way that no English teacher who considered development of a favorable attitude toward her subject would find acceptable. So the child gets an F for English (in spite of her knowledge, since attitude is the primary goal) because she has too much personal integrity to falsify her responses to the questionnaire about attitude toward English. For many students and parents this would be an intolerable state of affairs. One must then question whether it is sensible for attitudes to be our primary goals, and whether it is sensible to settle for the attitudes in which we are interested as being merely the consistencies among responses to questionnaire items about attitudes.

Should Attitudes Be Measured in Schools?

There is, however, another reason for teachers' being competent in attitude measurement and knowing the problems involved. Whether teachers *deliberately* set out to form attitudes in their pupils or not, the children's attitudes are being formed all the time, in school and out. One problem the teacher has is to determine whether her instruction is causing attitudes to develop incidentally, rather than deliberately, and what kinds of attitudes those are. For example, suppose that a new curriculum in physics is introduced in high school on the ground that in the past high school training in physics has not laid a sound foundation either for practical use of the knowledge or for continuing advanced instruction in physics. Now suppose that this new curriculum is shown to be effective in developing much more acceptable competencies in physics, but it also "turns off" the students so that now only one-tenth as many students are willing to study physics in high school. In all likelihood the physics teachers would regard that as an undesirable state of events and would seek to modify the new curriculum to make it more attractive or otherwise conducive to positive attitudes toward physics instruction. At least they might desire for attitude toward physics to be no worse as a result of the course. But they would not have known of the undesirable side effect on attitude unless they measured physics attitude somehow. (In this case, the measure was a very rough one, just counting how many students took physics before the new curriculum and after the new curriculum.) So teachers should know something about attitude measurement so that they can monitor the effects of their instruction and its modifications on attitudes of their students.

How Are Attitudes Measured?

There are many ways to measure attitudes, from very rough and coarse observations, such as counting the number of physics students in the new curriculum, to refined scales. We will learn about several techniques to illustrate some of the variety and to become acquainted with some of the problems. Attitude measurement is no simple matter unless, of course, the attitude is so strong that it is obvious.

ATTITUDE SCALES

Let us start with learning about how one might build an attitude scale. One technique, perhaps the most feasible for teachers, is to develop an attitude scale that requires the pupils to answer statements reflecting attitudes. Each student tells to what extent he agrees with each statement, i.e., he rates the statement. Then the ratings are summed together to give a number that reflects the direction and strength of his attitude. For instance, we might want to evaluate attitude toward poetry. We could have statements like:

I enjoy reading poetry aloud.
I enjoy reading poetry silently.
I would like to own a large number of poetry books.
I would like to take a course that would teach me to write poetry.
I would like to enter a poetry contest.

Each of the items should reflect a behavior or feeling that is a legitimate expectation as a result of the instruction. Each student would be presented with the list and asked to indicate for each statement the extent to which he agreed with it. Usually the following categories of response are offered for each item:

Strongly Agree
Agree
Undecided
Disagree
Strongly Disagree

For little children the wording of each item would have to be very simple, and it might be best to read each item to the child. Some device like having three large round "faces" before the child, one smiling, one frowning, and one with a straight line for a mouth, is a good idea. The child points at the face that indicates his feeling about the statement. Children at the earliest grades can learn to respond to positively stated items this way working on an individual basis with a teacher with whom they have rapport.

A scale is scored by giving 5 points for each time the student says Strongly Agree, 4 points for Agree, 3 for Undecided, 2 for Disagree, and 1 for each Strongly Disagree. (A parallel system would be used for three faces.) The sum of his number of points indicates the strength and direction of each student's attitude toward poetry.

We could have some statements negative in feeling about poetry in the set, such as:

I get nervous when I hear someone reading poetry aloud.

(We would assume that one of our expectations from instruction was development of an attitude that included hearing poetry read aloud.) We would have to reverse the scoring system for such items, giving 5 points to Strongly Disagree, and so on. It is recommended that in general an attitude scale have an equal number of positively and negatively worded statements since some people tend to agree with positive statements regardless of what they say. Also, since it has been found that one item on such a scale sometimes affects the responses on the next item, it is suggested that the positive and negative statements appear in a random order on the attitude questionnaire. Negatively stated items when used with the happy-faces response procedure will probably be too confusing to be useful.

WRITING ATTITUDE ITEMS

Writing items that will measure attitudes effectively is a bit tricky. Part of the trouble is that we do not know all the different factors that will influence how people will respond to an item, but we do know that attitude items are very sensitive to extraneous factors. Some of the factors that have been isolated are such things as (1) the connotations of words for different cultures, (2) the different frames of reference of different respondents, (3) the understandability of the question or of the issues involved, (4) whether a question is asked in the negative or positive direction, (5) whether the words "or not" are put at the end of the question, (6) whether one question precedes or follows some specific other question, (7) whether a question includes factors that make the respondent feel important, (8) whether technical words are used, (9) what kinds of responses are permitted (for instance, whether there is a neutral category or not), and so on. Even knowing all these factors we have the problem that we do not know for sure which way to ask the question to get the true reflection of opinion.

We do have some principles that have been recommended for many years, and they will be listed here. Basically, the item must be understandable, answerable, and interpretable. All kinds of ambiguity must be avoided — and that automatically means avoid the use of the word "not," and doubly avoid double negatives. It also means avoid long questions and questions that are not simple sentences. A common failing of the amateur is to put two or more elements into a single question, thoroughly frustrating the examinee who agrees with one part but not with the other. A simple example would be:

I like the teacher and the textbook in U.S. History this year.

More likely to get into an attitude instrument unnoticed is:

I like history this year because the textbook is good.

When you realize that research some years ago found that only 86% of adults gave the same responses three weeks apart to a factual item like whether they owned a car (Cantril, 1944), you can see how hard it would be to get consistent responses to complicated items. However, as with any kind of measurement, if we can't get consistent results there is no point in pursuing that way of measuring. Without consistency we have nothing.

Some additional suggestions for wording items are these:

1. Use words that the least fluent students who will take the questionnaire can understand and are familiar with.
2. Avoid any conditional clauses. Use simple sentences or questions.
3. Design the question to get at exactly what is wanted.
4. Avoid suggesting the answer, any particular answer, or a preferred answer, e.g., "Do you agree that busing improves relations between races."
5. Don't use catch words, stereotypes, or emotional words, such as *new*, as in, "I like the new mathematics course."
6. Try to allow for all possible answers that are likely to occur.

One of the best suggestions to help improve the items in questionnaires is to try them out before using them. A good tryout is to ask students like those who are going to be given the questionnaire to answer the items. See if they have any trouble with them. Ask them what they meant by their answers to see if that is what you thought their answers would mean. Even ask them how you could have written any troublesome question so that there would have been no confusion. Doing this with only a few students, a dozen or so, will often avoid a great deal of misinterpretation later.

Arranging Attitude Items

The arrangement of items is also important and there are a few suggestions available about arrangement.

1. Put the items in a logical order of sequence if there is one.
2. Ask general questions before specific questions if both kinds of questions are asked about a topic.
3. The first question or two should be easily answered and should be designed to avoid upsetting the student.
4. Sensitive questions or potentially embarrassing questions should be in the middle, not at either end.

5. Sensitive questions should be interspersed among nonsensitive questions so that they do not all come at once.

There are a variety of item types that can be used. One type was illustrated earlier. It asked the student to indicate whether he agreed or disagreed in various degrees with a statement. You can also ask directly how he feels when he engages in an activity, such as art. Possible answers might be: eager, anxious, bored, happy. The scoring for such an item introduces a complication. Often logic does not clearly tell us what weight or value should be given to each response. Does "eager" indicate a more positive attitude than "happy," and, if so, how much more? Since *rational keying* based on logic does not tell us what to do in such a situation, we resort to *empirical keying*. For empirical keying we must give the item to groups known to have different degrees or direction (or both) of attitude toward the object. We might give the item to a group of artists and a group of auto mechanics, presuming that on the average their attitudes toward art would be quite different. If more artists than mechanics choose the response, eager, that response gets a positive weight, say $+3$. If more artists than mechanics also say "happy," but the difference between the groups is not as great, happy may be given a weight of $+2$. If more mechanics than artists say "bored," that response may get a negative weight, say -2. Responses that do not differentiate between the groups get zero weight.

You can ask what the student does in certain situations and infer attitudes from his responses. For example, if a classical music program comes on the TV when you are watching, what do you do? Turn up the volume, change the channel, turn off the set, get up and get something to eat, and other similar activities would be possible answers. Notice two things about such questions, however. First, you must include all reasonable answers, but you don't want to suggest answers that the respondent would not otherwise think of. This requires a pretest of the item as an open-ended question to see what kinds of answers occur naturally. These become your alternative responses on the questionnaire. Second, you must not infer that the respondent actually does or would do what he says on the questionnaire. He may or he may not. It is well known that people often do not *act* the way they answer. All you want to find out is whether certain answers are given more often by people with certain attitudes or degrees of an attitude, and to develop a scoring plan accordingly. If you really want to know what the person would do, there is no acceptable way to find out other than to watch to see what he does. We ordinarily don't measure attitudes that way because it is so inconvenient.

It would seem relatively easy for a teacher to develop an attitude scale from the description so far, just as it seems to the naïve teacher a simple thing to construct an achievement test for her students. It is only when you learn enough to recognize the problems that you become sensitive to the need in achievement testing for such things as tables of specifications, item analyses, p values, discrimination values, sound use of specific determiners, and substantial numbers of items in teacher-made tests. The same is true with attitude measures.

REQUIREMENTS OF GOOD ATTITUDE SCALES

Let us look at some of the requirements for *good* attitude scales that make their development and use much more complicated than they appear to be at first glance.

First, while each *item* that a teacher might think up for an attitude scale might be relevant, for the *scale* to be a sound measure of the attitude, the set of items must represent all aspects of the attitude object, in our illustration, poetry. Have we left anything out about liking poetry? Undoubtedly we have. For instance, we did not mention liking to set poetry to music or to write verses that fit the sound and rhythm of an existing tune. Unless we have represented all aspects of the attitude object our attitude scale will not have *content validity* and will be relatively worthless.

It is not easy to evaluate the content validity of an attitude scale, but one device for helping to attain it is to start out development of a scale with a much larger number of statements than we expect to use, several hundred or so. We edit and cull these down to about 100 — those we expect to discriminate best between people at different points on the attitude. We then give the shortened list to students like ours and choose the 15 or 20 items for the final scale that are answered in the appropriate direction by people who get high positive scores on the total scale, and in the opposite direction by those who get low scores on the total scale. (For the initiated, this is the same as picking items that *correlate* highly with the total scale score or that have appropriate discrimination values for the different responses. This step provides us with *internal consistency* of the scale, i.e., the items tend to go together. An attitude scale should measure only one attitude, not confuse measurement of several.) Finally we develop the scoring system and try out this form again to be sure it works as a unit.

A good attitude scale should have items that represent the larger pool of items that might be asked, just as a good achievement test should contain items that represent a larger pool of test items that could be asked. So, we should really construct two forms of our attitude scale from the good items in our pool. To be sure that our scores are worthwhile we should get about the same score for a pupil on one form as on the other. And we should evaluate this by giving both forms to a substantial group of pupils and looking at the scatterplot for them or computing the correlation. This process is evaluating the *equivalent-forms reliability* of the scale. If we cannot generate at least two forms that agree from our item pool, it is doubtful that the attitude is worth measuring or that we have picked a very good way to measure it.

We should also find out how transitory our attitude is. To do this, we should test the attitude once, and then without attempting to change the attitude test it again a week or two later, or perhaps even longer. We might even give one form now and the other a month later and compare the scores by means of a scatterplot or correlation coefficient. If there is not a high relationship (combined *equivalent forms* and *retest reliability*), then it is doubtful that the attitude is worth worrying about, or else we have not measured it well enough to be useful.

Presumably we want to measure an attitude for some purpose. The purpose we set out as legitimate for all teachers was to monitor the effect of our instructional procedures. But, as was suggested earlier, we usually are not fundamentally interested in what students will say to a teacher on an attitude form. We are more interested in what they might do or not do related to the attitude object. But that is not what we have measured with our attitude scale. There is clear evidence that what people say on a scale or questionnaire is not necessarily similar to what they will do. So for a scale to be worthwhile we next have to find out whether what students say on our scale is related to the attitude they would express spontaneously and to the action they might take toward the attitude object.

The next step, then, in checking on whether we have usefully measured an attitude with our scale is usually to find *known groups*, that is, groups of people who are known spontaneously to express opposite attitudes toward the object or who are known to act differently toward the object. We give members of those known groups our attitude scale and see if they get very different average scores. If they do, we begin to be confident that our scale may measure the attitude usefully (have *construct validity*).[1] If they do not, it is back to the drawing board.

For the attitude toward poetry, members of a poetry club might be contrasted with some group much less likely to be generally interested in poetry, perhaps the basketball team. Students who enroll in an elective course in poetry have acted differently from those who elect no language or communication courses at all. A series of contrasts like this might make a sound construct validation basis for deciding whether our attitude-toward-poetry scale was a useful measure of what it claimed to be. Incidentally, it is recommended that the positive items on a scale be studied separately from the negative items in such a validation to be sure that both kinds of items behave the same way — as though they measured the same thing. Sometimes negative items that are written to correspond with positive ones turn out to be measuring some attitude other than the one initially sought.

You would think that these were enough problems, but there are more. Up to now we have assumed that the people you were using to develop your attitude measure were cooperative and helpful and had no reason to be concerned that their attitudes were being measured for some purpose. However, you may want to use your scale on people who will think that you are doing it for some reason. Now we get into the matter of accurate responding. Some of the people whose attitudes you are going to measure may not want you to have a good measure of their attitudes, especially if you are going to include attitude in your grade! They may even want you to think their attitudes are the opposite of what they really are. There is nothing to keep someone who hates poetry from answering your scale so that he looks like the greatest poetry lover in the school. Some of the people you want to measure may not deliberately set out to deceive you about their attitude, but it may be their nature to please (or displease) the teacher and unconsciously they will tend to make their scores come out so they please (or displease) you.

In some attitude scales in the past it has been found that people tended to answer the items in the direction that they thought was socially desirable, regardless of their own attitudes. Some attitude scales have been deliberately constructed so that the desirability of the items will not cloud the measurement of the attitude. But that is a very complicated business, not something that a teacher would be likely to do

---

[1] Construct validity refers to a measure's tendency to behave as we would expect it to behave in relation to other measures or operations. We expect a measure of weight to distinguish between objects that are hard to lift or easy to lift, between objects of similar size and shape that float on water and that sink, and between a loud and powerful explosion from a given weight of gunpowder and a softer and less violent explosion from a lesser weight of that kind of gunpowder. The weight measure, when it fits our expectations in all these and all similar ways, has great construct validity. (*Weight* is the "construct," logically, that we are measuring.) If an attitude measure behaves as we would expect it to behave in a wide variety of situations, it develops our respect as having construct validity. To the extent that it fails, due to faking, to inadequate content validity, or any other reasons, we distrust its construct validity.

along with all the rest of her activities. However, the problem of getting distorted results from the usual transparent set of items on an attitude scale is so great that such scales, by themselves, would be of little value if their purpose was to measure each student's attitude so that a grade could be based largely or even partially on it.

Even if a teacher were to desire to monitor the student's attitudes toward a new curriculum or classroom procedure, the results of scales such as these would be highly suspect unless the teacher had developed such an atmosphere of trust in her classroom that she could feel sure that the students would not be disposed, even unconsciously, to modify their answers to suit the situation. That level of trust can sometimes be achieved by taking several steps. First of all, assure the students clearly and categorically that the attitude scores will not be reflected in their grades. Even administer the attitude measure after the grades have been given, if possible. Second, let the students answer anonymously. Even better, let them answer on answer sheets that require only making black marks so that their handwriting cannot be identified. Third, have one of the students collect and shuffle the answer sheets. And fourth, never use the results for or against any student so that students come to respect your promise that they won't be used that way.

An alternative way of ascertaining information about attitudes is also possible, a way that is too cumbersome to be used for all attitudes, but that usually gets around the problem of faking when it can be applied.

NONREACTIVE MEASURES

One way to get around faking is to use what have been called *nonreactive* or *unobtrusive* measures. Those terms reflect the fact that our usual measuring instruments are obtrusive; that is, they are instruments presented to the student that tell him that now we are going to measure his attitude. He tends to react to the process of measurement. Suppose we simply watched his behavior, as when we noticed that students no longer took the physics course that we thought was so good for them. That measurement did not intrude into their stream of events. It did not stick out. The students did not even know that their attitude toward the course was being evaluated. They could not possibly react to the measurement, fake, respond in a socially desirable manner, etc.

There are a great variety of possibilities for developing measures of attitudes that are unobtrusive. One wag (Hallaman, 1974) has suggested that teacher interest in an in-service training program could be measured by counting the number of teachers who double-parked outside the building in which the program was being offered. You would also count, with additional scoring weight, the number who double-parked and left their motors running. Even greater scoring weight would be given to those who double-parked with their motors running and sent someone else into the building to see if the program was worthwhile. That is the idea of unobtrusive or nonreactive measurement. But, more realistically, physical traces can be examined. The amount of wear on books in the library concerning physics would be a measure to support or deny the soundness of a conclusion that students were turned off to physics by a new physics curriculum. The number of times paintings or books on painting are checked out in the library or bought in the bookstore gives clues to the extent to which art appreciation courses are effective in developing positive attitudes toward art objects. (The measure might be refined if separate counts are kept for students who took art appreciation during the *previous* quarter or semester. Even better if these can be compared with the number they purchased during the term prior to the appreciation course.) With proper precautions, you could also infer attitude toward instruction from such things as:

1. Frequency of lateness for class,
2. Frequency of absences from class,
3. Number of students attending optional activities,
4. Number of assignments handed in late (although, lateness might be due to extra care resulting from great interest),
5. Number choosing additional courses on the topic,
6. Degree of participation in clubs related to the topic, and
7. Number who indicate an interest in majoring in the area.

Other approaches can be used. The classic work of Hartshorne and May in the late 1920s on the willingness of children to deceive included a number of ingenious methods. For instance, coins were distributed for practice in arithmetic, and a record was made of those which failed to be returned. Students were allowed to grade their own exam papers (which had been collected, scored, and handed back with some excuse), and it was noted which responses were changed after the papers were handed back.

The teacher who is interested in using such procedures to study attitudes, or to evaluate the meaning of scores from an attitude scale she is developing, should study carefully the book by Webb and his colleagues entitled *Unobtrusive Measures: Nonreactive Research in the Social Sciences* (1966), for numerous examples and sound critical analysis of the use of this form of measurement. In general, they view these kinds of measures as supplements to measures such as questionnaires which are much more flexible. If the two forms of measurement yield supporting results, one is greatly reassured that his measurement of attitudes is sound. If the results conflict, he is warned that one or both may be misleading.

There is also the problem that not all would regard as ethical the measurement of people without their knowing that they are being studied. Probably not many would say that counting how many students elect to take physics and deciding from a great decrease in numbers that something is going wrong would be an unethical practice. But many more parents would be incensed if the teacher gave the pupils an opportunity to steal coins in an arithmetic lesson, and then noted which children did steal when given the opportunity. Probably even more parents would be upset if the teacher turned on a hidden tape recorder in her room when she left it briefly in order to find out who the troublemakers were and what kind of mischief they would try to cook up in her absence. The user of unobtrusive measures will have to struggle with these kinds of ethical problems just as the user of obtrusive measures will have to struggle with the problems of faking by those whose attitudes are presumably being measured. Obviously, the sound measurement of attitudes is no simple affair.

Opinion Measurement

Up to now we have talked about developing attitude scales and unobtrusive measures of attitudes for grading purposes (with the attendant problems) and for monitoring the development of attitudes. If one were willing to try to evaluate only rather clearly crystallized attitudes and to evaluate them for the class or group of students rather than for each individual student, a procedure that is often called opinion measurement could be used.

There is not a great gap between attitude and opinion measurement. Probably the main idea that differentiates the two is that in measuring opinions we usually seek only to know the percent of the group that reacts in a certain way, such as, what percent prefer a longer recess or what percent prefer to sit in a circle rather than in rows or what percent prefer a single teacher versus a team of teachers for a topic. Since we are not trying to measure how strongly an attitude is held or to measure direction and strength accurately for an individual person, the errors due to one person saying yes when he did not mean to are approximately cancelled by errors in the opposite direction by some other person, and we still have a fairly good idea of the group's position by the proportion who answer each way. Of course, we would be more confident if we had two or three questions about a topic that were answered similarly by similar proportions of people, since it is well known that even slight changes in the wording of an individual item can markedly change the proportion who respond in a particular way. But even one good question can reflect the group's opinion if the opinion is highly crystallized, that is, if the members have clear opinions that have been held for some time before the questionnaire is administered to them.

There are other subtle differences between the two methods. For instance, in collecting opinions one would be unlikely to ask a question like:

When you should be studying arithmetic, how do you feel about it?

That kind of item seems more appropriate as one of several items on an attitude scale. More appropriate for an opinion item in a school setting might be:

I think students should be chosen to clean erasers on the basis of their good behavior.

In the latter case, the teacher might just want to find out whether students as a group thought that cleaning erasers was a fun thing to do and was a suitable reward or whether they did not like it as an activity.

Most of the suggestions for writing and arranging items for attitude measurement are also appropriate for opinion measurement. However, there are a few differences. For instance, we don't get into distinctions between rational and empirical keying. In fact, we don't really key opinion items. We usually merely report the percent who make each response. Also, as we develop opinion items and pretest them to avoid ambiguity, it is a good idea to develop the tabulation procedure for the results at the same time. The results then will be as easy as possible to tabulate, and we won't find problems in tabulation that were not realized and could have been avoided if the item had been phrased differently. An example of what can happen if items are not carefully thought out is the final one on a questionnaire received by the author. The question was:

What are the three most important guiding principles which should shape academia?

Needless to say, the questionnaire was never answered. The wastebasket is the common and proper fate of bad questionnaires. But imagine trying to categorize and tabulate any responses received to such a question.

Tryout of items would prevent the asking of questions such as this one, which was also on a questionnaire received by the author:

The ideal committee size is: 7 9 11 13 Other_____.

Clearly, that question cannot be answered sensibly unless one knows at least the duties of the committee and the role it is to play. Questions like these in opinion questionnaires have brought the whole enterprise of collecting opinions in surveys into disrepute. But such incompetence is not necessary. Its prevention rests in careful planning and in pretesting before items are administered for the purposes of collecting data. With careful attention paid to item writing, item arrangement, data tabulation, and the collecting of data on the same issue from several different sources and approaches, the collection of opinion information may be more important in schools than the collection of attitude information.

A useful distinction can be made between the value of two-choice questions and multiple-choice questions on opinion items. A two-choice item might be something like:

I think the outside doors to the school should be kept locked to students until ten minutes before the first period starts.

  Yes_____ No_____

A multiple-choice item on the same topic might be:

How long before first period should the school's outside doors be opened to the students?

  a. As soon as students arrive
  b. One hour
  c. One-half hour
  d. Fifteen minutes
  e. Ten minutes

The former question, with only two choices, is recommended when the students hold clear opinions and the issue to be decided is clear. In other words, the students should be able to choose clearly which answer they want. The multiple-choice form should be used when opinions are not so clearly divided or when many people might find it hard to answer with only two choices.

With response options such as Agree, Undecided, Disagree, or such as Longer, the Same, Shorter, if a middle ground or neutral position is feasible as an answer it should be available. Attempts to force people to one side or the other by not providing a middle or neutral response only tend to distort the results. On the other hand, offering a middle ground on an issue in which opinions are not strongly held by most respondents will result in large numbers choosing the neutral response. The person who makes up the questionnaire must decide what is the best way to handle this problem in her own situation.

You might wonder why you should get so elaborate as to develop a pretested questionnaire in order to get your students' opinions about workaday matters such as how long classes should be, how many field trips should be taken, and so on. The alternative that occurs to many is just to ask the students. You could ask individual students as they are seen casually in the hall, or you could ask for a show of hands in class. But the problem with the former is that the students seen casually in the hall may not be a representative sample of the group. The students who come to see you certainly are not representative. So how should you get a sound evaluation of the group's opinion? The problem with going to the class for a show of hands is that students are so easily influenced by their peers. If a lot of hands seem to go up, many more will go up just because raising the hand seems like the thing to do. Opinions collected privately in a questionnaire may give a much more realistic reading of the group's true opinion.

SAMPLING

Though we can't get into it in depth here, a further word of caution should be inserted about getting representative samples of opinions. Most teachers will not have to worry about sampling if they measure attitudes or opinions with the kind of instruments we have been discussing. Presumably they will simply administer the instrument to everyone who is in attendance on a particular day, and they will choose a day on which there are relatively few absent, or they will get information from the absentees later. In sampling terms, they get data from the entire *population of interest*. However, if it is not the plan to get information from everyone, or nearly everyone, then it is essential that the sample from whom data are collected be representative. There is only one feasible way for teachers to do that. Some form of random sampling (or a close approximation to it) must be used. The essence of random sampling is that every person and every group of persons has an equal chance of being drawn in the sample. Groups of people who happen to be handy are not representative. They are called *samples of convenience*, and their results cannot at all be trusted to represent the target population.

If a sample is drawn at random (using procedures described in Van Dalen, 1973, p. 321), it is essential that sufficient follow-up be done that a very high percentage of the sample is reached, or else procedures must be introduced for estimating the bias that results from the sample's not being representative. About all we can say here on the topic is that opinion measurement in which only 60% or 70% or less of the population or sample (depending on which is being used) responds to the items is essentially worthless. Results from such abortive efforts should be considered to be pilot data at best, and they should be evaluated to see why better returns were not received. Then, with modifications, the survey should be repeated, or else the pilot data should simply be destroyed unreported, and the project abandoned.

Sources of Attitude Measures

Since attitude measurement has such a long history of study and is such a complicated affair if it is done soundly, it would seem that experts might have devised a number of standard procedures which could be bought, much as standardized achievement and aptitude tests can be bought from commercial publishers. This is not the case. Probably because there are so many attitudes that may be of interest, it apparently is not profitable to market many well-developed measurement procedures on a large scale.

However, there are places to which a teacher might turn to find scales that have already been developed and that can be used with permission (and occasionally even purchased). Devices and procedures other than scales are also recorded and described in reference works. The most useful references for school purposes are the following:

Johnson, O. G., and Bommarito, J. W. *Tests and Measurements in Child Development: A Handbook.* San Francisco: Jossey-Bass, 1971.

Shaw, M. E., and Wright, J. M. *Scales for the Measurement of Attitudes.* New York: McGraw-Hill, 1967.

Robinson, J. P., and Shaver, P. R. *Measures of Social-Psychological Attitudes.* Ann Arbor, Mich.: Institute for Social Research, University of Michigan, 1973.

Walker, D. K. *Socioemotional Measures for Preschool and Kindergarten Children.* San Francisco: Jossey-Bass, 1973.

The book by Johnson and Bommarito is a presentation of hundreds of measures of characteristics of children. These measures have never been published. Not all of them are attitude measures. Measures are included which are suitable for children between birth and age 12, and for which there is enough information available to enable other people to use the instrument effectively. While technical data on the quality of the measures were not required for the measure to be included in this reference, each measure had to at least be long enough that it would be possible to collect such data with a reasonable expectation that the instrument would show promise of being worthwhile. The actual measure is not included in this reference, but a description of it is. The description is not an evaluation. Evaluation is up to the reader, but the following information is given on each instrument:

Name of the measure

Author

Age of children for which it is appropriate

Characteristic measured

Source from which the measure may be obtained

Description of the measure

Reliability and validity information if it exists

Brief bibliography

The reference includes 20 measures of attitudes toward adults, 7 measures of attitudes toward other students, 14 measures of self-concepts, and half a dozen or so other attitude measures.

Shaw and Wright's book describes and presents the actual scales for hundreds of attitude measures, but it is not oriented toward children. The scales there are for the most part more appropriate for adults and secondary school students who can read the items fluently. This reference includes both published and unpublished scales, evaluations of attitude measurement in different areas, evaluations of the scales, and an extensive discussion of how scales are constructed. There are specific scales for such things as the following, which might interest teachers in elementary and secondary schools:

Attitude Toward Teaching

Attitude Toward Teaching as a Career

Attitude Toward Physical Education

Attitudes Toward Education

> Attitude Toward Intensive Competition in Team Games
> Competitive Attitude
> Attitude Toward a High School Education
> Attitude Toward Mathematics
> Attitude Toward Any Teacher
> Attitude Toward Teachers, Classroom, Study Hall, Study, High School, and School Rules.

Shaw and Wright are especially helpful in pointing out such things as the fact that many of these scales were developed many years ago, and they may no longer be appropriate without modification. Still, it may be better for a modern worker to take advantage of the work that has already been done in measuring a particular attitude than to start all over again.

The reference by Robinson and Shaver also presents actual scales for a wide variety of attitudes. They are classified, and there is a discussion of the general level of development of attitude measurement in each area. For example, in connection with measurement of one of the many attitude areas, the self-concept, it is pointed out that after all the years of research on, and with, this dimension, it is still not clear what it means. There are over two hundred scales for it in the literature, most of them used only once. Robinson and Shaver suggest that the reason for the proliferation is that the researchers on the topic are unwilling to face the measurement problems inherent in their work, a rather common failing. After an extended discussion in this vein, 19 different ways of measuring self-concept are presented. Each is described, evaluated, commented upon, and then the actual items are given.

Finally, the reference by Walker restricts itself to measures appropriate for the child from ages three to six. One hundred and forty-three measures are included, but some overlap those in other sources such as Johnson and Bommarito. The general style of presentation is parallel to that of Johnson and Bommarito. The actual instrument is not presented, but for each measure there is its title and date of publication or copyright, the author, the appropriate age range, the measurement technique used, sources in which the measure is described, address from which the measure can be obtained, a description of the instrument, how it is administered and scored, and technical data on its quality if such is available. Only 11 measures of attitudes are included, and most of them concern attitudes related to race. A separate section contains descriptions of 18 different measures of self-concept.

Summary

While the measurement of attitudes in order to monitor side effects of instructional procedures is important, it is not easy. The development of a sound attitude measure by a teacher is much more difficult than her development of a sound achievement test, which is no small task, itself. Not only does she have to write attitude items and analyze them using procedures similar to those used in the development of sound classroom achievement tests, but she also has to study the reliability (consistency and stability) of the scores, and the validity (for example, the ability to discriminate between groups whose attitudes are known) before the measure can be used.

If she has determined that her primary objective in instruction is to develop certain attitudes, then she should base her grades on measures of those attitudes, and the measures must be impervious to conscious and unconscious faking. Since that is an insurmountable obstacle for a teacher with attitude measures based on questions, she must resort to less efficient nonreactive measures of the desired attitudes.

If she is measuring attitudes in order to monitor side effects of instruction designed primarily to develop competence and knowledge, faking is less likely to be a problem, but it still may be wise to verify the validity of her questionnaire measures by corroborative evidence from nonreactive measures. Only after such thorough checking of her procedures can she routinely give her attitude measures to students and interpret their scores as measurements of their attitudes.

To do all that well would require a teacher to have the equivalent in training and competence to several specialized college courses in such things as attitude measurement or scaling, research design, and statistical analysis. Most teachers will not have that background, nor will they have the time and facilities to do the research necessary to develop an attitude scale that can be trusted to be reasonably sound and useful. The obvious thing for the teacher to attempt to do is to find measures that have already been proven. There are reference works that guide her to instruments, but usually they are still unproven — developed by people who did not take seriously the problems inherent in measuring attitudes. The scales presented in those references may not be much better than the first attempt that a teacher might make. Or the scales may have been created so long ago that they can no longer be trusted without research to verify their functioning. Or they may have been developed and used only once in one research project and never evaluated carefully or used again.

A teacher may want to measure students' opinions on various matters as well as, or instead of, their attitudes. To do this she might merely ask the appropriate questions by means of a questionnaire. Faking is less of a problem, and it is not necessary to try to develop complete scales, although several related questions about an issue may clarify and support one's interpretation of the group's opinion on a particular issue. The development of opinion items must be done carefully if the results are to be meaningful, and for sound interpretations data must be collected from a very large proportion of the target population or of a random sample from that population.

Obviously from the brief introduction to attitude and opinion measurement in this chapter, this kind of measurement is not something to be dashed off with abandon by the beginner. Good measurement of attitude or opinion is not a simple thing that any teacher can be expected to do satisfactorily without training or experience, and without extended time and effort.

References

Cantril, H. *Gauging public opinion.* Princeton, N.J.: Princeton University Press, 1944.

Hallaman, E. G. Measuring the effectiveness of in-service programs. *NCME Measurement News,* 1974, **18**, 9.

Johnson, O. G. & Bommarito, J. W. *Tests and measurements in child development: A handbook.* San Francisco: Jossey-Bass, 1971.

LaPiere, R. T. Attitudes vs. actions. *Social forces*, 1934, **13**, 230–37.

Robinson, J. P. & Shaver, P. R. *Measures of social-psychological attitudes*. Ann Arbor, Mich.: Institute for Social Research, University of Michigan, 1973.

Shaw, M. E. & Wright, J. M. *Scales for the measurement of attitudes*, New York: McGraw-Hill, 1967.

Van Dalen, D. B. *Understanding educational research, an introduction*. (3rd ed.) New York: McGraw-Hill, 1973.

Walker, D. K. *Socioemotional measures for preschool and kindergarten children*. San Francisco: Jossey-Bass, 1973.

Webb, E. J., Campbell, D. T., Schwartz, R. D., & Sechrest, L. *Unobtrusive measures: Nonreactive research in the social sciences*. Chicago: Rand McNally, 1966.

Index